STANDARD 2. Family–Teacher Partnerships and Community Connections

2a. Know about, understand, and value the diversity of families

2b. Collaborate as partners with families in young children's development and learning through respectful, reciprocal relationships and engagement.

2c. Use community resources to support young children's learning and development and to support families, and build partnerships between early learning settings, schools, and community organizations and agencies.

Chapter 1: *Case Study*, pp. 1–2. Families as Observers, p. 15; Portfolios, p. 18; Bioecological Theory, p. 9; Essential Needs Theory, p. 10.

Chapter 2: *Case Study*, pp. 23–24. Growth, p. 25; Development, p. 25; Brain Growth & Development, pp. 29–30; Attachment, pp. 32–33 ; Gender Awareness and Identity, pp. 34–35; Transactional Patterns of Development, p. 37.

Chapter 3: *Case study*, pp. 50–51; *Neuroscience & Brain Development*, p. 53. Risks to Fetal Health & Development, pp. 60–64; Post-partum Depression, p. 67.

Chapter 4: *Case study*, pp. 74–75. *Learning Activities*, pp. 80, 90, 97, 105.
  Video Features: Attachment, p. 98. *Daily Routines*, pp. 80, 88, 96, 104. *Positive Behavior Guidance*, pp. 107–108.

Chapter 5: *Case Study*, pp. 112–113; *Daily Routines*, pp. 119–120, 129–130. *Learning Activities*, pp. 120–121, 129–130. Social-Emotional Development, pp.117, 126. *Positive Behavior Guidance*, pp. 131–132.

Chapter 6: *Case Study*, pp. 137–138. *Neuroscience & Brain Development*, p. 148. *Learning Activities*, pp. 146, 154, 161–162. *Safety Concerns*, pp. 147–148, 155–156, 162–163. *Positive Behavior Guidance*, p. 163.

Chapter 7: *Case study*, pp. 169–170. *Learning Activities*, pp. 177–178, 186–187, 194–195. *Neuroscience & Brain Development*, pp. 180–181. *Safety Concerns*, pp. 177–178, 186–187, 194–195. *Positive Behavior Guidance*, p. 196.

Chapter 8: *Case study*, pp. 202–203. *Learning Activities*, pp. 210–211, 219. *Positive Behavior Guidance*, p. 221.

Chapter 9: *Case Study*, pp. 227–228. *Learning Activities*, pp., 234, 241–242, 247–248. *Safety Concerns*, pp. 235–236, 243, 248–249. *Positive Behavior Guidance*, p. 250.

Chapter 10: When to Seek Help, p. 263; Observing and Recording, pp. 264–265; Screening Tests, pp. 265–268.

STANDARD 3. Child Observation, Documentation, and Assessment

3a. Understand that assessments (formal and informal, formative and summative) are conducted to make informed choices about instruction and for planning in early learning settings.

3b. Know a wide range of types of assessments, their purposes, and their associated methods and tools.

3c. Use screening and assessment tools in ways that are ethically grounded and developmentally, ability, culturally, and linguistically appropriate in order to document developmental progress and promote positive outcomes for each child.

3d. Build assessment partnerships with families and professional colleagues.

Chapter 1: Data Gathering, pp. 13–14; Families as Observers, p. 15; Observation Methods, pp. 16–19.
  Video Features: Assessing Children's Development, p. 18., Portfolios, p. 18.

Chapter 3: *Video Features:* Prenatal Assessment, p. 60.

Chapter 4: *Video Features:* Newborn Reflex Development, p. 79, Fine Motor Development, p. 93, Assessing Language Development, p. 103. *Developmental Alerts*, pp. 82, 90, 99,106.

Chapter 5: *Developmental Alerts*, pp. 121, 130.

Chapter 6: *Developmental Alerts*, pp. 147, 155, 162.

Chapter 7: *Developmental Alerts*, pp. 178, 187–188, 195.

Chapter 8: *Developmental Alerts*, pp. 211, 220.

Chapter 9: *Developmental Alerts*, pp. 235, 242, 248.

Chapter 10: *Case Study*, pp. 256–257.
  Video Features: Including Children with Exceptionalities, p. 259; Assessing Children's Development, p. 266. Is There a Problem? pp. 262–263; When to Seek Help, p. 263; Information Gathering, pp. 264–268; Diagnosis and Referral, pp. 268–269.

STANDARD 4. Developmentally, Culturally, and Linguistically Appropriate Teaching Practices

4a. Understand and demonstrate positive, caring, supportive relationships and interactions as the foundation of early childhood educators' work with young children.

Chapter 1: Video Features: Culturally Responsive Teaching, p. 14.

Chapter 2: Age-level expectancies or Norms, pp. 27–28; Brain Growth and Development, pp. 29–30, Socio-Ecological Factors and Developmental Risk, pp. 36–37.
  Video Features: Brain Development in Infancy, p. 29. Typical Growth and Development, p. 28; Temperament, p. 33; Developmental Domains, pp. 38–43.

4b. Understand and use teaching skills that are responsive to the learning trajectories of young children and to the needs of each child, recognizing that differentiating instruction, incorporating play as a core teaching practice, and supporting the development of executive function skills are critical for young children.
 	
4c. Use a broad repertoire of developmentally appropriate, culturally and linguistically relevant, anti-bias, evidence-based teaching skills and strategies that reflect the principles of universal design for learning.
	Chapter 4: *Learning Activities*, pp. 80, 90, 97, 105. *Safety Concerns*, pp. 83, 91, 99, 107.
	    Video Features: Attachment, p. 98. *Positive Behavior Guidance*, pp. 107–108.
	Chapter 5: *Neuroscience & Brain Development*, pp. 127–128. *Learning Activities*, pp. 120–121, 129–130. *Safety Concerns*, pp. 122, 131. *Positive Behavior Guidance*, pp. 131–132.
	Chapter 6: *Learning Activities*, pp. 146, 154, 161–162. *Safety Concerns*, pp. 147–148, 155–156, 162–163. *Positive Behavior Guidance*, p. 163.
	Chapter 7: *Learning Activities*, pp. 177–178, 186–187, 194–195. *Safety Concerns*, pp. 179–180, 188, 195–196. *Positive Behavior Guidance*, p. 196.
	Chapter 8: *Learning Activities*, pp. 210–211, 219. *Safety Concerns*, pp. 211–212, 220–221. *Neuroscience & Brain Development*, pp. 212–213. *Positive Behavior Guidance*, p. 221.
	Chapter 9: *Learning Activities*, pp. 234, 241–242, 247–248. *Safety Concerns*, pp. 236–237, 243, 248–249.
	    Video Features: Understanding Adolescent Emotions, p. 233. *Neuroscience & Brain Development*, pp. 236–237. *Positive Behavior Guidance*, p. 250.
	Chapter 10: ***Video Features:*** Children with Developmental Disabilities in the Classroom, p. 264. Is There a Problem? pp. 262–263; When to Seek Help, p. 263; Screening Tests, pp. 265–267; IQ Tests, p. 267.

STANDARD 5. Knowledge, Application, and Integration of Academic Content in the Early Childhood Curriculum

5a. Understand content knowledge—the central concepts, methods and tools of inquiry, and structure—and resources for the academic disciplines in an early childhood curriculum. **5b.** Understand pedagogical content knowledge—how young children learn in each discipline—and how to use the teacher knowledge and practices described in Standards 1 through 4 to support young children's learning in each content area. **5c.** Modify teaching practices by applying, expanding, integrating, and updating their content knowledge in the disciplines, their knowledge of curriculum content resources, and their pedagogical content knowledge.	**Chapter 4:** ***Video Features:*** Early Infant Learning, p. 88; Fine Motor Development, p. 93, Attachment, p. 98. *Learning Activities*, pp. 81–82, 89–90, 97–98, 105–106. **Chapter 5:** ***Video Features:*** Speech and Language Development, p. 117; Toddlers' Cognitive Development, p. 118. *Learning Activities*, pp. 120–121, 129–130. **Chapter 6:** ***Video Features:*** Preschoolers' Motor Development, p. 142, Preschoolers' Language Development, p. 152; Social Skill Development, p. 159. *Learning Activities*, pp. 146, 154, 161–162. **Chapter 7:** ***Video Features:*** Cognitive Development, p. 174; Cognitive Development and Concrete Operations, p. 184. *Learning Activities*, pp. 177–178, 186–187, 194–195. **Chapter 8:** ***Video Features:*** Emotional Development and Bullying, p. 209; Middle Childhood and Cognitive Development, p. 217. *Learning Activities*, pp. 210–211, 219. **Chapter 9:** ***Video Features:*** Understanding Adolescent Emotions, p. 233; Technology and Learning, p. 239. *Learning Activities*, pp. 234, 241–242, 247–248.

STANDARD 6. Professionalism as an Early Childhood Educator

6a. Identify and involve themselves with the early childhood field and serve as informed advocates for young children, families, and the profession. **6b.** Know about and uphold ethical and other early childhood professional guidelines. **6c.** Use professional communication skills, including technology-mediated strategies, to effectively support young children's learning and development and to work with families and colleagues. **6d.** Engage in continuous, collaborative learning to inform praßctice. **6e.** Develop and sustain the habit of reflective and intentional practice in their daily work with young children and as members of the early childhood profession.	**Chapter 3:** Promoting Healthy Fetal Development, pp. 54. **Chapter 10:** Legislation Supporting Optimum Development, pp. 268–270; The Developmental Team, pp. 258–260.

Source: *NAEYC Professional Standards and Competencies for Early Childhood Educators,* copyright © 2020 by the National Association for the Education of Young Children. The complete position statement can be accessed at, https://www.naeyc.org/resources/position-statements professional-standards-competencies.

9th Edition

Developmental Profiles | Pre-Birth Through Adolescence

Lynn R. Marotz, Ph.D., R.N.

Professor Emerita
University of Kansas

CENGAGE

Australia • Brazil • Canada • Mexico • Singapore • United Kingdom • United States

Developmental Profiles: Pre-Birth Through Adolescence, **Ninth Edition**
Lynn R. Marotz

SVP, Higher Education Product Management:
Erin Joyner

VP, Product Management, Learning Experiences:
Thais Alencar

Product Director: Matthew Seeley

Product Manager: Bianca Fiorio

Product Assistant: Dallas Wilkes

Content Manager: Sibasis Pradhan, MPS Limited

Digital Delivery Quality Partner: Beth Ross

Director, Product Marketing: Neena Bali

Product Marketing Manager: Ian Hamilton

IP Analyst: Ashley Maynard

IP Project Manager: Anjali Kambli,
Lumina Datamatics Ltd.

Production Service: MPS Limited

Designer: Felicia Bennett

Cover Image Source: Ariel Skelley/Getty Images

Interior image Source: Strejman/
Shutterstock.com

Last three editions, as applicable: © 2016, © 2013, © 2010

For product information and technology assistance, contact us at
**Cengage Customer & Sales Support, 1-800-354-9706
or support.cengage.com.**

For permission to use material from this text or product, submit all requests online at **www.copyright.com.**

Library of Congress Control Number: 2021920079

ISBN: 978-0-357-62502-6

Cengage
200 Pier 4 Boulevard
Boston, MA 02210
USA

Cengage is a leading provider of customized learning solutions with employees residing in nearly 40 different countries and sales in more than 125 countries around the world. Find your local representative at **www.cengage.com.**

To learn more about Cengage platforms and services, register or access your online learning solution, or purchase materials for your course, visit **www.cengage.com.**

Notice to the Reader

Printed at CLDPC, USA, 12-21

Contents in Brief

Contents

Konstantin Christian/Shutterstock.com

3 • Prenatal Development   50

4 • Infancy: Birth to Twelve Months   74

iStock.com/FatCamera

5 • Toddlerhood: One- and Two-Year-Olds   112

iStock.com/stock_colors

8 • Middle Childhood: Nine-, Ten-, Eleven-, and Twelve-Year-Olds   202

9 • Adolescence: Thirteen- to Nineteen-Year-Olds   227

Architectural engineers know that a structurally sound building requires a strong foundation. Similarly, early childhood educators understand that children require a strong foundation if they are to develop to their fullest potential. The quality of children's environments, early learning opportunities, and adult support and encouragement play an influential role in shaping the groundwork upon which all future skill acquisition is built. When adults understand children's developmental needs, talents, and limitations, they are able to provide effective behavioral guidance and learning experiences that ultimately create a strong foundation.

Developmental Profiles: Pre-birth Through Adolescence is designed to be a concise and accessible resource for students, educators, service providers, and families. The ninth edition has been thoroughly revised and updated, yet it maintains the author's original purpose to provide a comprehensive yet nontechnical, easy-to-follow critical overview of children's development. It links contemporary empirical research, theory, and application to the guidance of children's behavior and the promotion of developmentally appropriate learning experiences.

Purpose and Philosophical Approach

The common practice of dividing infancy and childhood into age-related units of months and years may initially appear to distort the realities of human development. However, when describing developmental expectations, developmental progress, and exceptionalities, other systems seem to work even less well. Let it be stressed here, as it is again and again throughout the text, that *age specifications are only approximate markers derived from averages or norms*. In a way, they can be thought of as midpoints that are not intended to represent any one particular child. Rather, age expectations represent summary terms for skills that vary from child to child in form and time of acquisition. The truly important consideration in assessing a child's development is *sequence*. The essential question is not chronological age, but whether the child is progressing step by step in each developmental area. *Developmental Profiles* has long proven itself to be an invaluable resource in addressing this issue.

As in the previous editions, the early days, weeks, and months of infancy are examined in detail. New research findings on brain and early development clearly support the critical importance of this relatively short time span. What is now known about infants' capacity for learning is indeed amazing and counter to long-held assumptions that they are incapable of doing so until much later. Far from it!

The first year of life is essential for building a foundation of learning in every developmental domain. The vast array of new and complex behaviors that toddlers and preschoolers must learn in three or four short years is also monumental. At no other period in a person's lifetime will so much be expected in so short a time. Given that more infants and young children are enrolled in early childhood programs makes it essential that educators and service providers have a comprehensive understanding of how they grow, develop, and learn.

Respecting and working collaboratively with children's families remains a fundamental and underlying philosophy of *Developmental Profiles*. No matter how many hours children spend with caregivers or teachers in school each day, families still play the most significant and influential role in their lives. Families must be supported in their parenting efforts. They also must be encouraged to share their observations and concerns with teachers as this information is integral to each child's development and well-being. In turn, teachers and service providers must listen to families with focused and unbiased attention and respond with genuine interest and respect.

Partnerships with families become even more critical when an infant or older child is suspected of having a developmental disorder or delay. The *Developmental Alerts* identified for each age group can be especially useful to families, educators, and service providers for initiating a discussion about their concerns. Let it be emphasized, however, that under no circumstances should this book or any other book be considered an instrument for diagnosing a developmental problem. That is the role of professional clinicians and child development specialists.

Thus, the stated purposes of this text can be summed up as follows:

- To provide a concise overview of developmental principles
- To provide easily accessible information about what to expect at each developmental stage
- To suggest appropriate ways for adults to encourage and support children's learning and development
- To pinpoint warning signs of a possible developmental disorder or delay
- To suggest how and where to get help
- To describe cultural and environmental diversity in terms of its impact on the developmental process
- To emphasize the value of direct observation of children in their natural settings, whether in a classroom, early childhood program, or the child's own home
- To provide adults with the knowledge to help children achieve their individual potentials, develop a positive sense of self-esteem, and feel loved and respected
- To highlight contemporary child development theory and research

The Intended Audience

Teachers—caregivers, families, and service providers—play an essential role in guiding children's development. It is through their ability to foster learning and positive mental and physical health and to identify challenges that may interfere with developmental progress that adults ultimately make a difference in children's lives. Thus, *Developmental Profiles* is designed for adults who care for and work with children of all ages, including:

- Students and preservice teachers.
- Teachers in home-based settings, early childhood centers, Early Start and Head Start programs, public and private schools, and before- and after-school programs; home visitors and consultants; and nonparental caregivers in the child's home.

- Allied health professionals and service providers in nursing, nutrition, audiology, social work, physical and occupational therapy, psychology, medicine, language and speech therapy, and counseling who provide services for children and their families.

- Families, the most important contributors to a child's development.

Organization and Key Content

Developmental Profiles opens with a brief overview of major child development theories and principles. These chapters (1 and 2) serve as a refresher of basic concepts and provide background material on age-level expectancies for the chapters that follow. Chapter 3 is devoted to maternal and paternal practices that are essential for promoting healthy fetal development. Detailed word pictures of child and adolescent development across six developmental domains, including typical daily routines, safety alerts, developmental alerts, learning activities to promote brain development, and positive behavioral guidance are described in Chapters 4 through 9. Pages include color-coded tabs with age designations for quick, easy-to-locate reference. When and where to seek help if there are concerns about a child's developmental progress are discussed in Chapter 10. Cutting-edge neuroscience research about children's brain development is also included in each chapter. Developmental checklists and additional resource material of interest to families, educators, and service providers are provided in the appendices. This format encourages vigilance in identifying delays in their earliest stage and supports adults in creating developmentally appropriate interventions and learning opportunities for children of all ages.

Developmental Profiles provides nontechnical, key information about the following:

- What to expect of infants, young children, and adolescents at each succeeding developmental stage

- The ways in which all areas of development are intertwined and mutually supportive

- The unique pathway that each child follows in a developmental process that is alike, yet different, among children of a similar age

- Sequences, not age, being the critical concept in evaluating developmental progress

- The use of developmental norms in teaching, observing, and assessing children and in designing individualized as well as group learning experiences

New and Expanded Content

The ninth edition of *Developmental Profiles* continues to bring readers important content features that support understanding and practice in an easy-to-reference format:

- **Measurable Learning Objectives,** identified at the beginning of each chapter, highlight key concepts that are important for students to know and understand. After completing the chapter, students should be able to demonstrate how they can apply their new knowledge and skills. The learning objectives are also reflected in the end-of-chapter summary and review questions.

- *New* **NAEYC Standards:** The content in each chapter has been aligned to the new **National Association for the Education of Young Children Professional Preparation Standards (NAEYC)** standards. Relevant standards are identified at the beginning of each chapter, as well as in the standards correlation chart (inside cover), to help students make connections between what they are learning in the textbook and professional expectations. These callouts are also useful for program accreditation purposes.

- **Digital Downloads:** Downloadable and often customizable, these practical and professional resources allow students and practitioners to immediately implement and apply textbook content. The materials can be downloaded and retained for future use, enabling preservice teachers to begin building a library of practical, professional resources. Look for the **Digital Downloads** icon that identifies these items.

- *New* **TeachSource videos** feature footage from the classroom to help students relate key chapter content to real-life scenarios. Critical-thinking questions provide opportunities for in-class or online discussion and reflection.

- *New* **Spotlight on Neuroscience and Brain Development:** This feature, included in each chapter, draws attention to the latest neurocognitive research on critical issues (e.g., autism, breast-feeding, premature birth, maternal obesity, psychoactive stimulants, physical activity, early adversity) and the connections to children's brain development.

- **Did You Know?** Offers interesting facts in a marginal feature to arouse students' curiosity and interest in chapter content.

- *New* **Chapter to Practice:** Field-based exercises provide opportunities for students to apply developmental concepts learned in each chapter and to critique their experiences.

- *New* **What Do You See?** This feature is designed to reinforce students' observational skills by asking them to respond to what they see in a photograph.

- *New and expanded* **research on contemporary topics:** Additional material on brain development, attachment, cultural awareness and sensitivity, gender identity and sexual orientation, dual-language learners, observational skills, and strategies for supporting children's transitions has been incorporated throughout the book. Updated references reflect the latest empirical research on these subjects.

- **Concise developmental profiles:** Highlight children's sequential progress across six developmental domains, from prebirth to age nineteen in a bulleted format.

- *New* **Case Studies:** Presented at the onset of each chapter, the new case studies reflect the ethnic and family diversity experienced in today's schools. They set the stage for the chapter content that follows and are designed to help students relate what they learn to real-life situations. The **Case Study Connections** feature located at the end of each chapter includes questions that require students to reflect on and apply what they have learned.

- **Developmental Alerts** are highlighted at each age level to aid in the early identification of potential delays and/or developmental disorders that warrant further evaluation.

- **Daily Activities and Routines** typical at each age level are offered in each chapter to help families and teachers anticipate and respond appropriately to children's developmental interests and needs.

- **Positive Behavior Guidance sections** outline effective strategies for responding to children's behavior in a constructive manner to promote healthy social and emotional competence.

- **Learning Activities to Promote Brain Development** are available in digital format for easy downloading. These sections offer suggestions for developmentally appropriate learning experiences that can be used to promote children's curiosity, creativity, problem-solving abilities, and skill acquisition across all domains.

- *New* **Safety Alerts** reflect current safety concerns associated with each developmental stage and are designed to help adults create safe environments, maintain quality supervision, and support children's safety education.

- **Digital Download Developmental Checklists** are provided for each age group in Appendix A. The checklists are also available in digital format and can be downloaded for teachers, service providers, and families to use in monitoring children's developmental progress.

- *New* **Screening and Assessment Instruments:** An updated sampling of screening tests commonly used to evaluate infants', young children's, and adolescents' development are identified and described in an annotated listing (Appendix B).

- *New* **Resources:** An overview of early intervention, information, and technical assistance resources is provided in Appendix C. New online resource sites are also included at the end of each chapter.

New to This Edition

Each chapter has been updated in many ways. New photos, figures, content, research, and professional standards have been incorporated throughout the book. Some of the most significant changes include:

Chapter 1: *Child Development Theories and Data Gathering.* This chapter features new content aligned with the current NAEYC professional preparation standards. Information regarding e-portfolios and assessment has been expanded. The conduct of brain research and current findings are the topic of the *Spotlight on Neuroscience and Brain Development* feature.

Chapter 2: *Principles of Growth and Development.* This chapter features several new and expanded sections on attachment, socio-ecological factors and developmental risk, gender awareness and sexual identity, and eye gaze and its relationship to children's language development. New research has been added on exposure to adversity and its negative effects on children's brain development. New photos, research, and TeachSource videos are also provided in this chapter.

Chapter 3: *Prenatal Development.* Statistics, graphics, and photos have been updated in this chapter. New information on autism and paternal health, reproductive technologies, fetal development and maternal obesity, low birth weight infants and developmental outcomes, conditions that influence fetal development, and postpartum depression have been added.

Chapter 4: *Infancy: Birth to Twelve Months.* This chapter includes a new case study focused on family diversity, updated safety guidelines, new research findings, and information on social eye gaze and autism. A new *Spotlight on Neuroscience and Brain Development* addresses breast milk composition and its beneficial effects on infant brain development.

Chapter 5: *Toddlerhood: One- and Two-Year-Olds.* New research that adds to our understanding of children's language development, gender concept, media use, and cultural expectations is discussed. Safety guidelines have also been updated. A new *Spotlight on Neuroscience and Brain Development* examines the influence of music and participation in musical activities on the developing brain.

Chapter 6: *Early Childhood: Three-, Four-, and Five-Year-Olds.* This chapter includes new and expanded information on childhood fears and nightmares, reasoning and moral development (Theory of the Mind), gender and culture, friendships, and research on the origins of autism.

Chapter 7: *Early Childhood: Six-, Seven-, and Eight-Year-Olds.* New research on play-based learning, friendships, social-emotional development, and the effect of sleep on children's brain development and functioning have been added to this chapter.

Chapter 8: *Middle Childhood: Nine-, Ten-, Eleven-, and Twelve-Year-Olds.* Additional information and empirical research findings that address puberty, social-emotional development, safety concerns, and the impact of physical activity on neurocognitive functioning are included in this chapter.

Chapter 9: *Adolescence: Thirteen- to Nineteen-Year-Olds.* New content and research regarding culture and adolescent behavior, depression and suicide, and social-emotional development during adolescence have been added to this chapter. New research on psychoactive stimulants (e.g., cannabis, alcohol) and their effect on adolescent brain development and functioning is discussed in the *Spotlight on Neuroscience and Brain Development* feature.

Chapter 10: *When and Where to Seek Help.* New to this chapter are legislative updates, research on premature birth and neurocognitive development, and a video feature that discusses children with exceptionalities in inclusive classrooms.

Accompanying Teaching and Learning Resources

Online Instructor's Manual

An online Instructor's Manual accompanies this book. It contains information to assist instructors in designing their course, including discussion questions, teaching and learning activities, field experiences, learning objectives, and additional online resources. Additional online resources and assessments include:

- TeachSource videos of teachers teaching and children learning in real classrooms, accompanied by case study questions to assess students' understanding of the video concepts. All TeachSource videos can be found in the Cengage eBook for *Developmental Profiles*.

- Case scenarios requiring students to analyze typical teaching and learning situations and create a reasoned response to the issue(s) presented in the scenario, reflecting about and justifying the choices they made within the teaching scenario problem.

- Digital Download resources

PowerPoint® Lecture Slides

These vibrant Microsoft® PowerPoint lecture slides for each chapter assist you with your lecture by providing concept coverage using images, figures, and tables directly from the textbook!

Cengage Learning Testing Powered by Cognero

Cengage Learning Testing Powered by Cognero is a flexible online system that allows you to author, edit, and manage test bank content from multiple Cengage Learning solutions; create multiple test versions in an instant; and deliver tests from your LMS, your classroom, or wherever you want.

Acknowledgments

Once again, it has been my pleasure to work with a team of outstanding individuals at Cengage. I could always count on Lauren Whalen and Abby DeVeuve to provide excellent editorial guidance and a prompt response to my numerous questions. A special thank you is extended to Sibasis Pradhan at MPS Limited for his responsiveness, despite our considerable time differences, and exceptional editing and production. I would also like to acknowledge the many behind-the-scenes individuals who worked so diligently on the design, media, marketing, and production of another outstanding edition. Their tasks were more challenging than ever given the work-from-home conditions experienced during the pandemic, so thank you. Also, I want to acknowledge the reviewers for their insightful critiques and suggestions:

- Rebecca Castile, Spartanburg Community College
- Ericka Davis, Hinds Community College
- Shaunta Durr, Hinds Community College
- Nora Lee, Wayne Community College

Finally, I am grateful for my family's continued understanding and support....they mean the world to me!

ABOUT THE AUTHOR

Lynn R. Marotz, Ph.D., R.N., taught undergraduate and graduate courses in the Department of Applied Behavioral Science, University of Kansas, and served as the Associate Director of the Edna A. Hill Child Development Center for over 35 years. She worked closely with students in the early childhood teacher education program and offered courses in parenting, health/safety/nutrition for the young child, administration, and foundations of early childhood education.

Lynn has authored invited chapters on children's health and development, nutrition, and environmental safety in national and international publications and law books. She is also the author of *Health, Safety, and Nutrition for the Young Child, Parenting Today's Children: A Developmental Perspective, Early Childhood Leadership: Motivation, Inspiration, Empowerment,* and *By the Ages: Behavior & Development of Children Pre-birth Through Eight.* Her involvement in state policy development, health screenings, professional development training, working with families and allied health professionals, and the referral process is extensive. She has presented at international, national, and state conferences, and held appointments on national, state, and local committees and initiatives that advocate on children's and families' behalf. However, it is her daily interactions with children and their families, students, colleagues, and her beloved family that bring true insight, meaning, and balance to the material in this book.

Chapter 1

Child Development Theories and Data Gathering

Learning Objectives

After reading this chapter, you will be able to:

1-1 Compare and contrast the fundamental contemporary child development theories described in this chapter.

1-2 Explain why authentic assessment is the most developmentally appropriate method for evaluating children's progress.

1-3 Describe five methods that can be used for gathering observational data about children.

NAEYC NAEYC Professional Standards Linked to Chapter Content

1a and 1b: Child development and learning in context

2a: Family–teacher partnerships and community connections

3a, b, and c: Child observations, documentation, and assessment

Shortly after Tucker celebrated his first birthday, social workers removed him from his nineteen-year-old mother's home because of malnourishment and severe neglect. He was placed temporarily with an older couple who had long served as foster parents for many children. Several weeks after Tucker's initial placement, he was moved again to a different foster home where there were other children closer to his age. However, soon after Tucker arrived, the family decided that they no longer wanted to remain foster parents. This necessitated moving him yet again, and several additional times thereafter.

Tucker recently celebrated his fifth birthday and has been living with his current foster parents, Serena and James Martinez, for almost a year. They have two little girls of their own, ages four and six, and three additional foster children ranging in age from four to nine years. All the children are vigorous and outgoing except for Tucker, who seems to tire easily and is quite small for his age. Serena discussed her concerns with Tucker's pediatrician during his recent well-child checkup. When the nurse weighed and measured Tucker, he was only in the 30th percentile for height and weight, despite the fact that Serena says he eats far more than the other children.

Serena and James learned from their social worker that Tucker sat up, crawled, and eventually began to walk much later than most children his age. He continues to experience some motor delays, but is working with a therapist who believes that he is making good progress. Serena and James also have noted that Tucker seldom joins in play or conversation with the other children. However, they have occasionally overheard him holding lengthy and comprehensible discussions with his imaginary friend, Honey, at times when he thinks he is alone. The talk is usually about things he fears, possibly the root of recurring bad dreams from which he often wakes up screaming. Yet, despite his problems, Tucker is a kind and lovable child. He seizes any opportunity to curl up on Serena's lap, suck his thumb, and snuggle his free hand into hers. The Martinezes have come to love Tucker as one of their own and are currently in the process of formalizing his adoption.

Ask Yourself

- What aspects of Tucker's development pose a concern?
- In what ways are Serena and James attempting to meet Tucker's fundamental needs?

Children's development has interested philosophers and psychologists for decades (Figure 1-1). Early attempts to explain the origin of children's ideas and the processes involved in learning were derived primarily from personal observations and interpretations. Theories built solely on this information were later found to be incomplete, inconsistent, and vastly divergent in their explanations. The introduction of formalized scientific methodologies during the twentieth century enabled child development researchers to produce data that was more comprehensive, consistent,

Figure 1-1 Children's development has been the subject of study for many decades.

and reliable. Although many earlier theories were abandoned, significant differences of opinion regarding how children learned persisted among child development researchers.

It is unlikely that any one theory could ever adequately explain the complexities of human behavior. Each has contributed in some way to our understanding of children's development and reminds us that behavior is a product of multiple and complex factors. It is also important to remember that theories reflect the prevailing beliefs and conditions (e.g., social, economic, religious, and political) at a given historical point. As a result, existing children's development theories are often revisited and refined and are likely to continue changing over time.

Contemporary Theories

A longstanding debate in the child development field has centered on whether learning is the result of heredity (innate abilities) or environment (experiences). This argument is commonly referred to as the **nature vs. nurture** controversy (Honeycutt, 2019). Early philosophers, including Plato and Aristotle, believed that all behavior was biologically predetermined (nature). In other words, it was thought that children were born hardwired to think and act in specific ways. This conclusion was derived from the fact that most children learn to walk, talk, and feed themselves when they reach certain specific ages. By contrast, John Locke and other philosophers suggested that children were born with blank minds (*tabula rasa,* or clean slate) and that all behavior is learned and a product of one's environment and experiences (nurture).

Scientific advancements subsequently have criticized both theories for explaining human behavior in overly simplistic terms. Brain imaging studies, for example, have confirmed that development is not an either/or process. Rather, researchers have demonstrated that learning causes physical changes in the brain's structure and function. These changes are the product of complex interactions that occur between genetic materials (such as brain cells and an intact neurological system) and learning opportunities in the child's environment.

Much of our current knowledge about how children learn, grow, and mature is derived from several classical theories: maturational, psychoanalytic and psychosocial, cognitive-developmental, behaviorism and social learning, bioecological, and essential needs. An overview of the fundamental constructs associated with each theory follows.

Maturational Theory

Maturational theory focuses on a biological or *nature* approach to human development. All behavior is explained in terms of genetics and the biological changes that must occur before a child is able to perform certain skills; this capacity is often referred to as a stage of *biological readiness*. For example, maturational theory would argue that infants learn to walk only when their neurological system has matured sufficiently to permit this activity, regardless of any other factors, including opportunity or environment.

Arnold Gesell's historic research contributed significantly to our understanding of genetic influences on children's development. He believed that all development is governed primarily by internal forces of biologic and genetic origin (Dalton, 2005; Gesell & Ilg, 1949). This led to several notable publications in which he described children's achievements by age and explained them in ways that parents could understand and put into practice.

Few scientists would disagree that genetics play a critical role in human development and, in some cases, even has a limiting effect. For example, the genes that children inherit from their biological parents determine height, skin color, shoe size, hair color,

nature vs. nurture Refers to whether development is primarily due to biological– genetic forces (heredity– nature) or to external forces (environment–nurture).

What Do You See?

Development as a biological manifestation. Every child differs in terms of genetic makeup and daily experiences. How would Arnold Gesell explain any differences in the way these two children perform on this counting task?

and other distinguishing features. Genes are also responsible for chromosomal abnormalities, such as those causing Down syndrome, congenital deafness, vision defects, and a host of other limiting disorders. Neuroscientists have also identified biological differences associated with various personality traits (e.g., shyness, aggressiveness, agreeableness) as well as predispositions to certain mental health disorders (Montag et al., 2020; Poole et al., 2019).

Although most experts acknowledge that genetics are important to human development, they also do not accept it as the sole cause of behavior. Most experts believe that the maturational theory overlooks individual differences and the ways in which they influence learning experiences and outcomes. Yet it is interesting that some current educational practices, such as admission standards based on birth dates and "redshirting" (holding back) a child whose birthday falls close to a predetermined cutoff date, continue to accept a maturational position.

Gesell's contributions continue to serve a functional purpose despite some of this criticism. His observations have been translated into **norms**, or benchmarks that have proven useful for assessing and monitoring children's developmental progress. More recently, they have been incorporated into several commonly used screening tools, including the Ages and Stages, Denver Developmental Screening Test, and the Bayley Scales of Infant and Toddler Development. Scientists continue to update Gesell's original standards so that they more accurately reflect today's diverse population.

Psychoanalytic and Psychosocial Theory

Psychoanalytic and psychosocial theory postulates that much of human behavior is governed by unconscious processes, some of which are present at birth and others that develop over time. Sigmund Freud, considered the originator of psychoanalytic theory, believed that children's behavior is a reflection of their inner thoughts and sexual desires (Freud, 1923). He proposed a series of stages (e.g., oral, anal, phallic, latency, and genital) and suggested that children must resolve and satisfy certain emotional conflicts fully before they can advance to the next developmental phase. The degree to which these emotions are or are not fulfilled ultimately shapes the child's basic personality, which Freud believed was established during the first five years of life.

norms Age-level expectancies associated with the achievement of specific developmental skills.

Psychosocial theory is based on the work of Erik Erikson, who expanded on Freud's ideas about personality development. He, too, believed that each developmental stage is characterized by certain conflicts that must be resolved. After a successful resolution has been achieved, a person is motivated to undertake the next developmental challenge.

However, unlike Freud, Erikson's theory acknowledges the influence of environment and social interactions. He coined the term *ego identity* to describe an individual's conscious awareness of self (who I am in relation to others) and the lifelong changes that occur as a result of social interactions. Erikson was also the first to describe development across the life span by introducing his eight universal stages of human development (Erikson, 1950). The first four stages address the early years; the remaining four cover the span from adolescence to the later years:

- **Trust vs. mistrust (0–12 months)** Establishing a sense of trust with primary caregivers
- **Autonomy vs. shame and doubt (1–3 years)** Learning to gain control over some behaviors (e.g., eating, toileting, and sleeping) and developing a sense of autonomy or independence
- **Initiative vs. guilt (3–5 years)** Using social interaction to gain control over one's everyday world
- **Industry vs. inferiority (6–12 years)** Developing a sense of competence and pride through successful accomplishments
- **Identity vs. confusion (13–20 years)** Learning about self in relationship to others
- **Intimacy vs. isolation (20–35 years)** Exploring and forming intimate relationships
- **Generativity vs. stagnation (35–55 years)** Focusing on family, career, and ways of contributing to society
- **Integrity vs. despair (60s–death)** Reflecting on one's life and forming a sense of satisfaction or dissatisfaction

Psychoanalytic and psychosocial theories have contributed to our understanding of personality and social-emotional skills and their influence on all aspects of children's development. They also have helped us to better understand the universal challenges that children face at each stage and how to create environments that support children's social and emotional needs along a developmental continuum. However, critics suggest that the social expectations associated with various stages are too generic and may lack relevancy for all cultures.

Psychoanalytic and psychosocial theories are no longer as popular as they once were. However, they continue to foster research interests in areas such as caregiver consistency, attachment, morality, gifted education, play, cultural similarities and differences, and trauma's effects on children's development.

Cognitive-Developmental Theory

Jean Piaget was the first psychologist to study the qualitative and maturational changes that occur in children's cognitive development. He theorized that children were born with basic genetic capabilities that enabled them to construct knowledge and meaning through active exploration of their environment (Figure 1-2). The term **constructivism** often is used today to describe this mode of learning.

According to Piaget, children progress through four distinct stages of intellectual development, beginning in infancy and continuing into the late teens (Piaget, 1954):

- **Sensorimotor (birth–2 years)** The infant's reflexive behaviors gradually give way to intentional actions during the sensorimotor period. Young children explore and discover the world around themselves primarily through their senses.

Did You Know

.....Freud was the oldest of eight children and considered himself to be his mother's favorite, "darling Siggie"?

constructivism A learning approach in which individuals form their own meaning through active participation.

Figure 1-2 Jean Piaget believed that children learn through exploration and discovery.

Jennifer Murray/Pexels

They also begin to learn that they have the power to control some elements in their environment. For example, a toddler sees an object, picks it up, examines it while turning it around in his hands, and finally puts it into his mouth.

- **Preoperational (2–7 years)** Children begin thinking about things in their immediate environment in terms of symbols. For example, the three-year-old picks up a long stick, calls it a fishing pole, and pretends to catch a fish. This example also illustrates a second aspect of the preoperational stage (the emergence of language), which is another form of symbolic representation.
- **Concrete operational (7–11 years)** During this stage, children are developing the ability to comprehend and formulate ideas about their immediate world. Although their ideas remain quite simplistic and rigid, children are beginning to think logically, to anticipate outcomes, to classify objects, and to solve problems. These emerging *schema* (Piaget's term) lead to a rudimentary understanding of abstract concepts, such as those associated with math and spatial relationships.
- **Formal operational (11–15 years)** During this stage, children are able to use complex thinking skills to visualize and manipulate ideas and experiences in their heads without having immediate access to real or concrete objects (abstract thinking). In addition, they are able to think logically, weigh consequences, and use memory for problem solving.

Piaget alleged that children's cognitive development involves far more than the passive accumulation of new information. He described cognition as an active process defined by increasingly sophisticated thought processes that emerge as children transition from one developmental stage to the next. Piaget introduced several terms to describe these changes:

- *Schemas*—Mental patterns or categories (e.g., food, objects, places, or animals) that a child begins to form and use for organizing and storing information.
- *Assimilation*—The process of incorporating new information into preexisting schemas. For example, a carrot is food, and a rabbit is an animal.
- *Accommodation*—The process of modifying preconceived schemas or forming additional schemas based on new information. For example, a carrot is a vegetable, and a rabbit is a mammal.

- *Disequilibrium*—The period of confusion, conflict, tension, or all three that results when new information does not fit within existing schemas.
- *Equilibrium*—The process of using assimilation and accommodation to alleviate intellectual conflict.

Although experts have criticized some of Piaget's ideas, his contributions continue to influence contemporary educational practices, including discovery learning, the importance of play, peer teaching, and developmentally appropriate curriculum.

Lev Vygotsky (1986) also was interested in children's cognitive development, but he considered the processes involved in its formation to be different from those proposed by Piaget. He agreed with Piaget's notion that development follows a unique pattern and that children learn through active involvement and hands-on experiences. However, Vygotsky felt strongly that social and cultural environments (e.g., values, beliefs, and practices) shaped and ultimately determined the nature of children's learning. He believed that culture provided the mental framework for all thoughts and behavior, while language served as the mechanism for transmitting this information from one individual to another. For example, he explained that children initially learn how to behave in a certain way through a series of adult directives: "Don't touch," "Come here," "Eat this," "Stop that." As children begin to internalize social rules and cultural expectations and develop self-control, the nature of these directives gradually changes. Adults stop telling children what to do and shift their attention to encouraging and assisting the acquisition of new skills. Vygotsky referred to this as the **Zone of Proximal Development**.

Vygotsky also considered children's speech and language development a critical step in the socialization process. He believed that young children spend considerable time learning new words, thinking about their meanings, making associations, and forming an understanding about how they are to be used. Vygotsky observed that during this process, some children hold conversations with themselves as a way of thinking out loud. He referred to this stage as "self-talk," or inner speech, and suggested that the process provides children an opportunity to rehearse the meanings of words and how they function as communication tools before actually using them in social situations (Vygotsky, 1986).

Marie Montessori's ideas also have contributed to our understanding of cognitive-developmental theory. Trained as a pediatrician, she later became interested in educating children who were considered not capable of learning. She was convinced that all children had potential, but that traditional instructional methods might not always be effective. Her observations led to her belief that children learned best through a process of self-directed exploration. She designed a collection of sensory-based, self-correcting materials that required limited adult intervention. She also developed educational programs based on a philosophy that emphasized and encouraged children's natural curiosity and self-directed involvement in learning experiences.

Cognitive-developmental theorists have advanced our understanding of how children learn and construct meaning. They have raised educational awareness about differences in children's rate and style of learning and the importance of individualizing instruction to address each child's unique developmental needs. Their ideas have influenced policy formation and are evident in the position statement of the National Association for the Education of Young Children (NAEYC) on developmentally appropriate practice (DAP), as well as the philosophies of other educational organizations (NAEYC, 2020). For example, the concept and delivery of early intervention services is built on a foundation of cognitive theory. Children's cognitive development also continues to serve as a source of scientific study, particularly as it relates to curriculum, instructional methods, family involvement, social interaction, and the effects of cultural influence on children's development.

Did You Know ?

.....that Vygotsky was considered a genius of his time and often was referred to as the "Mozart of psychology"?

Zone of Proximal Development Vygotsky's term for tasks that initially prove too difficult for children to master by themselves but that they can perform with adult guidance or assistance.

Zone of Proximal Development

Adults intuitively use a variety of instructional methods to help children learn a new skill until they are able to perform it independently. Respond to the following questions after you have watched the learning video *5-11 Years: Lev Vygotsky, the Zone of Proximal Development and Scaffolding:*

1. What is the Zone of Proximal Development?

2. What role do adults play in this process?

3. What is scaffolding? How did the teacher illustrate this instructional concept in the video?

Behaviorism and Social Learning Theory

In its modern form, behaviorism and social learning theory stem from the works of B. F. Skinner and John B. Watson, who formulated a *nurture*, or environmental, approach to learning (Skinner, 1938). They argued that development, for the most part, involves a series of learned behaviors based on an individual's positive and negative interactions with the environment (Figure 1-3). For example, they would suggest that reinforcing a behavior typically causes it to be repeated. In other words, telling a child that he should be proud of the score on his spelling test is likely to motivate him to study even harder for the next one. However, the opposite is also true: giving in to a crying child's demands for a much-wanted toy may encourage her to repeat the behavior the next time she wants something. Ignoring the child's demands tends to reduce and eventually extinguish the behavior because there is no reinforcement (attention).

Skinner also explained how the association between two events (stimulus-response) results in learning. For example, a toddler bumps her head (stimulus) when she stands up under the table, so she abruptly ends the activity (response). A preschooler touches a hot pan (stimulus) and is careful to avoid repeating the same behavior (response). You promise to read a favorite book to your daughter (stimulus) if she picks up her toys (response), and she does so quickly.

Albert Bandura modified several of Skinner's earlier ideas when he formulated his own theory of social learning (Bandura, 1977). He viewed behavior as a combination of environmental influences (nature) and cognitive abilities (nurture). He also believed that children learned both positive and negative behaviors through observation and modeling (imitation). However, unlike Skinner, he did not agree that reinforcement was necessary

Figure 1-3 Social learning theory explains development as behavioral changes that result from observation and imitation.

to motivate or change behavior. He believed that children learned, for example, not to hit another child or not to take away a toy after having observed another child being punished for the same act.

Families and teachers employ the behavioral theory principles on a daily basis. They expect children to comply with requests and then reward or punish them accordingly. They model behavior that children are likely to imitate. They provide attention and encouragement, thus reinforcing the children's efforts (good or bad). Behavioral interventions also are commonly used in the treatment of behavior and developmental problems, such as aggression, feeding disorders, anger management, substance abuse, bullying, and obesity (Evans, Blossom, & Fite, 2020; Wood et al., 2020).

Bioecological Theory

There is little dispute among child development experts that environment has an influential effect on development. However, Urie Bronfenbrenner, a noted American scholar and psychologist, alleged that environment played a pivotal role in this process, especially during a child's early years. He proposed his ecological model of human development based upon this conviction and described environment from a multilayered, subsystem perspective: microsystems (e.g., face-to-face interactions with primary caregivers, siblings, and friends); mesosystems (e.g., school-home linkages and interactions with relatives); exosystems (e.g., mass media, parent's workplace, and social services); macrosystems (e.g., cultural values and customs, ethnicity, economic conditions, and politics); and chronosystems (e.g., changes that occur over time, such as moving to a new location, birth of a sibling, divorce, or a military deployment) (Bronfenbrenner, 1979) (Figure 1-4). Bronfenbrenner suggested that development is a product of the reciprocal interactions and relationships that an individual experiences across and within each of

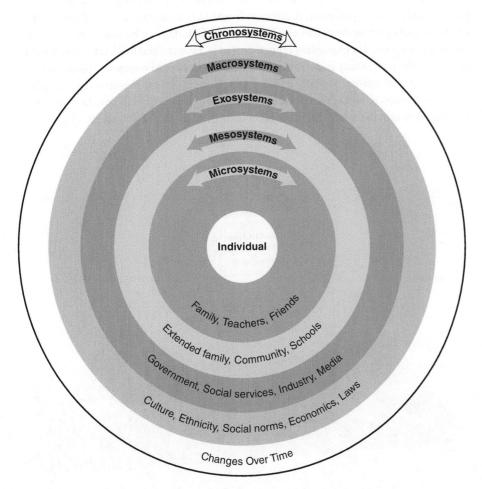

Figure 1-4 Bronfenbrenner's ecological model.

these subsystems. He also believed that as a result, developmental research was more insightful and meaningful when conducted in children's natural settings.

Bronfenbrenner later modified his original ideas to acknowledge and include the influence of biological factors. His revised bioecological model offers several unique perspectives on human development. First, it defines environment as a multilayered, interactive system and discards the notion that it can be treated as a single entity. Furthermore, it recognizes behavior as a product of the multiple, complex subsystems in which an individual participates. For example, poverty by itself may not limit a child's development if access to social services, high-quality schools, and a nurturing family are in place. Conversely, a child raised in a dysfunctional middle-class family may experience significant behavioral and developmental disorders. Bronfenbrenner's revised theory also emphasized the interactive nature of environment—that not only does environment affect an individual, but the nature of that environment is continuously changing in response to a person's behavior, age, and interactions.

The bioecological theory has had a significant impact on educational practices. It raised diversity awareness, which in turn has led to the development of bias-free curricula, assessment procedures, and play materials. Teacher education programs have also responded by addressing biased perspectives, social injustice, and the need to respect and respond to individual differences. The bioecological theory has also furthered our understanding of how environment and relationships shape a child's development and why family involvement and collaboration are essential in schools.

Maslow's Essential Needs Theory

Abraham Maslow, an American psychologist, attempted to describe human behavior from a motivational needs perspective (Maslow, 1968) (Figure 1-5). He believed that unmet physical and psychological needs drove an individual to take action to satisfy them. Only when one particular need was met or fulfilled would the individual be able to move on and pursue higher goals. For example, a hungry person is driven to find food; once that hunger is satisfied, the person may have the needed energy to work or to engage in a pleasurable or an educational activity. Similarly, a person who succeeds in securing an entry-level job may be motivated to seek additional training in order to perform better or to be considered for a promotion in the future. Maslow also believed that the inability to satisfy a higher

Figure 1-5 Maslow's hierarchy of essential needs.

need would cause the person to retreat temporarily to a lower and more comfortable level. For example, a child who is eager to make new friends but is rejected may withdraw temporarily until she regains her confidence and makes another attempt.

All children—those who are developing normally or typically and those who are gifted, have developmental disabilities, or are **at risk** for developing problems—have essential physiological and psychological needs in common. Only when these basic needs are met will a child be able to survive, thrive, and develop to his fullest potential.

Developmental psychologists have long considered the early years to be the most critical in the entire life span (Bruchhage et al., 2020). Their assumptions have been confirmed and documented many times over by contemporary neuroscientists. During these very early years, children learn most of the fundamental behaviors that characterize the human species—walking, talking, thinking, communicating, and socializing. Never again will the child grow as rapidly, change as dramatically, or be so totally dependent on adults to satisfy life's basic needs and opportunities for learning.

Essential needs—physical, psychological, and learning—are often separated for discussion purposes. However, it must be understood that they are mutually interrelated and interdependent. Meeting a child's physical needs while neglecting psychological needs may lead to serious developmental problems. The opposite also is true—children may experience difficulty in learning and getting along with others if they are being maltreated or their physical needs are neglected. Only when children's essential needs are being fully met will they continue to develop and become self-fulfilled, productive individuals (Jiang et al., 2020; McGuire & Jackson, 2020).

Physical Needs

- Adequate shelter and protection from harm (e.g., violence, neglect, and preventable injuries).
- Sufficient food that is nutritious and appropriate to the child's age.
- Clothing and shoes suitable to the climate and season.
- Preventive physical, mental, and dental health care that is accessible and affordable.
- Personal hygiene practices (e.g., hand-washing, brushing teeth, bathing).
- Rest and activity, in balance; opportunities for indoor and outdoor play.

Psychological Needs

- Affection and consistency: **nurturing** families and teachers who provide positive behavioral guidance.
- Safety, security, and trust: familiar surroundings with family and teachers who are dependable, protective, and responsive to the child's needs.
- **Reciprocal** exchanges that begin in earliest infancy; give-and-take interactions that convey trust, caring, and respect (Markova, Nguyen, & Hoehl, 2019).
- Appropriate adult expectations of what the child can and cannot do at each stage of development.
- Acceptance and positive attitudes shown toward the cultural, ethnic, language, or developmental differences (or all of them) that characterize the child and family.

Learning Needs

- Play opportunities that support early learning; freedom to explore and experiment within safe boundaries; limits that are stated clearly and maintained consistently (Schlesinger et al., 2020) (Figure 1-6).
- Access to **developmentally appropriate** learning experiences, environments, and play materials (McCollow & Hoffman, 2019; Taylor & Boyer, 2020).
- Opportunities that challenge and advance a child's skill development but do not lead to excessive frustration.

at risk A term describing children who may be more likely to have developmental impairments due to certain predisposing factors such as low birth weight (LBW), neglect, or maternal drug addiction.

essential needs Basic physical requirements such as food, shelter, and safety, as well as psychological needs, including love, security, and trust, which are required for survival and healthy development.

nurturing Refers to qualities of warmth, loving, caring, and attention to physical and emotional needs.

reciprocal Refers to exchanges between individuals or groups that are mutually beneficial (or hindering).

developmentally appropriate A term describing learning experiences that are individualized and based on a child's level of skills, abilities, and interests.

Figure 1-6 Children are continuously learning through their social interactions.

- Treatment of errors and delays in achieving a skill as important steps in the learning process, never as reasons for criticizing or ridiculing a child.
- Adults who demonstrate in their everyday lives the appropriate behaviors expected of the child, especially in language, social interactions, and ways of handling stress. Remember that adults serve as important role models for children; children learn far more from observing adults' behavior than from what they hear adults say.

Respect and Self-Esteem Needs

- A literacy-rich environment and inclusion in an active language "community" in which children can learn to communicate through sounds, gestures, signs, and, eventually, words and sentences (spoken, signed, or written).
- A supportive environment in which the child's efforts are encouraged and approved: "You picked up your crayons without being asked!"
- Acknowledgement of all accomplishments, small or large, and for errors as well as for successes: "Look at that! You put on your shirt without any help" (no mention of the button that was missed).
- Recognition that accomplishments and an "I can do it" attitude are important **intrinsic** motivators and essential components of a child's **self-esteem**: "You did a great job of pouring the juice without spilling!"
- Sincere attention drawn to what the child is doing well; using **descriptive praise** to help the child recognize and respect their own accomplishments: "You got your shoes on the right feet all by yourself!"
- Awareness of the effort and concentration that go into acquiring basic developmental skills; providing positive responses to each small step as a child works toward mastery of a complex skill, such as self-feeding with a spoon: "Good job! You took a small bite and it was easier to chew."

Only when children are healthy and have their basic or essential needs satisfied can we expect them to be ready and able to learn (Marotz, 2019). The critical nature of this relationship continues to be demonstrated in numerous research studies (Jirout et al., 2019; Loomis, 2020; Wang, Tian, & Huebner, 2019). The results have prompted support for policy and programs that assist families in meeting children's needs for nutritious food, health care (mental, physical, and oral), safe and nurturing homes, and educational opportunities that are accessible and meaningful. Examples include Head Start, school breakfast and lunch programs, Parents as Teachers, and Children's Health Insurance

intrinsic A feeling of personal satisfaction, pride, or pleasure.

self-esteem Feelings about one's self-worth.

descriptive praise Words or actions that describe to a child specifically what they are doing correctly or well.

Spotlight on **Neuroscience** and **Brain Development**

Why Conduct Brain Research? What Have We Learned?

Most of what previously was known about the brain and its role in children's development and disease was derived from observation and postmortem examinations. The introduction of noninvasive, three-dimensional computerized imaging technologies, such as positron emission tomography (PET), magnetic resonance imaging (MRI), and functional magnetic resonance imaging (fMRI), now has made it possible for scientists to study the living brain and to observe while it functions in real time. For example, Chen and colleagues (2020) and other scientists have discovered that the brain actually changes its activity pattern (plasticity) as a bilingual individual switches from one language to another.

Researchers are able to use imagining technologies to visualize an individual's brain circuitry and the way in which molecules interact to produce human behavior (Dufford, Kim, & Evans, 2020). They have also identified structural and chemical alterations that are associated with various neurodevelopmental disorders (e.g., autism, attention deficit hyperactivity disorder), neurological conditions (e.g., epilepsy, Parkinson's disease, Alzheimer's, posttraumatic stress disorder), and psychiatric disorders (e.g., depression, addiction, schizophrenia) (Edgar, 2020; Roos et al., 2020).

Neuroimaging studies continue to yield unprecedented findings that are rapidly advancing our understanding of how the brain's activity relates to learning and behavior. For example, normative changes are known to occur in the brain's electrical circuitry and cortical layers during adolescence. These alterations have been linked to a decrease in emotional awareness and impulse control which, in turn, increase an adolescent's risk for addiction (Fox, Karim, & Syed, 2020; Tervo-Clemmens et al., 2020). Abnormal changes in the brain's structural components have also been identified in children who are subjected to maltreatment, violence, and other environmental traumas (Killion & Weyandt, 2020; van Rooij et al., 2020). Neuroscientists have confirmed that these alterations influence children's individual learning rates and styles. They have also found that some instructional methods are more effective for teaching certain subjects, such as second languages, reading skills, and mathematical computation (Wilkey, Pollack, & Price, 2020).

These are but a sampling of the brain research discoveries that continue to improve our understanding of children's development and how best to support it. They also have had a significant impact on practices and policy decisions throughout the education, health care, and social justice systems.

Program (CHIP). Educators also understand this critical connection and devote substantial time and effort to ensuring that children and their families obtain supportive resources.

Data Gathering

What we know about children—how they grow and develop, how they learn, and how they interact with others—stems from firsthand observation. For decades, psychologists and educators have observed the daily activities of hundreds of infants and young children. They recorded what they saw and heard as children learned to walk, communicate, grasp basic science and math concepts, interact with peers, reason, and solve challenging problems. Their observations provided the foundation for what we now know about child development, effective teaching practices, curriculum models, and the significance of family–child relationships.

Early childhood educators continue to recognize the importance of gathering information about children's behavior and development and using it to enhance learning. Despite increasing pressures for standardized testing, documentation, and accountability issues in schools, teachers understand the value of observing children in their **naturalistic settings** (DeLuca et al., 2019; Pool & Hampshire, 2019). This approach, referred to as **authentic assessment**, is considered the most effective and

naturalistic settings Environments that are familiar and part of children's everyday experiences, such as classrooms, care arrangements, and the home.

authentic assessment A process of collecting and documenting information about children's developmental progress; data is gathered in children's naturalistic settings and from multiple sources.

▶❚❚ TeachSource **Video Connections**

Culturally Responsive Teaching

Children's development is shaped by an array of genetic and environmental factors. Acknowledging cultural differences is essential to recognizing and accepting children as unique individuals. Respond to the following questions after you have watched the learning video *Culturally Responsive Teaching: A Multicultural Lesson for Elementary Students*:

1. How would Urie Bronfenbrenner describe multiculturalism and its effect on children's learning?

2. Why do you think diversity should be addressed in the classroom?

3. In what ways are children more alike than different? Why is it important to remember that fact?

appropriate method for evaluating and supporting young children's development and learning (Mangione, Osborne, & Mendenhall, 2019).

Authentic assessment involves gathering performance-based evidence in the context of everyday settings and activities. Samples of children's products, family input, and teacher observations are collected continuously and systematically to document learning. This information provides an ongoing, comprehensive picture of a child's developmental progress and reduces the potential bias that results when decisions are based on a single evaluation measure. Authentic assessment also contributes to teachers' understanding of children's skills, abilities, and special needs against a background of the environmental factors that shape development (Danniels, Pyle, & DeLuca, 2020; Perry et al., 2020). Authentic assessment yields results that can be used to establish learning goals, design interventions, modify curriculum and instructional methods, and create responsive environments that effectively meet children's individual developmental and learning needs.

Teachers as Classroom Observers

Regularly scheduled monitoring and assessment of children's developmental progress are benchmarks of high-quality schools and early childhood programs. Observing, recording, and reviewing children's performance in the classroom and during outdoor play gives teachers insight into their accomplishments, progress, strengths, and limitations. Information acquired through observational methods is also beneficial for identifying children who have special talents, developmental delays, health issues, or behavioral problems that may require additional evaluation. In addition, teachers can use this information to design classroom experiences and environments that are developmentally appropriate and support children's individual learning needs.

What Do You See?

Observing children in naturalistic environments.
Teachers have many available options to use for assessing children's development. What developmental skills is the teacher in this photo able to evaluate? What advantages does observing the children in a classroom setting offer over conducting a formal assessment?

Figure 1-7 Providing meaningful learning experiences for children requires observing, involving, and exchanging information with their families.

iStock.com/SDI Productions

The ability to conduct and interpret meaningful observations requires that teachers be familiar with children's typical development so their expectations are accurate and realistic. They also must understand that family, culture, geographic, and linguistic differences can account for variations in what children know and are able to do. With time and practice, teachers become more proficient at identifying specific behaviors for observation, knowing what to look for, recording observations in an objective manner, interpreting their findings, and using the data to address children's individual needs.

Families as Observers

Families always should be welcome in their children's classroom, whether as scheduled observers or on a drop-in basis. They have a right to know what the children are learning and to ask questions. When family members arrange for a scheduled observation, they can be given a clipboard for noting points of interest or questions that they may want to ask about learning materials, teacher responses, or what seems to please or bother the children. A follow-up meeting should be arranged with the child's family to learn their thoughts about the classroom or program, to point out their child's positive qualities, and to share any mutual concerns about the child's progress.

It is important to always involve children's families in the assessment process and to encourage them to share their observations and questions. Families know and understand their children better than anyone else and see them behaving in almost every imaginable circumstance. They are aware of their children's likes and dislikes, joys and anxieties, and positive and negative qualities. As a result, they are often able to provide unique information about children's behavior, challenges, and talents that may be unknown to teachers. Most importantly, they may have specific goals that they want their children to achieve.

When schools create an atmosphere that encourages families to participate in the assessment process and to share information and concerns, everyone—children, families, and teachers—ultimately benefits (Figure 1-7). Ongoing communication with children's families can best be achieved in-person. However, the use of email, videoconferencing, and/or a secure classroom website can also be effective for communicating with those who experience scheduling conflicts, language obstacles, or other barriers that may limit their participation.

Observation Methods

Recorded observations assume many forms: anecdotal notes, running records and logs, time and event sampling, frequency and duration counts, checklists, rating scales, audio and video recordings, and portfolios. Each method is described briefly in the section that follows. Additional information on screening tests is available in Chapter 10, "When and Where to Seek Help," and Appendix B, "Selected Screening and Assessment Instruments."

Anecdotal Notes

Several times each day, the teacher takes a minute or so to write down a few relevant thoughts about what they see occurring. Bates, Schenck, and Hoover (2019) suggest that teachers carry index cards, Post-it notes, or a small notebook in their pocket to use for recording and organizing their observations. The teacher makes brief, dated entries about the **discrete behaviors** observed for a given child: "Played in block area for 5 minutes without hitting another child"; "Initiated conversation with teacher"; "Seemed anxious during the test."

Anecdotal notes provide a running record, or composite picture, of the child's developmental progress in one or more **domains** over a period of time. Teachers can use this information for a variety of intended purposes, including documenting a specific behavior, evaluating the effectiveness of an intervention, or determining if a child's development is progressing satisfactorily. When anecdotal notes are compiled chronologically across developmental domains, they also become a valuable tool for determining placements, writing progress reports, evaluating lesson plans, establishing learning goals, and sharing relevant information with families.

Time or Event Sampling

Sampling techniques enable a teacher to collect behavioral data on one or more children simultaneously during a given time frame or activity. For example, a teacher may be interested in learning which behaviors children use to resolve conflicts during free play: physical aggression (pa), verbal aggression (va), or cooperative problem solving (cps) skills. A simple score sheet can be developed for recording purposes, with children's names listed along one axis and the times and behavioral codes or categories identified along the other (Figure 1-8). A new sheet is dated and used for recording each day's observations.

A sampling approach often is used to obtain information about children's language development. Counts can be obtained during a live observation or from prerecorded audiotaped or videotaped sessions. An observer writes down every utterance exactly as the child says it. One purpose of the samplings, which are usually recorded for ten to fifteen minutes at a time over a monthlong period or so, is to track the child's speech and language progress. Another purpose is to see whether the child's language is functional. Is the child communicating effectively? Does the child get what they need and want by using language? No other behavior (except communicative gestures or facial grimaces) is recorded, although brief notations may be made (e.g., that other children rarely respond to the child's verbal overtures).

Language samples are invaluable for monitoring developmental progress, planning individualized programs, and/or determining if additional intervention services are needed. They are also effective for recalling humorous quips or insightful statements that the child has made.

discrete behaviors Actions that can be observed and described clearly, such as hitting, pulling hair, laughing, or spitting.

domains Areas of development such as physical, motor, social-emotional, and speech and language.

_____ date						Activity: Free Play					

Code:
  pa – physical aggression
  va – verbal aggression
  cps – cooperative play/problem solving

Child	8:30 a.m.			8:40 a.m.			8:50 a.m.			9:00 a.m.		
	pa	va	cps	pa	va	cps	pa	va	cps	pa	va	cps
LaShauna												
Jose												
Markie												
Winston												

Total: pa ___   va ___   cps ___

Figure 1-8 Time sampling form.

Frequency and Duration Counts

When concerns about a specific aspect of a child's behavior arise, teachers first must determine how often the behavior occurs (frequency) or how long it continues (duration) (Figure 1-9). Observations are made and data recorded while teachers go about their daily tasks. One form of frequency count simply requires the teacher to make a tally mark every time the child engages in the specified behavior. A count might reveal that a two-year-old child who was said to cry or hit "all the time" was actually doing so only once or twice per morning, and some mornings not at all. Electronic or inexpensive digital handheld counters can be used to record behaviors that occur at a high rate. Frequency counts yield objective information that can help teachers determine if a problem indeed exists.

A duration count measures the amount of time that a child engages in a particular behavior. For example, a teacher might simply jot down the time when a child enters and leaves a learning center or activity. Another example would be penciling (unobtrusively) on a corner of a painting or collage the time that the child started and finished the project; or the teacher might note when a child's tantrum began and ended. Duration counts are helpful for deciding whether interventions are needed to increase or decrease a specific behavior.

Child's name: Findley A.
Week of: June 7–11, 2021
Observer: Juanita M.
Behavior observed: Not attending/distracting other children

Figure 1-9 Sample frequency and duration counts.

Activity:	Mon	Tues	Wed	Thurs	Fri	Comments
Morning circle	II	0	II	I	III	
Afternoon circle	III	II	IIII	0	III	

Assessing Children's Development

Adults are able to support and guide children's development when they have appropriate information about a child's progress and expected achievements. Respond to the following questions after you have watched the learning video *Portfolio Assessment: Elementary Classroom*:

1. What does portfolio assessment involve?

2. What information does it provide that may not be obtainable from other assessment methods?

3. In what ways can teachers and families use portfolio assessment results to support learning?

Checklists and Rating Scales

Checklists permit a teacher or other observer to quickly record the occurrence of certain skills or behaviors. For example, in infant centers, many firsts can be checked off: the day Josie first smiled, rolled over, or walked alone. In preschools, a checklist can be an effective method for monitoring children's skill acquisition. The date can be inserted as teachers check off when, for example, Carmella correctly identified and matched her primary colors; when Jayson built a tower of eight one-inch cubes; or when Sophia zipped up her own jacket. Teachers may wish to construct their own checklists to reflect unique program objectives. The lists, whether teacher-made or commercial, can be simple or detailed, depending on the need (see Appendix A, "Developmental Checklists").

Rating scales, like checklists, usually are designed to target specific behaviors (Figure 1-10). They provide an efficient method for recording teacher observations and later retrieving that information in a meaningful way.

Portfolios

Representative examples of a child's work—drawings, digital photographs of a special block structure or science project, notes describing manipulative activities completed, audiotapes of conversations and language samples, and digital video of a class play or a child's attempts at learning a new skill—offer another effective method for monitoring children's developmental progress (Habeeb & Ebrahim, 2019; Pahlevi, Rosy, & Ranu, 2018). Teachers select materials that represent a child's learning across all developmental domains and assemble them in an individual portfolio. Children also should be invited to choose items for inclusion and to review the collection from time to time. This step affords children an opportunity to explain their ideas and engage in self-assessment.

Information obtained from teacher observations and conversations with families should also be included in this collection, as they provide additional insight and meaning to the child's products.

Figure 1-10 Sample rating scale form.

Child's name: Findley A.

Date: _____

Task:	Not Yet	Attempts/Not always accurate	Usually accurate	Proficient	Comments (observer/date):
Identifies numbers 1–10					
Arranges numbers 1–10 in correct order					
Counts from 1–10 with prompting					
Counts from 1–10 without prompting					
Writes numbers 1–10					

Portfolio contents should be reviewed and updated periodically to reflect children's changing interests, skill mastery, the need for additional instruction, or all three. The items serve as a visual resource that can be shared with families during conferences to illustrate children's unique strengths and progress. Portfolios are also useful for identifying environmental and/or instructional improvements that may be needed to support children's continued development and learning.

More teachers are adopting the use of e-portfolios for assessment purposes (Hooker, 2019). This format improves the ability to include digital examples of children's work, share contents with families, and accompany a child from grade to grade. It has been noted that children also tend to become more engaged in the assessment process and able to reflect on their own learning experiences and progress.

Summary

1-1 Current knowledge of child development is a composite of human development theories: maturational, psychoanalytic, psychosocial, cognitive-developmental, behaviorism and social learning, bioecological, and essential needs.

- All theories concur that meeting children's basic physical and psychological needs is a powerful determinant of optimum development.
- Current explanations about how children grow and develop rarely rely on any one exclusive theory. Each theory has made major contributions to our understanding of children's behavior.
- Scientists view human development as a product of biological and environmental interactions; they dismiss the nature vs. nurture question as improbable as an either/or proposition.

1-2 Teachers and families play an important role in gathering and contributing information about children's growth and development.

- Authentic assessments provide a comprehensive understanding of children's unique interests, abilities, talents, and needs.
- The process of documenting children's behavior enables teachers to make necessary adjustments in their curricula and instructional methods to improve and support learning.

1-3 Methods commonly used for monitoring children's developmental progress include observation, anecdotal notes, time/event sampling, frequency and duration counts, checklists, rating scales, and portfolios.

Key Terms

nature vs. nurture **p. 3**

norms **p. 4**

constructivism **p. 5**

Zone of Proximal
    development **p. 7**

at risk **p. 11**

essential needs **p. 11**

nurturing **p. 11**

reciprocal **p. 11**

developmentally
    appropriate **p. 11**

intrinsic **p. 12**

self-esteem **p. 12**

descriptive praise **p. 12**

naturalistic settings **p. 13**

authentic assessment **p. 13**

discrete behaviors **p. 16**

domains **p. 16**

Apply What You Have Learned

A. Case Study Connections

Reread the developmental sketch about Tucker at the beginning of the chapter and answer the following questions.

1. What conditions or circumstances may have influenced Tucker's developmental progress to date? Explain your answer based on the theories described in this chapter.

2. Although Tucker's motor development has been somewhat delayed, he has learned to sit up, crawl, stand, walk, and eventually run. Which is more important to consider in his case, the fact that he was older than is typical when he learned these skills, or that he has developed them in this particular order? Explain.

3. Based on the brief description of Tucker and his current foster family, what reciprocal effect(s) might you anticipate when he crawls up onto his mother's lap? How would Skinner and Bandura explain this response?

B. Review Questions

1. What is the nature vs. nature controversy? How does it contribute to our understanding of children's development?

2. What are some behaviors that children would be likely to exhibit during each of the first five stages of Erikson's developmental theory (infancy–adolescence)?

3. In what ways does the maturational theory differ from the cognitive-developmental theory?

4. What is behaviorism, and how does it explain why a child might continue to refuse eating despite repeated warnings from her mother?

5. What data collection method(s) would you use to confirm or refute your suspicions about a child's ability to complete a specific task?

C. Your Turn: Chapter to Practice

1. Use Bronfenbrenner's ecological model to diagram the environmental factors that have influenced your development. Interview a friend or colleague and repeat this exercise. In what ways are the two models similar? Different?

2. Develop five schemas for the word *apple*.

3. Select an age-specific speech-language milestone (see the section "Speech and Language Development," in Chapters 4–9). Conduct a ten-minute observation with a child of this age and record the data using anecdotal notes. Repeat the exercise (with the same child and milestone) using a time or event sampling method. Compare and contrast your experiences with each of the assessment tools. What did you like or dislike about each method?

4. Determine where developmental screenings are conducted in your community. Contact the agency and make arrangements to observe or volunteer to assist with a screening session.

Online Resources

Children's Defense Fund

The Children's Defense Fund is a private, nonprofit organization that serves as a national voice for children, especially those who have disabilities, live in poverty, or are of minority backgrounds. They support policy and programs designed to help children succeed in life.

Council for Exceptional Children (CEC)

The Council for Exceptional Children (CEC) is the largest international professional organization dedicated to advocating and improving educational outcomes for persons with exceptionalities, disabilities, giftedness, or all three.

National Center for Cultural Competence (NCCC)

The National Center for Cultural Competence (NCCC), located at the Georgetown University Center for Child and Human Development, conducts research and provides national leadership, consultation, training, assessment tools, and resource information for agency personnel, health professionals, educators, and family advocates.

Society for Research in Child Development (SRCD)

The stated mission of the Society for Research in Child Development (SRCD) is to support, organize, and disseminate interdisciplinary, child development research findings. Their publications include *Child Development, Child Development Perspectives, Monographs, and Social Policy Report.*

References

Bandura, A. (1977). *Social learning theory.* New York: General Learning Press.

Bates, C. C., Schenck, S. M., & Hoover, H. J. (2019). Anecdotal records: Practical strategies for taking meaningful notes. *Young Children, 74*(3), 14–19.

Bronfenbrenner, U. (1979). *The ecology of human development: Experiments by nature and design.* Cambridge, MA: Harvard University Press.

Bruchhage, M. M., Ngo, G., Schneider, N., D'Sa, V., & Deon, S. C. (2020). Functional connectivity correlates of infant and early childhood cognitive development. *Brain Structure and Function, 225*(2), 669–681.

Chen, M., Ma, F., Wu, J., Li, S., Zhang, Z., Fu, Y., Lu, C., & Guo, T. (2020, May). Individual differences in language proficiency shape the neural plasticity of language control in bilingual language production. *Journal of Neurolinguistics, 54,* 100887. https://doi.org/10.1016/j.jneuroling.2020.100887

Dalton, T. (2005). Arnold Gesell and the maturation controversy. *Integrative Psychological & Behavioral Science, 40*(4), 182–204.

Danniels, E., Pyle, A., & DeLuca, C. (2020). The role of technology in supporting classroom assessment in play-based kindergarten. *Teaching and Teacher Education, 88,* 102966. https://doi.org/10.1016/j.tate.2019.102966

DeLuca, C., Pyle, A., Valiquette, A., & LaPointe-McEwan, D. (2020). New directions for kindergarten education: Embedding assessment in play-based learning. *The Elementary School Journal, 120*(3), 455–479.

Dufford, A. J., Kim, P., & Evans, G. W. (2020). The impact of childhood poverty on brain health: Emerging evidence from neuroimaging across the lifespan. *International Review of Neurobiology, 150,* 77–105.

Edgar, J. C. (2020). Identifying electrophysiological markers of autism spectrum disorder and schizophrenia against a backdrop of normal brain development. *Psychiatry and Clinical Neurosciences, 74*(1), 1–11.

Erikson, E. (1950). *Childhood and society.* New York: Vintage.

Evans, S. C., Blossom, J. B., & Fite, P. J. (2020). Exploring longitudinal mechanisms of irritability in children: Implications for cognitive behavioral intervention. *Behavior Therapy, 51*(2), 238–252.

Fox, H. C., Karim, A., & Syed, S. A. (2020). Bio-behavioral indices of emotion regulation: Potential targets for treatment of addiction. *Current Addiction Reports, 7,* 333–343.

Freud, S. (1923). *The Ego and the Id.* Vienna, Austria: W. W. Norton & Company.

Gesell, A., & Ilg, F. (1949). *Child development.* New York: Harper.

Habeeb, K. M., & Ebrahim, A. H. (2019). Impact of e-portfolios on teacher assessment and student performance on learning science concepts in kindergarten. *Education Information Technologies, 24*(3), 1661–1679.

Honeycutt, H. (2019, September 30). Nature and nurture as an enduring tension in the history of psychology. *Oxford Research Encyclopedia of Psychology.* https://doi.org/10.1093/acrefore/9780190236557.013.518

Hooker, T. (2019). Using ePortfolios in early childhood education: Recalling, reconnecting, restarting and learning. *Journal of Early Childhood Research, 17*(4), 376–391.

Jiang, H., Justice, L. M., Purtell, K. M., & Bates, R. (2020). Exposure to environmental toxicants and early language development for children reared in low-income households. *Clinical Pediatrics, 59*(6), 557–565.

Jirout, J., LoCasale-Crouch, J., Turnbull, K., Gu, Y., Cubides, M., Garzione, S., Evans, T.M., Weltman, A.L., & Kranz, S. (2019). How lifestyle factors affect cognitive and executive function and ability to learn in children. *Nutrients, 11*(8), 1953. doi:10.3390/nu11081953.

Killion, B. E., & Weyandt, L. L. (2020). Brain structure in childhood maltreatment related PTSD across the lifespan: A systematic review. *Applied Neuropsychology; Child, 9*(1), 68–82.

Loomis, A. M. (2020, April 6). Effects of household and environmental adversity on indices of self-regulation for Latino and African American preschool children: Closing the school readiness gap. *Early Education and Development, 31*(1), 1– 21.

Mangione, P. L., Osborne, T., & Mendenhall, H. (2019). How learning progressions help teachers support children's development and learning. *Young Children, 74*(3), 20–25.

Markova, G., Nguyen, T., & Hoehl, S. (2019, September 18). Neurobehavioral interpersonal synchrony in early development: The role of interactional rhythms. *Frontiers in Psychology.* Retrieved from https://www.frontiersin.org/articles/10.3389/fpsyg.2019.02078/full.

Marotz, L. R. (2019). *Health, safety, and nutrition for the young child* (10th ed.). Boston, MA: Cengage Learning.

Maslow, A. (1968). *Toward a psychology of being* (2nd ed.). New York: Van Nostrand Reinhold.

McCollow, M. M., & Hoffman, H. H. (2019). Supporting social development in young children with disabilities: Building a practitioner's toolkit. *Early Childhood Education Journal, 47*(3), 309–320.

McGuire, A., & Jackson, Y. (2020). The role of trauma type and age in the relation between trauma exposure and intelligence. *Child Maltreatment, 25*(2), 192–202.

Montag, C., Ebstein, R. P., Jawinski, P., & Marke, S. (2020). Molecular genetics in psychology and personality neuroscience: On candidate genes, genome wide scans, and new research strategies. *Neuroscience & Biobehavioral Reviews, 118*, 163–174.

National Association for the Education of Young Children (NAEYC). (2020). Developmentally Appropriate Practice (DAP) position statement (4th ed.). Retrieved from https://www.naeyc.org/resources/position-statements.

Pahlevi, T., Rosy, B., & Ranu, E. M. (2018). A scientific approach based on portfolio assessment for autonom problem solving. *International Journal of Educational Research Review, 3*(2), 29–36.

Perry, N. E., Lisaingo, S., Yee, N., Parent, N., Wan, X., & Muis, K. (2020). Collaborating with teachers to design and implement assessments for self-regulated learning in the context of authentic classroom writing tasks. *Assessment in Education: Principles, Policy & Practice, 27*(4), 416–443.

Piaget, J. (1954). *The construction of reality in the child.* New York: Basic Books.

Pool, J. L., & Hampshire, P. (2019). Planning for authentic assessment using unstructured and structured observation in the preschool classroom. *Young Exceptional Children, 23*(3), 143–156.

Poole, K. L., Santesso, D. L., Van Lieshout, R. J., & Schmidt, L. A. (2019). Frontal brain asymmetry and the trajectory of shyness across the early school years. *Journal of Abnormal Child Psychology, 47*(7), 1253–1263.

Roos, A., Fouche, J., du Toit, S., du Plessis, S., Stein, D. J., & Donald, K. A. (2020). Structural brain network development in children following prenatal methamphetamine exposure. *Journal of Comparative Neurology, 528*(11), 1856– 1863.

Schlesinger, M. A., Hassinger-Das, B., Zosh, M., Sawyer, J., Evans, N., & Hirsh- Pasek, K. (2020). Cognitive behavioral science behind the value of play: Leveraging everyday experiences to promote play, learning, and positive interactions. *Journal of Infant, Child, and Adolescent Psychotherapy, 19*(2), 202– 216.

Skinner, B. F. (1938). *The behavior of organisms: An experimental analysis.* New York: Appleton-Century.

Taylor, M. E., & Boyer, W. (2020). Play-based learning: Evidence-based research to improve children's learning experiences in the kindergarten classroom. *Early Childhood Education Journal, 48*(10), 127–133.

Tervo-Clemmens, B., Quach, A., Calabro, F. J., Foran, W., & Luna, B. (2020). Meta-analysis and review of functional neuroimaging differences underlying adolescent vulnerability to substance use. *NeuroImage, 209*, 116476. https://doi.org/10.1016/j.neuroimage.2019.116476

van Rooij, S. J., Smith, R. D., Stenson, A. F., Ely, T. D., Yan, X., Tottenham, N., Stevens, J. S., & Jovanovic, T. (2020). Increased activation of the fear neurocircuitry in children exposed to violence. *Depression & Anxiety, 37*(4), 303– 312.

Vygotsky, L. (1986). *Thought and language* (2nd ed.). Cambridge, MA: MIT Press.

Wang, Y., Tian, L., & Huebner, E. S. (2019). Basic psychological needs satisfaction at school, behavioral school engagement, and academic achievement: Longitudinal reciprocal relations among elementary school students. *Contemporary Educational Psychology, 56*, 130–139.

Wilkey, E. D., Pollack, C., & Price, G. R. (2020). Dyscalculia and typical math achievement are associated with individual differences in number-specific executive function. *Child Development, 91*(2), 596–619.

Wood, J. J., Kendall, P. C., Wood, K. S., Kerns, C. M., Seltzer, M., Small, B. J., Lewin, A. B., & Storch, E. A. (2020). Cognitive behavioral treatments for anxiety in children with autism spectrum disorder: A randomized clinical trial. *JAMA Psychiatry, 77*(5), 474–483.

Chapter 2

Principles of Growth and Development

Learning Objectives

After reading this chapter, you will be able to:

2-1 Define growth and development as separate concepts and provide at least two examples of each.

2-2 Defend this statement: "Sequence, not age, is the important factor in evaluating a child's developmental progress."

2-3 Identify and briefly describe the six major developmental domains that are the focus of this text.

NAEYC NAEYC Professional Standards Linked to Chapter Content

1a, 1b, and 1c: Child development and learning in context
2a: Family–teacher partnerships and community connections
4a and 4b: Developmentally, culturally, and linguistically appropriate teaching practices

Dakota and Liselli, identical twins soon to be three years old, weighed in at a little over four pounds each at birth. Despite having being born two months early and considered to be low-birth-weight infants, both are now strong and healthy. They look alike in almost every way, with dark brown eyes, thick eyelashes, and high cheekbones. Dakota and Liselli's young parents recently moved with their twins to a nearby state where they would begin to attend college.

Although Dakota and Liselli behave alike in many ways, there are also noticeable differences. Since early infancy, Dakota has been more physically active. She slept less, ate more, sat up, crawled, and walked alone weeks before Liselli (or other babies her age, for that matter). She has also been more adventuresome in attempting new experiences, such as learning to swim and riding a tricycle. Liselli, on the other hand, was the first to smile, play peek-a-boo, and say recognizable words. She now uses complete sentences and has considerable letter, word, and number recognition skills. She likes to "read" to

Dakota and acts as her interpreter when Dakota can't make herself understood. In turn, Dakota is first to protect and comfort Liselli whenever she is hurt or frightened.

Dakota and Liselli's parents enrolled the girls in a Head Start program conveniently located on the college campus. During a recent health screening session, Liselli failed her initial vision test and was referred to an eye specialist for additional evaluation. The optometrist determined that Liselli is nearsighted and requires corrective glasses. Although the girls were initially reluctant to join in group activities, they are beginning to make several "friends" but still seldom venture too far from one another.

Ask Yourself

- From the brief descriptions of Dakota and Liselli, which developmental characteristics can be attributed solely to genetic makeup?
- In what ways may environment account for differences in the girls' development?
- How do Dakota and Liselli's motor skills differ?

Basic Patterns and Concepts

Groups of children of approximately the same age, across all cultures, appear to be remarkably similar in size, shape, and developmental abilities. However, closer observation also reveals a wide range of individual differences within these groups (Figure 2-1). Both similarities and differences depend on a child's unique patterns of growth and development. What defines this complementary process of *growth and development*? Why do children experience this progression differently? Although these terms are often used interchangeably, they do not describe identical concepts.

Figure 2-1 Children's development includes a wide range of individual differences.

Monstera/Pexels

24

Growth

Growth refers to specific physical changes and increases in the child's size. An increase in cell numbers and enlargement of existing cells are responsible for the observable gains in a child's height, weight, **head circumference**, shoe size, length of arms and legs, body shape, and many other notable changes. Growth also lends itself to direct and fairly reliable measurement.

The growth process continues throughout the life span, although the rate varies by age. For example, growth occurs rapidly during infancy and adolescence but is typically much slower and less dramatic in the toddler and middle school years. The body continues to repair and replace its cells throughout adulthood, even into old age, although much less vigorously during these times.

Growth is a sensitive indicator of a child's overall wellness. Genetic growth parameters are set prior to birth, but it is the interaction with environmental factors that ultimately determines whether this potential will be realized. Children who have access to a nutritious diet, nurturing care, medical treatment, and opportunities for play and physical activity are most likely to achieve optimal growth. By contrast, children who are exposed to toxic environmental conditions, such as poverty, maltreatment, food insecurity, or lack of health care are at greater risk for delayed or stunted growth (Black, Trude, & Lutter, 2020; Raiten & Bremer, 2020).

Development

Development refers to an increase in complexity—a change from the relatively simple to the more complex and advanced. This process involves an orderly progression along a continuum or pathway over time. Little by little, knowledge, behaviors, and skills are learned and refined. Although the developmental sequence across domains is basically the same for all children, the rate and degree of attainment can vary greatly from child to child.

The progressive acquisition of developmental skills involves a dynamic interaction of biological and environmental factors (nature *and* nurture). Neurological, muscular, and skeletal systems must reach a certain functional maturity before a child is capable of learning a particular skill. At the same time, the social, cultural, ethnic, and linguistic context in which a child is growing up influences what is likely to be learned (Figure 2-2). Collectively, these factors account for the wide range of individual differences observed in children's developmental progress. For example, families in many cultures encourage

Tatiana Syrikova/Pexels

Figure 2-2 Learning to walk is a complex developmental and maturational process.

growth Physical changes leading to an increase in size.

head circumference Measurement of the head taken at its largest point (across the forehead, around the back of the head, and returning to the starting point).

development Refers to an increase in complexity, from simple to more complicated and detailed.

their children to begin crawling, walking, and self-feeding at an early age, whereas in other cultures, the early acquisition of these skills is not highly valued or supported. Children living in poor, inner-urban neighborhoods may have delayed motor skills due to fewer safe opportunities for organized and spontaneous outdoor play.

Developmental Milestones

Major markers or points of accomplishment are referred to as *developmental milestones.* They provide a functional guide that can be useful for tracking the emergence of children's motor, social, cognitive, and language skills. Milestones represent behaviors that appear in somewhat orderly steps and within fairly predictable age ranges for typically developing children. For example, almost every child begins to smile socially by ten to twelve weeks and to speak a first word or two at around twelve months. These achievements are only two of the many significant behavioral indications that a child's developmental progress is on track. When children fail to achieve one or more developmental milestones within a reasonable time frame, careful and systematic monitoring by a child development specialist or health care provider is necessary.

Sitting, walking, and talking are examples of developmental milestones that depend on biological maturation, yet these skills do not develop independently of the environment. For example, learning to walk requires muscle strength and coordination. In addition, it requires an environment that encourages practice, not only of walking as it emerges but also of the behaviors and skills that precede walking, such as rolling over, sitting up, and standing. It is also important to recognize that differences in children's biological makeup affect the ways in which they experience and respond to their environment. For example, a hearing loss may significantly alter a child's concept of language, interest in talking, and development of linguistic skills, even if the child lives in a literacy-rich environment.

Sequences of Development

A sequence of development is composed of predictable steps along a developmental pathway common to the majority of children. This process sometimes is referred to as **continuity**. Children must be able to roll over before they can sit, and sit before they can stand. *The critical consideration is the order in which children acquire these developmental skills, not their age in months and years.* The appropriate sequence in each developmental area is an important indication that the child is moving steadily forward along a sound developmental continuum (Figure 2-3). For example, in language development, it does not matter how many words a child speaks by two years of age. What is important is that the child has progressed from cooing and babbling to jabbering (inflected **jargon**) to syllable production. The two- or three-year-old who has progressed through these stages usually also produces words and sentences within a reasonable period of time.

Some scientists explain children's development from a different point of view, believing that development occurs in a series of stages rather than as a gradual progression from simple to complex. They refer to this process as **discontinuity**. For example, rolling over, sitting up, and standing are considered distinct and abrupt steps that precede walking. It isn't necessary for a child to perfect one skill set before attempting another that may be more advanced.

In any case, developmental progress is rarely a smooth and even process. Irregularities, such as periods of **stammering** or the onset of a **food jag**, are not uncommon. Regression, or taking a step or two backward now and then, is also perfectly normal and to be expected. For example, a child who has been toilet trained for some time may begin to have accidents at times of stress, such as starting school or welcoming a new sibling into the family. An older child may resort to hitting or become verbally aggressive following a family move or a parent's divorce. Children are usually able to overcome these temporary setbacks and to gradually move on when adults provide them with compassionate support, understanding, and direction.

continuity Developmental progress that gradually becomes increasingly refined and complex.

jargon Unintelligible speech; in young children, it usually includes sounds and inflections of the native language.

discontinuity Development that occurs in irregular periods or stages; not a smooth, continuous process.

stammering To speak in an interrupted or repetitive pattern; not to be confused with stuttering.

food jag A period when only certain foods are preferred or accepted.

Figure 2-3 Typical motor development sequence.

Age-Level Expectancies or Norms

Age-level expectancies can be thought of as **chronological**, or age-related, levels of development. Psychologists, including Gesell, Piaget, and Erikson, conducted hundreds of systematic observations of infants and children of various ages. Analyses of their findings represent the average or typical age at which many specifically described developmental skills are acquired by most children in a given culture (Gesell & Ilg, 1949; Piaget, 1954). This average age is often referred to as the *norm*. Thus, a child's development may be described as at the norm, above the norm, or below the norm. For example, a child who begins walking at eight months is ahead of the norm (twelve to fifteen months), whereas a child who does not walk until twenty months is considered to be below the norm.

Age-level expectancies *always represent a range and never an exact point in time* when specific skills are most likely to be achieved. Therefore, profiles described in this text (age expectancies for specific skills) always must be interpreted as approximate midpoints on a range of months (as in the example on walking, the range is from eight to twenty months, with the midpoint at fourteen months). Once again, a reminder: It is *sequence*, not age, that is the important factor in evaluating a child's progress (Estrada et al., 2019; Kabha & Berger, 2020; Monier & Droit-Volet, 2019).

In real life, no child is typical in every way. The range of skills and the age at which skills are attained show great individual and cultural variation. Relevant again is the example of walking—one infant may begin at eight months and another not until twenty months (many months apart on either side of the norm). No two children grow and develop at exactly the same rate, nor do they perform in exactly the same way. For example, there are a half-dozen ways to creep and crawl. Most children, however, use what is referred to as *contralateral locomotion*, an opposite knee–hand method of getting

chronological Refers to events or dates occurring in sequence over the passage of time.

about prior to walking. Yet, some normally walking two-year-olds never crawl, indicating a distinct variation in typical development.

Organization and Reorganization

Development can be thought of as a series of phases. Spurts of rapid growth and development often are followed by a period of disorganization. During this time, the child works to regain confidence by practicing a new skill until it is mastered. Once this has been achieved, the child seems to recover and move into a period of reorganization. It is not uncommon for children to demonstrate behavior problems or even regression during these phases. Perhaps a new baby has become an active and engaging older infant who is now the center of family attention. At the same time, mother may expect three-year-old brother to help dress himself in the morning. He may begin to have tantrums over minor frustrations, and for the time being, revert to babyish ways and lose his hard-won bladder control. In most instances, these periods are relatively short-lived. Almost always, the three-year-old will learn more age-appropriate ways of gaining attention if given adequate adult encouragement and support.

Typical Growth and Development

In terms of development, the words **typical** and *normal* often are used interchangeably to describe the acquisition of certain skills and behaviors according to a predictable rate and sequence. However, as previously stated, the range of typical behaviors within each developmental domain is broad and includes mild variations and simple irregularities, such as the three-year-old who stutters or the twelve-month-old who learns to walk without having crawled. The use of these terms also oversimplifies the concept. Normal or typical development implies:

- An integrated process governing change in size, **neurological** structure, and behavioral complexity.
- A cumulative or building-block process in which each new aspect of growth or development includes and builds on earlier changes; each accomplishment is necessary to the acquisition of the next set of skills.
- A continuous process of give and take (reciprocity) between the child and the environment, each changing the other in a variety of ways. For example, the four-year-old drops a glass and breaks it, and the parent scolds the child. Both events—the broken glass and the adult's displeasure—are environmental changes that the child triggered. From this experience, the child might learn to hold on more firmly next time, which constitutes a change in both the child's and the adult's behavior—fewer broken glasses, thus less adult displeasure.

Interrelatedness of Developmental Domains

Discussions about development usually focus on several major domains: physical, motor, perceptual, cognitive, social-emotional, and language. However, no single area develops independently of the others. Every skill a child attempts, whether simple or complex, requires a mix of developmental abilities. Social skills are a prime example. Why are some young children said to have good social skills? Often the answer is because they play well with other children and are sought out as playmates. To be a preferred playmate, a child must have many skills, all of them interrelated and interdependent. For example, a four-year-old should be able to:

- Run, jump, climb, and build with blocks (good motor skills)
- Ask for, explain, and describe what is going on (good language skills)

typical Refers to the achievement of certain skills according to a fairly predictable sequence, although with many individual variations.

neurological Refers to the brain and nervous system.

What Do You See?

The interplay of developmental domains. Multiple domains are actively involved in the completion of any task, from dressing oneself to putting together a puzzle. Look closely, and identify the developmental skills and domains required for this child to thread the string through the block successfully.

- Recognize similarities and differences among play materials and thus be able to select appropriate materials in a joint building project (good perceptual skills)
- Problem-solve, conceptualize, and plan ahead in cooperative play ventures (good cognitive skills)

Every developmental area is well represented in the preceding example, even though social development was the primary area under consideration. A significant delay in any one domain is likely to disrupt typical developmental progression in the others. For this reason, it is important to always monitor children's developmental progress across all domains.

Brain Growth and Development

Brain maturation lays the foundation for all other aspects of a child's development. Growth and development of the fetal brain is rapid, exceedingly complex, and influenced by a combination of maternal environment and genetics (see Chapter 3, "Prenatal Development"). Healthy conditions and maternal lifestyle practices foster optimal brain formation, whereas adverse conditions, such as fetal exposure to alcohol, smoke, or maternal depression, can have a negative effect and place the child at lifelong risk (Estrada et al., 2019; Kabha & Berger, 2020; Monier & Droit-Volet, 2019).

A child's brain continues to grow and to be shaped through the daily interaction of genetic materials and daily experiences. Infants are born with an excess of brain cells (neurons)—an estimated 10 billion—more than adults have or will ever need! However, these

▶❚❚ **TeachSource Video Connections**

Source: https://www.youtube.com/watch?v=m_5u8-0Sh6A.

Brain Development in Infancy

Early brain development sets the stage for future learning and success. Adults play a critical role in fostering this early development by providing young children with enrichment opportunities, positive support, and consistent nurturing and care. Respond to the following questions after you have watched the video *Serve and Return Interaction Shapes Brain Circuitry.*

1. What triggers the formation of neural connections?
2. What type of learning experiences can adults provide to promote children's brain development?

neurons are relatively nonfunctional until connections are established and organized into purposeful networks. **Neural connections** are formed when chemical and electrical reactions in the brain are activated by sensory input and learning experiences. Once established, these neural connections enable brain cells to communicate with one another and to perform purposeful activities (Figure 2-4). Each time an experience is repeated, the neural connection becomes stronger. For example, consider the infant who is initially unable to feed himself, then learns to hold a cup and spoon after much practice, and eventually is able to eat a meal without giving much thought to the mechanics involved.

Children's brains continue to increase in size as neurons grow larger and neural connections become more complex. An infant's brain triples in weight by the end of the first year; a toddler's brain weighs approximately three-fourths that of an adult's. Growth is especially remarkable during the first three or four years, when the brain is most flexible and receptive to learning. This quality, known as **plasticity**, accounts for the young child's unique ability to acquire skills quickly (Reh et al., 2020). It explains, for example, why a four-year-old who is learning English as a second language is able to understand and converse in a significantly shorter period of time than an adult would require.

Weak or seldom-used connections are eliminated gradually through a natural process known as **pruning** in order to make room for active cells and expanding networks. Selective pruning begins in earnest at around age 10 and peaks in early puberty. This "use it or lose it" process is ongoing throughout an individual's life, although it occurs at a slower pace with aging. It explains why infants who are born with the capability of reproducing sounds in any language eventually learn to communicate in their own native language but not in any of the others; or why one child becomes an outstanding pianist while another excels at playing sports or chess.

Research has revealed an amazing relationship that exists between a child's brain development and language acquisition (Adibpour et al., 2020; Laing & Bergelson, 2020). For example, infants not only take in the sounds of the language they are hearing, but they also replicate them, complete with a dialect. Furthermore, the dialect is maintained without change for years to come. It is as if, in the case of language development, the brain will not easily sever connections made in the earliest months and years of life, regardless of subsequent changes in language environments.

neural connections Organized linkages formed between brain cells as a result of learning.

plasticity The brain's ability to change and reorganize its structure as a result of learning.

pruning The process of eliminating unused neurons and neural connections to strengthen those that the child is actively using.

Figure 2-4 Neural connections become stronger through repetition of an activity or behavior.

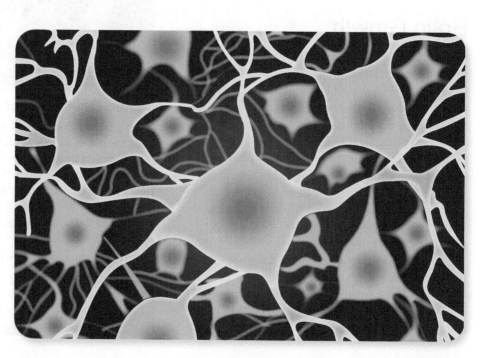

It has long been thought that the child's brain simply continues to mature and increase in complexity because of ongoing experiences. However, neuroscientists used modern technologies to examine the adolescent brain and have discovered that this isn't the case. What they found was that a new layer of gray matter forms on the brain's frontal lobes during adolescence. Their discovery is especially significant because this particular region of the brain is responsible for regulating emotion, impulsivity, and decision-making processes (Xu et al., 2020). Once again, new neural connections must be established in these areas through repeated experience, refinement, and pruning before they are able to perform with any degree of consistency and adultlike sophistication. This finding helps explain why adolescents are more likely to engage in risk-taking behaviors and to make seemingly irrational decisions that adults often find puzzling (McIlvain et al., 2020).

Again, it is critical to remember that the interplay of genetic materials and daily experiences—positive as well as negative—determine how the brain's architectural structure ultimately forms. For example, growing up in a neglectful or chaotic home environment can alter the structure of neural connections and wire a child's brain for instinctive survival rather than for cognitive tasks. In contrast, a positive, supportive home environment and opportunities for learning are conducive to healthy brain development. However, an impairment may influence the way in which a child experiences and interprets everyday activities and also affect the brain's structure differently.

Spotlight on **Neuroscience** and **Brain Development**

Early Adversity and Atypical Brain Development

Researchers have long focused on adversity and its negative effects on individual health outcomes, disease, and longevity. More recently, they have turned their attention to how children's neurocognitive development is affected. What they have learned is that growing up in a disadvantaged or toxic environment changes the brain's size, physical structure, and organization (Dufford, Kim, & Evans, 2020; Nelson & Gabard-Durnam, 2020). These deviations significantly compromise memory, attention, language, and self-regulation abilities and set children on a negative trajectory for the rest of their lives (Jiang et al., 2020; Rod et al., 2020).

Approximately 35.2 million people in the United States, including 5.3 million children under age eighteen, lived in food-insecure households in 2019 (USDA, 2020) (Figure 2-5). Insufficient food and poor prenatal diet combined with poverty-related stress are factors known to have an adverse effect on fetal growth and brain development (Fitzgerald, Hor, & Drake, 2020; Franke et al., 2020). These children often continue to grow up in economically disadvantaged homes and, thus, face a higher incidence of maltreatment, a lack of reading and play materials, violent neighborhoods, and unsafe, unpredictable housing.

Chronic exposure to adversity and toxic stress eventually alters the way in which neural connections are established in the brain, preparing it for basic existence rather than for learning. The combined effect of early structural and learning deficits seriously limits children's development, leaves them unprepared for school, and interferes with academic achievement (Loomis, 2021; Tooley et al., 2020). It also increases children's likelihood of developing serious behavioral and mental health problems later in life (Franke et al., 2020; Gete, Waller, & Mishra, 2021). Perhaps it would be more appropriate to classify adversity as a disease rather than a social problem. It affects a large segment of the population, has observable symptoms caused by environmental factors, impairs an individual's ability to function, and can be transmitted from one person to another.

(continued)

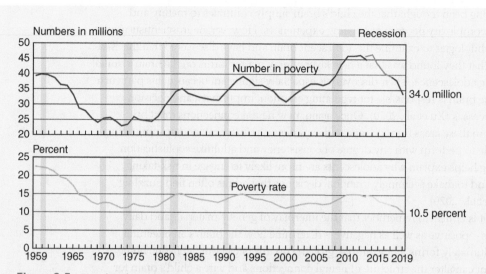

Figure 2-5 Number living in poverty and poverty rate: 1959 to 2019.

Source: U.S. Census Bureau, Current Population Survey, 1960–2020 Annual Social and Economic Supplements, https://www.census.gov/library/publications/2020/demo/p60-270.html.

What are the connections?

1. How might children's early adversity exposure contribute to chronic school failure?
2. What intervention services and assistance programs are needed to help mitigate poverty's early and cyclical effects on children's development?

Attachment

Theorists have suggested that infants and their parents are innately driven to form an emotional connection with one another. This **attachment** process is thought to be a protective response and one that improves an infant's chances for survival. A secure attachment also plays an important role in social-emotional and brain development and enables children to explore and gradually move beyond a caregiver's comfort and protection.

Freud concluded that attachments were formed as a result of a mother's feeding relationship with her infant. This idea was later dispelled by Harlow and Zimmermann (1958), who suggested that infants have a biological or "tactile need" to be touched and held. The resulting comfort and security they experience is considered essential to an attachment formation. Erikson (1968) hypothesized that attachment relationships were established during the child's first year of life and were based on a child's feelings of trust vs. mistrust.

The idea that infants are programmed instinctively to form an emotional connection with a primary caregiver was also fundamental to Bowlby's (1969, 1988) theory of attachment. He suggested that this relationship forms in stages and becomes increasingly focused, purposeful, and insightful as children's cognitive and motor skills advance:

- Birth to 2 months – Infant shows no preference for a specific caregiver; responds similarly to anyone who satisfies their needs.
- 2 to 8 months – Infant begins to recognize and respond to a preferred caregiver.
- 8 to 24 months – Child forms a strong connection with specific caregivers; becomes wary and distressed when approached by other persons, which are expressions of **separation anxiety**.
- 24 months and beyond – Child develops some emotional understanding of other people's feelings and objectives and begins to reciprocate; continues to maintain physical closeness with preferred caregivers.

attachment A strong emotional connection usually formed between a child and parent(s).

separation anxiety Extreme fear or distress that a child experiences when separated from their primary caregiver; occurs most commonly between 9 and 24 months-of-age.

Few had questioned whether there were individual differences in the quality of children's attachment until Ainsworth (1979) developed her "Strange Situation" experiment. She conducted a series of observations in which (1) a toddler played in a room when the mother was present, (2) the mother left and a stranger entered the room and, finally, (3) the child and mother were reunited. Ainsworth concluded from the data that there were significant differences in the attachment quality among children. She described three attachment styles, and later added a fourth, based on the degree of security or insecurity that individual children displayed:

- *Securely attached* – Children continued to play after their mother left the room and the stranger appeared.
- *Insecure avoidant* – Children hesitated momentarily when their mother left the room, acknowledged the stranger when they entered the room, but then continued to play.
- *Insecure resistant* – Children become alarmed and distressed, clung to their mother, and cried inconsolably when she attempted to leave; they stopped playing until their mother returned to the room, then clung to her once again.
- *Insecure disorganized* – Children appeared confused, fearful, and unsure of what to do. They stopped playing, then appeared to be upset (e.g., thrashing about, crying, unable to be comforted) when she returned.

A secure attachment relationship is formed and strengthened through consistent, caring, and supportive interactions between a child and their parent or primary caregiver. Researchers have found that children are also capable of forming meaningful attachments with multiple caregivers and that each contributes different, but important, qualities to the child's development (Brown & Cox, 2020; Fernandes et al., 2020). Child–adult attachment relationships are a reflection of cultural values and, thus, assumptions about their nature must be made with caution (Granqvist, 2021; Strand, 2020; Strand, Vossen, & Savage, 2019).

Many variables can interfere with attachment strength and stability. Women who experience unwanted pregnancy, previous pregnancy loss, a lack of partner support, or postpartum depression are less likely to form a healthy attachment with their infant (Landi et al., 2020; Rollè et al., 2020). Medical conditions may limit a mother's ability to care for her infant and to establish a secure emotional bond. A mismatch in child–parent temperaments may increase negative interactions and result in a dysfunctional attachment (Augustine & Stifter, 2019; Carrasco, Delgado, & Holgado-Tello, 2020). The early identification of potential risk factors and implementation of attachment-focused interventions is, thus, essential for promoting a healthy parent–child relationship.

Temperament

The term *temperament* refers to the genetic foundation of an individual's personality (Zwir et al., 2020). It describes psychological qualities that are characteristic of a person's emotional reactions and regulation, such as intensity, disposition or mood, and persistence. Temperament also accounts for children's individual physiological differences in behavior patterns, including activity level, predictability, emotionality, and manner of reacting and adapting to unfamiliar experiences (Figure 2-6). Thomas and Chess (1977) categorized and labeled these behaviors as the "easy" child, the "difficult" child, and the "slow-to-warm" child. They found that approximately 65 percent of children fall into one of these three categories: 40 percent of children are considered "easy," 15 percent are regarded as "slow-to-warm," and 10 percent are seen as "difficult." The remaining 35 percent of children may exhibit characteristics in more than one category.

Anete Lusina/Pexels

Figure 2-6 A child's temperament can influence the nature of parent–child interactions.

Subsequent studies have noted that such characteristic patterns are generally stable and persist into adulthood (Tang et al., 2020). Some researchers suggest that the socialization process (i.e., parental responses, cultural expectations, peer relationships) may influence the way a child ultimately expresses these behaviors (Super et al., 2020; Wagers & Kiel, 2019). Maturation also plays a critical role in children's ability to exercise greater emotional control and respond in a more positive manner.

It is important to understand that temperament also affects the way in which a child experiences everyday activity. For example, a difficult child may be hard to please and react intensely or tantrum when things don't go his way. He may find it difficult to adjust to a new teacher or school and act out to express his displeasure. By contrast, an easy child may pout for a few minutes when told she can't have an ice cream cone, but then quickly turn her attention to the puppy playing in a neighbor's yard. A three-year-old who is slow-to-warm may require extra time to separate from his parents when they leave him at the preschool. In each case, it is easy to understand how a child's temperament may also influence the nature of an adult's response. Parents of difficult children may avoid situations that are likely to elicit an explosive outburst. In contrast, a smiling, easygoing toddler may invite unsolicited hugs and adult attention.

Categorical labels must be used cautiously when they are applied to children's behavior. Labeling a moody child as "difficult" or "slow-to-warm" may influence the expectations that an adult has for that child and reinforce the very behavior in question. For example, a slow-to-warm child may evoke few displays of affection from others. As a result, she may identify this as rejection, making it even more difficult for this child to act warm and outgoing.

Adult temperament must also be considered in this equation because it influences the way in which a child's behavior is perceived. For example, a short-fused parent may overreact to a curious toddler who continues to pull pots and pans from the cabinet despite an earlier warning, whereas an easygoing parent may understand that this is typical behavior and encourage the toddler's curiosity. In each case, adult temperament contributes to the contrast in perception and initial response to the toddler's behavior. Each reaction conveys an important message that continuously influences and shapes the child's behavior (Kälin & Roebers, 2021).

Gender Awareness and Identity

What does it mean to be a boy or a girl? Early in life, young children begin to develop a concept of gender and gender identity appropriate to their culture. Each boy and girl develops a set of behaviors, attitudes, beliefs, and commitments that are defined, directly or indirectly, as acceptable male or female attributes (McLean et al., 2020). In addition, children typically play out gender roles that reflect customary practices.

Several theoretical perspectives have been advanced over the years to explain children's gender identity formation. Freud's psychoanalytic theory suggested that children are initially attracted to the opposite-sex parent and later identify with the same-sex parent when they become sexually uncomfortable (Oedipus complex) (Freud, 1924). Most modern theorists do not agree with this concept. The social learning theory of gender advocates that children learn male or female behaviors through observation and imitation (Bandura, 1977), but critics consider this approach overly passive and suggest that it perpetuates male and female stereotyping.

Cognitive-developmental theorists believe that children play an active role (e.g., observing, imitating, and experiencing) in gender concept formation (Kohlberg, 1966). However, they also acknowledge maturational and biological differences (male/female) as influencing the way in which gender-relevant information is interpreted and internalized. Preferred-gender ideas are further socialized through continuous peer and adult feedback. For example, a five-year-old girl may be told to "act like a lady" or an eight-year-old boy may be chastised by his friends for choosing a girl to be on their kickball team.

Each theoretical approach has contributed to a contemporary understanding of gender and gender identity—that a child's sense of maleness or femaleness involves a complex interaction of biological, cognitive, and socialization processes, including cultural expectations, daily experiences, family values, adult role models, playmates and play opportunities, toys, and media exposure (Ristori et al., 2020; Shroeder & Liben, 2021).

Children's concept of gender is formed in stages. Infants, for example, are able to distinguish the difference between male and female voices and faces. Toddlers become aware of physical differences between boys and girls and begin to show a preference for same-sex playmates. Between two and three years of age, children are able to label themselves correctly as girls or boys. Their toy selections and play often reflect gender role stereotyping (e.g., mothers feed babies, while dads go to work) (Davis & Hines, 2020). Parents may begin treating children differently at this point—perhaps more tender and nurturing with girls, while reinforcing boys for their toughness and independent behaviors.

Gender stability is generally achieved by three to four years of age. That is, children distinguish themselves and others as being a boy or a girl based upon appearance: "Girls have long hair," "Boys have short hair"; "Girls wear pink, boys don't." However, they continue to believe that a person's gender can be changed depending upon the situation (Kohlberg, 1966). For example, a girl can become a "daddy" by simply dressing up in pants, T-shirt, and a hat. Three- and four-year-olds also begin labeling toys and activities as being either for girls or boys. Gender constancy becomes apparent between five and seven years of age. At this point, children accept that gender is permanent and unchangeable. It is important that children's gender identity be supported at each stage because it influences all aspects of development, including self-concept, self-esteem, academic performance, and mental health.

Children's sexual identity is usually well-established by middle childhood (Figure 2-7). Occasionally, a child may experience ideas and behaviors that do not necessarily conform to their assigned gender at birth (Diamond, 2020). They may identify more with another gender and struggle psychologically to accept (or even deny) their own sexuality. Adolescent boys are more likely than girls to feel significant parental and peer pressure to conform to gender-stereotyped norms. As a result, they tend to experience more behavioral problems, bullying, and psychological disorders when their behavior is nonconforming (van Beusekom et al., 2020).

Scientists have explored a number of factors, including genetic abnormalities, hormonal disturbances during fetal development, environmental influences, and

Figure 2-7 Sexual orientation is usually well established by middle childhood.

personal choice in an attempt to explain gender nonconformity, but they have been unable to determine a definitive cause. It is important to understand that a child's sexual identity cannot be changed. Some children experience considerable psychological confusion and inner turmoil (gender dysphoria) in their attempts to comprehend what is occurring. What they need most is acceptance, understanding, and nonjudgmental love and support. Participation in individual and family therapy is often also beneficial.

Socio-Ecological Factors and Developmental Risk

All aspects of a child's development, starting at conception, are subject to the environmental influence of family and home, community, and society at large. Some factors promote optimum development; others may serve as temporary barriers, or even cause abnormalities that interfere with typical progress. The following are but a few examples of powerful **socio-ecological** factors:

- A family's financial resources
- Adequacy and availability of nutritious food and safe housing (Dunn, 2020)
- Cultural values and practices (Cote & Bornstein, 2021)
- Prenatal and postnatal access to medical care for mother and child
- Parents' level of education, especially that of the mother, being a major predictor of a child's academic achievement (Schochet, Johnson, & Ryan, 2020)
- A family's understanding of its roles and responsibilities before and after the infant's birth (Marotz & Kupzyk, 2018)
- Family communication and child-rearing practices (supportive or punitive, nurturing or neglectful); family stress (Duong et al., 2021)
- Family structure—single- or two-parent, blended, or extended family; grandparent with primary parenting role; same-sex parent(s); foster or adoptive homes

socio-ecological Refers to the interactive exchanges that occur between children and their family, other significant adults, and everything in the broader community that affects their lives.

Differences in the way each of these factors are experienced ultimately result in a child being unlike any other child. Some children grow up in conditions that support optimum growth and development. Others are born into situations that are harmful to their early development and, thus, may be considered *at risk*. For example, premature birth and low birth weight are two conditions known to increase a child's risk for physical impairments, learning disabilities, behavioral problems, or all three. Nagy and colleagues (2021) noted that these children often have poorer executive function and lower intelligence. Chung, Chou, and Brown (2020) found that premature infants are more likely to have sensory, motor, behavioral, and/or cognitive deficits that require early intervention.

The risk for developmental delays is also greater among children born to mothers outside of the "normal" age range (e.g., very young teenagers or women in their forties) or those who are significantly depressed. Chronic exposure to domestic violence, maltreatment, or poverty also increases a child's potential for significant behavioral and developmental problems (Dodaj, 2020). Children subjected to harsh physical punishment, such as repeated spanking, exhibit more learning problems, aggressive behaviors, and lower academic potential, the latter expressed as a lower intelligence quotient (IQ) (Giannotti et al., 2020).

Complex interactions among socio-ecological factors and their effects on children's development present unique challenges. Successful interventions require a comprehensive approach and understanding of the individual, family, and community variables that are involved and operating on different levels. For example, improving a child's access to nutritious food without also addressing other critical issues such as living in an unsafe neighborhood or attending a poorly-funded school is unlikely to be effective in changing the child's lifelong trajectory.

TeachSource Video Connections

Observing Piaget's Conservation Task in Kindergarten

It is important for teachers at all grade levels to be familiar with basic child development theories. Although many were proposed decades ago, their contributions remain relevant and applicable to today's children. Respond to the following questions after you have watched the learning video, *Child Development Theories: Observing Piaget's Conservation Task in Kindergarten*.

1. In what ways do children ultimately benefit from teachers' understanding of the major child development theories?

2. What are anecdotal notes? How can a teacher use this information to support children's learning?

3. How did differences in each of the children's language skills influence their ability to answer the teacher's questions?

4. What other factors may explain why each child appears to be at a different stage in their understanding of the conservation concept?

Transactional Patterns of Development

From birth, children influence the behavior of their adult caretakers (e.g., parents, families, teachers). In turn, these same adults exert a significant influence on children's behavior and development. For example, a calm, cuddly infant expresses her needs in a clear and predictable fashion. This infant begins life with personal–social experiences that are quite different from those of a tense, colicky infant whose sleeping and eating patterns are highly irregular and often stressful for his parents. This complex **transactional process** of bidirectional give and take between children and their families and daily events is ongoing and continually changing, and results in developmental experiences that shape each child's unique qualities.

Infants and young children thrive when adults respond promptly and positively, at least a fair amount of the time, to appropriate things that a child says and does. Researchers have shown repeatedly that children develop healthier self-concepts as well as earlier and better language, cognitive, and social skills when they are raised by adults who are caring, consistent, and supportive (Bornstein, Putnick, & Esposito, 2020; Leung & Susking, 2020).

transactional process The give-and-take relationship between children, their primary caregivers, and daily events that influences each other's behavior and developmental outcomes.

Figure 2-8 A vision impairment is an example of a developmental deviation.

Atypical Growth and Development

The term *atypical* describes children who have developmental differences, deviations, or marked delays—children whose development appears to be incomplete or inconsistent with typical patterns and sequences. There are many causes of atypical development, including genetic errors, poor health, inadequate nutrition, injury, and too few or poor-quality opportunities for learning.

Abnormal development in one area may or may not interfere with development in other areas. However, the child with developmental delays might perform in one or more areas of development as a much younger child does. For example, a three-year-old who is still babbling, with no recognizable words, is an example of a child with delayed development. This condition need not be disabling unless the child never develops **functional language**. The term *developmental deviation* describes an aspect of development that is different from what is expected in typical development (Figure 2-8). For example, the child born with a missing finger or a profound hearing loss has a developmental deviation. The child with a missing finger is not likely to be disabled. In contrast, the child who is deaf will experience significant developmental delays unless early and intensive intervention is obtained.

In any event, the concepts and principles described in this chapter apply to the child with developmental differences, as well as to the child who is said to be developing typically. However, one always must be cautious not to make judgments about a child's development without first being sensitive to cultural, ethnic, socioeconomic, language, and gender variations that may account for any differences (Trawick-Smith, 2017). Most important, it also must be remembered that a child who experiences any type of developmental problem still has the same fundamental needs as all other children.

Developmental Domains

A framework is needed to describe and accurately assess children's developmental progress. In this book, six major domains or developmental areas are addressed: physical, motor, perceptual, cognitive, speech and language, and social-emotional. Each domain includes the many skills and behaviors that will be discussed in the developmental profiles that are the major focus of this book (Chapters 4–9). Although these developmental areas are separated for the purpose of this discussion, they cannot be separated from one another in reality. Each is integrally related to, and **interdependent** with, each of the others in the overall developmental process.

Developmental profiles, or word pictures, are useful for assessing both the immediate and ongoing status of children's skills and behavior. It is important to remember that the rate of development is uneven and occasionally unpredictable across areas. For example, the language and social skills of infants and toddlers are typically less well developed than is their ability to move about. Also, children's individual achievements can vary across developmental areas: a child may walk late but talk early. Again, an important reminder: Development in any of the domains depends in large part

functional language Language that allows children to get what they need or want.

interdependent Affecting or influencing development in multiple domains.

on children having appropriate stimulation and adequately supported opportunities to learn. Additionally, the types of learning experiences that individual children encounter are highly variable and reflect cultural, socioeconomic, and family values.

Physical Development and Growth

The physical development and growth domain governs the major tasks of infancy and childhood. Understanding the patterns and sequences of physical development is essential to being effective parents, teachers, and service providers. Healthy growth and development, not adult pressure or coaching, is what makes new learning and behavior possible. Adult pressure cannot hurry the process and, in fact, is more likely to be counterproductive. A seven-month-old infant cannot be toilet trained; the **sphincter** muscles are not yet developed sufficiently to exert such control. Nor can the majority of kindergartners catch or kick a ball skillfully; such coordination is impossible given a five- or six-year-old's stage of physical and motor development, yet many of us have seen a coach or family member reduce a child to tears for failing to catch or kick a ball.

Governed by heredity and greatly influenced by environmental conditions, physical development and growth are highly individualized processes. They are responsible for changes in body shape and proportion, as well as for overall body size. Growth, especially of the brain, occurs more rapidly during prenatal development and the first year than at any other time. Growth is also intricately related to progress in other developmental areas. It is responsible for increasing the muscle strength necessary for movement, coordinating vision and motor control, and synchronizing neurological and muscular activity in gaining bladder and bowel control. A child's growth is also closely linked to nutritional status and ethnicity (Bartels et al., 2020). Thus, the state of a child's physical development serves as a fairly reliable index of general health and well-being. Physical growth also plays a direct role in determining whether children are likely to achieve their full cognitive and academic potentials.

Motor Development

The child's ability to move about and control various body parts are major functions of the motor development domain. Refinements in motor development depend on brain maturation, input from the *sensory system*, increased bulk and number of muscle fibers, a

sphincter The muscles necessary to accomplish bowel and bladder control.

What Do You See?

Motor development. Motor development proceeds in a fairly predictable and orderly manner. What stage is the infant in this photo exhibiting? What activities would encourage and support this phase of his motor development?

© GROW/Cengage Learning

healthy nervous system, and opportunities for practice. This holistic approach contrasts markedly with the way that early developmentalists such as Gesell viewed the emergence of motor skills. They described motor development as a purely maturational process, governed almost entirely by instructions in the individual's genetic code (nature). Today's developmental psychologists consider such an explanation misleading and incomplete. Their research suggests, for example, that when young children show an interest in using a spoon to feed themselves, it is always accompanied by improved eye–hand coordination (to direct the spoon to the mouth), motivation (liking and wanting to eat what is on the spoon), and the drive to imitate what others are doing. In other words, the environment [that is, experience (nurture)] plays a major role in the emergence of new motor skills.

Motor activity during very early infancy is purely **reflexive** and gradually disappears as children develop **voluntary** control over their movements. Failure of these earliest reflexes to phase out at appropriate times in the **developmental sequence** may be an indication of neurological problems (see Chapter 4, "Infancy"). In such cases, medical evaluation should be sought. Three principles govern motor development:

1. **Cephalocaudal**—Bone and muscular development that proceeds from head to toe. The infant first learns to control muscles that support the head and neck, then the trunk, and later, those that allow reaching. Muscles for walking develop last.
2. **Proximodistal**—Bone and muscular development that begins with improved control of muscles nearest the central portion of the body, gradually extending outward and away from the midpoint to the extremities (arms and legs). For example, control of the head and neck is achieved before the child is able to pick up an object with thumb and forefinger (pincer grasp or finger–thumb opposition).
3. **Refinement**—Muscular development that progresses from the general to the specific in both **gross motor** and **fine motor** abilities. In the refinement of a gross motor skill, for example, a two-year-old might attempt to throw a ball but achieves little distance or control. The same child, within a few short years, is likely to pitch a ball over home plate with considerable speed and accuracy. As an instance of a fine motor skill, compare the self-feeding efforts of a toddler with those of an eight-year-old who is motivated (for whatever reason) to display good table manners.

Perceptual Development

The increasingly complex way that a child learns and uses information received through the senses—sight, hearing, touch, smell, taste, and body position—forms the basis of perceptual development. It might be said that perception is a significant factor that determines and orchestrates the functioning of the various senses, singly or in combination. The perceptual process also enables the individual to focus on what is relevant at a particular moment and to screen out whatever is irrelevant: Which details are important? Which differences should be noted? Which should be ignored? Perceptual development involves three important functions:

1. *Multisensory*—Information is generally received through more than one sensory system at a time. For example, when listening to a speaker, we use sight (watching facial expressions and gestures) and sound (listening to the words) (Maitre et al., 2020).
2. *Habituation*— This term refers to a person's ability to concentrate on a specific task while ignoring everything else. For example, a child who is focused on reading a book of interest may be completely unaware of a classmate's conversation, a dog's continuous barking, or music playing in the background. In other words, the repetition of these sounds gradually becomes so familiar that they no longer attract the child's interest or attention. As a result, the child is able to tune out things around her and devote full attention to what is most immediately important.

reflexive Refers to movements resulting from impulses of the nervous system that cannot be controlled by the individual.

voluntary Refers to movements that can be willed and purposively controlled and initiated by the individual.

developmental sequence A continuum of predictable steps along a developmental pathway of skill achievement.

cephalocaudal Refers to bone and muscular development that proceeds from head to toe.

proximodistal Refers to bone and muscular development that begins closest to the trunk, gradually moving outward to the extremities.

refinement Progressive improvement in the ability to perform fine and gross motor skills.

gross motor Refers to large muscle movements such as locomotor skills (walking, skipping, or swimming) and nonlocomotive movements (sitting, pushing and pulling, or squatting).

fine motor Refers to small muscle movements; also referred to as *manipulative skills;* includes the ability to stack blocks, button and zip clothing, hold and use a pencil, and brush teeth.

3. *Sensory integration*—This process involves translating **sensory information** into functional behavior (Wallace, Woynaroski, & Stevenson, 2020). For example, the five-year-old sees and hears a car coming and waits for it to pass before crossing the street; the adolescent lets her soup cool before proceeding to eat it.

The basic perceptual system is in place at birth. Through experience, learning, and maturation, it develops into a smoothly coordinated operation for processing complex information from multiple senses. As a result, children can sort shapes according to size and color and make fine discriminations, or hear and distinguish the difference among initial sounds in rhyming words such as *rake, cake,* and *lake.* The sensory system also enables each of us to respond appropriately to different messages and signals, such as smiling in response to a smile or keeping quiet in response to a frown.

Cognitive Development

The cognitive development domain addresses the expansion of a child's intellect or mental abilities. Cognition involves recognizing, processing, and organizing information and then using it appropriately. The cognitive process includes such mental activities as discovering, interpreting, sorting, classifying, and remembering. For preschool and school-aged children, it means evaluating ideas, making judgments, solving complex problems, understanding rules and concepts, anticipating, and visualizing possibilities or consequences.

Cognitive development is an ongoing process of interaction between the child and his perceptual view of objects or events in the environment (Piaget, 1954). It is probably safe to say that neither cognitive nor perceptual development can proceed independently of each other. Cognitive skills always overlap with both perceptual and motor development. Early in the second year, the emergence of speech and language adds yet another dimension.

The development of cognition begins with the primitive or reflexive behaviors that support survival and early learning in the healthy newborn. One example of very early learning is when a mother playfully sticks out her tongue several times and the infant begins to imitate her. This and other early behaviors led developmental psychologists to ponder the many striking similarities in how infants and children learn. During the 1950s, repeated observations of such similarities led Piaget to formulate his four stages of cognitive development: sensorimotor, preoperational, concrete operations, and formal operations (see Chapter 1, "Child Development Theories and Data Gathering").

Language Development

Language is often defined as a system of symbols, spoken, written, and gestural (e.g., waving, smiling, scowling, and cowering) that enables us to communicate and socialize with one another. It allows the expression and sharing of ideas, feelings, and desires. Language gives meaning to words and, thus, is also essential for thinking and problem-solving processes.

Normal language development is regular and sequential and depends on maturation as well as on learning opportunities. The first year of life is called the *prelinguistic* or *prelanguage phase.* The child is totally dependent upon body movements and sounds, such as crying and laughing, to convey needs and feelings. This is followed during the second year by the *linguistic* or *language stage,* in which speech becomes the primary mode for communicating. Over the next three or four years, the child learns to put words together to form simple and then compound sentences that make sense to others because he has learned the appropriate grammatical constructions. Between five and seven years of age, most children have become skilled at conveying their thoughts and

Did You Know

?

...the media industry incorporates basic elements of perceptual development (e.g., multisensory information, habituation, repetition, and sensory integration) to assure that cartoons and programming appeal to and hold children's attention?

Did You Know

?

...that infants younger than two months show evidence of receptive language? They prefer and attend to repetition, sounds that rhyme, and their mother's voice.

sensory information Information received through the five sensory organs: eyes, ears, nose, mouth, and skin.

Figure 2-9 Most five-year-olds are able to express their thoughts clearly and with correct grammar.

Monkey Business Images/Shutterstock.com

ideas verbally (Figure 2-9). Many children at this age have a vocabulary of 14,000 words or more, which can double or triple during middle childhood depending on a child's literacy environment.

Most children seem to understand a variety of words, concepts, and relationships long before they have the words to describe them. This ability is referred to as **receptive language**, which precedes **expressive language** (the ability to speak words to describe and explain). Speech and language development is closely related to the child's general cognitive, social, perceptual, and neuromuscular development. Language development and the rules that address how it is to be used are also influenced by the type of language that children hear in their homes, schools, and community (Johnson & White, 2019; Leung, Hernandez, & Suskind, 2020).

Eye gaze plays an important role in early language development. It enables infants to begin learning about objects, forming word associations and committing them to memory, especially when gaze is accompanied with words (Çetinçelik, Rowland, & Snijders, 2021). Infants as young as six months are able to focus on an object for longer periods and to follow its movement. Scientists have noted that infants who are later diagnosed with autism spectrum disorders experience a steep decline in eye gazing ability before their third birthday (Bacon et al., 2020; Gangi et al., 2021). These findings suggest that eye gaze may provide a reliable screening method for the early detection of autism disorders and potential language delays.

Social and Emotional Development

This is a complex and broad domain that addresses how children feel about themselves and their relationships with others. It refers to children's behaviors, the way they respond to play and learning activities, and their attachments to family members, caregivers, teachers, and friends. Social and emotional development unfolds across multiple, interconnected areas, including:

- gender roles
- temperament
- morality
- attachment
- empathy

receptive language Understanding words that are heard.

expressive language Words used to verbalize thoughts and feelings.

- risk and resilience
- social and cultural rules and expectations
- self-awareness
- self-regulation

The foundation of children's social and emotional development begins to form shortly after birth and advances quickly during the early years. Neuroscientists have identified unique neural pathways that enable infants to establish the connections that are essential for their survival and learning (Meltzoff & Marshall, 2018; Ruba & Pollak, 2020). Within months, young infants are able to discriminate between objects and people and respond differently to facial expressions, vocalizations, and body movements (Addabbo et al., 2020). By age two, intentional verbalizations and behaviors are used to initiate, imitate, and participate in reciprocal interactions with caregivers.

Older infants and toddlers become increasingly aware of their own behavior and its effect on others. They begin to engage in **social referencing** to determine how their actions are perceived and what adjustments may be needed to gain approval. For example, a toddler may look at his father before deciding whether or not to open the cabinet door. Gradually, children use this information to modify their actions, regulate their emotions, abide by social expectations, and engage in acceptable, goal-directed behaviors (Reschke, Walle, & Dukes, 2020).

Researchers have noted a number of positive associations between children's social-emotional competence and improved school readiness, higher academic achievement, greater resilience, better long-term mental health, and fewer behavior problems (MacCann et al., 2020; Ursache et al., 2020; Wells et al., 2020). Children who have developed effective social and emotional skills are more likely to make sound decisions and establish meaningful relationships. These findings reinforce the importance of supporting children's social and emotional learning during the early years and beyond.

It must be remembered that children develop at different rates when describing social and emotional development. Individual differences in genetic and cultural backgrounds, health status, living arrangements, family interactions, and daily experiences within the larger community continuously shape and reshape children's social and emotional skills. Consequently, no two children can ever be exactly alike, not in social and emotional development or in any other developmental area.

▶❚❚ TeachSource **Video Connections**

Temperament and Personality Development

Temperament is considered one component of an individual's personality. It influences a person's feelings and behavior. It explains, in part, why infants and toddlers differ in their emotional perceptions and responses to caregivers and the environment. Respond to the following questions after you have watched the learning video *0–2 Years: Temperament in Infants and Toddlers:*

1. What determines a child's temperament?
2. Which terms did parents in the video use to describe their child's temperament?
3. How does a child's temperament influence the transactional process of parenting?
4. How would you describe your own temperament?
5. Do you think there are cultural differences in temperament? Explain.

Age Divisions

The age divisions shown in Table 2-1 and used throughout this book are commonly referred to by many child development specialists when describing significant changes within developmental areas.

Age divisions are to be used with extreme caution and great flexibility when dealing with children. They are based on the average achievements, abilities, and behaviors of

social referencing Observing another person's expressions to determine what they may be thinking or how they are likely to respond.

Table 2-1 Common Age Divisions

Infancy	Birth to 1 month
	1–4 months
	4–8 months
	8–12 months
Toddlerhood	12–24 months
	24–36 months
Early childhood	3–5 years
	6–8 years
Middle childhood	9–12 years
Adolescence	13–14 years
	15–16 years
	17–19 years

large numbers of children at various stages of development. As stated again and again, there is great variation from one child to another.

The step-by-step development detailed in Chapters 4–9 speaks to the importance of understanding that it is sequential acquisition, *not* age, that indicates the developmental progress in each domain and in each child's overall development.

Summary

2-1 Growth and development are influenced by a child's unique genetic makeup and the quality of the everyday environment, which includes nurturing, health care, nutrition, and learning opportunities.

- The term *growth* describes physical changes that occur in a child's size.
- The term *development* refers to the acquisition of increasingly complex skills.

2-2 Sequential acquisition, not age, is the critical factor in assessing a child's developmental progress.

- The accepted range of normalcy is broad and recognizes that each child is unique.
- A child should progress in a relatively orderly manner through each step in a given developmental area, even though it may be somewhat earlier or later than most children of a similar age.

2-3 Each child's well-being depends on having their basic needs met and opportunities to acquire essential skills across the six developmental domains: physical, motor, perceptual, cognitive, language, and social-emotional.

- Although the six domains are separated for discussion purposes, they are interwoven and interdependent during the developmental years and throughout life.
- All children have the same basic needs for nutrients, protection, safety, attention, and nurturing, regardless of their special abilities, limitations, or challenges.

Key Terms

growth **p. 25**

head circumference **p. 25**

development **p. 25**

continuity **p. 26**

jargon **p. 26**

discontinuity **p. 26**

stammering **p. 26**

food jag **p. 26**

chronological **p.27**

typical **p. 28**

neurological **p. 28**

neural connections **p. 30**

plasticity **p. 30**

pruning **p. 30**

attachment **p. 32**

separation anxiety **p. 32**

socio-ecological **p. 36**

transactional process **p. 37**

functional language **p. 38**

interdependent **p. 38**

sphincter **p. 39**

reflexive **p. 40**

voluntary **p. 40**

developmental sequence **p. 40**

cephalocaudal **p. 40**

proximodistal **p. 40**

refinement **p. 40**

gross motor **p. 40**

fine motor **p. 40**

sensory information **p. 41**

receptive language **p. 42**

expressive language **p. 42**

social referencing **p. 43**

Apply What You Have Learned

A. Case Study Connections

Reread the developmental sketch about Dakota and Liselli presented at the beginning of this chapter and answer the following questions:

1. In what ways do Dakota and Liselli differ in terms of their personal–social development? Given that they are identical twins, what factors may explain these differences?

2. According to Piaget, which stage of cognitive development are the twins, who are almost three years old, currently experiencing? Give an example of this concept from the descriptions of Dakota and Liselli.

3. Should you expect Dakota and Liselli to grow and develop in exactly the same way and at exactly the same rate just because they are identical twins? Explain. How would developmental theorists account for these differences (see Chapter 1)?

B. Review Questions

1. Explain how the concepts of growth and development differ.

2. Identify and discuss three factors that contribute to atypical development.

3. Discuss the role that environment plays in children's brain development.

4. Define the term *perceptual information* and provide three examples to illustrate this concept.

5. Explain why you might not need to be concerned about a toddler who was learning to walk but now insists on only crawling.

6. What are developmental milestones, and what purpose do they serve?

C. Your Turn: Chapter to Practice

1. Visit your local library and select twenty children's books at random. Evaluate the nature of the pictures/illustrations and narrative content in each book to determine if it perpetuates gender stereotyping. Describe your findings.

2. Visit a shopping mall or restaurant and observe parents interacting with their children for approximately an hour. In each case, record the child's behavior and

the nature of the adult response. In what ways are temperament and transactional processes illustrated in each of these situations?

3. Tommy's father arrives to pick up his son from preschool and immediately becomes upset when he sees Tommy wearing a ballerina's tutu and high heels. He confronts the head teacher and wants her to explain why they have allowed his son to "dress like a girl." If you were that teacher, how would you respond to the father's question?

Online Resources

Centers for Disease Control and Prevention

Extensive information on children's development, developmental screening, and positive parenting is provided in lay terms and an easy-to-access format (e.g., podcasts, videos, and print materials).

Eunice Kennedy Shriver National Institute of Child Health and Human Development

Research and information dissemination on children's development and the prevention of developmental disabilities are this organization's primary goals.

National Center for Children in Poverty

This national center is affiliated with Columbia University. Databases, fact sheets, and community interventions for improving the lives of families and children who live in poverty are available on their website. You can also access the respected research journal *Child Care and Early Education Research Connections*, which is published by this organization.

References

Addabbo, M., Vacaru, S. V., Meyer, M., & Hunnius, S. (2020). "Something in the way you move": Infants are sensitive to emotions conveyed in action kinematics. *Developmental Science, 23*(1), e12873.

Adibpour, P., Lebenberg, J., Kabdebon, C., Dehaene-Lambertz, & Dubois, J. (2020). Anatomo-functional correlates of auditory development in infancy. *Developmental Cognitive Neuroscience, 42*, 100752. https://doi.org/10.1016/j.dcn.2019.100752

Ainsworth, M. S. (1979). Infant–mother attachment. *American Psychologist, 34*(10), 932–937. https://doi.org/10.1037/0003-066X.34.10.932

Augustine, M. E., & Stifter, C. A. (2019). Children's behavioral self-regulation and conscience: Roles of child temperament, parenting, and parenting context. *Journal of Applied Developmental Psychology, 63*, 54–64.

Bacon, E. C., Moore, A., Lee, Q., Barnes, C. C., Courchesne, E., & Pierce, K. (2020). Identifying prognostic markers in autism spectrum disorder using eye tracking. *Autism, 24*(3), 658–669.

Bandura, A. (1977). *Social learning theory*. Englewood Cliffs, NJ: Prentice Hall.

Bartels, H. C., O'Connor, C., Segurado, R., Mason, O., Mehegan, J., Geraghty, A. A., O'Brien, E., Walsh, J., & McAuliffe, F. (2020). Fetal growth trajectories and their association with maternal and child characteristics. *The Journal of Maternal-Fetal & Neonatal Medicine, 33*(14), 2427–2433.

Black, M. M., Trude, A. C., & Lutter, C. K. (2020). All children thrive: Integration of nutrition and early childhood development. *Annual Review of Nutrition, 40*(1), 375–406.

Bornstein, M. H., Putnick, D. L., & Esposito, G. (2020). Skill–experience transactions across development: Bidirectional relations between child core language and the child's home learning environment. *Developmental Psychology, 56*(10), 1842–1854.

Bowlby, J. (1969). *Attachment and loss*. Volume 1. Attachment. (2nd ed.). New York: Basic Books.

Bowlby, J. (1988). *A secure base: Parent-child attachment and healthy human development*. New York: Basic Book.

Brown, G. L., & Cox, M. J. (2020). Pleasure in parenting and father-child attachment security. *Attachment & Human Development, 22*(1), 51–65.

Carrasco, M., A., Delgado, B., & Holgado-Tello, F. P. (2020). Children's temperament: A bridge between mother's parenting and aggression. *International Journal of Environmental Research and Public Health, 17*(17), 6382. https://doi.org/10.3390/ijerph17176382

Çetinçelik, M., Rowland, C. F., & Snijders, T. M. (2021). Do the eyes have it? A systematic review on the role of eye gaze in infant language development. *Frontiers in Psychology, 11*, 589096. http://hdl.handle.net/21.11116/0000-0007-86BF-B

Chung, E. H., Chou, J., & Brown, K. A. (2020). Neurodevelopmental outcomes of preterm infants: A recent literature review. *Translational Pediatrics, 9*(Suppl 1), S3–S8. https://doi.org/10.21037/tp.2019.09.10

Cote, L. R., & Bornstein, M. H. (2021). Three cultural contrasts in search of specificities and commonalities: Acculturation in Japanese, South American, and South Korean immigrant families. *Journal of Applied Developmental Psychology, 73*(2), 1242. https://doi.org/10.1016/j.appdev.2021.101242

Davis, J. T., & Hines, M. (2020). How large are gender differences in toy preferences? A systematic review and meta-analysis of toy preference research. *Archives of Sexual Behavior, 49*(2), 373–394.

Diamond, L. M. (2020). Gender fluidity and nonbinary gender identities among children and adolescents. *Child Development Perspectives, 14*(2), 110–115.

Dodaj, A. (2020). Children witnessing domestic violence. *Journal of Children's Services, 15*(3), 161–174.

Dufford, A. J., Kim, P., & Evans, G. W. (2020). The impact of childhood poverty on brain health: Emerging evidence from neuroimaging across the lifespan. *International Review of Neurobiology, 150*, 77–105.

Dunn, J. R. (2020). Housing and healthy child development: Known and potential impacts of interventions. *Annual Review of Public Health, 41*, 381–396.

Duong, H. T., Monahan, J. L., Kollar, L. M., & Klevens, J. (2021). Identifying knowledge, self-efficacy and response efficacy of alternative discipline strategies among low-income Black, Latino and White parents. *Health Education Research*, cyaa053. https://doi.org/10.1093/her/cyaa053

Erikson, E. H. (1968). *Identity: Youth and crisis.* New York: W. W. Norton & Company.

Estrada, E., Ferrer, E., Román, F. J., Karama, S., & Colom, R. (2019). Time-lagged associations between cognitive and cortical development from childhood to early adulthood. *Developmental Psychology, 55*(6), 1338–1352.

Fernandes, C., Monteiro, L., Santos, A. J., Fernandes, M., Antunes, M., Vaughn, B. E., & Veríssimo, M. (2020). Early father–child and mother–child attachment relationships: Contributions to preschoolers' social competence. *Attachment & Human Development, 22*(6), 687–704.

Fitzgerald, E., Hor, K., & Drake, A. J. (2020). Maternal influences on fetal brain development: The role of nutrition, infection and stress, and the potential for intergenerational consequences. *Early Human Development, 150*, 105190. https://doi.org/10.1016/j.earlhumdev.2020.105190

Franke, K., Van den Bergh, B. R., de Rooij, S. R., Kroegel, N., Nathanielsz, P. W., Rakers, F., Roseboom, T. J., Witte, O. W., & Schwab, M. (2020). Effects of maternal stress and nutrient restriction during gestation on offspring neuroanatomy in humans. *Neuroscience & Biobehavioral Reviews, 117*, 5–25.

Freud, S. (1924). *The dissolution of the Oedipus complex.* Standard Edition, 19, 172–179.

Gangi, D. N., Boterberg, S., Schwichtenberg, A. J., Solis, E., Young, G. S., Iosif, A., & Ozonoff, S. (2021). Declining gaze to faces in infants developing autism spectrum disorder: Evidence from two independent cohorts. *Child Development.* https://doi.org/10.1111/cdev.134

Gesell, A., & Ilg, F. (1949). *Child development.* New York: Harper.

Gete, D. G., Waller, M., & Mishra, G. D. (2021). Pre-pregnancy diet quality and its association with offspring behavioral problems. *European Journal of Nutrition, 60*(1), 503–515.

Giannotti, M., Mills, R., Kisely, S., Najman, J., & Abajobir, A. (2020). Long-term cognitive, psychological, and health outcomes associated with child abuse and neglect. *Pediatrics, 136*(4), e20200438. https://doi.org/10.1542/peds.2020-0438

Granqvist, P. (2021). Attachment, culture, and gene-culture co-evolution: Expanding the evolutionary toolbox of attachment theory. *Attachment & Human Development, 23*(1), 90–113.

Harlow, H. F., & Zimmermann, R. R. (1958). The development of affective responsiveness in infant monkeys. *Proceedings of the American Philosophical Society, 102*, 501–509.

Jiang, H., Justice, L. M., Purtell, K. M., & Bates, R. (2020). Exposure to environmental toxicants and early language development for children reared in low-income households. *Clinical Pediatrics, 59*(6), 557–565.

Johnson, E. K., & White, K. S. (2019). Developmental sociolinguistics: Children's acquisition of language variation. *WIREs Cognitive Science, 11*(1), e1515. https://doi.org/10.1002/wcs.1515

Kabha, L., & Berger, A. (2020). The sequence of acquisition for theory of mind concepts: The combined effect of both cultural and environmental factors. *Cognitive Development, 54*, 100852. https://doi.org/10.1016/j.cogdev.2020.100852

Kälin, S., & Roebers, C. M. (2021). Self-regulation in preschool children: Factor structure of different measures of effortful control and executive functions. *Journal of Cognition and Development, 22*(1), 1–20.

Kohlberg, L. (1966). A cognitive-developmental analysis of children's sex-role concepts and attitudes. In E. E. Mccoby (Ed.), *The development of sex differences.* Stanford, CA: Stanford University Press.

Laing, C., & Bergelson, E. (2020). From babble to words: Infants' early productions match words and objects in their environment. *Cognitive Psychology, 122*, 101308. https://doi.org/10.1016/j.cogpsych.2020.101308

Landi, I., Giannotti, M., Venuti, P., & de Falco, S. (2020). Maternal and family predictors of infant psychological development in at-risk families: A multilevel longitudinal study. *Research in Nursing & Health, 43*(1), 17–27. https://doi.org/10.1002/nur.21989

Leung, C. Y., Hernandez, M. W., & Suskind, D. L. (2020). Enriching home language environment among families from low-SES backgrounds: A randomized controlled trial of a home visiting curriculum. *Early Childhood Research Quarterly, 50*(1), 24–35.

Leung, C. Y., & Suskind, D. L. (2020). What parents know matters: Parental knowledge at birth predicts caregiving behaviors at 9 months. *The Journal of Pediatrics, 221*, 72–80.

Loomis, A. M. (2021). Effects of household and environmental adversity on indices of self-regulation for Latino and African American preschool children: Closing the school readiness gap. *Education and Development, 32*(2), 228–248.

MacCann, C., Jiang, Y., Brown, L. E., Double, K. S., Bucich, M., & Minbashian, A. (2020). Emotional intelligence predicts academic performance: A meta-analysis. *Psychological Bulletin, 146*(2), 150–186.

Maitre, N. L., Key, A. P., Slaughter, J. C., Yoder, P. J., Neel, M. L., Richard, C., Wallace, M. T., & Murray, M. M. (2020). Neonatal multisensory processing in preterm and term infants predicts sensory reactivity and internalizing tendencies in early childhood. *Brain Topography, 33*(5), 586–599.

Marotz, L. R., & Kupzyk, S. (2018). *Parenting today's children*. Boston, MA: Wadsworth.

McIlvain, G., Clements, R. G., Magoon, E. M., Spielberg, J. M., Telzer, E. H., & Johnson, C. L. (2020). Viscoelasticity of reward and control systems in adolescent risk taking. *NeuroImage, 215*, 116850. https://doi.org/10.1016/j.neuroimage.2020.116850

McLean, K. C., Boggs, S., Haraldsson, K., Lowe, A., Fordham, C., Byers, S., & Syed, M. (2020). Personal identity development in cultural context: The socialization of master narratives about the gendered life course. *International Journal of Behavioral Development, 44*(2), 116–126.

Meltzoff, A., & Marshall, P. J. (2018). Human infant imitation as a social survival circuit. *Current Opinion in Behavioral Sciences, 24*, 130–136.

Monier, F., & Droit-Volet, S. (2019). Development of sensorimotor synchronization abilities: Motor and cognitive components. *Child Neuropsychology, 25*(8), 1043–1062.

Nagy, A., Kalmár, M., Beke, A. B., Gráf, R., & Horváth, E. (2021). Intelligence and executive function of school-age preterm children in function of birth weight and perinatal complication. *Applied Neuropsychology: Child, 10*(1), 1–12. https://doi.org/10.1080/21622965.2020.1866571

Nelson, C. A., & Gabard-Durnam, L. J. (2020). Early adversity and critical periods: Neurodevelopmental consequences of violating the expectable environment. *Trends in Neurosciences, 43*(3), 133–143.

Piaget, J. (1954). *The construction of reality in the child*. New York: Basic Books.

Raiten, D. J., & Bremer, A. A. (2020). Exploring the nutritional ecology of stunting: New approaches to an old problem. *Nutrients, 12*(2), 371. https://doi.org/10.3390/nu12020371

Reh, R. K., Dias, B. G., Nelson, C. A., Kaufer, D., Werker, J. F., Kolb, B., Levine, J. D., & Hensch, T. K. (2020). Critical period regulation across multiple timescales. *Proceedings of the National Academy of Sciences of the United States of America, 117*(38), 23242–23251.

Reschke, P. J., Walle, E. A., & Dukes, D. (2020). Did you mean to do that? Infants use emotional communication to infer and re-enact others' intended actions. *Cognition and Emotion, 34*(7), 1473–1479.

Ristori, J., Cocchetti, C., Romani, A., Mazzoli, F., Vignozzi, L., Maggi, M., & Fisher, A. D. (2020). Brain sex differences related to gender identity development: Genes or hormones? *International Journal of Molecular Sciences, 21*(6), 2123. https://doi.org/10.3390/ijms21062123

Rod, N. H., Bengtsson, J., Budtz-Jørgensen, E., Clipet-Jensen, C., Taylor-Robinson, D., Andersen, A. N., Dich, N., & Rieckmann, A. (2020). Trajectories of childhood adversity and mortality in early adulthood: A population-based cohort study. *Lancet, 396*(10249), 489–497.

Rollè, L., Giordana, M., Santoniccolo, F., & Trombetta, T. (2020). Prenatal attachment and perinatal depression: A systematic review. *International Journal of Environmental Research and Public Health, 17*(8), 2644. https://doi.org/10.3390/ijerph17082644

Ruba, A. L., & Pollak, S. D. (2020). The development of emotion reasoning in infancy and early childhood. *Annual Review of Developmental Psychology, 2*, 503–531.

Schochet, O. N., Johnson, A. D., & Ryan, R. M. (2020). The relationship between increases in low-income mothers' education and children's early outcomes: Variation by developmental stage and domain. *Children and Youth Services Review, 109*, 104705. https://doi.org/10.1016/j.childyouth.2019.104705

Schroeder, K. M., & Liben, L. S. (2021). Felt pressure to conform to cultural gender roles: Correlates and consequences. *Sex Roles, 84*(1), 125–138.

Strand, P. S. (2020). The security-seeking impulse and the unification of attachment and culture. *Psychological Review, 127*(5), 778–791.

Strand, P. S., Vossen, J. J., & Savage, E. (2019). Culture and child attachment patterns: A behavioral systems synthesis. *Perspective on Behavior Science, 42*(4), 835–850.

Super, C. M., Harkness, S. Bonichini, S., Welles, B., Zylicz, P. O., Bermúdez, M. R., & Palacious, J. (2020). Developmental continuity and change in the cultural construction of the "difficult child": A study in six western cultures. *New Directions for Child and Adolescent Development, 2020*(170), 43–68.

Tang, A., Crawford, H., Morales, S., Degnan, K. A., Pine, D. S., & Fox, N. A. (2020). Infant behavioral inhibition predicts personality and social outcomes three decades later. *Proceedings of the National Academy of Sciences of the United States of America, 117*(18), 9800–9807.

Thomas, A., & Chess, S. (1977). *Temperament and development*. New York: Brunner/Mazel.

Tooley, U. A., Mackey, A. P., Ciric, R., Ruparel, K., Moore, T. M., Gur, R. C., Satterthwaite, T. D., & Bassett, D. S. (2020). Associations between neighborhood SES and functional brain network development. *Cerebral Cortex, 30*(1), 1–19.

Trawick-Smith, J. (2017). *Early childhood development: A multicultural perspective* (7th ed.). Upper Saddle River, NJ: Pearson.

United States Department of Agriculture (USDA). (2020). *Food security status of U.S. households with children in 2019*. Retrieved from https://www.ers.usda.gov/topics/food-nutrition-assistance/food-security-in-the-us/key-statistics-graphics.aspx.

Ursache, A., Gouley, K. K., Dawson-McClure, S., Barajas-Gonzalez, R. G., Calzada, E. J., Goldfeld, K. S., & Brotman, L. M. (2020). Early emotion knowledge and later academic achievement among children in historically disinvested neighborhoods. *Child Development, 91*(6), e1249–e1266. https://doi.org/10.1111/cdev.13432

van Beusekom, G., Collier, K. L., Bos, H. M., Sandfort, T. G., & Overbeek, G. (2020). Gender nonconformity and peer victimization: Sex and sexual attraction differences by age. *The Journal of Sex Research, 57*(2), 234–246.

Wagers, K. B., & Kiel, E. J. (2019). The influence of parenting and temperament on empathy development in toddlers. *Journal of Family Psychology, 33*(4), 391–400.

Wallace, M. T., Woynaroski, T. G., & Stevenson, R. A. (2020). Multisensory integration as a window into orderly and disrupted cognition and communication. *Annual Review of Psychology, 71*, 193–219.

Wells, A. E., Hunnikin, L. M., Ash, D. P., & van Goozen, S. H. (2020). Low self-esteem and impairments in emotion recognition predict behavioural problems in children. *Journal of Psychopathology and Behavioral Assessment, 42*, 693–701.

Xu, W., Ying, F., Luo, Y., Zhang, X., & Li, Z. (2020). Cross-sectional exploration of brain functional connectivity in the triadic development model of adolescents. *Brain Imaging and Behavior.* https://doi.org/10.1007/s11682-020-00379-3

Zwir, I., Arnedo, J., Del-Val, C., Pulkki-Råback, L., Konte, B., Yang, S. S., Romero-Zaliz, R., Hintsanen, M., Cloninger, K. M., Garcia, D., Svrakic, D. M., Rozsa, S., Martinez, M., Lyytikäinen, L. P., Giegling, I., Kähönen, M., Hernandez-Cuervo, H., Seppälä, I., Raitoharju, E., ... & Cloninger, C. R. (2020). Uncovering the complex genetics of human temperament. *Molecular Psychiatry, 25*(10), 2275–2294.

Konstantin Christian/Shutterstock.com

Chapter 3

Prenatal Development

Learning Objectives

After reading this chapter, you will be able to:

3-1 Describe the developmental changes that occur during the germinal, embryonic, and fetal stages of pregnancy.

3-2 Describe at least four practices that a mother should follow throughout pregnancy to improve her chances of giving birth to a healthy infant.

3-3 Name five teratogens and describe their preventive measures.

3-4 Identify several changes that signal the onset of active labor.

3-5 Define maternal depression and discuss its potential impact on infant development.

NAEYC NAEYC Professional Standards Linked to Chapter Content

1b: Child development and learning in context
2a: Family–teacher partnerships and community connections
6e: Professionalism as an early childhood educator

Anna and Miguel were elated when they learned that she was seven weeks pregnant. Six months earlier, Anna experienced a miscarriage during her third month of pregnancy. At the time, Anna's doctor advised her to stop smoking before attempting future pregnancies. Although she was not able to quit completely, she significantly reduced the number of cigarettes smoked to no more than two or three a day. Anna also has tried to improve her diet by eating more fruits and vegetables and eliminating all alcohol consumption. She enrolled in a beginner's yoga class and walks with Miguel on weekends to control her weight and relieve stress.

When Anna and Miguel shared their exciting news with family members, everyone had advice for preventing another miscarriage. Her mother insisted that Anna rest and avoid any type of activity, including cleaning the house and cooking. Miguel's grandmother advised Anna to eat all that she could "because now you're eating for two." She also told Anna not to drink too much milk because "it will make the baby's complexion lighter in color" and to avoid strawberries because "they can cause a red birthmark." Her sister discouraged Anna from continuing her job at the bank because she had heard that stress could cause miscarriage and affect the infant's personality. However, Anna's job provides a needed source of income. Anna appreciates everyone's well-intended suggestions, but she is convinced that everything will be okay this time around.

Ask Yourself

- What lifestyle changes has Anna made to improve her chances of giving birth to a healthy infant? Are there other things she also might try?
- Do you think Anna should follow the advice that her friends and family have offered? Why or why not?

Each of the approximately 266 days of prenatal development (from **conception** to birth) is critical to producing a healthy newborn. **Genes** inherited from the infant's biological mother and father determine all physical characteristics, as well as many abnormalities. Studies have suggested that even **temperament** may have a biological basis (Cloninger, et al., 2019). However, because it is the mother who provides everything physically essential (as well as harmful) to the growing fetus, she plays a major role in promoting its healthy development. Her personal health, nutrition, and lifestyle before and during pregnancy strongly influence the birth of a healthy infant. In addition, researchers have determined that a father's health, personal habits, and his caring support for the mother throughout the pregnancy contribute to the unborn infant's development (Kasman et al., 2020; Watkins et al., 2020). Thus, it is important for every potential parent to be familiar with the patterns of normal prenatal development, as well as with practices that promote and interfere with this process (Figure 3-1).

Figure 3-1 A mother's and father's lifestyles have a direct influence on their infant's development.

The Developmental Process

The prenatal period is commonly divided into stages. In obstetrical practice, pregnancy is described in terms of trimesters, each consisting of three calendar months:

- First trimester—Conception through the third month
- Second trimester—Fourth through the sixth month
- Third trimester—Seventh through the ninth month

Pregnancy can also be discussed in terms of fetal development (Table 3-1). This approach emphasizes the critical changes that occur week by week and encompasses three stages as well:

- Germinal
- Embryonic
- Fetal

The *germinal stage* refers to the first fourteen days of pregnancy. The union of an ovum and sperm produces a **zygote**. Cell division begins within twenty-four hours

conception The joining of a single egg or ovum from the female and a single sperm from the male.

genes Genetic material that carries codes, or information, for all inherited characteristics.

temperament An individual's characteristic manner or style of response to everyday events, including degree of interest, activity level, and regulation of behavior.

zygote The cell formed as a result of conception; called a zygote for the first fourteen days.

Table 3-1 Characteristics of Fetal Development

2 weeks	• Cell division results in an embryo consisting of 16 cells.
3–8 weeks	• Structures necessary to support the developing embryo have formed: placenta, chorionic sac, amniotic fluid, and umbilical cord. • Embryonic cell layers begin to specialize, developing into major internal organs and systems, as well as external structures. • First bone cells appear. • Less than 1 inch (2.54 cm) in length at eight weeks.
12 weeks	• Weighs approximately 1–2 ounces (0.029–0.006 kg) and is nearly 3 inches (7.6 cm) in length. • Sex organs develop; baby's gender can be determined. • Kidneys begin to function. • Arms, legs, fingers, and toes are well defined and movable. • Makes facial expressions (e.g., smiles and frowns), looks around, and is able to suck and swallow.
16 weeks	• Weighs about 5 ounces (0.14 kg) and is 6 inches (15.2 cm) in length. • Sucks thumb. • Moves about actively; mother may begin to feel baby's movement (called *quickening*). • Has strong heartbeat that can be heard.
20 weeks	• Weighs nearly 1 pound (0.46 kg) and has grown to approximately 11–12 inches (27.9–30.5 cm) in length (approximately half of baby's birth length). • Experiences occasional hiccups. • Eyelashes, eyebrows, and hair forming; eyes remain closed.
24 weeks	• Weight doubles to about 1.5–2 pounds (0.68–0.90 kg) and length increases to 12–14 inches (30.5–35.6 cm). • Eyes are well formed, often open; responds to light and sound. • Grasp reflex develops. • Skin is wrinkled, thin, and covered with soft hair called *lanugo* and a white, greasy, protective substance called *vernix caseosa*.
28 weeks	• Weighs about 3–3.5 pounds (1.4–1.6 kg); grows to approximately 16–17 inches (40.6–43 cm) in length. • Develops a sleep/wake pattern. • Remains very active; kicks and pokes mother's ribs and abdomen. • Able to survive if born prematurely, although lungs are not yet fully developed.
32 weeks	• Weighs approximately 5–6 pounds (2.3–2.7 kg) and is 17–18 inches in length (43–45.7 cm). • Baby takes iron and calcium from mother's diet to build up reserve stores. • Becomes less active due to larger size and less room for moving about.
36–38 weeks	• Weighs an average of 7–8 pounds (3.2–3.6 kg) at birth; length is approximately 19–21 inches (48–53.3 cm). • Moves into final position (usually head down) in preparation for birth. • Loses most of lanugo; skin still somewhat wrinkled and red. • Is much less active (because there is now little room in which to move about). • Body systems are more mature (especially the lungs and heart), thus increasing baby's chances of survival at birth.

implantation The attachment of the blastocyst to the wall of the mother's uterus; occurs around the twelfth day.

and gradually forms a pinhead-size mass of specialized cells called a *blastocyst*. Around the fourteenth day, this small mass attaches itself to the wall of the mother's uterus. Successful attachment (**implantation**) marks the beginning of the **embryo** and the embryonic stage. Approximately two-thirds of zygotes survive this phase and continue to develop.

The *embryonic stage* includes the third through the eighth week of a pregnancy and is a critical period for the developing fetus. Cell division continues and forms specialized cell layers that are responsible for producing all major organs and systems, including the heart, lungs, digestive system, and brain. Many of these structures will be functional near the end of this period. For example, embryonic blood begins to flow through the fetus's primitive cardiovascular system (heart and blood vessels) in the fourth to the fifth week.

During this time, other important changes also take place. When implantation is completed, a **placenta** begins to form. This organ serves four major functions:

- It supplies nutrients and hormones to the fetus.
- It removes fetal waste products throughout the pregnancy.
- It filters many harmful substances, as well as some viruses and other disease-causing organisms. (Unfortunately, many medications and chemicals can pass through the placenta's filtering system.)
- It acts as a temporary immune system by supplying the fetus with the same antibodies that the mother produces against certain infectious diseases. (In most instances, the infant is protected for approximately six months following birth.)

An umbilical cord, containing two arteries and one vein, develops as the placenta forms and establishes a linkage between the fetus, its mother, and the outside world. From this point on, the fetus is affected by the mother's health and lifestyle and, via the placenta, begins to share everything the mother experiences and takes into her body. During this early stage, the fetus is especially vulnerable if exposed to certain chemical substances, such as alcohol,

embryo The cell mass from the time of implantation through the eighth week of pregnancy.

placenta A specialized lining that forms inside the uterus during pregnancy to support and nourish the developing fetus.

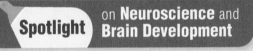

Maternal Obesity and Fetal Brain Development

Throughout the world, rates of obesity and overweight continue to rise among women of reproductive age. Obesity during pregnancy increases a woman's risk of developing serious health complications, such as extreme fatigue, high blood pressure, gestational diabetes, sleep disorders, heart and lung problems, premature birth, and miscarriage (Davis, 2020; Saravanan, 2020).

Scientists are learning that maternal overweight and obesity also have detrimental effects on fetal health and brain development. Advanced imaging technologies, such as magnetic resonance imaging (MRI), ultrasound, and magnetoencephalography are being used to examine fetal brain structure formation and activity. Abnormal neural connections between various brain regions have been identified in infants, particularly males, who are born to overweight mothers (Cirulli, Musillo, & Berry, 2020; Spann et al., 2020). Atypical brain activity patterns have been observed in fetuses of mothers who developed gestational diabetes (Avci et al., 2020). Malformations have also been noted in an area of the fetal brain (hippocampus) that is associated with learning, memory, and emotional regulation (Alves et al., 2020).

Researchers attribute these aberrations to an inflammation of the placenta that occurs with gestational diabetes. Inflammation disrupts the placenta's role in hormone production and the delivery of nutrients essential for healthy fetal brain and neurological development. It is becoming increasingly evident that long-term consequences are associated with these brain abnormalities, including autism spectrum disorders, learning and behavior problems, and neuropsychiatric disorders (Lahti-Pulkkinen et al., 2020; Shapiro et al., 2020).

These findings, in addition to others, underline the importance of moderating weight gain by following a nutritious diet and engaging in physical activity throughout pregnancy. Mothers and their infants are more likely to experience a healthier outcome.

What are the connections?

1. What is gestational diabetes and how can it affect fetal brain development?
2. What steps can mothers take prior to and during pregnancy to avoid gaining excess weight?

cigarette smoke, medications or other drugs (Table 3-2), or infectious illnesses (Table 3-3) that enter the mother's body. Exposure to any of these substances can damage developing fetal organs and systems and increase the risk of irreversible birth defects.

The *fetal stage* refers to the period between the ninth week and the onset of labor and delivery (around the fortieth week). Most fetal systems and structures are now formed, and this final and longest period is devoted to continued growth and maturation. By seven months, a fetus is capable of surviving birth. During the final two months, few developmental changes occur. Instead, the fetus undergoes rapid and important increases in weight and size by adding layers of fat. For example, a seven-month-old fetus who weighs 2 to 3 pounds (0.9 to 1.4 kg) will gain approximately a half-pound (0.23 kg) per week until birth. Body systems are also maturing and growing stronger, thus improving the fetus's chances of surviving outside the mother's body.

Promoting Healthy Fetal Development

Critical aspects of fetal development take place during the earliest days of pregnancy. Because the mother may not yet know that she is pregnant, it is important that both parents follow healthy lifestyle practices throughout their reproductive years, whether they are trying to have a baby or not. Researchers have identified many practices that can improve a mother's chances of giving birth to a healthy infant, including:

- Obtaining early prenatal care
- Following a nutritious diet
- Maintaining a moderate weight gain
- Obtaining adequate sleep and rest
- Avoiding excessive stress
- Having a positive emotional attitude
- Planning pregnancies when a mother is in her twenties to thirties and in good health
- Participating in daily physical activity
- Limiting exposure to teratogens such as drugs, alcohol, tobacco, high dose radiation, and environmental chemicals
- Allowing a two-year interval between pregnancies (Haight et al., 2019; WHO, 2007)

Prenatal Care

Medically supervised prenatal care is critical for ensuring the development of a healthy infant (Figure 3-2). Arrangements for this care should be made as soon as a woman suspects that she may be pregnant. Women should not rely solely on home pregnancy tests before seeking medical care because the results are not always accurate, especially during the early days and weeks. During the initial visit to a health-care provider, pregnancy can be confirmed (or refuted), immunizations can be updated, and any medical problems that the mother may have can be evaluated and treated. In addition, the parents-to-be can be counseled on practices that influence fetal development. For example, mothers may be encouraged to participate in a program of regular noncontact physical activity or to take prenatal vitamins. (So long as there are no complications to the pregnancy, regular exercise can improve weight control, circulation, muscle tone, and elimination and is believed to contribute to an easier labor and delivery.)

At present, approximately 77 percent of women in the United States receive prenatal care during their first trimester of pregnancy (Osterman

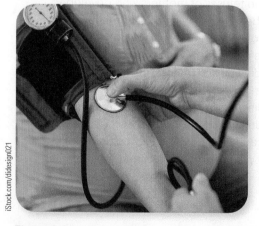

iStock.com/didesign021

Figure 3-2 Early and regular prenatal care is essential for a healthy pregnancy and infant.

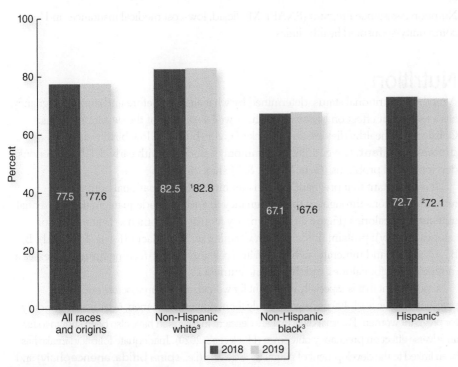

Figure 3-3 Timing of prenatal care initiation.

Source: Centers for Disease Control and Prevention, National Center for Health Statistics, Natality. Retrieved from https://www.cdc.gov/nchs/data/databriefs/db387-H.pdf.

[1]Significant increase from 2018 (*p* < 0.05).
[2]Significant decline from 2018 (*p* < 0.05).
[3]Significant difference between all race and Hispanic-origin groups (*p* < 0.05).

& Martin, 2018) (Figure 3-3). Efforts to increase this number are identified as a significant public health objective in the Healthy People 2030 national agenda. Failure to obtain early and regular prenatal care is often associated with an increase in medical complications, preterm births, **low birth weight (LBW)** infants, fetal death, and disabilities (Figure 3-4). Poverty and a lack of health insurance are often cited as factors that limit a mother's access to essential medical care, as well as to her understanding about its importance. Language barriers, differences in cultural beliefs, being a teen mother, and ethnicity are also identified as inhibiting factors (Wong & Kitsantas, 2020). Consequently, continued efforts must be made to improve mothers' awareness of government-sponsored programs such as the national Women, Infants, and Children (WIC) supplemental food program, Supplemental

low birth weight (LBW) An infant who weighs less than 5.5 pounds (2,500 grams) at the time of birth.

Figure 3-4 Percent of infants born with low birth weight.

Source: National Center for Health Statistics, National Vital Statistics System. Retrieved from https://www.cdc.gov/nchs/products/databriefs/db306.htm.

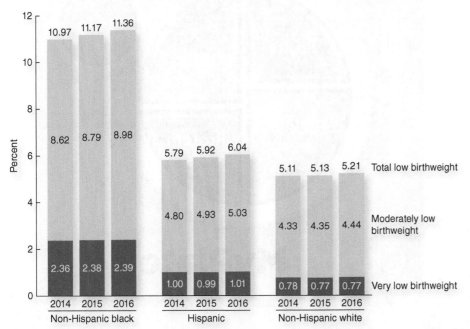

Nutrition Assistance Program (SNAP), Medicaid, low-cost medical insurance, and community-sponsored health clinics.

Nutrition

A mother's nutritional status, determined by what she eats before and during pregnancy, has a significant effect on her own health, as well as on that of the developing fetus. Consuming a healthy diet lessens the risk of giving birth to a low birth weight or **premature infant**, two conditions commonly associated with early death and serious developmental problems (Gete, Waller, & Mishra, 2020).

It is important that pregnant women continue to follow national nutrition recommendations throughout their pregnancy to ensure an adequate intake of essential nutrients and calories (Figure 3-5). Pregnancy increases a woman's dietary need for calories (energy); protein; fluids; certain vitamins such as folacin (folate, folic acid), B_6, B_{12}, C, and D; and minerals such as iron and calcium. Breast-feeding further increases a mother's need for calories and these same nutrients.

One nutrient that is especially important for women to consume before and during pregnancy is folic acid: 400 micrograms daily for nonpregnant women, 600 micrograms daily for pregnant women. Paternal diets that are deficient in folic acid have also been shown to have an adverse effect on pregnancy outcomes (Hoek et al., 2020). Inadequate folic acid intake has been linked to the development of neural tube defects (i.e., **spina bifida**, **anencephaly**) and **cleft lip/cleft palate** deformities in infants (Li et al., 2020; Steele, Kim, & Finnell, 2020).

Folic acid is a B vitamin found abundantly in many foods, especially raw, leafy green vegetables, dried beans, lentils, peas, avocado, eggs, and orange juice. Food manufacturers are currently required to add folic acid to all enriched grain products, such as pastas, rice, breads, crackers, and breakfast cereals. This measure has contributed to a significant reduction in folate deficiencies among women and men of reproductive age and, in turn, the incidence preventable birth defects in infants (Kancherla et al., 2021).

Although vitamin supplements are generally prescribed, they must not be considered a substitute for a nutritious diet. They lack essential protein, calories, and other important

premature infant An infant born before thirty-seven weeks following conception.

spina bifida A birth defect caused by a malformation of the infant's spinal column.

anencephaly A birth defect resulting in malformation of the skull and brain; portions of these structures might be missing at birth.

cleft lip/cleft palate Incomplete closure of the lip, palate (roof of the mouth), or both, resulting in a disfiguring deformity.

Figure 3-5 Daily food plans for pregnant and breast-feeding mothers are available on this interactive tool.

Source: U.S. Department of Agriculture. Retrieved from https://www.myplate.gov/.

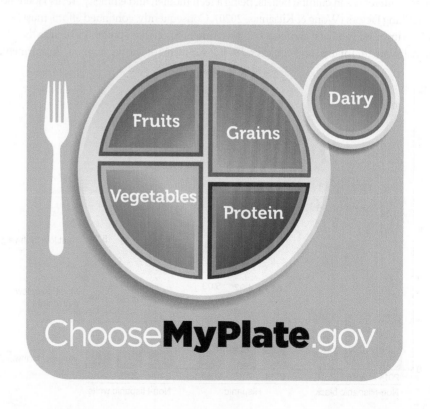

What Do You See?

Maternal diet and fetal development.
What a mother eats and drinks in the months before and throughout pregnancy has a direct influence on her infant's development. Which food items in this photo will supply folacin? What role does this B vitamin play in fetal development?

Tetra Images/Brand X Pictures/Getty Images

nutrients found in most foods. These nutrients are required for healthy fetal development and also improve the absorption and utilization of vitamins and minerals taken in tablet form. Herbal preparations are not recommended due to a lack of sufficient information about their value and safety during pregnancy (Illamola et al., 2019).

Several groups, including the U.S. Food & Drug Administration (FDA), have advised young children and women who are contemplating pregnancy, pregnant, or breast-feeding to limit their intake of certain fish and seafood varieties due to potential mercury and pesticide contamination (U.S. FDA, 2020). However, because fish are low in calories and a rich source of high-quality protein and essential fats, researchers suggest that the benefits of including them in one's diet may outweigh the potential risks. They encourage women and young children to limit their seafood consumption to no more than 8 to 12 ounces per week and to choose healthier and safer options (Figure 3-6). Consumers also

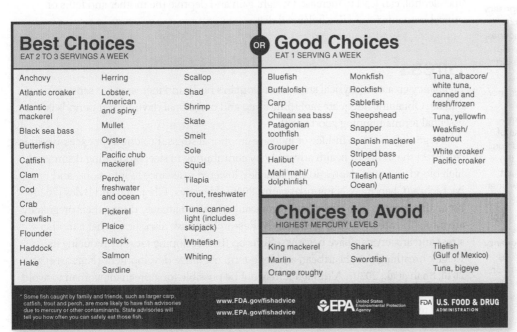

Figure 3-6 Advice about eating fish.

Source: U.S. Food & Drug Administration. Advice about eating fish. Retrieved from https://www.fda.gov/food/consumers/advice-about-eating-fish.

are encouraged to check with authorities before eating fish caught in local rivers and lakes to determine whether mercury or other hazardous chemical contamination is a concern.

Weight

What is the optimum weight gain during pregnancy? Most medical practitioners agree that a woman of normal weight [i.e., having a healthy body mass index (BMI)] should ideally gain between 25 and 35 pounds (10 and 14 kg) over the nine-month period (CDC, 2020). Insufficient maternal weight gain increases the chances of giving birth to a **small-for-gestational age infant** (Meinich & Trovik, 2020). These infants experience a greater risk for premature birth, cognitive and motor impairments, infection, and death. They are also more likely to experience behavior problems, depression, anxiety, and hyperactivity during their lifetime (Litt et al., 2020; Tore et al., 2020).

Women who are overweight or obese before they become pregnant or gain too much weight during pregnancy are at high risk of developing significant medical complications, including sleep apnea, **gestational diabetes**, **preeclampsia**, **eclampsia**, and **gestational hypertension** (Bicocca et al., 2020). They are also more likely to experience preterm births and pregnancy loss (e.g., miscarriage, stillborn). Infants born to mothers who are overweight have a higher incidence of heart and neural tube defects and of developing asthma, diabetes, and/or obesity later in life (Husin et al., 2020). At present, approximately 50 percent of pregnant women in the United States are considered obese (Davis, 2020). Interventions to help women lose weight before becoming pregnant and maintain a healthy weight during pregnancy are, thus, critical to achieving improved health outcomes for mothers and their infants.

Following a diet that is nutritionally adequate helps to ensure optimum weight gain. Including the recommended servings of a wide variety of fruits and vegetables supplies the vitamins essential for fetal growth (vitamins A and C) and fiber to decrease constipation. Choosing low-fat dairy products and lean meats and plant proteins (e.g., dried beans, legumes, and whole grains) aids in moderating caloric intake while providing key minerals (e.g., iron and calcium) required for the infant's and mother's health. Consuming too many empty calories, such as those found in junk foods, sweets, and alcohol, can lead to increased weight gain and deprive the mother and fetus of critical nutrients found in a balanced diet.

Stress

Pregnancy creates a physical strain on a woman's body and increases her sense of fatigue. Obtaining adequate nighttime sleep and occasional daytime rest periods is, thus, essential for maintaining good health.

Pregnancy can also induce or increase emotional stress. Prolonged or excessive stress can affect the mother's health adversely by contributing to sleep and eating disorders, high blood pressure, depression, headaches, lowered resistance to infections, and backaches (Chandra & Nanjundaswamy, 2020). Hendryx, Chojenta, and Byles (2020) noted that women who experience significant stress and anxiety during their pregnancy are more likely to give birth prematurely. Researchers have also shown that a mother's stress and anxiety can have negative effects on the developing fetus by reducing its weight, breathing rate, heartbeat, and long-term cognitive development (Nazzari et al., 2020; Shah et al., 2020). Although it may not be possible for a pregnant woman to avoid all exposure to stress, anxiety, and fatigue, the ill effects often can be minimized with proper rest, nutrition, and engagement in physical activity.

Did You Know ?

...the average age of first-time mothers in the United States is 26.4 years, which is younger than for women in many other developed countries?

small-for-gestational age infant An infant whose weight and length are significantly less at birth than an infant of the same gestational age.

gestational diabetes A form of diabetes that occurs only during pregnancy and places the fetus at increased risk; often associated with excess maternal weight gain, a family history of diabetes, and certain ethnicities (e.g., Latina, Native American, African American, Asian, Pacific Islander).

preeclampsia A serious maternal condition linked to the development of high blood pressure after the 20th week of pregnancy. Symptoms include headache, swelling, nausea, vision changes, and fluid retention; kidney and liver failure and premature birth may occur unless treated.

eclampsia A serious pregnancy complication related to preeclampsia. Causes and symptoms are the same as those of preeclampsia with the addition of seizures, agitation, and the potential for stroke. Pregnant teens, older women, and women of color are at highest risk.

gestational hypertension High blood pressure that develops after the 20th week of pregnancy. Symptoms include headache, swelling, nausea, fluid retention, and vision changes. Pregnant teens, older women, and women of color are at highest risk.

Age

A woman's age at the time of conception is an important factor in fetal development. Numerous studies conclude that the mid-twenties to early thirties are the optimum years for childbearing. Teenage mothers experience a rate of premature births, LBW infants, infant deaths, and infants born with developmental disabilities that is nearly double that for all mothers (Wong et al., 2020). These problems often are attributed to inadequate prenatal care, poor nutrition and housing, substance use, or all three. In addition, the immaturity of a teen mother's reproductive system and her lack of basic knowledge about how best to care for her own personal needs frequently place these infants at increased risk.

Advanced maternal age (late thirties and beyond) presents a different set of health concerns. The quality of genetic material contained in the **ova** continues to deteriorate as a woman ages, increasing the probability of miscarriage, infant mortality, and certain birth defects such as Down syndrome (Zhang et al., 2020a; Zhang et al., 2019). Older women are also more likely to experience multiple-birth pregnancies, medical complications during pregnancy, and birthing difficulties. However, medical advances continue to improve their chances of giving birth to a healthy infant.

Advanced paternal age has also been shown to have an adverse effect on conception and fetal health outcomes. Infertility and miscarriage rates increase as sperm quality declines with age (du Fossé et al., 2020). Researchers have also noted that the incidence of autism spectrum disorders, cancers, and some chromosomal abnormalities is significantly higher among the children of older biological fathers (Brandt et al., 2019; Rieske & Matson, 2020).

Improved knowledge and technology have contributed to a reduction in fetal risk for mothers of all ages. Genetic counseling, ultrasound scanning **(sonogram)**, **chorionic villus sampling (CVS)**, **amniocentesis**, and new noninvasive prenatal screening (NIPS) tests enable medical personnel to monitor fetal growth and detect more than 800 specific genetic disorders earlier than had been possible in the past (Carbone et al., 2021; Sabbagh & Van den Veyver, 2020; Yang & Tan, 2020). These procedures have proven to be especially beneficial for women who elect to delay childbearing until their late thirties and early forties.

Although the risks of pregnancy are undeniably greater for older women and teenagers, the problems often have as much to do with limited knowledge and poverty as with age. (Exceptions include chromosomal abnormalities such as Down and Turner syndromes.) Regardless of maternal age, a significant number of fetal problems are closely associated with a lack of medical care, an unhealthy diet, substandard housing, substance abuse, and limited education, all often closely associated with poverty. Spacing pregnancies at least two years apart also improves the mother's health and chances of carrying a subsequent pregnancy to full term (Gupta et al., 2019; Haight et al., 2019). The optimal spacing of pregnancies is so important to the reduction of preterm births that it has been addressed by the World Health Organization (WHO) and in the Healthy People 2030 objectives (DHHS, 2020).

Assisted reproductive technologies (ART), such as in vitro fertilization, have become increasingly successful and affordable procedures for treating infertility. The most common complications associated with these techniques are **ectopic pregnancy**, premature delivery, and multiple births. Some researchers have also noted a moderate risk of congenital deformities, intellectual disability, and autism in children born to mothers who have undergone various forms of ART (Starbird & Crawford, 2019; Wen et al., 2020; Zhao et al., 2020).

Did You Know
?
...the youngest mother recorded to give birth following natural conception was 5 1/2 years old (1939) and the oldest was 59 years (1997)? Birth complications and congenital defects are more common among mothers at both ends of the age spectrum.

ova Female reproductive cells (eggs) that contain reproductive materials.

sonogram A visual image of the developing fetus, created by directing high-frequency sound waves (ultrasound) at the mother's uterus; the procedure is used to determine fetal age and physical abnormalities.

chorionic villus sampling (CVS) A genetic-screening procedure in which a needle is inserted and cells removed from the outer layer of the placenta; performed between the eighth and twelfth weeks to detect some genetic disorders, such as Down syndrome.

amniocentesis Genetic-screening procedure in which a needle is inserted through the mother's abdomen into the sac of fluids surrounding the fetus to detect abnormalities such as Down syndrome or spina bifida; usually performed between the twelfth and sixteenth weeks.

ectopic pregnancy Pregnancy that occurs when a fertilized egg attaches itself outside the uterus, most often in one of the fallopian tubes located between the ovaries and uterus.

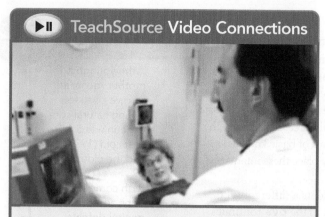

TeachSource Video Connections

Prenatal Assessment

Several procedures are available to help detect some genetic abnormalities during pregnancy. Each test has its advantages and limitations, and such tests may present the family with a difficult decision if a genetic condition is detected. Respond to the following questions after you have watched the learning video *0–2 Years: Prenatal Assessment*:

1. How is a sonogram performed, and for what purpose it is used?
2. What is an amniocentesis, and what risks are associated with this procedure?
3. How common are genetic abnormalities?
4. What ethical and moral dilemmas may some prenatal screenings present for parents and/or health-care providers?

Risks to Fetal Health and Development

Birth defects are a major cause of infant mortality in the United States (Almli et al., 2020). However, less than 3 percent of infants are born with a significant birth defect each year. An additional 3 percent have abnormalities that will be identified later in life. Fewer than 25 percent of these infants have a condition that has a genetic origin. The remainder are thought to be caused by a combination of genetic, environmental, and undetermined factors.

Much is known about lifestyle practices that improve a mother's chances of having a healthy infant. However, there is also evidence to suggest that a number of environmental substances called **teratogens** can have adverse effects on the unborn child. Several are especially damaging during the earliest weeks, often before a woman realizes that she is pregnant. It is during these sensitive or critical periods that various fetal structures and major organ systems are forming rapidly and, thus, are most sensitive to the effects of any harmful substance. For example, the heart is most vulnerable between the third and sixth weeks; the palate, from the sixth to eighth weeks. Extensive research has identified a number of major teratogens, including:

- Alcohol consumption
- Maternal and paternal smoking and vaping
- Addictive drugs (e.g., cocaine, heroin, amphetamines, marijuana)
- Hazardous chemicals (e.g., mercury, lead, carbon monoxide, polychlorinated biphenols [PCBs], paint solvents)
- Pesticides and insecticides
- Some prescribed medications (Table 3-2)
- Maternal infections (Table 3-3)
- Radiation, such as x-rays
- Obesity

Researchers continue to study other potential links between environmental factors and birth defects. To date, many findings are still considered to be inconclusive, controversial, or both. Some of the factors being investigated include:

- Prolonged exposure to high temperatures (hot baths, saunas, hot tubs)
- Herbal supplements, cannabis, and over-the-counter medications and vitamins (Paul et al., 2021; Stanley et al., 2019)
- Exposure to electromagnetic fields such as those created by cell phones, computers, microwave ovens, and power lines (Mansuori, Alihemmati, & Mesbahi, 2020)
- Aspartame, stevia, and other artificial sweeteners
- Cooking smoke and consumption of grilled meats (Yang et al., 2020)
- Hazardous waste sites
- Indoor air quality

teratogens Harmful agents that can cause fetal damage (e.g., malformations, neurological, and behavioral problems) during the prenatal period.

The relationship between teratogen exposure and fetal damage is not always clear or direct. Several factors can influence a teratogen's harmful effect on fetal development,

vadimguzhva/iStock/Getty Images

including the amount and method of exposure (dose), fetal age (timing), and genetic makeup of the mother and fetus. Women who are contemplating pregnancy should take measures to avoid unnecessary contact with known teratogens that can cross the placental barrier. As noted earlier, fetal organs and body systems are especially vulnerable to these agents during the early weeks following conception. This is not to suggest that there is ever a completely safe time period. Even during the later months, fetal growth can be negatively affected by maternal exposure to or use of substances mentioned here and in the following sections. There is also evidence to suggest that some teratogens can have a lifelong effect on an individual's health (Gentner & Leppert, 2019; Joseph et al., 2020).

Alcohol

Alcohol consumption during pregnancy is known to have serious consequences for both the mother and the developing fetus. Warnings to this effect appear on the labels of all alcoholic products. Mothers who consume alcohol during pregnancy experience a greater risk of miscarriages, stillbirths, premature infants, and LBW infants (Sundermann et al., 2021). The incidence of fetal death is also significantly higher. Because alcoholic beverages contain only calories and no nutrients, consuming them on a regular or binge basis can limit the mother's dietary intake of essential protein, vitamins, and minerals necessary for her well-being and that of her infant.

Alcohol is also a potentially toxic teratogen that can have a wide range of irreversible adverse effects on a fetus's physical and brain development (Hemingway et al., 2020; Zhang et al., 2020b). Because mother and infant share a common circulatory system (through the placenta and umbilical cord), both are affected by any alcohol that is consumed. However, alcohol remains in the fetal circulatory system twice as long as in that of the mother. It is especially damaging to the fetus during the critical first trimester of pregnancy when most body structures and organs, especially the brain, heart, and neurological system, are forming.

Prenatal exposure to alcohol can result in conditions commonly referred to as fetal alcohol spectrum disorders (FASDs). Heavy or binge drinking is associated with a preventable condition known as *fetal alcohol syndrome (FAS)*, which causes intellectual disabilities and growth retardation, behavior and learning problems, poor motor coordination, heart defects, characteristic facial deformities (e.g., eyes set wide apart, shortened eye lids, or flattened nose), and speech impairment (NIAAA, 2020). Moderate alcohol consumption is associated with a milder form of this condition known as fetal alcohol effect (FAE). These children often exhibit a wide range of developmental, psychological, and neurobehavioral disorders (Lees et al., 2020). When alcohol is consumed later in the pregnancy, it typically interferes with proper fetal growth.

Precisely how much alcohol might be damaging to an unborn child is difficult to determine. Researchers have reported reduced brain size and a range of neurobehavioral deficits linked to any fetal alcohol exposure (Mattson, Bernes, & Doyle, 2019). Most likely, the relationship between alcohol and fetal damage is more complex than it might initially appear. *Thus, no amount of alcohol is considered safe to consume during pregnancy.*

Smoking

Many pregnant women continue to smoke despite warnings issued by the U.S. surgeon general and those printed on all tobacco products (Figure 3-7). Researchers have determined that even smoking as few as one or two cigarettes a day can have adverse effects on fetal development (Liu et al., 2020). Smokeless tobacco and e-cigarettes are not considered safe alternatives because they contain many of the same chemicals present in regular cigarettes (Kim & Oancea, 2020).

Maternal smoking has been linked to a variety of fetal malformations and birth complications (Philips et al., 2020). Toxic substances in cigarette smoke, including nicotine, tars, ammonia, carbon monoxide, and other chemicals, cross the placental barrier and interfere with normal fetal development. For example, carbon monoxide reduces the amount of oxygen available to the fetus and damages fetal DNA (Sifat et al., 2020). This early oxygen deprivation seems to correlate with learning and behavioral problems, especially as these children reach school age.

Mothers who smoke during pregnancy experience a higher rate of miscarriage, premature births, stillborn infants, and LBW infants. Their infants are addicted to the nicotine and undergo a period of withdrawal following birth. They are also three times more likely to die from sudden infant death syndrome (SIDS) and experience a range of acute and chronic respiratory problems (e.g., allergies, asthma, colds, croup, and bronchitis) (Bednarczuk, Milner, & Greenough, 2020).

Figure 3-7 Percent of women who smoke anytime during pregnancy.

Source: NCHS, National Vital Statistics System, Natality. Retrieved from https://www.cdc.gov/nchs/products /databriefs/db305.htm.

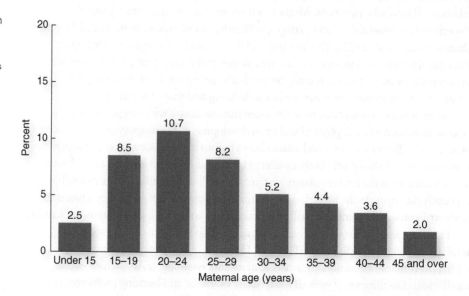

Table 3-2 Examples of Potentially Teratogenic Drugs

- Analgesics (more than an occasional dose of aspirin or ibuprofen)
- Antibiotics (particularly tetracyclines and streptomycin)
- Anticonvulsants (such as Dilantin)
- Anticoagulants (used to thin the blood, such as Coumadin)
- Antidepressants
- Antihistamines
- Antihypertensives (used to treat high blood pressure)
- Anti-neoplastic drugs (used to treat cancers and some forms of arthritis, such as Methotrexate)
- Antiviral agents
- Hormones [such as diethylstilbesterol (DES) and progesterin]
- Large doses of vitamin A [in excess of 10,000 international units (IU); includes some acne treatments such as Accutane and Retin-A]
- Thyroid and anti-thyroid drugs
- Diet pills
- Nicotine
- Cocaine, heroin, marijuana, and methadone

The incidence of attention deficit and other conduct disorders is also significantly higher among these children.

Paternal smoking prior to and during a woman's pregnancy has also been identified as a significant contributing factor to fetal birth defects (Zhou et al., 2020). In addition, it is known to increase children's risk for developing several chronic conditions, including childhood cancers, asthma, diabetes, cardiovascular disease, and obesity (Cao, Lu, & Lu, 2020; Philips et al., 2020).

Environmental Chemicals

Numerous chemicals and drugs are known to be detrimental to healthy fetal development. These substances range from prescription and nonprescription medications to pesticides, fertilizers, metals, air pollution, and street drugs (Kharbanda et al., 2020; Park et al., 2020) (Table 3-2). Some cause severe malformations, such as missing or deformed limbs or facial features. Others can lead to fetal death (spontaneous abortion), premature birth, or lifelong behavioral and learning disabilities.

Racial, ethnic, socioeconomic, and geographical disparities place some pregnant women at greater risk for chemical exposure. For example, Varshavsky and colleagues (2020) noted that non-Hispanic Black women are often exposed to higher levels of flame-retardant chemicals, present in drapes, furniture, and carpeting, that have been banned in the United States since 2004. Cushing and colleagues (2020) found that women who live in neighborhoods near oil refineries and fracking operations are exposed to chemicals that increase their risk of giving birth prematurely.

Not all exposed fetuses will be affected in the same manner or to the same degree. The nature and severity of an infant's abnormalities seem to be influenced by the timing of exposure during fetal development, the amount and type of substance, the mother's general state of health, and maternal and fetal genetics. In many cases, researchers are not able to provide a definitive answer about which drugs and chemicals (if any) have absolutely no harmful effects on the developing fetus. Thus, women who are or may

Did You Know ?

...that the supplement and herbal industries are unregulated in this country? Ingredients may not be present in amounts listed on the label and scientific evidence supporting their safety and use is often lacking.

Table 3-3 Examples of Potentially Teratogenic Communicable Diseases

- Chicken pox
- Cytomegalovirus (CMV)
- Fifth disease
- Herpes
- Human immunodeficiency virus (HIV)
- Mumps
- Rubella (German measles)
- Syphilis
- Toxoplasmosis

Note: Information about any of these infectious diseases can be found on the CDC website (*www.cdc.gov*).

become pregnant are encouraged to check with their medical provider before using any chemical substance or medication (prescription or nonprescription).

Communicable Diseases

Although the placenta effectively filters out many infectious organisms, it does not prevent all disease-causing agents from reaching the unborn child. Whether a fetus will be affected (and, if so, the resulting abnormality) depends upon the particular disease and stage of pregnancy when the infection occurs (Table 3-3). For example, researchers have noted that women who had a cold or flu and fever shortly before or during early pregnancy were at greater risk of giving birth to an infant with a neural tube, heart, or other congenital defect (Graham, 2020; Wang et al., 2021). A pregnant woman who develops rubella (German measles) during the first four to eight weeks following conception is at high risk for giving birth to an infant who may have heart problems and be deaf, blind, or both (an example of the extreme vulnerability of the fetus during its earliest weeks). *Note:* Rubella can be controlled if women who do not have natural immunity are immunized following a pregnancy or not less than three to four months prior to becoming pregnant.

The coronavirus (COVID-19) epidemic has raised new concerns about its potential effect on maternal health and fetal development. Emerging studies have reported a slight increase in rates of preterm and cesarean births among women who contracted the virus during their pregnancy (Wong, Khong, & Tan, 2021). However, the majority of infants born to these mothers appear to be relatively unaffected (Dashraath et al., 2021). Researchers have found that the placenta may provide some antiviral properties that protect the fetus.

The percentage of fetuses who are exposed to infectious agents and develop congenital abnormalities is relatively small. It is still unknown as to why some fetuses are affected and others are not. What is reasonably certain is that pregnant women who are well nourished, have regular prenatal care, are generally healthy, and avoid addictive substances have a higher probability of giving birth to a strong and healthy infant.

Chronic Health Disorders

Women who have chronic health conditions, such as asthma, pre-diabetes or diabetes, obesity, or some autoimmune disorders (i.e., thyroid, lupus) are at increased risk for adverse pregnancy outcomes. Their disorders are often more difficult to manage due to the hormonal changes that occur during pregnancy. These women also experience higher rates of infertility, premature delivery, pregnancy loss, and infant birth defects (Liu et al., 2019; Ponnusamy, 2020).

Chronic depression and anxiety are also known to present additional risks for maternal health and fetal development. For example, Smith, Twynstra, and Seabrook (2020) noted a significant increase in preterm births among these mothers. Their infants often displayed excessive crying and experienced more behavioral and mental health problems later in life. Perhaps more notable are the structural abnormalities that researchers have identified in the fetal brain. Wu and colleagues (2021) describe these alterations as typical of a fear response that can have lasting effects on children's language, cognitive, and motor development.

Despite these findings, it is important to understand that not all infants born to mothers who have a chronic health disorder will experience adverse effects. Much remains to be learned about how these conditions may affect fetal development. What must be remembered is the importance of assuring that all pregnant women, especially those who experience chronic disorders, have access to high-quality medical supervision and follow healthy lifestyle practices.

An Infant's Arrival: Labor and Delivery

For most women, childbirth is a natural process that follows months of anticipation and preparation. Several birthing options are available to families today, including birthing centers, hospitals, and home deliveries with physicians or certified nurse midwives in attendance. Although the fundamental labor and delivery process is similar for most mothers-to-be, the actual experience is often unique. Labor and delivery can occur prematurely, on time, or beyond a mother's expected due date, be long or short in duration, be considered relatively easy or difficult, and occur with or without complications.

The onset of labor is usually signaled by several physical changes. Approximately two weeks before labor begins, the mother may notice that she is carrying the infant lower in her abdomen. This occurs as the infant's head drops down into the birth canal in preparation for delivery and is commonly referred to as *lightening*. The mother also may note that the mild contractions (Braxton-Hicks) she has experienced throughout her pregnancy are becoming stronger and more regular as they prepare the birth canal for delivery. When active labor begins, she may experience a small amount of bloody discharge as the mucus plug that has protected the birth canal opening for nine months becomes dislodged. Some mothers also have a leaking of amniotic fluid if the sac surrounding the fetus tears or breaks in the early stages of labor.

The normal birthing process is divided into three stages. The first and longest stage lasts approximately fourteen to seventeen hours for first-time mothers and six to eight hours for subsequent births. During this stage, contractions slowly cause the diameter of the **cervix** to expand (dilate) in preparation for delivery. Stage two lasts approximately thirty to ninety minutes and begins when the cervix is completely dilated and ends when the infant is delivered. Contractions become more intense and painful throughout this stage. When the infant is born, the umbilical cord is clamped, and the infant begins to function independently. Some medical researchers suggest that clamping be delayed for several minutes following birth, especially for low birth weight or premature infants, to reduce the incidence of anemia (Yunis et al., 2021). The third and final birthing stage

cervix The lower portion of the uterus that opens into the vagina.

begins after the infant arrives and ends when the placenta is delivered; this stage usually lasts only a few minutes.

The majority of births proceed normally and without complications. However, a small percentage of deliveries may require some form of medical intervention. In less than 5 percent of live births, the infant descends feet or buttocks first (rather than headfirst) into the birth canal. This situation may require a **cesarean section (C-section)** to be performed. A C-section may also be necessary when labor does not progress, the mother's birth canal is too small, the umbilical cord prolapses, or a medical problem such as fetal distress develops.

Throughout the birth process, the infant is monitored closely for signs of distress. Heart rate is checked with a stethoscope or ultrasound device (Doppler) or by placing a tiny electrode on the infant's head. Immediately following birth, the newborn's condition is assessed at one minute and again at five minutes, using the Apgar scoring system (Figure 3-8). The infant receives a score between 0 and 2 in each of five categories: appearance, pulse, grimace, activity, and respirations. A score of 8 or better is considered normal (Apgar, 1953). The Apgar scale provides a reliable measure of how well the infant is doing at the time, but it is not a predictor of future health or developmental problems.

Healthy mothers and infants are typically released from the hospital within one to two days following the birth. Mothers who have had a C-section or experienced health complications may remain in the hospital for several days longer. Infants born prematurely or LBW will remain hospitalized until they are healthy enough to go home.

Cultural differences can influence how a mother and her family perceive pregnancy and an infant's birth (Klann & Wong, 2020; Mathur, Morris, & McNamara, 2020). Some groups view pregnancy and delivery as normal events that require little special attention or recognition. Others consider a child's birth an experience to be shared by extended family members. Myths and beliefs about everything from the mother's diet to how she responds to physical discomforts, sexuality, and daily living routines also differ by cultural group (Ahmad, Nor, & Daud, 2019). Although these views may differ from your own, it is important to show respect and support for the family. In cases where cultural practices may cause harm to the mother or her fetus, families should be directed to professional health care providers and reliable information sources.

cesarean section (C- section) The delivery of an infant through an incision in the mother's abdomen and uterus.

Figure 3-8 Apgar scoring system for evaluating newborns.

Source: Adapted from Apgar (1953).

	0	1	2
Appearance (skin color)	Bluish or pale	Pink, except extremities	Pink all over
Pulse	None	Fewer than 100 beats/minute	Greater than 100 beats/minute
Grimace (reflex response)	None	Makes some facial response	Strong response: cries, coughs, or sneezes
Activity (muscle tone)	Limp	Weak flexion of extremities	Active movement
Respiration (breathing)	None	Slow and/or irregular	Regular; strong cry

Post-partum Depression

New mothers often undergo a range of mixed emotions following an infant's birth. Feelings of exhilaration, uncertainty, anxiety, and overwhelming fatigue may come and go at a moment's notice. Mood swings, commonly referred to as the *baby blues,* are often experienced several days after delivery. Symptoms can include weepiness, sadness, anxiety, difficulty sleeping, lack of energy, appetite loss, irritability, or all of these. Hormonal changes, lack of sleep, and added responsibilities are thought to trigger these feelings, which typically improve within several weeks. Compassionate support from family members and friends, moderate exercise, adequate rest, and a healthy diet can help to ease temporary discomforts. However, a doctor should be consulted if symptoms are severe or persist because this could be a sign of postpartum depression (PPD).

It is estimated that fewer than 10 to 15 percent of new mothers experience signs of PPD within the first year following delivery (Bauman et al., 2020). However, this rate varies by geographical area, with significantly higher rates in some regions of the United States. Women who experience unintended pregnancy, poverty, domestic partner abuse, fetal loss, unhealthy behaviors (e.g., drinking, smoking, illicit drugs) during pregnancy, birth complications, are younger than age twenty, or lack social support are at increased risk for developing PPD (Hutchens & Kearney, 2020). The rate is also significantly higher for women who suffer from chronic depression prior to and during their pregnancy.

The symptoms of PPD are far more serious than baby blues. They can include hallucinations, thoughts of harming the infant, hopelessness, and/or suicide. PPD can last three to twelve months and has been shown to interfere with the quality of maternal care, emotional attachment, and breastfeeding (Dias & Figueiredo, 2020). It can also have an adverse effect on an infant's sleep and eating behaviors and language and social-emotional development (Brookman et al., 2020).

Although PPD is a universal phenomenon, much of what is known about the disorder and its treatment is based on Western cultures. However, comparable symptoms and protective measures are described in cross-cultural literature (Haque & Malebranche, 2020; Recto, 2019). For example, varying lengths of maternal and newborn confinement are practiced in many cultures to avoid harmful spirits and prevent illness (Evagorou, Arvaniti, & Samakouri, 2016). Somali women, for example, often wear garlic earrings following delivery to ward off the "evil eye." Women in Muslim and Arab cultures describe symptoms of PPD and attribute them to Jinn, or supernatural spirits that enter and take over the body (Al-Krenawi, 2019). As societies become increasingly diverse, it is important to understand the cultural differences that influence and shape the concept of motherhood.

Summary

3-1 A human pregnancy requires approximately 266 days (nine months) from conception until an infant is fully developed.

- Germinal stage—Zygote is formed; cell division begins and develops into a blastocyst.

- Embryonic stage—Embryo attaches to the uterine wall, cell division continues, the placenta develops, and all major organs and systems are formed.

- Fetal stage—Fetal systems continue to grow and mature; fetus gains weight and prepares for birth.

3-2 The mother's general health, age, quality of diet, emotional state, physical fitness, and support system influence healthy fetal development.

continued on following page

Summary

- Exposure to environmental factors (teratogens), such as certain infectious illnesses, alcohol, addictive drugs, smoking, and some medications (prescription and over-the-counter drugs) are known to have a harmful effect on fetal development.

- Mothers can take steps to improve their chances of having a healthy pregnancy and infant by obtaining routine prenatal care, following a nutritious diet, gaining an appropriate amount of weight (not too much or too little), participating in daily physical activity, avoiding teratogens, and maintaining a positive state of mental health.

3-3 Substances capable of interfering with healthy fetal development include alcohol; cigarettes, e-cigarettes, and secondhand smoke; addictive drugs; certain chemicals and pesticides; some medications; infectious agents; radiation; and chronic health conditions, including obesity.

3-4 Changes associated with impending delivery include lightening, contractions that increase in intensity and regularity, and bloody discharge. Some mothers also experience a leaking of amniotic fluid prior to or at the onset of labor.

3-5 A small percentage of new mothers will develop PPD, which can affect the quality of care provided and mother-infant attachment.

- Researchers have also determined that maternal depression can interfere with the infant's language and social-emotional development.

- PPD requires prompt medical treatment.

Key Terms

conception **p. 51**
genes **p. 51**
temperament **p. 51**
zygote **p. 51**
implantation **p. 52**
embryo **p. 52**
placenta **p. 53**
low birth weight (LBW) **p. 55**
premature infant **p. 56**

spina bifida **p. 56**
anencephaly **p. 56**
cleft lip/cleft palate **p. 56**
small-for-gestational age infant **p. 58**
gestational diabetes **p. 58**
preeclampsia **p. 58**
eclampsia **p. 58**
gestational hypertension **p. 58**

ova **p. 59**
sonogram **p. 59**
chorionic villus sampling (CVS) **p. 59**
amniocentesis **p. 59**
ectopic pregnancy **p. 59**
teratogens **p. 60**
cervix **p. 65**
cesarean section (C-section) **p. 66**

Apply What You Have Learned

A. Case Study Connections

Reread the developmental sketch about Anna and Miguel presented at the beginning of this chapter and answer the following questions:

1. At what point is Anna likely to begin feeling the baby move?

2. What practices should Anna avoid during pregnancy to improve her chances of having a healthy infant?

3. What negative effects might Anna's smoking have on her pregnancy?

4. Which nutrients are especially important for Anna to include in her daily diet?

5. In what ways is Anna's Latina heritage influencing her pregnancy?

B. Review Questions

1. Discuss three practices that promote a healthy pregnancy.

2. Describe three factors that appear to be hazardous to fetal development.

3. Identify one characteristic or change in fetal development that occurs during each month of pregnancy.

4. What role(s) does the placenta perform during pregnancy?

5. What characteristics would you expect to observe in a child who has FAS? Explain how this condition can be prevented.

C. Your Turn: Chapter to Practice

1. Select one of the following cultural groups: Hispanic/Latina, Asian, Native American, Middle Eastern, African American, or other group of personal or local interest. Interview several mothers to learn more about their views on pregnancy, unique practices associated with pregnancy and birthing, and the role that children play in a family. Share your findings with the class.

2. Make arrangements to observe at a local WIC clinic. What services do they offer in addition to nutrition? Who is eligible to receive services? Write a brief paper summarizing your experience.

3. Organize and/or participate in a local food drive. Note how many food recipients are pregnant women and young children. What do these numbers suggest?

4. As a group, develop a one-hour class focused on healthy practices for mothers who are pregnant or contemplating pregnancy. Make arrangements to present your session to a group of pregnant women in your community. Evaluate the effectiveness of the presentation and make recommendations for improvement.

Online Resources

March of Dimes
This organization is devoted to supporting families and fostering healthy infant births. Information about positive lifestyle practices for parents to follow before, during, and after pregnancy can be accessed on this site.

Medline Plus
The National Institutes of Health (NIH) provide an abundance of information on topics related to reproduction and pregnancy.

Office of Women's Health
Extensive information about pregnancy, prenatal care, birthing, breast-feeding, and family legislation are provided in terms that are easy to understand.

Postpartum Support International
Numerous resources for families and professionals are provided in multiple languages. Links to state organizations can also be accessed from this site.

References

Ahmad, N., Nor, S. F., & Daud, F. (2019). Understanding myths in pregnancy and childbirth and the potential adverse consequences: A systematic review. *Malaysian Journal of Medical Sciences, 26*(4), 17–27.

Al-Krenawi, A. (2019). The role of cultural beliefs on mental health treatment. *Arab Journal of Psychiatry, 30*(2), 89–99.

Almli, L. M., Ely, D. M., Ailes, E. C., Abouk, R., Grosse, S. D., Isenburg, J. L., Waldron, D. B., & Reefhuis, J. (2020). Infant mortality attributable to birth defects — United States, 2003–2017. *Morbidity and Mortality Weekly Report (MMWR), 69*, 25–29.

Alves, J. M., Luo, S., Chow, T., Herting, M., Xiang, A. H., & Page, K. A. (2020). Sex differences in the association between prenatal exposure to maternal obesity and hippocampal volume in children. *Brain and Behavior, 10*(2), e.01522. https://doi.org/10.1002/brb3.1522

Apgar, V. (1953). Proposal for a new method of evaluation of the newborn infant. *Current Researches in Anesthesia & Analgesia, 32*(4), 260–267.

Avci, R., Whittington, J. R., Blossom, S. J., Escalona-Vargas, D., Siegel, E. R., Preissl, H. T., & Eswaran, H. (2020). Studying the effect of maternal pregestational diabetes on fetal neurodevelopment using magnetoencephalography. *Clinical EEG and Neuroscience, 51*(5), 331–338.

Bauman, B. L., Ko, J. Y., Cox, S., D'Angelo, D. V., Warner, L., Folger, S., Tevendale, H. D., Coy, K. C., Harrison, L., & Barfield, W. D. (2020). *Vital Signs*: Postpartum depressive symptoms and provider discussions about perinatal depression—United States, 2018. *Morbidity and Mortality Weekly Report (MMWR), 69*(19), 575–581. https://doi.org/10.15585/mmwr.mm6919a2

Bednarczuk, N., Milner, A., & Greenough, A. (2020). The role of maternal smoking in sudden infant death pathogenesis. *Frontiers in Neurology, 11*, e586068. https://doi.org/10.3389/fneur.2020.586068

Bicocca, M. J., Mendez-Figueroa, H., Suneet, C., & Sibai, B. (2020). Maternal obesity and the risk of early-onset and late-onset hypertensive disorders of pregnancy. *Obstetrics & Gynecology, 136*(1), 118–127.

Brandt, J. S., Ithier, M. A., Rosen, T., & Ashkinadze, E. (2019). Advanced paternal age, infertility, and reproductive risks: A review of the literature. *Prenatal Diagnosis, 39*(2), 81–87.

Brookman, R., Kalashnikova, M., Conti, J., Rattanasone, N. X., Grant, K., Demuth, K., & Burnham, D. (2020). Depression and anxiety in the postnatal period: An examination of infants' home language environment, vocalizations, and expressive language abilities. *Child Development, 91*(6), e1211–e1230. https://doi.org/10.1111/cdev.13421

Cao, Y., Lu, J., & Lu, J. (2020). Paternal smoking before conception and during pregnancy is associated with an increased risk of childhood acute lymphoblastic leukemia: A systematic review and meta-analysis of 17 case-control studies. *Journal of Pediatric Hematology/Oncology, 42*(1), 32–40.

Carbone, L., Cariati, F., Sarno, L., Conforti, A., Fagnulo, F., Strina, I., Pastore, L., Maruotti, G. M., & Alviggi, C. (2021). Non-invasive prenatal testing: Current perspectives and future challenges. *Genes, 12*(1), 1–12.

Centers for Disease Control and Prevention (CDC). (2020). Weight gain during pregnancy. Retrieved from https://www.cdc.gov/reproductivehealth/maternalinfanthealth/pregnancy-weight-gain.htm#recommendations.

Chandra, P. S., & Nanjundaswamy, M. H. (2020). Pregnancy specific anxiety: An underrecognized problem. *World Psychiatry, 19*(3), 336–337.

Cirulli, F., Musillo, C., & Berry, A. (2020). Maternal obesity as a risk factor for brain development and mental health in the offspring. *Neuroscience, 447*(1), 122–135.

Cloninger, C. R., Cloninger, K. M., Zwir, I., & Keltikangas-Järvinen, L. (2019). The complex genetics and biology of human temperament: A review of traditional concepts in relation to new molecular findings. *Translational Psychiatry, 9*(1), 290. https://doi.org/10.1038/s41398-019-0621-4

Cushing, L. J., Vavra-Musser, Chau, K., Franklin, M., & Johnson, J. E. (2020). Flaring from unconventional oil and gas development and birth outcomes in the Eagle Ford shale in South Texas. *Environmental Health Perspectives, 128*(7), 1–9.

Dashraath, P., Wong, J. L., Lim, M. X., Lim, L. M., Li, S., Biswas, A., Choolani, M., Mattar, C., & Su, L. L. (2021). Coronavirus disease 2019 (COVID-19) pandemic and pregnancy. *American Journal of Obstetrics and Gynecology, 222*(6), 521–531.

Davis, A. M. (2020). Collateral damage: Maternal obesity during pregnancy continues to rise. *Obstetrical & Gynecological Survey, 75*(1), 39–49.

Dias, C. C., & Figueiredo, B. (2020). Mother's prenatal and postpartum depression symptoms and infant's sleep problems at 6 months. *Infant Mental Health Journal, 41*(5), 614–627.

du Fossé, N. A., van der Hoorn, M. P., van Lith, J. M., le Cessie, S., & Lashley, E. E. (2020). Advanced paternal age is associated with an increased risk of spontaneous miscarriage: A systematic review and meta-analysis. *Human Reproductive Update, 26*(5), 650–669.

Evagorou, O., Arvaniti, A., & Samakouri, M. (2016). Cross-cultural approach of postpartum depression: Manifestations, practices, risk factors and therapeutic interventions. Therapeutic Interventions. *Psychiatric Quarterly, 87*(1), 129–154.

Gentner, M. B., & Leppert, M. L. (2019). Environmental influences on health and development: Nutrition, substance exposure, and adverse childhood experiences. *Developmental Medicine & Child Neurology, 61*(9), 1008–1014.

Gete, D. G., Waller, M., & Mishra, G. D. (2020). Effects of maternal diets on preterm birth and low birth weight: A systematic review. *British Journal of Nutrition, 123*(4), 446–461.

Graham, J. M. (2020). Update on the gestational effects of maternal hyperthermia. *Birth Defects Research, 112*(12), 943–952.

Gupta, P. M., Freedman, A. A., Kramer, M. R., Goldenberg, R. L., Willinger, M., Stoll, B. J., Silver, R. M., Dudley, D. J., Parker, C. B., & Hogue, C. J. (2019). Interpregnancy interval and risk of stillbirth: A population-based case control study. *Annals of Epidemiology, 35*, 35–41.

Haight, S. C., Hogue, C. J., Raskind-Hood, C. L., & Ahrens, K. A. (2019). Short interpregnancy intervals and adverse pregnancy outcomes by maternal age in the United States. *Annals of Epidemiology, 31*, 38–44.

Haque, S., & Malebranche, M. (2020). Impact of culture on refugee women's conceptualization and experience of postpartum depression in high-income countries of resettlement: A scoping review. *PLoS ONE, 15*(9), e0238109. https://doi.org/10.1371/journal.pone.0238109

Hemingway, A. S., Davies, J. K., Jirikowic, T., & Olson, E. M. (2020). What proportion of the brain structural and functional abnormalities observed among children with fetal alcohol spectrum disorder is explained by their prenatal alcohol exposure and their other prenatal and postnatal risks? *Advances in Pediatric Research, 7*(41), 2–16.

Hendryx, M., Chojenta, C., & Byles, J. E. (2020). Latent class analysis of low birth weight and preterm delivery among Australian women. *Journal of Pediatrics, 218*, 42–48.e1. https://doi.org/10.1016/j.jpeds.2019.11.007

Hoek, J., Steegers-Theunissen, R. P., Willemsen, S. P., & Schoenmakers, S. (2020). Paternal folate status and sperm quality, pregnancy outcomes, and epigenetics: A systematic review and meta-analysis. *Molecular Nutrition & Food Research, 64*(9), 1900696. https://doi.org/10.1002/mnfr.201900696

Husin, H. M., Schleger, F., Bauer, I., Fehlert, E., Kiefer-Schmidt, I., Weiss, M., Kagan, K. O., Brucker, S., Pauluschke-Fröhlich, J., Eswaran, H., Häring, H. U., Fritsche, A., & Preissl, H. (2020). Maternal weight, weight gain, and metabolism are associated with changes in fetal heart rate and variability. *Obesity, 28*(1), 114–121.

Hutchens, B. F., & Kearney, J. (2020). Risk factors for postpartum depression: An umbrella review. *Journal of Midwifery & Women's Health, 65*(1), 96–108.

Illamola, S. M., Amaeze, O. U., Krepkova, L. V., Birnbaum, A. K., Karanam, A., Job, K. M., Bortnikova, V. V., Sherwin, C. M., & Enioutina, E. Y. (2019). Use of herbal medicine by pregnant women: What physicians need to know. *Frontiers in Pharmacology, 10*, 1483. http://doi.org/10.3389/fphar.2019.01483

Joseph, R., Brady, E., Hudson, M. E., & Moran, M. M. (2020). Perinatal substance exposure and long-term outcomes in children: A literature review. *Pediatric Nursing, 46*(4), 163–173.

Kancherla, V., Wagh, K., Pachón, H., & Oakley, G. P. (2021). A 2019 global update on folic acid-preventable spina bifida and anencephaly. *Birth Defects Research, 113*(1), 77–89.

Kasman, A. M., Zhang, C. A., Shufeng, L., & Stevenson, D. K. (2020). Association of preconception paternal health on perinatal outcomes: Analysis of U.S. claims data. *Fertility and Sterility, 113*(5), 947–954.

Kharbanda, E. O., Vazquez-Benitez, G., Kunin-Batson, A., Nordin, J. D., Olsen, A., & Romitti, P. A. (2020). Birth and early developmental screening outcomes associated with cannabis exposure during pregnancy. *Journal of Perinatology, 40*(3), 473–480.

Kim, S., & Oancea, S. C. (2020). Electronic cigarettes may not be a "safer alternative" of conventional cigarettes during pregnancy: Evidence from the nationally representative PRAMS data. *BMC Pregnancy and Childbirth, 20*(1), 557. https://doi.org/10.1186/s12884-020-03247-6

Klann, E., M., & Wong, Y. J. (2020). A pregnancy decision-making model: Psychological, relational, and cultural factors affecting unintended pregnancy. *Psychology of Women Quarterly, 44*(2), 170–186.

Lahti-Pulkkinen, M., Girchenko, P., Tuovinen, S., Sammallahti, S., Reynolds, R. M., Lahti, J., Heinonen, K., Lipsanen, J., Hämäläinen, E., Villa, P. M., Kajantie, E., Laivuori, H., & Räikkönen, K. (2020). Maternal hypertensive pregnancy disorders and mental disorders in children. *Hypertension, 75*(6), 1429–1438.

Lees, B., Mewton, L., Jacobus, J., Valadez, E. A., Stapinski, L. A., Teesson, M., Tapert, S. F., & Squeglia, L. M. (2020). Association of prenatal alcohol exposure with psychological, behavioral, and neurodevelopmental outcomes in children from the Adolescent Brain Cognitive Development Study. *The American Journal of Psychiatry, 177*(11), 1060–1072.

Li, Q., Xu, L., Jia, X., Saleem, K., Zaib, T., Wenjing, S., & Fu, S. (2020). SNPs in folate pathway are associated with the risk of nonsyndromic cleft lip with or without cleft palate, a meta-analysis. *Bioscience Reports, 40*(3), BSR20194261. https://doi.org/10.1042/BSR20194261

Litt, J. S., Minich, N., Taylor, H. G., & Tiemeier, H. (2020). The inter-relationships of extremely low birth weight, asthma, and behavior: A study of common cause, mediation, and moderation. *Academic Pediatrics, 20*(7), 975–982.

Liu, B., Xu, G., Sun, Y., Du, Y., Gao, R., Snetselaar, L. G., Santillan, M. K., & Bao, W. (2019). Association between maternal pre-pregnancy obesity and preterm birth according to maternal age and race or ethnicity: A population-based study. *The Lancet: Diabetes & Endocrinology, 7*(9), 707–714.

Liu, B., Xu, G., Sun, Y., Qiu, X., Ryckman, K. K., Yu, Y., Snetselaar, L. G., & Bao, W. (2020). Maternal cigarette smoking before and during pregnancy and the risk of preterm birth: A dose–response analysis of 25 million mother–infant pairs. *PLoS Med, 17*(8), e1003158. https://doi.org/10.1371/journal.pmed.1003158

Mansuori, E., Alihemmati, A., & Mesbahi, A. (2020). An overview on the effects of power frequency electromagnetic field exposure on the female reproduction system, pregnancy outcome and fetal development. *Journal of Medicinal and Chemical Sciences, 3*(1), 60–70.

Mathur, V. A., Morris, T., & McNamara, K. (2020). Cultural conceptions of women's labor pain and labor pain management: A mixed-method analysis. *Social Science & Medicine, 261,* 113240. https://doi.org/10.1016/j.socscimed.2020.113240

Mattson, S. N., Bernes, G. A., & Doyle, L. R. (2019). Fetal alcohol spectrum disorders: A review of neurobehavioral deficits associated with prenatal alcohol exposure. *Alcoholism: Clinical and Experimental Research, 43*(6), 1046–1062.

Meinich, T., & Trovik, J. (2020). Early maternal weight gain as a risk factor for SGA in pregnancies with hyperemesis gravidarum: A 15-year hospital cohort study. *BMC Pregnancy and Childbirth, 20*(1), 255. https://doi.org/10.1186/s12884-020-02947-3

National Institute of Alcohol Abuse and Alcoholism (NIAAA). (2020). Fetal alcohol exposure. Retrieved from https://www.niaaa.nih.gov/publications/brochures-and-fact-sheets/fetal-alcohol-exposure.

Nazzari, S., Fearon, P., Rice, F., Ciceri, F., Molteni, M., & Frigerio, A. (2020). Neuroendocrine and immune markers of maternal stress during pregnancy and infant cognitive development. *Developmental Psychobiology, 62*(8), 1100–1110.

Osterman, M. J., & Martin, J. A. (2018). Timing and adequacy of prenatal care in the United States, 2016. *National Vital Statistics Reports, 67*(3). U.S. Department of Health and Human Services (HHS). Centers for Disease Control and Prevention. National Center for Health Statistics National Vital Statistics System. Retrieved from https://www.cdc.gov/nchs/data/nvsr/nvsr67/nvsr67_03.pdf.

Park, A. S., Ritz, B., Yu, F., Cockburn, M., & Heck, J. E. (2020). Prenatal pesticide exposure and childhood leukemia – A California statewide case-control study. *International Journal of Hygiene and Environmental Health, 226,* 113486. https://doi.org/10.1016/j.ijheh.2020.113486

Paul, S. E., Hatoum, A. S., Fine, J. D., Johnson E. C., Hansen, I. Karcher, N. R., Moreau, A. L., Bondy, E. Qu, Y., Carter, E. B., Rogers, C. E., Agrawal, A., Barch, D. M., & Bogdan, R. (2021). Associations between prenatal cannabis exposure and childhood outcomes. Results from the ABCD study. *JAMA, 78*(1), 64–76.

Philips, E. M., Santos, S., Trasande, L., Aurrekoetxea, J. J., Barros, H., von Berg, A., Bergstrom, A., Bird, P. K., Brescianini, S., Chaoimh, C. N., Charles, M. A., Chatzi, L., Chevrier, C., Chrousos, G. P., Costet, N., Criswell, R., Crozier, S., Eggesbø, M., Fantini, M. P., ... & Jaddoe, V. W. (2020). Changes in parental smoking during pregnancy and risks of adverse birth outcomes and childhood overweight in Europe and North America: An individual participant data meta-analysis of 229,000 singleton births. *PLoS Medicine, 17*(8): e1003182. https://doi.org/10.1371/journal.pmed.1003182

Ponnusamy, S. (2020). Gestational diabetes: Opportunities for improving maternal and child health. *The Lancet: Diabetes & Endocrinology, 8*(9), 793–800.

Recto, P. (2019). Mexican-American adolescents' views on factors that facilitate recognition and help-seeking for perinatal depression. *Issues in Mental Health Nursing, 40*(9), 821–824.

Rieske, R. D., & Matson, J. L. (2020). Paternal age at conception and the relationship with severity of autism symptoms. *Developmental Neurorehabilitation, 23*(5), 265–270.

Sabbagh, R., & Van den Veyver, I. B. (2020). The current and future impact of genome-wide sequencing on fetal precision medicine. *Human Genetics, 139*(9), 1121–1130.

Saravanan, P. (2020). Gestational diabetes: Opportunities for improving maternal and child health. *Lancet Diabetes Endocrinology, 8*(9),793–800.

Shah, Z., Pal, P., Pal, G. K., Papa, D., & Bharadwaj, B. (2020). Assessment of the association of heart rate variability and baroreflex sensitivity with depressive symptoms and stress experienced by women in pregnancy. *Journal of Affective Disorders, 277*(1), 503–509.

Shapiro, A. L., Moore, B. F., Sutton, B., Wilkening, G., Stence, N., Dabelea, D., & Tregellas, J. R. (2020). In utero exposure to maternal overweight or obesity is associated with altered offspring brain function in middle childhood. *Obesity, 28*(9), 1718–1725.

Sifat, A. E., Nozohouri, S., Villalba, H., Al Shoyaib, A., Vaidya, B., Karamyan, V. T., & Abbruscato, T. (2020). Prenatal electronic cigarette exposure decreases brain glucose utilization and worsens outcome in offspring hypoxic–ischemic brain injury. *Journal of Neurochemistry, 153*(1), 63–79.

Smith, A., Twynstra, J., & Seabrook, J. A. (2020). Antenatal depression and offspring health outcomes. *Obstetric Medicine, 13*(2), 55–61.

Spann, M. N., Scheinost, D., Feng, T., Barbato, K., Lee, S., Monk, C., & Peterson, B. S. (2020). Association of maternal prepregnancy body mass index with fetal growth and neonatal thalamic brain connectivity among adolescent and young women. *JAMA Network Open, 3*(11), e2024661. https://doi.org/10.1001/jamanetworkopen.2020.24661

Stanley, A. Y., Durham, C. O., Sterrett, J. J., & Wallace, J. B. (2019). Safety of over-the-counter medications in pregnancy. *The American Journal of Maternal/Child Nursing (MCN), 44*(4), 196–205.

Starbird, E., & Crawford, K. (2019). Timing and spacing of pregnancy: Reducing mortality among women and their children. *Global Health: Science & Practice, 7*(Suppl 2), S211–S214. Retrieved from https://www.ncbi.nlm.nih.gov/pmc/articles/PMC6711626/.

Steele, J. W., Kim, S. E., & Finnell, R. H. (2020). One-carbon metabolism and folate transporter genes: Do they factor prominently in the genetic etiology of neural tube defects? *Biochimie,173,* 27–32.

Sundermann, A. C., Edwards, D. R., Slaughter, J. C., Wu, P., Jones, S. H., Torstenson, E. S., & Hartmann, K. E. (2021). Week-by-week alcohol consumption in early pregnancy and spontaneous abortion risk: A prospective cohort study. *American Journal of Obstetrics and Gynecology, 224*(1), 97.e1–97.e16. https://doi.org/10.1016/j.ajog.2020.07.012

Tore, E. C., Antoniou, E. E., de Groot, R.H., Gielen, M., Godschalk, R. W., Roumeliotaki, T., Smits, L., Southwood, T. R., Spaanderman, M. E., Stratakis, N., Vafeiadi, M., Chatzi, V. L., & Zeegers, M. P. (2020). Gestational weight gain by maternal pre-pregnancy BMI and childhood problem behaviours in school-age years: A pooled analysis of two European birth cohorts. *Maternal and Child Health Journal, 24*(10), 1288–1298.

U.S. Food & Drug Administration (FDA). (2020). *Advice about eating fish.* Retrieved from https://www.fda.gov/food/consumers/advice-about-eating-fish.

U.S. Department of Health and Human Services (DHHS). (2020). *Healthy People 2030.* Retrieved from https://health.gov/healthypeople.

Varshavsky, J. R., Sen, S., Robinson, J. F., Smith, S. C., Frankenfield, J., Wang, Y., Yeh, G., Park, J. S., Fisher, S. J., & Woodruff, T. J. (2020). Racial/ethnic and geographic differences in polybrominated diphenyl ether (PBDE) levels across maternal, placental, and fetal tissues during mid-gestation. *Science Reports, 10*, 12247. https://doi.org/10.1038/s41598-020-69067-y

Wang, C. -L., Liu, Y. -Y., Wu, C. -H., Wang, C. -Y., Wang, C. -H., & Long, C. -Y. (2021). Impact of COVID-19 on pregnancy. *International Journal of Medical Sciences, 18*(3), 763–767. https://doi.org/10.7150/ijms.49923

Watkins, A. J., Rubini, E., Hosier, E. D., & Morgan, H. L. (2020). Paternal programming of offspring health. *Early Human Development, 150*, 105185. https://doi.org/10.1016/j.earlhumdev.2020.105185

Wen, S. W., Miao, Q., Taljaard, M., Lougheed, J., Gaudet, L., Davies, M., Lanes, A., Leader, A., Corsi, D. J., Sprague, A. E., & Walker, M. (2020). Associations of assisted reproductive technology and twin pregnancy with risk of congenital heart defects. *JAMA Pediatrics, 174*(5), 446–454.

Wong, P. C., & Kitsantas, P. (2020). A review of maternal mortality and quality of care in the USA. *The Journal of Maternal-Fetal & Neonatal Medicine, 33*(19), 3355–3367.

Wong, S. P., Twynstra, J., Gilliland, J. A., Cook, J. L., & Seabrook, J. A. (2020). Risk factors and birth outcomes associated with teenage pregnancy: A Canadian sample. *Journal of Pediatric and Adolescent Gynecology, 33*(2), 153–159.

Wong, Y. P., Khong, T. Y., & Tan, G. C. (2021). The effects of COVID-19 on placenta and pregnancy: What do we know so far? *Diagnostics, 11*(1), 1–13.

World Health Organization (WHO). (2007). *Report of a WHO technical consultation on birth spacing: Geneva, Switzerland 13-15 June 2005.* World Health Organization. Retrieved from https://apps.who.int/iris/handle/10665/69855.

Wu, Y., Zhang, H., Wang, C., Brockman, B. F., Chong, Y. -S., Shek, L. P., Gluckman, P. D., Meaney, M. J., Fortier, M. V., & Qiu, A. (2021). Inflammatory modulation of the associations between prenatal maternal depression and neonatal brain. *Neuropsychopharmacology, 46*, 470–477.

Yang, L., Shang, L., Wang, S., Yang, W., Huang, L., Qi, C., Gurcan, A., Yang, Z., & Chung, M. C. (2020). The association between prenatal exposure to polycyclic aromatic hydrocarbons and birth weight: A meta-analysis. *PLoS One, 15*(8): e0236708. https://doi.org/10.1371/journal.pone.0236708

Yang, L., & Tan, W. C. (2020). Prenatal screening in the era of non-invasive prenatal testing: A nationwide cross-sectional survey of obstetrician knowledge, attitudes and clinical practice. *BMC Pregnancy and Childbirth, 20*(1), 579. https://doi.org/10.1186/s12884-020-03279-y

Yunis, M., Nour, I., Gibreel, A., Darwish, M., Sarhan, M., Shouman, B., & Nasef, N. (2021). Effect of delayed cord clamping on stem cell transfusion and hematological parameters in preterm infants with placental insufficiency: A pilot randomized trial. *European Journal of Pediatrics, 180*(1), 157–166.

Zhang, J., Xiaoyan, L., Chen, L., Zhang, S., Zhang, X., Hao, C., & Miao, Y. (2020a). Advanced maternal age alters expression of maternal effect genes that are essential for human oocyte quality. *Aging, 12*(4), 3950–3961.

Zhang, R., Chen, X., Wang, D., Chen, X., Wang, C., Zhang, Y., Xu, M., & Yu, J. (2019). Prevalence of chromosomal abnormalities identified by copy number variation sequencing in high-risk pregnancies, spontaneous abortions, and suspected genetic disorders. *Journal of International Medical Research, 47*(3), 1169–1178.

Zhang, S., Wang, L., Yang, T., Chen, L., Zhao, L., Wang, T., Chen, L., Ye, Z., Zheng, Z., & Qin, J. (2020b). Parental alcohol consumption and the risk of congenital heart diseases in offspring: An updated systematic review and meta-analysis. *European Journal of Preventive Cardiology, 27*(4), 410–421.

Zhao, J., Yan, Y., Huang, X., & Li, Y. (2020). Do the children born after assisted reproductive technology have an increased risk of birth defects? A systematic review and meta-analysis. *The Journal of Maternal-Fetal & Neonatal Medicine, 33*(2), 322–333.

Zhou, Q., Zhang, S., Wang, Q., Shen, H., Zhang, Y., Tian, W., & Li, X. (2020). Association between preconception paternal smoking and birth defects in offspring: Evidence from the database of the National Free Preconception Health Examination project in China. *BJOG, 127*(11), 1358–1364.

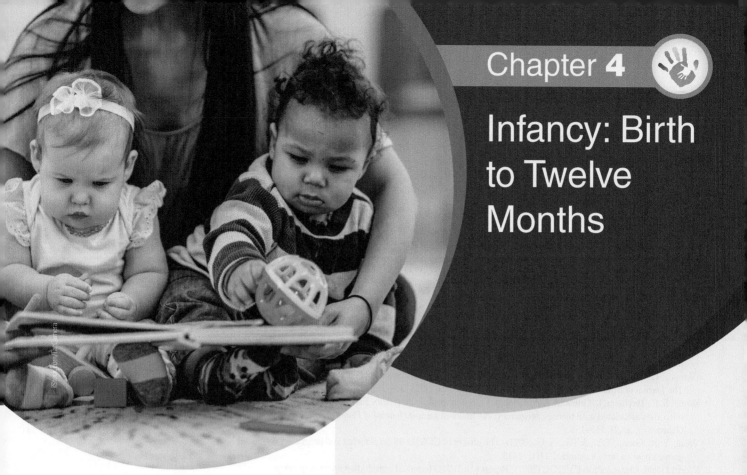
iStock.com/FatCamera

Chapter 4

Infancy: Birth to Twelve Months

Learning Objectives

After reading this chapter, you will be able to:

4-1 Define the term *reflexive motor activity* and provide examples that are observable in newborns.

4-2 Explain why the statement "Babies can't learn" is a myth, and describe activities that promote infants' cognitive development.

4-3 Identify several ways in which infants communicate with adults during each developmental stage described in this chapter.

4-4 Describe the phenomenon known as *stranger anxiety.*

NAEYC NAEYC Professional Standards Linked to Chapter Content

1a, 1b, and 1c: Child development and learning in context

2a and 2c: Family–teacher partnerships and community connections

3a and 3c: Child observations, documentation, and assessment

4a, 4b, and 4c: Developmentally, culturally, and linguistically appropriate teaching practices

5b: Knowledge, application, and integration of academic content in the early childhood curriculum

Julie and Danielle (aka "Danny") were married two years ago. Julie recently gave birth to a healthy 7 pound 10 ounce baby girl following several months of assisted reproductive treatments. The new parents are ecstatic and find joy in every "coo" and movement their now six-week-old daughter, Harper, makes. They are fascinated by how quickly she seems to be changing and learning each day. They have watched Harper try to raise up while lying on her tummy, turn her head when the family's cat meows, and make pleasurable cooing sounds during times when a story is being read.

Julie and Danny are fortunate to have jobs that provide twelve weeks of paid maternity and paternity benefits. This time has allowed them to bond with their infant and adjust to new parenting responsibilities. However, Julie feels pressured to return to her job before the twelve weeks are over. She is the head coach of the local high school girls' softball team, and their conference season is about to begin. Danny is employed by a local non-profit organization and has made arrangements to work only part-time for the next year or two.

Julie and Danny are struggling with the idea of placing Harper in an early childhood program on days when they are both working. They have concerns about the quality of care, nurturing, and support that she would receive. Their friends have recommended several places, but none have had an available opening for an infant. The wife of one of Julie's colleagues recently retired from her cook position at a local restaurant and has offered to care for Harper until her parents can find an acceptable and affordable placement.

Ask Yourself

- In what ways are Harper and her parents beginning to form a strong emotional bond with one another other?
- What activities are Julie and Danny engaging in now with Harper that will support her future language development?

The Newborn (Birth to One Month)

The healthy newborn infant is truly amazing. Within moments of birth, infants begin to adapt to an outside world that is radically different from the one experienced **in utero**. The newborn's systems for breathing, eating, eliminating, and regulating body temperature are functional and ready to take over at the time of birth. However, the infant remains completely dependent upon adults for survival because these systems are still relatively immature and require time to develop fully.

The newborn's motor development (movement) is both reflexive and protective. There is no voluntary control of the body during the early weeks. Although newborn infants sleep most of the time, they do not lack awareness. They are sensitive to their environment and have unique methods of responding to it. Crying is their primary method for communicating needs and emotions. Perceptual and cognitive abilities are present, although they are primitive and relatively difficult to distinguish from one another during the initial weeks following birth (Guellaï et al., 2020). Yet, newborns are taking in information and learning about the people and world around them every minute that they are awake.

in utero Latin term for "in the mother's uterus."

Developmental Profiles and Growth Patterns

Growth and Physical Characteristics

The newborn's physical characteristics are distinct from those of a slightly older infant. All infants are born with relatively light-colored skin that gradually darkens to a shade characteristic of their genetic makeup. At birth, the newborn's skin usually appears quite wrinkled. Within the first few days that follow, it becomes dry and is likely to peel, especially around the hands, ankles, and feet. The infant's skin remains

Developmental Profiles and Growth Patterns *(continued)*

sensitive and prone to rashes and acne-like breakouts for several months. Some newborns may also develop **jaundice** during the first days or weeks following birth.

The newborn's eyelids often appear swollen and closed for several days following birth, but this soon disappears. Swelling may be due to the birth process and/or preventive antibiotic ointment that is placed in a newborn's eyes. Hearing is well-developed and acute at the time of birth. All infants in the United States have their hearing tested before leaving the hospital or birthing center. Fewer than 3 out of every 1,000 newborns are identified with a hearing loss. However, this rate is significantly higher among infants who are born prematurely or with a developmental disorder.

Breast and genital enlargement are common in both male and female infants and are caused by maternal hormones that have been transferred to the fetus prior to birth. The infant's head may have an unusual shape as a result of the delivery process, but it gradually resumes a normal appearance within weeks. Hair color and amount vary; some infants are born with negligible hair, while others may have an abundance of it. Initial hair is often lost during the early weeks and replaced with new growth that may have a different texture and color. Additional physical characteristics include the following:

- Weighs approximately 6.5–9 pounds (3.0–4.1 kg) at birth; females weigh approximately 7 pounds (3.2 kg), and males weigh approximately 7.5 pounds (3.4 kg).

- Loses 5 to 7 percent of birth weight in the days immediately following delivery.

- Gains an average of 5–6 ounces (0.14–0.17 kg) per week during the first month.

- Is approximately 19–21 inches (48.3–53.3 cm) in length at birth.

- Breathes at a rate of approximately thirty to fifty respirations per minute; breathing can be somewhat irregular in both rhythm and rate.

- Chest appears small, cylindrical, and nearly the same size as the head.

- Normal body temperature ranges from 96°F to 99°F (35.6°C–37.2°C); fluctuations are normal during the early weeks; body temperature begins to stabilize as the system matures and a fat layer develops beneath the skin.

- Skin is sensitive to touch, especially on the newborn's hands and around the mouth.

- Head appears large in proportion to the body and accounts for nearly one-quarter of the total body length.

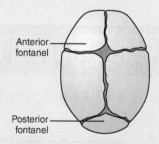

Figure 4-1 Head circumference is measured to monitor brain growth.

- Head circumference averages 12.5–14.5 inches (31.7–36.8 cm) at birth (Figure 4-1).

- "Soft" spots (called **fontanels**) are located on the top (anterior) and back (posterior) of the newborn's head (Figure 4-2).

- Tongue appears large in proportion to the mouth.

- Cries without tears; eyes are extremely sensitive to light. Sees only outlines and shapes; is unable to move eyes intentionally or to focus on objects more than 10–12 inches (25.4–30.5 cm) away (AOA, 2021).

- Hears well; is especially responsive to voices.

Anterior fontanel

Posterior fontanel

Figure 4-2 Location of fontanels.

jaundice A yellow discoloration of the infant's skin and eyes caused by excess bilirubin (a yellow pigment that results when red blood cells are broken down in the liver) circulating in the bloodstream.

fontanels Small openings (sometimes called "soft spots") in the infant's skull bones; covered with soft tissue; eventually, they close.

Developmental Profiles and Growth Patterns (continued)

Motor Development

The newborn's primitive motor skills are purely reflexive movements or automatic responses that are designed for protection and survival. Sucking, for example, ensures that the infant obtains critical nutrients. During the coming weeks, the newborn gradually develops some purposeful or voluntary behaviors as the central nervous system matures and several of the early reflexes begin to fade away. Any failure of reflexes to fade according to schedule may be an early indication of neurological problems that can result in learning and behavior disorders (Gieysztor, Choińska, & Paprocka-Borowicz, 2018). During the first month, the typically developing newborn exhibits the following behaviors:

- Engages in motor activity that is primarily reflexive (Figure 4-3):

Appears	swallow,* gag,* cough,* yawn,* blink suck rooting Moro (startle) grasp stepping plantar elimination tonic neck reflex (TNR)	Landau tear* (cries with tears)	parachute palmar grasp pincer grasp				
(Age)	(birth)	(1–4 mos)	(4–8 mos)	(8–12 mos)	(12–18 mos)	(18–24 mos)	(3–4 years)
Disappears		grasp suck (becomes voluntary) step root tonic neck reflex (TNR)	Moro (startle)	palmar grasp plantar reflex	Landau	parachute	elimination (becomes voluntary)

* Permanent; present throughout person's lifetime.

Figure 4-3 **Summary of reflexes.**

- Swallowing, sucking, gagging, coughing, yawning, blinking, and elimination reflexes are present at birth.

- The rooting reflex is triggered by gently touching the sensitive skin around the cheek and mouth; the infant turns toward the cheek that is being stroked.

- The Moro (startle) reflex is set off by a sudden loud noise or touch, such as bumping of the crib or quick lowering of the infant's position (as if dropping); in this reflex, both arms are thrown open and away from the body, then quickly brought back together over the chest.

- The grasping reflex occurs when the infant tightly curls their fingers around an object placed in their hand.

- The stepping reflex involves the infant moving the feet up and down in walking-like movements when held upright with feet touching a firm surface (Figure 4-4).

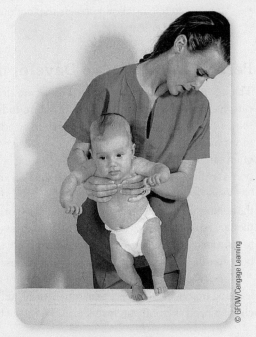

© GFCW/Cengage Learning

Figure 4-4 **Stepping reflex.**

Developmental Profiles and Growth Patterns *(continued)*

- The tonic neck reflex (TNR) occurs when the infant, in supine (face-up) position, extends the arm and leg on the same side toward which the head is turned, while the opposite arm and leg are flexed (pulled in toward the body). This is sometimes called the *fencing position* (Figure 4-5).

- The plantar reflex is initiated when pressure is placed against the ball of the infant's foot, causing the toes to curl.

- Maintains "fetal" position (with the back flexed or rounded, extremities held close to the body, and knees drawn up), especially when asleep.

- Holds hands in a fist; does not reach for objects.

- When held in a prone (facedown) position, the infant's head falls lower than the horizontal line of the body, with hips flexed and arms and legs extending downward (Figure 4-6).

- Has good muscle tone in the upper body when supported under the arms.

- Turns head from side to side when placed in a prone position.

- **Pupils** dilate (enlarge) and constrict (become smaller) in response to light.

- Eyes do not always work together and may appear crossed at times.

- Attempts to track (follow) objects that are out of their direct line of vision; unable to coordinate eye and hand movements.

Figure 4-5 The tonic neck reflex (TNR).

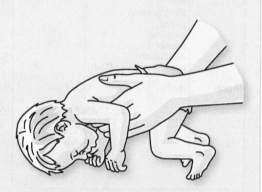

Figure 4-6 Prone suspension.

Perceptual-Cognitive Development

The newborn's perceptual-cognitive skills are designed to capture and hold the attention of family and caregivers and to gain some sense of the surrounding environment. Hearing is the most well-developed of the senses and is nearly equivalent to that of an adult's. Newborns can distinguish and respond differently to various sounds; they are especially responsive to their mother's voice (Uchida-Ota et al., 2019). They often can be soothed with quiet sounds (cooing or humming) and movements (rocking or swaying). Newborns are also responsive to touch, with the skin around the mouth and hands being especially sensitive.

Vision is present, although it is quite limited and will take several years to develop fully. Newborns see only the outline of an object (including faces) and are not able to detect any of its detail (AOA, 2021). For this reason, they are especially attracted to bright, high-contrast (black-and-white) geometric designs. The infant's inability to coordinate eye movements often causes eyes to wander or appear crossed. An infant may momentarily focus both eyes on an object (especially a face) that is close and moving slowly (Buiatti et al., 2019).

From the earliest days of life, newborns are absorbing information through all of their senses and learning from what they see, hear, touch, taste, and smell. Thus, the newborn's cognitive behaviors can be characterized as being purely reflexive. They take the form of sucking, startle responses, grimacing, flailing

pupil The small, dark, central portion of the eye.

Developmental Profiles and Growth Patterns *(continued)*

of arms and legs, and uncontrolled eye movements, all of which overlap with perceptual responses. During the first month, the newborn does the following:

- Blinks in response to a fast-approaching object.

- Follows a slowly moving object through a complete 180° arc.

- Follows an object moved vertically if it is held close to their face [i.e., 10–15 inches (25.4–38.1 cm)].

- Continues looking about, even in the dark.

- Begins to study their own hand when lying in the TNR position.

- Hears as well at birth as do most adults (with the exception of quiet sounds); hearing is more developed and acute than is vision.

- Prefers to listen to their mother's voice rather than an unfamiliar person's; opens eyes and looks toward the mother.

- Often synchronizes body movements to the speech patterns of the parents or primary caregivers.

- Distinguishes some tastes; shows preference for sweet liquids.

- Has a keen sense of smell at birth; turns toward preferred odors (i.e., sweet, breast milk, mother) and away from strong or unpleasant odors (Adam-Darque et al., 2018; Loos, Reger, & Schaal, 2019).

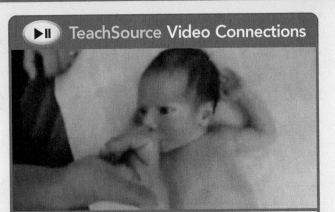

▶❚❚ TeachSource Video Connections

Newborn Reflex Development

Initially, newborns are not capable of purposeful movement. However, this does not suggest that they are passive individuals. Reflexes serve important protective functions and gradually give way to increasingly complex motor development. Respond to the following questions after you have watched the learning video *0–2 Years: The Newborn and Reflex Development:*

1. Which involuntary reflexes are considered critical for the infant's survival?

2. What does it indicate when one or more of the infant's reflexes are absent, do not fade at the correct time, or reappear later?

3. How does the infant's reflex system affect early cognitive development?

Speech and Language Development

The beginnings of speech and language development can be identified in several of the newborn's reflexes. These include the bite–release action, which occurs when the infant's gums are rubbed; the rooting reflex; and the sucking reflex. In addition, the newborn communicates directly and indirectly in a number of other ways:

- Cries and fusses to express discomfort and/or needs (e.g., hunger, cold or too warm, diaper change, desire to be held or laid down due to overstimulation).

- Reacts to loud noises by blinking, moving, stopping a movement, shifting eyes about, or exhibiting a startle response.

- Shows a preference for certain sounds, such as quiet music and human voices, by calming down or quieting.

Developmental Profiles and Growth Patterns *(continued)*

- Turns head to locate voices and other nearby sounds.
- Makes occasional sounds other than crying.

Social-Emotional Development

Newborns possess a variety of built-in social skills. They are able to indicate needs and distress (by crying or fussing) and to detect some caregiver reactions (Addabbo et al., 2020). For example, an infant may become agitated, tense, or both when they sense that an adult is angry, frustrated, or hurried. The infant thrives on feelings of security and soon displays a sense of attachment to primary caregivers who meet this need. The newborn exhibits the following:

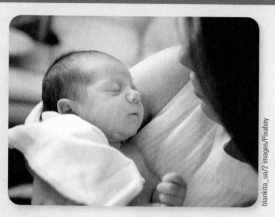

Figure 4-7 **Newborns spend most of their time sleeping.**

- Experiences a brief period of calm alertness immediately following birth; gazes at their parents and listens to their voices.
- Sleeps 17–19 hours per day; is gradually awake and responsive for longer periods (Figure 4-7).
- Likes to be held close and cuddled when awake; opens eyes and looks toward the mother.
- Shows qualities of individuality; each infant varies in how they respond or fail to respond to similar situations.
- Begins to establish an emotional attachment, or a **bonding** relationship, with parents and primary caregivers; opens eyes; relaxes body tension.
- Develops a gradual sense of security and trust with the parents and primary caregivers; is able to sense caregiver differences and responds accordingly. For example, an infant may become tense with an adult who is unfamiliar or uncomfortable with them.

DAILY ROUTINES

Eating

- Takes six to ten feedings, totaling approximately 18–22 ounces (532–660 ml) per 24 hours at the beginning of this period; later, the number of feedings decreases to five to six, while the total amount consumed increases to approximately 30 ounces (887 ml).
- Drinks 2–4 ounces (59–118 ml) of breast milk or formula per feeding; may take 25–30 minutes to complete a feeding and fall asleep toward the end.
- Expresses the need for food by crying.
- Benefits from being fed in an upright position; this practice reduces the risk of choking and of developing ear infections (Marotz, 2020).

bonding The establishment of a close, loving relationship between an infant and adults (usually the mother and father); sometimes called attachment.

DAILY ROUTINES *(continued)*

Toileting, Bathing, and Dressing

- Signals the need for a diaper change by crying. (If crying does not stop when diaper is changed, another cause, such as hunger or other discomfort, should be sought.)
- Enjoys bath; keeps eyes open, coos, and relaxes body tension when placed in warm water.
- Expresses displeasure (fusses, cries) when clothes are pulled over head (hence, it is best to avoid over-the-head clothes).
- Prefers to be wrapped firmly (swaddled) in a blanket; coos, stops crying, and relaxes muscle tension; swaddling seems to foster a sense of security and comfort.
- Has one to four bowel movements per day.

Sleeping

- Begins to sleep four to six periods per 24 hours after the first few days following birth; one of these might be 5–7 hours in length.
- Cries sometimes before falling asleep (usually stops if the infant is held and rocked briefly).
- *Always place an infant on their back, on a firm mattress, and in a smoke-free room for sleeping to reduce the risk of sudden infant death syndrome (SIDS) and sudden unexplained infant death (SUID). Remove* all *bedding and toys from the crib and surrounding sleeping area. Dress the infant lightly to avoid overheating. Breastfeeding and placing an infant's crib in a parent's room for the first year are practices also known to reduce the risk of SIDS and SUID* (CDC, 2020).

Play and Social Activities

- Prefers light and brightness; may fuss if turned away from a light source.
- Stares at faces in close visual range [10–12 inches (25.4–30.5 cm)].
- Signals the need for social stimulation by crying; stops when picked up or put in an infant seat close to people, voices, and movement.
- Is content to lie on their back much of the time.
- Needs to be forewarned (e.g., touched or spoken to) before being picked up to avoid being startled.
- Enjoys lots of touching and holding; however, may become fussy with too much handling or overstimulation.
- Enjoys the en face (face-to-face) position (Guellaï et al., 2020).

learning activities to promote **brain development**

Newborns begin learning from the moment they are born. Their primary mode of learning is sensory—soothing voices, gentle handling, responsive attention, quiet music, or familiar smells associated with nourishment and comforting touch. Newborns are intrigued with faces, although they are not yet able to see them in detail.

Developmentally appropriate applications for families and teachers:

- Respond with gentle and dependable attention to an infant's cries so the infant feels secure and begins to develop trust. (Infants always cry for a reason; crying

learning activities *(continued)*

signals a need.) Stroking the skin gently may soothe and relax the infant. Repositioning may bring comfort. Swaddling may provide a feeling of security.

- Make eye contact when the infant is in an alert state. Bring your face close [10–15 inches (25.4–38 cm)] to the infant's so they can see it. Make faces or stick out and wiggle your tongue; both are activities that infants often imitate. (Imitation is an important avenue for early learning.)

- Talk and sing to the infant often and in a normal voice during feedings, diapering, and bathing activities; vary your voice tone and rhythm of speech.

- Play quiet background music; music can have a calming effect (for caregivers also) and has been shown to improve infant feeding and sleeping patterns.

- Show delight in the infant's responsiveness: smile, laugh, and comment. (Mutual responsiveness and social turn-taking will be the bases for all teaching and learning in the months and years ahead.)

- Show the infant simple pictures (as previously noted, infants are attracted to high-contrast, black-and-white geometric designs and faces); gently move a stuffed animal or toy into the baby's visual pathway approximately 10–15 inches (25–37.5 cm) from the face to encourage visual tracking; hang toys or a mobile within the infant's visual range (and change the positioning often—novelty increases interest).

- Take cues from the infant; too much stimulation can be as distressing as too little; stop activities temporarily if the infant begins to cry, becomes fussy, or loses interest.

TeachSource Digital Download

developmental **alerts**

Did You Know ?

...that suffocation is the number one cause of unintentional death among infants younger than one year?

Check with a health-care provider or early childhood specialist if, by one month of age, the infant does *not*:

- Show alarm or startle responses to loud noise.
- Suck and swallow with ease.
- Increase height, weight, and head circumference.
- Grasp with equal strength in both hands.
- Make eye contact when awake and being held.
- Roll head from side to side when placed on stomach.
- Express needs and emotions with distinctive cries and patterns of vocalizations that can be distinguished from one another.
- Stop crying or become soothed (relaxed) most times when picked up and held.

Note: Cultural differences may alter the timetable when some developmental skills are acquired. Expanded Developmental Alerts Checklists appear in Appendix A and also are available as digital downloads.

safety concerns

Parents and caregivers should complete first aid and cardiopulmonary resuscitation (CPR) training before caring for an infant. Smoke and carbon monoxide detectors should be installed near the infant's room and tested monthly to be sure they are in working order. It is also important to remain alert to new safety issues that may emerge as the infant continues to grow and develop.

1–4 months

Burns

- Never heat bottles in a microwave oven; hot spots can form in the liquid and burn the infant's mouth.
- Set the temperature of the hot water heater so that it is no higher than 120°F (49°C).
- Always check the water temperature before bathing an infant. Infants have thinner skin that burns in a matter of seconds.

Choking

- Learn CPR.
- Always hold the infant in an upright position during feedings; do not prop bottles.

Suffocation

- Provide a firm mattress that fits crib snugly; there should be less than a two-finger width gap between the mattress and crib sides to prevent the infant from becoming entrapped.
- *Always* put infants to sleep on their back; this practice reduces the risk of SIDS. Remove all bedding and soft items from the infant's crib (e.g., blankets, toys, or pillows).
- Do not use infant sleep positioners; sling carriers are also not recommended for use with newborns due to the risk of suffocation.

Transportation

- Always use an approved, rear-facing carrier installed in the vehicle's back seat whenever transporting an infant. Check the Consumer Product Safety Commission's website (www.cpsc.gov) for safety feature recommendations and recalls; always install the carrier according to the manufacturer's guidelines.

One to Four Months

During these early months, the wonders of infancy continue to unfold. Growth proceeds at a rapid pace. Body systems are fairly well stabilized, with temperature, breathing patterns, and heart rate becoming more regular. Motor skills improve as strength and voluntary muscle control increase. Longer periods of wakefulness encourage the infant's social-emotional development. Social responsiveness begins to appear as infants practice and enjoy using their eyes to explore the environment (Keemink, Keshavarzi-Pour, & Kelly, 2019; Wass et al., 2020). They soon are able to maintain eye contact, smile momentarily, and imitate simple facial expressions. As social awareness develops, the infant continues to establish a sense of trust and emotional attachment to parents and primary caregivers.

Although crying remains a primary mode for communicating and gaining adult attention, more complex communication skills are beginning to emerge. Different crying patterns are used to express distinct needs (e.g., discomfort, hunger, fatigue, frustration). Infants soon find great pleasure in imitating the speech sounds and gestures of others (Vainio, 2019). Cooing and babbling often begin around two months of age and represent an important step in the acquisition of language and give-and-take social interaction with others.

Learning occurs continuously throughout the infant's waking hours as newly acquired skills are used for exploring and gathering information about a still new and unfamiliar environment (Figure 4-8). It is important to remember that perceptual, cognitive, and motor developments are closely interrelated and nearly impossible to differentiate during these early months. However, the rate and attainment of skills in these domains is also

Figure 4-8 Infants are gathering information and learning every waking moment.

1–4
months

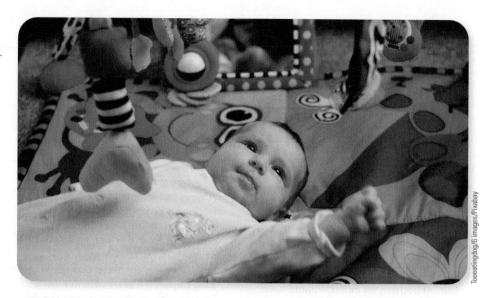

Toeeatingdog/6 images/Pixabay

highly influenced by cultural differences in expectations, environmental opportunities, and parenting practices (Adolph & Hoch, 2019; Rowe & Weisleder, 2020). For example, an infant confined to a crib or playpen for long hours with only limited human interaction cannot be expected to develop in a typical manner. Development across all domains is supported when infants are provided with numerous and varied opportunities for learning (see *Learning Activities to Promote Brain Development*).

Developmental Profiles and Growth Patterns

Growth and Physical Characteristics

- Averages 20–27 inches (50.8–68.6 cm) in length; grows approximately 1 inch (2.54 cm) per month (measured with the infant lying on their back, from the top of the head to the bottom of the heels, with knees straight and feet flexed).
- Weighs an average of 8–16 pounds (3.6–7.3 kg); females weigh slightly less than males.
- Gains approximately 1/4–1/2 pound (0.11–0.22 kg) per week.
- Breathes at a rate of approximately thirty to forty breaths per minute; rate increases significantly during periods of crying or activity.
- Normal body temperature ranges from 96.4°F–99.6°F (35.7°C–37.5°C).
- Head and chest circumference are nearly equal.
- Head circumference increases approximately 3/4 inch (1.9 cm) during the first and second months and 5/8 inch (1.6 cm) during months three and four. Increases are an important indication of continued brain growth and development.
- Continues to breathe using abdominal muscles.
- The posterior fontanel closes by the second month; the anterior fontanel closes to approximately 1/2 inch (1.3 cm).
- The skin remains sensitive and easily irritated.
- The arms and legs are of equal length, size, and shape, and are easily flexed and extended.
- The legs may appear slightly bowed; feet appear flat, with no arch.
- Cries with tears.
- Begins moving eyes together in unison (binocular vision).

Developmental Profiles and Growth Patterns *(continued)*

Motor Development

- Reflexive motor behaviors change as follows (Figure 4-3):
  - The tonic neck and stepping reflexes disappear.
  - The rooting and sucking reflexes are well developed.
  - The swallowing reflex and tongue movements are still immature; infant continues to drool and is not able to move food (other than milk) to the back of the mouth.
  - The grasp reflex gradually disappears.
  - The Landau reflex appears near the middle of this period: when the infant is held in a prone (facedown) position, the head is held upright and legs are fully extended.
  - Grabs onto small objects using the entire hand (palmar grasp); however, strength is insufficient to hold onto items for long at the beginning of this period (Chinn et al., 2019).
- Holds hands in an open or semi-open position much of the time.
- Muscle tone and development are equal for boys and girls.
- Movements tend to be large and jerky, gradually becoming smoother and more purposeful as muscle strength and control improve.
- Raises the head and upper body on the arms when in a prone position.
- Turns head from side to side when in a supine (face up) position; near the end of this period, can hold head up and in line with the body.
- Shows greater activity level in upper body parts: clasps hands above the face; waves arms about; reaches for objects.
- Begins rolling from the front to the back by turning the head to one side and allowing the trunk to follow. Near the end of this period, the infant can roll from front to back to side at will.
- Can be pulled to a sitting position, with considerable head lag and rounded back at the beginning of this period. Later, can be positioned to sit with minimal head support. By four months, most infants can sit with support, holding their heads steady and backs fairly erect; enjoys sitting in an infant seat or being held on an adult's lap.

Perceptual-Cognitive Development

- Fixates on a moving object held at a distance of 12 inches (30.5 cm); smoother visual tracking of objects across a 180° pathway, vertically, and horizontally.
- Continues to gaze in the direction of moving objects that have disappeared from sight (Figure 4-9).
- Exhibits some sense of size, color, and shape recognition of familiar objects in what Piaget refers to as **object permanence** (Piaget, 1954).

Figure 4-9 An infant continues to look for an object that has disappeared.

object permanence Piaget's sensorimotor stage in which infants understand that an object exists even when it is not in sight.

Developmental Profiles and Growth Patterns *(continued)*

1–4 months

What Do You See?

Early motor development. This two-month-old infant is beginning to learn about purposeful movement. What motor skills is she displaying? What other developmental abilities is she using to make this happen?

- Moves eyes from one object to another.
- Focuses on a small object and reaches for it; watches own hand movements intently.
- Alternates looking at an object, at one or both hands, and then back at the immediate environment—for example, recognizes own bottle even when bottle is turned around, thus presenting a different shape.
- Ignores (does not search for) a bottle that falls out of a crib or a toy hidden under a blanket: "out of sight, out of mind." (The infant has not yet fully developed object permanence.)
- Imitates gestures that are modeled: bye-bye, patting head.
- Hits at an object closest to the right or left hand with some degree of accuracy.
- Looks in the direction of a sound source (sound localization).
- Connects sound and rhythms with movement by moving or jiggling in time to music, singing, or chanting.
- Distinguishes parent's face from a stranger's face when other cues, such as voice, touch, or smell are also available (Addabbo et al., 2020; Durand et al., 2020).
- Attempts to keep a toy in motion by repeating arm or leg movements that started the toy moving in the first place.
- Begins to mouth objects (Figure 4-10).

Speech and Language Development

- Reacts (stops whimpering, startles) to sounds, such as a voice, rattle, or doorbell. Later, will search for a sound source by turning the head and looking in the direction of a sound.

Figure 4-10 Most objects end up in the infant's mouth.

Developmental Profiles and Growth Patterns *(continued)*

- Coordinates vocalizing, looking, and body movements in face-to-face exchanges with the parent or primary caregiver; can follow and lead to keep communication going.
- Babbles or coos when spoken to or smiled at; even infants who are deaf begin to babble (Long et al., 2020).
- Coos, using single vowel sounds (e.g., *ah, eh, uh*); also imitates their own sounds and vowel sounds produced by others.
- Laughs out loud.

1–4 months

Social-Emotional Development

- Imitates, maintains, terminates, and avoids interactions—for example, infants can turn at will toward or away from a person or situation.
- Reacts differently to variations in adult voices; for example, may frown or appear tense or anxious if voices are loud, angry, or unfamiliar.
- Enjoys (i.e., relaxes, quiets) being held and cuddled at times other than feeding and bedtime.
- Coos, gurgles, and squeals when awake.
- Smiles in response to a friendly face or voice when awake; smiling during sleep is thought to be reflexive.
- Entertains self for brief periods by playing with fingers, hands, and toes.
- Enjoys familiar routines, such as being bathed and having the diaper changed.
- Shows delight (i.e., squeals, laughs) in play that involves gentle tickling, laughing, and "peek-a-boo."
- Cries less often; stops crying when the parent or primary caregiver approaches.
- Recognizes and reaches out to familiar faces and objects, such as father or bottle; reacts by waving arms and squealing with excitement.

What Do You See?

Promoting language development. Surrounding infants with a literacy-rich environment promotes early language development, curiosity, cognitive abilities, and social skills. In what ways have these teachers created a classroom environment that supports developmentally appropriate emergent literacy?

Developmental Profiles and Growth Patterns *(continued)*

▶❚❚ TeachSource Video Connections

Early Infant Learning

It is probably true that we will never again learn as much as infants do during their first year of life! Every experience creates an opportunity for infants to acquire new information or learn something different about the world around them. In turn, additional neural connections are formed and strengthened. Respond to the following questions after you have watched the learning video *0–2 Years: Early Learning in Infants and Toddlers:*

1. What sensory systems does the infant use to gather information for learning?

2. What behavior does the term *habituation* describe?

3. Why is it important to provide infants with a variety of different toys and activities from time to time?

DAILY ROUTINES

Eating

- Takes five to eight feedings [5–6 ounces (148–177 ml) each] per day; may eat more often if fed on demand.
- Begins fussing before anticipated feeding times; may suck on hand and become restless; does not always cry to signal the need to eat.
- Needs only a little assistance in getting the nipple to the mouth; may begin to help the caregiver by using own hands to guide the nipple or to hold onto the bottle.
- Sucks vigorously; may choke on occasion due to vigorous and enthusiastic sucking.
- Becomes impatient if the bottle or breast continues to be offered once hunger is satisfied.
- Requires only breast milk or formula to meet all nutrient needs; is not ready to eat solid foods.

DAILY ROUTINES *(continued)*

Toileting, Bathing, and Dressing

- Enjoys bath time on most occasions; kicks, laughs, and splashes.
- Has one or two bowel movements per day; may skip a day on occasion.
- Begins to establish a regular time or pattern for bowel movements.

Sleeping

- Averages 14–17 hours of sleep per day; often awake for two or three periods during the daytime.
- Falls asleep for the night soon after the evening feeding.
- Begins to sleep through the night; many infants do not sleep more than six hours at a stretch for several more months.
- May begin thumb-sucking during this period.
- Begins to entertain self before falling asleep: "talks," plays with hands or feet, jiggles crib (Figure 4-11).

Play and Social Activity

- Spends waking periods engaged in physical activity: kicking, turning head from side to side, clasping hands together, grasping objects.
- Vocalizes with delight; becomes more "talkative."
- Smiles and coos when being talked and sung to; may cry when the social interaction ends.
- Appears content when awake and alone (for short periods of time).

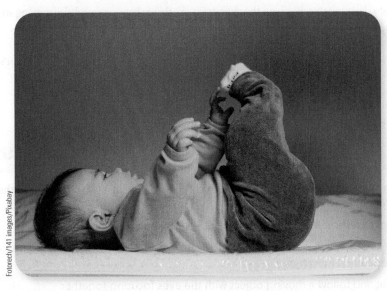

Figure 4-11 Infants often entertain themselves before falling asleep.

Fotorech/141 images/Pixabay

learning activities to promote **brain development**

Infants are becoming increasingly aware of their environment. They are learning about cause and effect through communication, movement, problem solving, and intentional behavior.

1–4 months

learning activities *(continued)*

Developmentally appropriate applications for families and teachers:

- Imitate the infant's vocalizations and faces (i.e., grunting, smacking, yawning, squinting, frowning). When the infant begins to smile, smile back and sometimes remark, "You are smiling! Happy baby!"

- Sing songs and read to the baby from magazines, books, or whatever is of interest to you; it is the sound of your voice and your closeness that matter.

- Play simplified peek-a-boo (hold a cloth in front of your face, drop it, and say "peek-a-boo"); repeat if the baby shows interest.

- Gently stretch and flex the infant's arms and legs while making up an accompanying song; later, start a gentle "bicycling" or arm-swaying activity.

- Touch the infant's hand with a small toy* (soft rattles or other quiet noisemakers are especially good); encourage the baby to grasp the toy.

- Walk around a room holding the infant, touching and naming objects. Stand with the baby in front of a mirror, touching and naming facial features: "Baby's mouth, Daddy's mouth. Baby's eye, Mommy's eye."

- Position an unbreakable mirror near the crib so the baby can look and talk to their reflection.

- Hang brightly colored or geometric pictures (black-and-white) or objects near the baby's crib; change often to maintain the baby's interest and attention.

- Fasten small bells (securely) to the baby's booties; this helps the baby to localize sounds while also learning that they have the ability to make things happen simply by moving about.

TeachSource Digital Download

*Rule of Fist: Toys and other objects given to an infant should be no smaller than the infant's fist (1.5 inches; 3.8 cm) to prevent choking or swallowing.

developmental **alerts**

Check with a health-care provider or early childhood specialist if, by four months of age, the infant does *not:*

- Continue to show steady gains in height, weight, and head circumference.

- Smile in response to the smiles of others. (The social smile is a significant developmental milestone.)

- Gaze at and follow a moving object with the eyes focusing together.

- Bring hands together over the mid-chest (a significant neurological milestone).

- Turn head to locate sounds.

- Begin to raise head and upper body when placed on the stomach.

- Reach for objects or familiar persons; begin to mouth objects.

- Coo or make babbling sounds.

Note: Cultural differences may alter the timetable when some developmental skills are acquired. Expanded Developmental Alerts Checklists appear in Appendix A and are also available as digital downloads.

safety concerns

Continue to implement the safety practices described for the previous stages, and always be aware of new safety issues as the infant continues to grow and develop. Be sure that the infant's immunizations are all current.

1–4 months

Burns
- Do not bring hot beverages or appliances near the infant.
- Check the temperature of bottles carefully (if warming formula or breast milk) before offering them to an infant.

Choking and Suffocation
- Check rattles and stuffed toys for small parts that could become detached. Purchase only toys larger than 1.5 inches (3.75 cm) in diameter and without small parts (e.g., eyes and buttons) that could become detached.
- Place all small items, strings, and cords out of the infant's reach.
- Remove all plastic bags and balloons from the infant's environment.

Falls
- Attend to the infant at all times whenever they are placed on an elevated surface (such as changing table, sofa, counter, or bed); the infant may begin to turn over or roll unexpectedly.
- Always set an infant carrier on the floor (not on the table or countertop) and securely fasten safety straps.

Sharp Objects
- Keep pins and other sharp objects out of the infant's reach.
- Check nursery furniture for sharp or protruding edges; purchase only furnishings and toys that comply with federal safety standards (see the "Online Resources" section at the end of this chapter).

Spotlight on **Neuroscience** and **Brain Development**

Infant Brain Development and Breast Milk

The brain undergoes its most rapid growth and development during the first year of a child's life. The long-chain polyunsaturated fatty acids (PUFAs) in breast milk are known to optimize its structural formation and enhance children's neurocognitive development and intelligence (Lenehan et al., 2020; Van Dael, 2021). Some formula manufacturers are now adding PUFAs to their products based on the results of numerous studies. However, encouraging and supporting more mothers to breastfeed their infants, so long as they are able, is preferrable and has unquestionable short- and long-term advantages for children's brain potential, overall health, and optimal development. Mothers also experience many physical and psychological benefits.

Bauer et al. (2020) noted a positive correlation between the length of time an infant was breast-fed and beneficial changes in white matter neural pathway development. These differences were associated with improved verbal memory and language performance. Similar findings have been reported by other scientists who have established a strong link between exclusive breastfeeding and children's advanced language, cognitive, and motor competencies (Guzzardi et al., 2020; Tinius et al., 2020). Researchers have noted that these benefits are especially significant for infants who are born low birth weight or prematurely.

Low breastfeeding rates have been reported among mothers of color, especially non-Hispanic Black women (Louis-Jacques et al., 2020). This has raised concerns about the negative effects this could potentially have on children's development and future academic performance (Orozco et al., 2020). Although women identify many reasons for not breastfeeding, the most common themes relate to personal beliefs and misconceptions, a lack of social support, discrimination, and economic insecurities (Gyamfi et al., 2021). Clearly, renewed efforts are needed to reduce the disparity in breastfeeding rates among these populations and ensure that all children experience a healthy beginning.

4–8 months

Four to Eight Months

Between four and eight months, infants are developing a wide range of skills and greater ability to use their bodies for purposeful activities. They seem to be busy every waking moment, manipulating and mouthing toys and other objects. They move easily from spontaneous, self-initiated activities to social activities initiated by others (Figure 4-12). They "talk" all the time, with more variety and complexity of vowel and consonant sounds. They initiate social interactions and respond to all types of cues (i.e., facial expressions, gestures, and sounds) and the comings and goings of everyone in their world. In other words, they are becoming more self-confident in their ability to explore, manipulate, and control the surrounding environment.

Although all infants experience the same fundamental human emotions, parenting practices in each culture shape the ways in which they are expressed. For example, prolonged mutual eye gaze is considered a sign of disrespect in some cultures. Parents in these cultures are more likely to limit eye contact with their infants and to interact more often through touch, holding, and vocalizations. In many Western cultures where direct eye contact is highly valued and practiced, infants are more likely to fixate on a caregiver's eyes and mouth. Any gradual decline in an infant's ability to maintain social attention or eye gaze may be an early sign of an autism spectrum disorder (de Araújo et al., 2020; Gangi et al., 2021).

Figure 4-12 Infants become more sociable and verbal between four and eight months of age.

Developmental Profiles and Growth Patterns

Growth and Physical Characteristics

- Gains approximately 1 pound (2.2 kg) per month in weight; doubles original birth weight by eight months.

- Increases length by approximately 1/2 inch (1.3 cm) per month; average length is 27.5–29 inches (69.8–73.7 cm).

- Head circumference increases by an average of 3/8 inch (0.95 cm) per month until six to seven months of age; growth then slows to approximately 3/16 inch (0.47 cm) per month. Continued gains are a sign of healthy brain growth and development.

- Takes approximately twenty-five to fifty breaths per minute, depending upon the activity; rate and patterns vary from infant to infant; breathing is abdominal.

- Begins to develop teeth, with upper and lower incisors erupting first.

- Moves eyes in unison; follows movement across the room.

- Color vision is now evident (AOA, 2021).

- Gums may become red and swollen as teeth begin to erupt; may be accompanied by increased drooling, chewing, biting, and mouthing of objects.

- Legs often appear bowed; bowing gradually disappears as the infant grows older and begins to walk.

- True eye color is established.

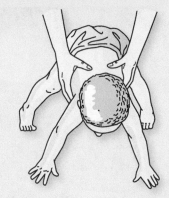

Figure 4-13 The parachute reflex.

4–8 months

Motor Development

- Reflexive behaviors are changing (Figure 4-3).

  - The blinking reflex is well established.

  - The sucking reflex becomes voluntary.

  - The Moro reflex disappears.

  - The parachute reflex appears toward the end of this stage: when held in a prone, horizontal position and lowered suddenly, the infant throws out their arms as a protective measure (Figure 4-13).

  - The swallowing reflex (a more complex form of swallowing that involves tongue movement against the roof of the mouth) appears; this allows the infant to move solid foods from the front to the back of the mouth for swallowing.

▶️ **TeachSource Video Connections**

Fine Motor Development

Motor development proceeds rapidly during the first year. Infants' motor abilities advance quickly from a reflexive stage to one that permits them to move about, explore, and manipulate their environment. Their ability to hold, poke, shake, transfer, and reach for objects with intention increases as hand-eye coordination improves. Respond to the following questions after you have watched the learning video *0–2 Years: Fine Motor Development for Infants and Toddlers*:

1. What is a pincer grip? How does a pincer grip differ from an ulnar or a palmar grasp?

2. What purpose do improving fine motor skills and coordination serve?

3. How might cultural differences influence an infant's motor development?

4–8 months

Developmental Profiles and Growth Patterns *(continued)*

Figure 4-14 Infants are able to sit alone by supporting themselves.

- Reaches for objects with both arms simultaneously; later reaches with one hand or the other.
- Transfers objects from one hand to the other; still grasps objects using the entire hand (palmar grasp).
- Handles, shakes, and pounds objects; puts everything into the mouth.
- Helps to hold onto the bottle during feedings; if breast-fed, may place a hand on the breast.
- Sits alone without support, holding the head erect and the back straight, with the arms propped forward for support (Figure 4-14).

Figure 4-15 The pincer grip.

- Pulls self into a crawling position by rising up on the arms and drawing the knees up beneath the body; rocks back and forth, but generally does not move forward.
- Rolls over from front to back and back to front.
- Begins scooting backward, sometimes accidentally, when placed on the stomach; soon learns to crawl forward.
- Shows delight in being placed in a standing position, especially on someone's lap; laughs and jumps in place.
- Begins to pick up objects using finger and thumb (pincer grip) near the end of this period (Figure 4-15).

Perceptual-Cognitive Development

- Turns toward and locates familiar voices and sounds; this behavior can be used for informal testing of an infant's hearing.
- Focuses the eyes on small objects and reaches for them accurately with either hand.
- Uses the hands, mouth, and eyes in coordination to explore own body, toys, and surroundings.
- Imitates actions, such as "pat-a-cake," waving "bye-bye," and playing "peek-a-boo."
- Shows evidence of **depth perception**; becomes tense, resistant, and fearful of falling from high places, such as changing tables and stairs.

depth perception The ability to determine the relative distance of objects from the observer; recognition of objects as being multi-dimensional.

Developmental Profiles and Growth Patterns *(continued)*

- Looks over the side of a crib or highchair for objects dropped; delights in repeatedly throwing objects overboard for an adult or older sibling to retrieve.
- Searches for a toy or food that has been partially hidden under a cloth or behind a screen; beginning to understand that objects continue to exist even when they cannot be seen. (Piaget refers to this characteristic as *object permanence*.)
- Shows greater interest in holding and manipulating three-dimensional objects rather than simply looking at a picture of the same items (Woods et al., 2021).
- Handles and explores objects in a variety of ways: visually, turning them around, feeling all surfaces, banging, and shaking.
- Picks up an inverted object (for instance, begins to recognize a cup even when it is positioned differently) (Johnson & Moore, 2020).
- Ignores a second toy or drops a toy in one hand when presented with a new one; unable to deal with more than one toy at a time.
- Plays actively with small toys such as rattles or blocks.
- Bangs objects together playfully; thumps a spoon or toy on the table.
- Continues to put everything into the mouth.
- Establishes full attachment to the mother or primary caregiver(s): seeks out and prefers to be held by this adult, which coincides with a growing understanding of object permanence.

4–8 months

Speech and Language Development

- Responds appropriately to name and simple requests such as "Come," "Eat," and "Wave bye-bye."
- Imitates some nonspeech sounds, such as coughing, tongue clicking, and lip smacking.
- Produces a full range of vowels and some consonants: *r, s, z, th,* and *w.*
- Responds to variations in an adult's tone of voice—anger, playfulness, sadness, or frustration.
- Expresses emotions, such as pleasure, satisfaction, and anger, by making different sounds.
- "Talks" to toys and objects.
- Babbles by repeating the same syllable in a series: *ba, ba, ba.*
- Reacts differently to noises, such as a phone ringing, door slamming, toilet flushing, or dog barking; may begin to cry, whimper, or look to the parent or caregiver for reassurance.

Social-Emotional Development

- Delights in observing surroundings; continuously watches people and activities.
- Becomes more outgoing and social in nature: smiles, coos, reaches out, and seeks adult attention.
- Distinguishes among and responds differently to teachers, parents, siblings, and people who are unfamiliar.
- Responds differently and appropriately to facial expressions: e.g., frowns and smiles.
- Imitates facial expressions, actions, and sounds (Figure 4-16).
- Remains friendly toward strangers at the beginning of this stage; later, is reluctant to be approached by or left with strangers and may exhibit **stranger anxiety**. Displays considerable distress: cries,

stranger anxiety A cross-cultural phenomenon in which infants begin to show distress or fear when approached by persons other than their primary caregivers.

Developmental Profiles and Growth Patterns *(continued)*

4–8 months

clings to the parents, and refuses to let go. Infants who are raised in cultures where multiple family members provide care are less likely to experience a strong reaction when parents leave.

- Enjoys being held and cuddled; indicates desire to be picked up by raising arms and vocalizing.

- Establishes a trust relationship with family members and teachers if physical and emotional needs are met consistently; by six months, begins to show preference for the primary caregiver.

- Laughs out loud.

- Becomes upset if a toy or other objects are taken away.

- Seeks attention by using body movements, verbalizations, or both.

Figure 4-16 The infant delights in imitating adult made sounds.

DAILY ROUTINES

Eating

- Adjusts feeding times to the family's schedule; usually takes three to four feedings per day, each 6–8 ounces (144–237 ml), depending on sleep schedule.

- *Caution:* Infants should not be allowed to drink formula or juice from a bottle or to nurse for an extended time. Extensive decay can develop when teeth are in prolonged contact with the sugars in these fluids and cause a condition known as baby bottle tooth decay (BBTD). A small amount of water offered after feedings rinses the teeth and reduces this risk.

- Shows excitement (squeals, wiggles, licks lips) when food is viewed; is interested in "assisting" with feedings; reaches for the cup and spoon while being fed.

- Is able to wait a half hour or more after awakening for the first morning feeding.

- Has less need for sucking.

- Begins to accept a small amount of semisolid pureed foods, such as cereal and vegetables, at around six months. Food should be placed well back on the tongue to prevent the infant from pushing it back out (if placed on the tip).

- Closes mouth firmly, pushes away, or turns the head when hunger is satisfied (satiety). It is important to acknowledge the infant's signals and to cease the feeding.

Toileting, Bathing, and Dressing

- Prefers being free of clothes; may fuss while being dressed.

- Splashes vigorously with both hands (and sometimes feet as well) during bath time.

DAILY ROUTINES *(continued)*

- Moves hands constantly; nothing within reach is safe from being spilled, placed in the mouth, or dashed to the floor.
- Pulls off own socks; plays with snaps, zippers, and Velcro closures on clothing.
- Has one bowel movement per day as a general rule, often at about the same time.
- Urinates often and in large quantities; female infants tend to have longer intervals between wetting.

Sleeping

- Awakens early in the morning; usually falls asleep soon after the evening meal.
- Begins to give up the need for a late-night feeding.
- Sleeps 11–13 hours through the night.
- Takes two or three naps per day. (However, there is great variability among infants in terms of frequency and length of naps.)

Play and Social Activity

- Enjoys lying on the back; arches back, kicks, and stretches legs upward, grasps the feet and brings them to the mouth.
- Looks at his own hands with interest and delight; may squeal or gaze at them intently.
- Plays with soft, squeaky toys and rattles; puts them in the mouth and chews on them.
- "Talks" happily to self: gurgles, growls, makes high squealing sounds.
- Differentiates between people: lively with those who are familiar, may ignore or become anxious with unfamiliar persons.
- Likes rhythmic activities: being bounced, jiggled, or swayed about gently.

4–8 months

learning activities to promote **brain development**

Infants need a safe environment where they are free to move about, investigate their surroundings, and practice newly emerging motor skills. Talking, singing, and reading to infants also promote important language and brain development.

Developmentally appropriate applications for families and teachers:

- Gradually elaborate on earlier activities: imitate the infant's sounds, facial expressions, and body movements; point to body parts and name them out loud; look in the mirror together and make faces; read, talk, and sing to the baby throughout the day.
- Provide toys, rattles, and household items that are of different colors and textures and make noise as the baby shakes or waves them about (a set of measuring spoons or plastic keys, shaker cans, squeak toys)—but remember the *Rule of Fist*.
- Place toys slightly out of reach to encourage the infant's movement (physical activity) and eye–hand coordination (Jacquey et al., 2020).
- Read aloud and often to the baby—even the evening newspaper or your favorite magazine will do. Infants will not understand what you are saying, but they begin to learn about word sounds and patterns, voice inflections, facial expressions, and that reading is an enjoyable experience.

4–8 months

learning activities *(continued)*

- Repeat the infant's name during all kinds of activities so that they begin to recognize it: "*Ethan* has a big smile." "*Stella's* eyes are wide open." "*Tyrel* looks sleepy."

- Play, dance, and move around with the baby to music on the radio, television, or a CD; vary the tempo and movement: gentle jiggling, dancing, or turning in circles; dance in front of the mirror, describing movements to the infant. *Note:* Do not toss infants up into the air. This can cause a serious brain injury.

- Sing all types of songs to the baby—silly songs, lullabies, popular tunes; encourage the infant to "sing" along and to imitate your movements and sounds (Falk et al., 2021).

- Allow plenty of time for the baby's bath. This activity provides important opportunities for reinforcing learning across developmental areas, including movement, sensory experiences, language, social interaction, and relaxation.

- Play "This little piggy," "Where's baby's (nose, eye, hand . . .)," and other simple games invented on the spot, such as taking turns at shaking rattles, gently rubbing foreheads, or clapping hands.

- Encourage the infant to touch and explore different textures. Cut small squares from a variety of fabrics (e.g., rough, smooth, soft, ridged, woven, silky); or crinkle up sheets of different types of paper (e.g., typing, construction, gift wrap, newspaper, and aluminum foil).

TeachSource Digital Download

▶❚❚ TeachSource **Video Connections**

Attachment

Attachment is a special emotional bond formed between parents and infants through a process of give-and-take interactions. It develops as infants and parents begin to synchronize their response patterns. Studies have shown that attachment helps infants build a sense of trust and is essential for future social-emotional development. Respond to the following questions after you have watched the learning video *0–2 Years: Attachment in Infants and Toddlers:*

1. What can parents do to foster the attachment process?

2. What is a reciprocal relationship, and what purpose does it serve?

3. Why do infants develop stranger anxiety?

4. How can families and teachers help infants to get through this phase?

developmental **alerts**

Check with a health-care provider or early childhood specialist if, by eight months of age, the infant does *not:*

- Show an even, steady increase in weight, height, and head size (growth that is too slow or too rapid is cause for concern).
- Explore their own hands and objects placed in their hands.
- Hold and shake a rattle.
- Smile, babble, and laugh out loud.
- Search for hidden objects.
- Begin to pick up objects using a pincer grip.
- Have an interest in playing games such as pat-a-cake and peek-a-boo.
- Show interest in or respond to new or unusual sounds.
- Reach for and grasp objects.
- Sit alone.
- Begin to eat some solid (pureed) foods.

Note: Cultural differences may alter the timetable when some developmental skills are acquired. Expanded Developmental Alerts Checklists appear in Appendix A and are also available as digital downloads.

4–8 months

safety **concerns**

Continue to implement the safety practices described for the previous stages, and always be aware of new safety issues as the infant continues to grow and develop.

Burns

- Keep electrical cords out of reach and electrical outlets covered; inspect the condition of electrical cords and replace or remove them if worn or frayed.
- Take precautions to protect infants from accidentally touching hot objects (e.g., oven or fireplace doors, space heaters, candles, curling irons, burning cigarettes, and hot beverage cups).

Falls

- Use approved safety gates to protect infants from tumbling down stairs; gates are also useful for keeping the infant confined to an area for supervision.
- Always fasten the restraining strap when the infant is placed in a highchair, stroller, or grocery cart.

- Always raise crib sides to their maximum height and lock them when the baby is in bed.

Poisons

- Use safety latches on cabinet doors and drawers where potentially poisonous substances (i.e., medications, laundry and cleaning supplies, cosmetics, hand sanitizer, or garden chemicals) are stored.

Strangulation

- Never fasten teethers or pacifiers on a cord or around the infant's neck; avoid clothing with drawstrings or ribbons.
- Remove crib gyms and mobiles after the infant reaches five months or begins pushing up on hands and knees.
- Use a wireless baby monitor (audio or video) to check on the infant during sleep.

Eight to Twelve Months

Figure 4-17 Older infants enjoy adult attention.

© GFOW/Cengage Learning

8–12 months

Between eight and twelve months of age, the infant is gearing up for two major developmental events—walking and talking. These milestones usually begin around the infant's first birthday, although cultural background may influence the acquisition rate and nature of these early skills (Adolph & Hoch, 2019).). For example, early walking is often valued in Western cultures, and parents spend considerable time encouraging this behavior. In contrast, infants raised in many South American and African societies are often carried in slings or on their mother's back and, consequently, learn to walk several months later.

Delayed motor development, such as walking, may be associated with certain medical conditions, chromosomal abnormalities, prematurity and low birth weight, birth injuries, and autism spectrum disorders (Poro et al., 2020; Reindal et al., 2020). These children should be monitored closely so that intervention services can be initiated early and as needed. During this stage, infants are also beginning to develop fine motor skills as evidenced by their increasing ability to pick up, manipulate, and release small objects in their hand.

Infants at this age are also becoming extremely sociable. They find ways to be the center of attention and to win approval and applause from family and friends (Figure 4-17). When applause is forthcoming, the infant joins in with delight. The ability to imitate improves, serving two purposes: to extend social interactions and to help the child learn many new skills and behaviors in the months of rapid development that lie ahead (Over, 2020; Salvadori et al., 2021). However, it is important to remember that individual attention is not highly valued in all cultures. As a result, infants in some environments may not be encouraged or reinforced for their attention-getting efforts and gradually will be socialized to blend into the group.

Developmental Profiles and Growth Patterns

Growth and Physical Characteristics

- Grows at a slower rate than during the previous months; averages an increase of 1/2 inch (1.3 cm) in length per month. Length is approximately 1 1/2 times the birth length by the first birthday.

- Weight increases by approximately 1 pound (0.5 kg) per month; birth weight nearly triples by one year of age: infants weigh an average of 21 pounds (9.6 kg).

- Respiration rates vary with activity: typically, twenty to forty-five breaths per minute.

- Body temperature ranges from 96.4°F–99.6°F (35.7°C–37.5°C); environmental conditions, weather, activity, and clothing affect variations in temperature.

- The circumferences of the head and chest remain equal.

- The anterior fontanel begins to close.

- Approximately four upper and four lower incisors and two lower molars erupt.

- The arms and hands are more developed than the feet and legs (cephalocaudal development); hands appear large in proportion to other body parts.

- The legs may continue to appear bowed.

- The feet appear flat because the arch has not yet developed fully.

Developmental Profiles and Growth Patterns *(continued)*

- Visual acuity is approximately 20/100; can see distant objects [15–20 feet (4.6–6 m) away] and point to them.
- Both eyes work in unison (true binocular coordination).

Motor Development

- Reaches with one hand leading to grasp an offered object or toy (Fagard et al., 2020). Manipulates objects, transferring them from one hand to the other.
- Explores new objects by poking with one finger.
- Uses a deliberate pincer grip to pick up small objects, toys, and finger foods.
- Stacks objects; also places objects inside one another.
- Releases objects or toys by dropping or throwing; cannot intentionally put an object down.
- Begins pulling self to a standing position.
- Begins to stand alone, leaning on furniture for support; moves or "cruises" around obstacles by side-stepping (Adolph & Hoch, 2019).
- Maintains good balance when sitting; can shift positions without falling.
- Creeps on hands and knees or hands and feet; crawls up and down stairs.
- Walks with adult support, holding onto an adult's hand; may begin to walk alone.

8–12 months

Perceptual-Cognitive Development

- Watches people, objects, and activities in the immediate environment.
- Shows awareness of distant objects (15–20 feet away) by pointing at them.
- Responds to hearing tests (voice localization); however, loses interest quickly and therefore, the results of this informal testing approach may not always be accurate.
- Begins to understand the meaning of some words (receptive language) as evidenced by use of appropriate gestures or behavioral response (Stewart, Vigil, & Carlson, 2021).
- Follows simple instructions, such as "Wave bye-bye" or "Clap your hands."
- Reaches for toys that are visible but out of reach.
- Puts everything into their mouth (Figure 4-18).
- Continues to drop the first item when other toys or items are offered.
- Recognizes the reversal of an object: a cup that is upside down is still a cup (Johnson & Moore, 2020).
- Imitates activities, such as hitting two blocks together or playing pat-a-cake.

Figure 4-18 Safety becomes an important issue as the infant gains mobility.

Developmental Profiles and Growth Patterns *(continued)*

What Do You **See?**

Integration of developmental domains. The achievement of even simple tasks requires the collaborative efforts of multiple developmental skills. Look closely at the little boy in this picture. What developmental domains are involved in his effort to pick up this ball?

techlescuk/139 images/Pixabay

8–12 months

- Drops toys intentionally and repeatedly; looks in the direction of a fallen object; delights in having an adult or sibling pick up an object, only to throw it overboard again.

- Exhibits some relational discrimination, such as identifying items that are the same/different (Hespos et al., 2021).

- Shows the appropriate use of everyday items: pretends to drink from a cup, puts on a necklace, hugs a doll, brushes own hair, makes a stuffed animal "walk."

- Shows some sense of spatial relationships: puts a block into a container and takes it out when requested to do so.

- Begins to show an understanding of causality—for example, hands a musical toy back to an adult to have it rewound when the music stops playing.

- Shows some awareness of the functional relationship of objects: puts a spoon into mouth, uses a brush to smooth hair, turns the pages of a book.

- Searches for a completely hidden toy or object by the end of this period.

Speech and Language Development

- Babbles or jabbers deliberately to initiate social interaction; may shout to attract attention, listen, and then shout again if no one responds.

- Nods head to indicate "no" and might occasionally do so for "yes."

- Responds by looking for the source of the voice when name is called.

- Babbles in sentence-like sequences, "*ma ma ma ma*," "*ba ba ba*"; followed later by jargon (syllables and sounds common to many languages, uttered with language-like inflection).

- Waves bye-bye; claps hands when asked.

- Says "*da-da*" and "*ma-ma*" (or equivalents in other languages).

Developmental Profiles and Growth Patterns *(continued)*

- Reproduces sounds similar to those that the infant already has learned to make; often sounds are directed to no one in particular; also imitates motor noises, tongue clicking, lip smacking, and coughing when encouraged to do so by an adult; (Long et al., 2020).

- Enjoys rhymes and simple songs; vocalizes and dances to music.

- Hands a toy or an object to an adult when appropriate gestures accompany the request.

Social-Emotional Development

- Continues to exhibit a definite fear of unfamiliar persons (stranger anxiety); clings to or hides behind a parent or primary caregiver; may begin to resist being away from familiar adults (separation anxiety) (Brand, Escobar, & Patrick, 2020) (Figure 4-19). Infants raised in extended families may not exhibit the same negative reaction.

- Wants an adult to be in constant sight; may cry and search the room when no one is immediately visible.

- Enjoys being nearby and included in daily activities of family members and teachers; is becoming more sociable and outgoing.

- Enjoys novel experiences and opportunities to examine new objects.

▶❚❚ **TeachSource Video Connections**

Assessing Language Development

Language provides a means for expressing pleasure, wants, and needs. Encouraging and supporting early language development creates important neural connections in the infant's brain that are critical for future vocabulary, writing, and reading skills. Respond to the following questions after you have watched the learning video *Observing and Monitoring Language Development in Infants: The Importance of Assessment:*

1. Why is it important to assess an infant's language development several times during the year?

2. At approximately what age can you expect an infant to begin understanding and responding to requests?

3. What prelinguistic skills did the infants in this video (in the main feature) display?

4. What language-promoting activities would you encourage families to implement at home, based on what you observed in the video?

8–12 months

- Expresses a need to be picked up and held by extending arms upward, crying, or clinging to an adult's legs.

- Begins to exhibit assertiveness by resisting a caregiver's requests; may kick, scream, toss toys, or throw self on the floor.

- Offers toys and objects to others.

- Often becomes attached to a favorite toy or blanket, and cries when it is missing.

- Looks up and smiles at a person who is speaking upon hearing name.

Developmental Profiles and Growth Patterns *(continued)*

8–12 months

Did You Know ❓

… stranger anxiety is a universally observed phenomenon that occurs across cultures and genders? Cultural differences in child-rearing practices and temperament influence the degree of anxiety that children may experience.

Figure 4-19 Infants may begin to show fear of adults other than their primary caregivers (stranger anxiety).

Oswald El-saboath/Pexels

- Repeats behaviors that get attention; jabbers continuously.
- Carries out simple directions and requests; understands the meaning of "No," "Yes," "Come here," and other common phrases.

DAILY ROUTINES

Eating

- Eats three meals per day, plus mid-morning or mid-afternoon snacks such as juice, fruit, crackers, and cereal. Enjoys eating with family members; usually has a good appetite.
- Begins to refuse bottle; shows greater interest in drinking from a cup.
- Learns to drink from a cup; wants to hold it alone; will even tilt head backward to get the last drop.
- Begins to eat finger foods; may remove food from mouth, look at it, and put it back in.
- Develops certain food likes and dislikes.
- Is continuously active during feedings; the infant's hands may be so busy that a toy is needed for each hand to prevent a cup or dish from being overturned or food grabbed and tossed.
- Sweeps food off of tray with hand when no longer hungry.

Toileting, Bathing, and Dressing

- Enjoys bath time; splashes and plays with the washcloth, soap, and water toys.
- Delights in letting water drip from a sponge or washcloth; pours water from cup to cup.
- Shows great interest in pulling off hats, shoes, and socks.
- Fusses when diaper needs changing; may pull off a soiled or wet diaper.
- Cooperates to some degree while being dressed; puts the arms in armholes when asked, may even extend the legs to have pants put on.
- Has one or two bowel movements per day.
- Remains dry after nap on occasion.

DAILY ROUTINES *(continued)*

Sleeping

- Goes to bed willingly but may not fall asleep immediately; plays or walks around in crib before eventually falling asleep.
- Sleeps until early morning.
- Plays alone and quietly for 15–30 minutes after awakening; may call out for parent or caregiver and begin to make demanding noises, signaling the need to be up and about.
- Plays actively in the crib when awake; the crib sides must be up and securely fastened at all times to protect the infant from injury.
- Takes one afternoon nap most days; length varies from infant to infant.

Play and Social Activities

- Enjoys large motor activities: pulling to a standing position, cruising, standing alone, creeping.
- Places things on own head, such as a basket, bowl, or cup; finds this very funny and expects others to notice and laugh.
- Puts nesting objects, such as pans or cups, in and out of each other: places toys in a container and them dumps them out.
- Enjoys hiding behind chairs to play "Where's baby?"
- Throws things on the floor and expects them to be returned.
- Shows interest in opening and closing doors and cupboards.
- Hands an object to an adult upon request; expects to have it returned immediately.
- Responds to "no-no" by stopping the activity. Later in this period, the infant might smile, laugh, and resume the inappropriate behavior, thus turning it into a game.

8–12 months

learning activities to promote **brain development**

Infants now enjoy activities that involve movement, imitation, reciprocal actions, cause-effect, and repetition. Music, stories read aloud, rhyming, and back-and-forth conversation reinforce early cognitive, language, and social development.

Developmentally appropriate applications for families and teachers:

- Continue to elaborate on previously suggested activities; sing, read, talk, play simple games (rolling a ball, stacking objects), and encourage the infant's efforts.
- Always follow the infant's lead whenever they initiate a new response or invent a new version of a familiar game (the roots of creativity).
- Provide safe floor space close to the parent or caregiver; learning to sit, crawl, stand, and explore are an infant's major tasks during these months.
- Look at photo albums together and talk about everyday happenings in the baby's life.
- Read from sturdy, brightly colored picture books, allowing the infant to help hold the book and turn pages. Point to pictures and label the object to help infants begin to make associations; "Soft brown kitten," "Happy puppy," "Big red pail."

8–12
months

learning activities *(continued)*

- Talk about routine activities as they are unfolding, naming and emphasizing key words: "Let's *wash your hands* before you eat." "Here is the *soap*," "Let's get your hands all *wet*."

- Give the baby simple instructions: "Pat Mommy's head," "Point to baby's nose," "Find Daddy's ear."

- Allow adequate time for a response; if the infant seems interested but does not respond, demonstrate the request.

- Accept the infant's newly invented game of dropping things off a highchair or out of the crib; act surprised, laugh, return dropped object, and do not scold. This is the baby's way of learning about cause and effect, gravity, and adults' patience.

- Encourage infants to fill a container with small toys, blocks, or other items and then empty it out. (The *Rule of Fist* still applies.)

- Provide push-and-pull toys, toys with wheels, and large textured balls to roll back and forth. (Helping to unpack canned foods and rolling them across the kitchen floor is also an all-time favorite game!) Activity cubes provide opportunities for manipulation and discovery.

TeachSource Digital Download

developmental **alerts**

Check with a health-care provider or early childhood specialist if, by twelve months of age, the infant does *not*:

- Blink when fast-moving objects approach the eyes.

- Begin to develop teeth.

- Imitate simple sounds.

- Follow simple verbal requests: "Come," "Bye-bye."

- Pull self to a standing position.

- Transfer objects from hand to hand.

- Show any anxiety toward strangers by crying or refusing to be held.

- Interact playfully with parents, caregivers, and siblings.

- Feed self; hold a bottle or cup; pick up and eat finger foods.

- Creep or crawl on hands and knees.

Note: Cultural differences may alter the timetable when some developmental skills are acquired. Expanded Developmental Alerts Checklists appear in Appendix A and are also available as digital downloads.

safety concerns

Continue to implement the safety practices described for the previous stages, and always be aware of new safety issues as the infant continues to grow and develop.

Choking and Poisoning

- Cut finger foods into small pieces (1/4 inch [0.63 cm] or smaller). Avoid sticky foods (e.g., raisins, caramels, or peanut butter) and hard foods (e.g., raw vegetables, hard candies, or nuts).
- Keep small objects such as buttons, dry pet food, coins, pen tops, and small batteries out of reach; keep garbage cans closed tightly. Any item that can fit through a toilet paper tube is too small for young children to play with.
- Store laundry and dishwashing soaps (and pods), cleaning supplies, personal care items, and garden chemicals in a locked cabinet.
- Hang purses and backpacks up high to prevent the infant's access to medications, cosmetics, coins, hand sanitizer, or small sharp objects.

Drowning

- Remove unsupervised water sources, including bath water, outdoor fountains, pet dishes, and wading pools. Place safety devices on toilet lids.
- Enclose pools with fences and latched gates; install alarms on windows and doors. Never leave a young child unsupervised in a pool or bathtub, even briefly to answer the telephone.

Falls

- Always strap infants into highchairs, grocery carts, and strollers and on changing tables. Never allow them to stand up in or on these objects (unless you are holding onto the infant).
- Keep the crib sides up and locked at all times.
- Pad the sharp corners and edges of furniture and cabinet doors.
- Place safety gates across stairs.

Strangulation

- Purchase clothing, such as jackets, with elastic instead of pull strings in the hoods.
- Fasten cords on all blinds and curtains up high and out of a child's reach.

Suffocation

- Keep plastic bags and wrappings out of the infant's reach; knot and discard them immediately.
- Remove any latex balloons (only Mylar balloons are safe); small pieces of latex can obstruct the airway and, thus, pose a serious choking and suffocation hazard.
- Remove lids from airtight containers such as plastic storage tubs and toy chests.

8–12 months

positive behavior guidance

There are several things that adults must understand about infants' behavior: they depend on adults to satisfy all their basic needs; crying is their primary mode of communication; they cannot be spoiled; and they should not be punished. Because caring for an infant can be stressful at times, it is important that adults take care of themselves, learn self-control, and practice anger management skills so they are able to respond in a positive manner.

Newborns

- Always respond to their cries with love, gentle handling, and calming words to build feelings of trust and security.

One to four months

- Help infants learn to soothe and quiet themselves: hold, cuddle, or rock them gently; wrap them snuggly in a blanket; massage their skin; offer a pacifier (some infants prefer their thumbs).

positive behavior **guidance** (continued)

Four to eight months

- Maintain consistent eating and sleeping schedules to reduce crying and fussiness.
- Create a safe environment; eliminate items and situations that could be potentially harmful to mobile infants.
- Convey a sense of calm when responding to a fussy infant.

Eight to twelve months

- Introduce the word "No" (spoken gently) to correct infants when they are doing something that could result in harm. If necessary, pick up and move the infant to a safe area until corrective measures can be taken, but do not punish them.
- Distract or redirect the infant to an appropriate activity rather than scolding.
- Give attention when an infant is behaving appropriately: "You rolled the ball really far," "You came when Daddy asked."

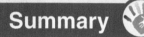

Summary

4-1 Newborns have almost no intentional or purposeful control over their motor abilities; thus, these actions are referred to as *reflexive movements*, which include:

- Swallowing, sucking, gagging, coughing, yawning, blinking, and elimination
- Rooting, in which the infant turns when skin around check is touched
- Moro (startle), in which the infant throws open the arms when surprised by loud noise or touch
- Grasping, in which the infant tightly curls fingers around an object
- Stepping, in which walking-like movements occur when the infant's feet touch a firm surface.

4-2 The first year marks one of the most important stages of brain development:

- Infants are learning continuously about the people and environment around them.
- Learning opportunities increase the number and strength of neural connections in the infant's brain.
- Learning is influenced by genetics, culture, environment, and adult expectations.

4-3 Initially, infants communicate through crying, eye contact, social smiling, and muscle tension (or relaxation). Later, infants begin to coo and babble, imitate adult expressions, respond to name and simple commands, and produce simple word sequences (i.e., "*ma ma ma*" or "*da da da*").

4-4 Infants begin to exhibit stranger anxiety at around nine and ten months of age; this is a normal developmental phenomenon. Observable behaviors include considerable distress and anxiety, crying, clinging, and reluctance to let a primary caregiver out of sight.

Key Terms

in utero **p. 75**

jaundice **p. 76**

fontanels **p. 76**

pupil **p. 78**

bonding **p. 80**

object permanence **p. 85**

depth perception **p. 94**

stranger anxiety **p. 95**

Apply What You Have Learned

A. Case Study Connections

Reread the developmental sketch about Harper and her parents, Julie and Danny, presented at the beginning of this chapter and answer the following questions:

1. In what ways is Harper's motor development likely to change by the time she turns seven months of age?

2. Would you expect Harper to experience stranger anxiety if her parents don't enroll her in an early childhood program until she turns eight or nine months? Explain.

3. How would you respond to Harper's parents if they expressed concern about her lack of interest in pulling herself to a standing position or taking any steps by her first birthday?

B. Review Questions

1. Explain why a ten-month-old infant might begin fussing and refusing to be left with a familiar babysitter.

2. Identify and discuss three informal methods for determining whether a newborn's hearing is functional.

3. Identify three newborn reflexes that typically disappear by one year of age. Why should you be concerned if they do not fade according to schedule?

4. What activities can families and teachers engage in with infants to promote and reinforce early motor skills?

5. Identify three perceptual-cognitive skills that appear during late infancy (8–12 months) and provide a behavioral example that illustrates each.

C. Your Turn: Chapter to Practice

1. Arrange to visit four or five early childhood programs (e.g., centers, homes) that accept infants in your community. Before you go, research and learn about the features typically associated with high-quality programs (these are posted on many early childhood professional organization websites). Briefly summarize your observations and personal reaction to each site. If you were the parent of a six-month-old, how would you describe this experience?

2. Prepare a list of five developmentally appropriate activities for infants; each activity should involve and reinforce at least two different forms of learning (visual, auditory, tactile, or hand–eye coordination).

3. Compile a list of ten recommended storybooks that parents could read to their infants. Identify and describe the features that make each book an appealing and developmentally appropriate choice.

Online Resources

Child Care Aware® of America
This organization advocates on behalf of all early childhood educators. Extensive information, resources, and tools are available to help providers operate effective programs. Parents and families can access current information and guidelines to help them identify high quality care programs in their area. Child Care Aware also works closely with the United States military and assists families with child care fees and respite care.

Early Head Start National Resource Center
The Early Head Start National Resource Center, operated by Zero to Three, serves as a repository for timely information, professional expertise, and technical assistance to Early Head Start educators and families. Extensive resources on topics ranging from culture, school readiness, and assessment to family engagement, children's health, and policy can be accessed from this site.

HealthyChildren.org
The American Academy of Pediatrics (APA) supports this website and offers professional information on a variety of children's health, safety, and nutrition topics. The *Ages & Stages*, *Healthy Living*, *News*, and *Search*, sections are especially useful.

Safe to Sleep
The Safe to Sleep campaign is an ongoing national effort to raise awareness about SIDS prevention. Facts about SIDS, preventive measures, research findings, informational videos, and printable resources are available in English and Spanish.

References

Adam-Darque, A., Grouiller, F., Vasung, L., Leuchter, R. H., Pollien, P., Lazeyras, F., & Hüppi, P. S. (2018). fMRI-based neuronal response to new odorants in the newborn brain. *Cerebral Cortex, 28*(8), 2901–2907.

Addabbo, M., Vacaru, S. V., Meyer, M., & Hunnius, S. (2020). "Something in the way you move": Infants are sensitive to emotions conveyed in action kinematics. *Developmental Science, 23*(1), e12873. https://doi.org/10.1111/desc.12873

Adolph, K. E., & Hoch, J. E. (2019). Motor development: Embodied, embedded, enculturated, and enabling. *Annual Review of Psychology, 70*, 141–164.

American Optometric Association (AOA). (2021). Infant vision: Birth to 24 months of age. Retrieved from https://www.aoa.org/healthy-eyes/eye-health-for-life/infant-vision?sso=y.

Bauer, C. E., Lewis, J. W., Brefczynski-Lewis, J., Frum, C., Schade, M. M., Haut, M. W., & Montgomery-Downs, H. E. (2020). Breastfeeding duration is associated with regional, not global, differences in white matter tracts. *Brain Sciences, 10*(1), 19. https://doi.org/10.3390/brainsci10010019

Brand, R. J., Escobar, K., & Patrick, A. M. (2020). Coincidence or cascade? The temporal relation between locomotor behaviors and the emergence of stranger anxiety. *Infant Behavior and Development, 58*, 101423. https://doi.org/10.1016/j.infbeh.2020.101423

Buiatti, M., Di Giorgio, E., Piazza, M., Polloni, C., Menna, G., Taddei, F., Baldo, E., & Vallortigara, G. (2019). Cortical route for facelike pattern processing in human newborns. *Proceedings of the National Academy of Sciences of the United States of America, 116*(10), 4625–4630.

Centers for Disease Control and Prevention (CDC). (2020). *Sudden Unexpected Infant Death and Sudden Infant Death Syndrome.* Retrieved from https://www.cdc.gov/sids/index.htm.

Chinn, L. K., Noonan, C. F., Hoffmann, M., & Lockman, J. J. (2019). Development of infant reaching strategies to tactile targets on the face. *Frontiers in Psychology, 10*, 9. https://doi.org/10.3389/fpsyg.2019.00009

de Araújo, M. F., de Castro, W. A., Nishimaru, H., Urakawa, S., Ono, T., & Nishijo, H. (2020). Performance in a gaze-cueing task is associated with autistic traits. *AIMS Neuroscience, 8*(1), 148–160.

Durand, K., Schaal, B., Goubet, N., Lewkowicz, D. J., & Baudouin, J-Y. (2020). Does any mother's body odor stimulate interest in mother's face in 4-month-old infants? *Infancy, 25*(2), 151–164.

Fagard, J., Corbetta, D., Somogyi, E., Safar, A., & Bernard, C. (2020). Right-handed one day, right-handed the next day? *Laterality, 25*(4), 455–468.

Falk, S., Fasolo, M., Genovese, G., Romero-Lauro, L., & Franco, F. (2021). Sing for me, Mama! Infants' discrimination of novel vowels in song. *Infancy, 26*(2), 248–270.

Gangi, D. N., Boterberg, S., Schwichtenberg, A. J., Solis, E., Young, G. S., Iosif, A., & Ozonoff, S. (2021). Declining gaze to faces in infants developing autism spectrum disorder: Evidence from two independent cohorts. *Child Development, 92*(3), e285–e295. https://doi:.org/ 10.1111/cdev.13471

Gieysztor, E. Z., Choińska, A. M., & Paprocka-Borowicz, M. (2018). Persistence of primitive reflexes and associated motor problems in healthy preschool children. *Archives of Medical Science, 14*(1), 167–173.

Guellaï, B., Hausberger, M., Chopin, A., & Streri, A. (2020). Premises of social cognition: Newborns are sensitive to a direct *versus* a faraway gaze. *Scientific Reports, 10*(1), 9726. https://doi.org/10.1038/s41598-020-66576-8

Guzzardi, M. A., Granziera, F., Sanguinetti, E., Ditaranto, F., Muratori, F., & Iozzo, P. (2020). Exclusive breastfeeding predicts higher hearing-language development in girls of preschool age. *Nutrients, 12*(8), 2320. http://dx.doi.org/10.3390/nu12082320

Gyamfi, A., O'Neill, B., Henderson, W. A., & Lucas, R. (2021). Black/African American breastfeeding experience: Cultural, sociological, and health dimensions through an equity lens. *Breastfeeding Medicine, 16*(2), 103–111.

Hespos, S., Gentner, D., Anderson, E., & Shivaram, A. (2021). The origins of *same/different* discrimination in human infants. *Current Opinion in Behavioral Sciences, 37*(1), 69–74.

Jacquey, L., Fagard, J., Esseily, R., & O'Regan, J. K. (2020). Detection of sensorimotor contingencies in infants before the age of 1 year: A comprehensive review. *Developmental Psychology, 56*(7), 1233–1251.

Johnson, S. P., & Moore, D. S. (2020). Spatial thinking in infancy: Origins and development of mental rotation between 3 and 10 months of age. *Cognitive Research: Principles and Implications, 5*(1), 10. https://doi.org/10.1186/s41235-020-00212-x

Keemink, J. R., Keshavarzi-Pour, M. J., & Kelly, D. J. (2019). Infants' responses to interactive gaze-contingent faces in a novel and naturalistic eye-tracking paradigm. *Developmental Psychology, 55*(7), 1362–1371.

Lenehan, S. M., Boylan, G. B., Livingstone, V., Fogarty, L., Twomey, D. M., Nikolovski, J., Irvine, A. D., Kiely, M., Kenny, L. C., Hourihane, J. O., & Murray, D. M. (2020). The impact of short-term predominate breastfeeding on cognitive outcome at 5 years. *Acta Paediatrica, 109*(5), 982–988.

Long, H. L., Bowman, D., Yoo, H., Burkhardt-Reed, M. M., Bene, E. R., & Oller, D. K. (2020). Social and non-social functions of infant vocalizations. *PLos One, 15*(8), e0224956. https://doi.org/10.1371/journal.pone.0224956

Loos, H. M., Reger, D., & Schaal, B. (2019). The odour of human milk: Its chemical variability and detection by newborns. *Physiology & Behavior, 199*, 88–99.

Louis-Jacques, A. F., Marhefka, S. L., Brumley, J., Schafer, E. J., Taylor, T. I., Brown, A. J., Livingston, T. A., Spatz, D. L., & Miller, E. M. (2020). Historical antecedents of breastfeeding for African American women: From pre-colonial period to the mid-twentieth century. *Journal of Racial and Ethnic Health Disparities, 7*, 1003–1012.

Marotz, L. R. (2020). *Health, safety, and nutrition for the young child.* (10th ed.). Boston, MA: Cengage.

Orozco, J., Echeverria, S. E., Armah, S. M., & Dharod, J. M. (2020). Household food insecurity, breastfeeding, and related feeding practices in US infants and toddlers: Results for HNANES 2009-2014. *Journal of Nutrition Education and Behavior, 52*(6), 588–594.

Over, H. (2020). The social function of imitation in development. *Annual Review of Developmental Psychology, 2*(1), 93–109.

Piaget, A. (1954). *The construction of reality in the child.* New York: Basic Books.

Porro, M., Fontana, C., Giannì, M. L., Pesenti, N., Boggini, T., De Carli, A., De Bon, G., Lucco, G., Mosca, F., Fumagalli, M., & Picciolini, O. (2020). Early detection of general movements trajectories in very low birth weight infants. *Science Reports, 10*, 13290. https://doi.org/10.1038/s41598-020-70003-3

Reindal, L., Nærland, T., Weidle, B., Lyderssen, S., Andreassen, O. A., & Sund, A. M. (2020). Age of first walking and associations with symptom severity in children with suspected or diagnosed autism spectrum disorder. *Journal of Autism and Developmental Disorders, 50*(9), 3216–3232.

Rowe, M. L., & Weisleder, A. (2020). Language development in context. *Annual Review of Developmental Psychology, 2*, 201–223.

Salvadori, E. A., Colonnesi, C., Vonk, H. S., Oort, F. J., & Aktar, E. (2021). Infant emotional mimicry of strangers: Associations with parent emotional mimicry, parent-infant mutual attention, and parent dispositional affective empathy. *The International Journal of Environmental Research and Public Health, 18*(2), 654. https://doi.org/10.3390/ijerph18020654

Stewart, J. R., Vigil, D. C., & Carlson, R. (2021). Frequency of gesture use and language in typically developing prelinguistic children. *Infant Behavior and Development, 62*, 101527. https://doi.org/10.1016/j.infbeh.2021.101527

Tinius, R., Rajendran, N., Miller, L., Menke, B., Esslinger, K., Maples, J., & Furgal, K. (2020). Maternal factors related to infant motor development at 4 months of age. *Breastfeeding Medicine, 15*(2), 90–95.

Uchida-Ota, M., Arimitsu, T., Tsuzuki, D., Dan, I., Ikeda, K., Takahashi, T., & Minagawa, Y. (2019). Maternal speech shapes the cerebral frontotemporal network in neonates: A hemodynamic functional connectivity study. *Developmental Cognitive Neuroscience, 39*, 100701. https://doi.org/10.1016/j.dcn.2019.10071

Vainio, L. (2019). Connection between movements of mouth and hand: Perspectives on development and evolution of speech. *Neuroscience & Biobehavioral Reviews, 100*, 211–223.

Van Dael, P. (2021). Role of n-3 long-chain polyunsaturated fatty acids in human nutrition and health: Review of recent studies and recommendations. *Nutrition Research and Practice, 15*, e8. https://doi.org/10.4162/nrp.2021.15.e8

Wass, S. V., Whitehorn, M., Haresign, I. M., Phillips, E., & Leong, V. (2020). Interpersonal neural entrainment during early social interaction. *Trends in Cognitive Science, 24*(4), 329–342.

Woods, R. J., Johnson, K. M., Honsa, E., Westrom, S., & Lammers, S. M. (2021). Infants distinguish and represent pattern as an object feature from externally generated patterns superimposed on real, 3-dimensional objects' surfaces. *Infancy, 26*(1), 63–83.

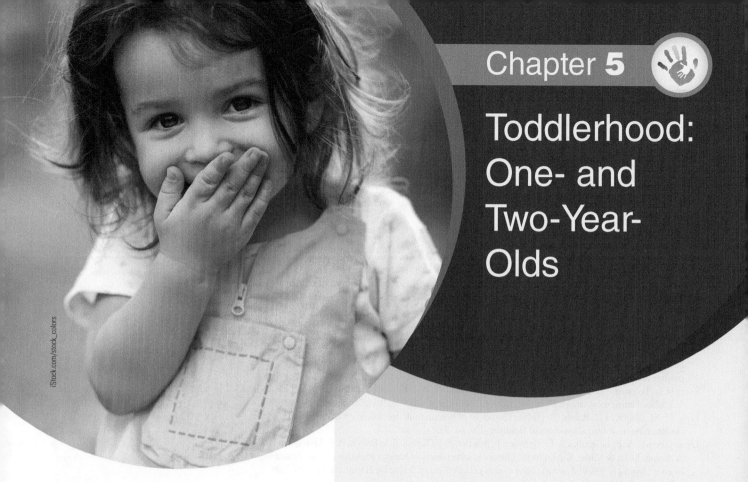

Chapter 5

Toddlerhood: One- and Two-Year-Olds

Learning Objectives

After reading this chapter, you will be able to:

5-1 Define the concept of egocentricity and provide an example.

5-2 Describe the motor abilities of a typical one-year-old and two-year-old.

5-3 Define the terms *holophrastic speech* and *telegraphic speech* and give an example of each.

5-4 Provide two illustrations of the two-year-old's improved understanding of size and spatial relationships.

5-5 Explain why two-year-olds are often described as picky or fussy eaters.

NAEYC NAEYC Professional Standards Linked to Chapter Content

1a, 1b, 1c, and 1d: Child development and learning in context

2a and 2c: Family–teacher partnerships and community connections

3a, 3b, and 3c: Child observations, documentation, and assessment

4a and 4b: Developmentally, culturally, and linguistically appropriate teaching practices

5b: Knowledge, application, and integration of academic content in the early childhood curriculum

Alandra and her husband divorced last year when their son, Darrius, was just eighteen months old. Darrius and his mother now live in a small apartment just a few blocks away from his grandmother's house. As a single parent, Alandra often feels overwhelmed by the burdens of working evenings at a local restaurant and caring for her now-two-year-old son. Darrius spends his mornings playing alone in his bedroom or watching television while his mother sleeps. When he tires of playing with the few toys in his room, he often heads to the kitchen and begins pulling things from the drawers and cabinets. His activity usually awakens his mother and results in a scolding and an occasional spanking. Books, magazines, and newspapers are notably absent in their apartment. Alandra has little interest in reading and prefers to get her news from television. She occasionally takes Darrius to a neighborhood park, where most of the equipment is old, in poor condition, and designed for older children. Darrius usually ends up playing alone in the sandbox with any Styrofoam cups, plastic spoons, and sticks that he can find lying around, while his mother chats with her friends.

Darrius adores his father and spends every other weekend at his house. However, when he returns home, Alandra finds Darrius unmanageable and disobedient. She blames her ex-husband for their son's behavior problems, and they often end up arguing about it in front of Darrius. His grandmother is concerned about the effect the divorce and co-parenting arrangement may be having on Darrius's development. He utters only two or three words that anyone can understand and shows little interest in the children's books that his grandmother borrows from her neighbor. Lately, Darrius has become increasingly aggressive—hitting, yelling, and throwing objects—whenever he is frustrated. He refuses to help dress himself when asked, is defiant when told to get ready for bed, and usually runs the other way when his mother calls for him to come.

Ask Yourself

- Do you think Alandra should be concerned about Darrius's language skills? Explain.
- What suggestions, considering the family's limited financial resources, could you offer to Alandra for encouraging Darrius's language development?
- In what ways may his environment be contributing to Darrius's problematic behavior?

One- and Two-Year-Olds

Did You Know ?

... toddlers are at extremely high risk for death and unintentional injury due to their lack of fear?

Toddlers are dynamos, full of unlimited energy, enthusiasm, and curiosity. Although their rate of growth slows significantly during this stage, important developmental changes are taking place. The toddler begins this period with the limited motor, social, language, and cognitive abilities of an infant and ends it with the relatively sophisticated skills of a young child.

Toddlers' improving motor skills allow them to navigate, explore, and test their surroundings. However, this newly emerging mobility is also likely to result in frequent bumps, falls, and other injuries due to toddlers' limited control and understanding of cause and effect. There are also times when their motor skills are not as advanced as their intentions and may lead to considerable frustration.

Toddlers begin to show interest in books and having an adult read to them. Vocabulary is acquired at a fairly rapid pace and permits toddlers to engage in more complex thinking and communication patterns. "No" becomes a favorite word, and it is used frequently and emphatically to express wants, needs, and frustration.

Defiant behaviors, such as tantrums, hitting, biting, and negative verbalizations often increase in frequency as toddlers begin testing and asserting their independence. Toddlers also have a limited understanding of social conventions and expectations and positive ways to express frustration. Although adults may find these behaviors troublesome at times, they mark the beginning of a significant developmental transition. Erik Erikson described this stage as an important step in helping children achieve a sense of **autonomy** and degree of personal control over their environment (Erikson, 1959). However, early independence is not encouraged across all cultures. For example, many Asian, Latino, and Native American cultures socialize children to be obedient, to submit to authority, and to show respect toward others, especially their elders (Pham, Luui, & Rollock, 2020; Suizzo, Tedford, & McManus, 2019). These behaviors are believed to be vital for enabling families and groups to live and work together in harmony.

autonomy A sense of self as being separate from others.

113

The One-Year-Old

The ability to stand upright and toddle from place to place enables one-year-olds to begin learning about the world around them. They become talkers and doers, stopping only for much-needed meals and bedtimes. Their curiosity mounts, their skills become increasingly advanced, and their energy level seems never-ending. One-year-olds believe that everything and everyone exists for their sole benefit (Piaget & Inhelder, 1967). Eventually, this **egocentricity** or self-centeredness, gives way to a gradual respect for others. However, for now, one-year-olds are satisfied to declare everything "mine." They prefer to play alone (**solitary play**), observing and imitating the actions of other children rather than joining in.

egocentricity Believing that everything and everyone is there for your personal benefit.

solitary play Playing alone.

Developmental Profiles and Growth Patterns

Growth and Physical Characteristics

- Grows at a considerably slower rate during this period.
- Gains approximately 2–3 inches (5.0–7.6 cm) in height per year; toddlers reach an average height of 32–35 inches (81.3–88.9 cm).
- Weighs approximately 21–27 pounds (9.6–12.3 kg); gains 1/4–1/2 pound (0.13–0.25 kg) per month; weight is now approximately triple the child's birth weight.
- Breathes at a rate of 22–30 respirations per minute; rate varies with emotional state and activity.
- Heart rate (pulse) is approximately 80–110 beats per minute.
- Head size increases slowly; the head grows approximately 1/2 inch (1.3 cm) every six months; anterior fontanel is nearly closed at eighteen months as the bones of the skull thicken.
- Chest circumference is larger than the head circumference.
- Teeth begin to erupt rapidly; six to ten new teeth appear during this period.
- Legs still may appear bowed.
- Body shape begins to change; toddlers gradually develop a more adultlike appearance but remain top-heavy; abdomen protrudes; back is swayed.
- Visual acuity is approximately 20/60.

Motor Development

- Crawls skillfully and quickly to a desired location.
- Stands alone with the feet spread apart, legs stiffened, and arms extended for support.
- Gets to the feet unaided.
- Walks unassisted near the end of this period (most children); is still somewhat unsteady and falls often; not always able to maneuver successfully around obstacles such as furniture or toys.
- Uses furniture to lower self to floor; collapses backward into a sitting position or falls forward on hands and then sits.
- Releases an object voluntarily.
- Enjoys pushing or pulling toys while walking.
- Picks up objects and throws them repeatedly; direction becomes more deliberate.
- Attempts to run (with stiff legs); has difficulty stopping and usually just drops to the floor.

Developmental Profiles and Growth Patterns *(continued)*

Figure 5-1 Toddlers use whole-arm movements when drawing or painting.

- Crawls upstairs on all fours; goes downstairs backward in the same position.
- Sits in a small chair.
- Carries toys from place to place.
- Uses crayons and markers for scribbling; holds crayon in entire hand and draws with whole-arm movement (Figure 5-1).
- Helps feed self; wants to hold own spoon (often upside down) and cup; not always accurate at directing utensils into the mouth; frequent spills should be expected.
- Helps turn pages of a book during story time.
- Stacks two to four objects with reasonable accuracy.

Perceptual-Cognitive Development

- Enjoys object-hiding activities:
  - Early in this period, the toddler always searches in the same location for a hidden object (if the child has watched the object being hidden). Later, the child will search in several locations (Kim, Sodian, & Proust, 2020).
  - Hands an object back to the adult, indicating a desire to have it hidden again.

- Passes an object to the other hand when offered a second object (this is referred to as *crossing the midline*—an important neurological development (Hadders-Algra, 2018). Infrequent midline crossing has been observed in children who are later diagnosed with ADHD (Begum et al., 2020).

- Manages three to four objects by setting one aside (on the lap or floor) when presented with another.
- Studies objects by holding and manipulating them in both hands; puts toys in mouth less often.
- Enjoys looking at picture books; gazes at, and points to, illustrations (Figure 5-2).

Figure 5-2 Toddlers enjoy listening to stories and looking at pictures.

1-year-old

Developmental Profiles and Growth Patterns *(continued)*

- Demonstrates an understanding of functional relationships (objects that belong together):
  - Puts a spoon in a bowl and then uses spoon, pretending to eat.
  - Pounds wooden pegs with a toy hammer.
  - Tries to make a doll stand up and "walk."
- Shows or offers a toy for another person to look at.
- Names many everyday objects.
- Shows an increasing understanding of spatial and form discrimination (puts all large pegs in a pegboard; places three geometric shapes in a large formboard or puzzle) (Uhlenberg & Geiken, 2021).
- Places several small items (e.g., blocks, clothespins, or cereal pieces) in a container or bottle and then delights in dumping them out.
- Attempts to make mechanical objects work after watching someone else do so.
- Uses some facial expressions, but they are not always accurate representations.
- Imitates gestures.

Speech and Language Development

- Produces considerable jargon (i.e., puts sounds and words together into speechlike [inflected] patterns).
- Uses one word to convey an entire thought (**holophrastic speech**); the meaning depends upon the inflection ("me" might be used to request more cookies or express a desire to feed themselves). Later, the toddler produces two-word phrases to express a complete thought (**telegraphic speech**) ("more cookie," "Daddy bye-bye").
- Follows simple directions ("Give Daddy the book"; "Come here") (Figure 5-3).
- Points to familiar persons, animals, and toys when asked.
- Understands and identifies three body parts when someone names them (**receptive language**); "Show me your nose (toe, ear, tongue, finger)."
- Indicates a few desired objects and activities by name ("bye-bye," "cookie," "story," "blanket"); verbal request is often accompanied by an insistent gesture.
- Responds to simple questions with "Yes" or "No" and appropriate head movement.
- Produces speech that is 25–50 percent **intelligible** during this period. Late talking has been linked to persistent language delay disorders in older children (Morgan et al., 2020).
- Locates familiar objects upon request (if the child knows their usual location).

Figure 5-3 Toddlers understand and respond to simple questions and requests.

---

holophrastic speech Using a single word to express a complete thought.

telegraphic speech Uttering two-word phrases to convey a complete thought.

receptive language Understanding words that are heard.

intelligible Language that can be understood by others.

Developmental Profiles and Growth Patterns *(continued)*

1-year-old

- Acquires and uses five to fifty words (**expressive language**); typically, these are words that refer to the names of familiar objects (e.g., animals, food, and toys); bilingual toddlers tend to have smaller total vocabularies at this point (Diaz, Borjas, & Farrar, 2021; Florit et al., 2021).

- Uses gestures, such as pointing or pulling, to direct adult attention.

- Enjoys rhymes and songs; tries to join in; dances and sings along.

- Seems aware of reciprocal (back-and-forth) aspects of conversational exchanges; engages in some vocal turn-taking, such as making and imitating sounds.

Social-Emotional Development

- Remains friendly toward others, although the toddler still may be shy; usually less wary of strangers (Yeary, 2020).

- Becomes anxious or cries when parent or parents leave or are out of sight.

- Helps to pick up and put away toys when asked.

- Plays alone for short periods.

- Enjoys being held and read to.

- Observes and imitates the actions of others (i.e., adults, peers) during play (Quinn & Kidd, 2019; Stout et al., 2021).

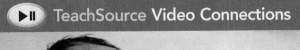

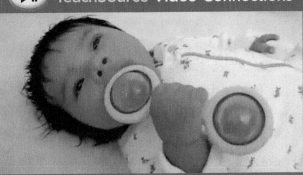

Speech and Language Development

One-year-olds are learning that language is a functional tool, useful for making requests, informing adults about their needs, and letting others know where they stand—sometimes quite emphatically! Perhaps even more significant is their level of understanding, which far exceeds their ability to use spoken language. Respond to the following questions after you have watched the learning video *0–2 Years: Observation Module for Infants and Toddlers* (focus your attention on the one-year-old in the last one-third of the clip):

1. Were you able to understand all of what the toddler was saying? Why do you think her mother was able to do so?

2. Would you consider the toddler's speech and language skills to be developmentally typical for a one-year-old?

3. What behaviors did the toddler exhibit that would suggest she is in a stage of autonomy?

- Is eager for adult attention; likes to know that an adult is near; gives hugs and kisses.

- Recognizes self in mirror.

- Enjoys the companionship of other children but seldom engages in cooperative play; still prefers to play alone.

- Begins to assert independence; often refuses to cooperate with daily routines that once were enjoyable: may resist getting dressed, putting on shoes, eating, taking a bath when asked. Wants to try doing things without any adult help.

- Cries and resorts to tantrums on occasion when things go wrong or if overly tired, hungry, or frustrated (Bastien, Tétreault, & Bernier, 2020). Frequency of tantrums tends to decrease as toddlers' verbal skills improve (Gandolfi & Viterbori, 2020; Rantalainen et al., 2021).

expressive language Words used to verbalize thoughts and feelings.

1-year-old

Developmental Profiles and Growth Patterns *(continued)*

- Shows a growing curiosity about people and surroundings (approaches and talks to strangers; wanders away when left unattended; searches through cabinets).
- Begins to understand gender labels (i.e., boy, girl) and correctly identify own gender.

What Do You See?

Toddler development. Toddlers are entering a stage of increased awareness, but they are not always ready to play cooperatively with other children. What type of play does this boy appear to be absorbed in? Is this typical? How might you expect him to react if another child tried to help him build the tower higher?

▶❚❚ TeachSource Video Connections

Toddlers' Cognitive Development

Children younger than two years learn about their world primarily through their senses. Hand one-year-olds a new toy, and they might look it over, shake it, pound it on the table, and then pop it into their mouths (if it is small enough). Two-year-olds begin to utilize a whole new set of emerging abilities for learning. Respond to the following questions after you have watched the learning video *Infants and Toddlers: Cognitive Development and Imaginative Play*:

1. What advanced cognitive skills are the two-year-olds in this video exhibiting?
2. What instructional strategies is the teacher using to foster and reinforce the children's learning?
3. Could the teacher expect to achieve the same learning outcomes if the children were one-year-olds instead of two-year-olds? Explain.

Did You Know ?

...that until the twentieth century, fathers ignored their children and did not participate in their care or upbringing until they had reached the age of seven?

DAILY ROUTINES

Eating

- Has a much smaller appetite than as an infant; neither requires nor wants a large amount of food due to a slower growth rate; lunch is often the preferred meal (Marotz, 2020).
- Goes on occasional **food jags** (willing to eat only a few preferred foods, such as peanut butter and jelly sandwiches or macaroni and cheese); resists trying unfamiliar foods (**neophobia**); sometimes described as a picky or fussy eater (Johnson & Moding, 2020; Watson, Costantini, & Clegg, 2020).
- Holds food in mouth without swallowing it on occasion; this usually indicates that the child does not need or want more to eat.
- Uses a spoon with some degree of skill (if hungry and interested in eating); often resorts to eating with hands if foods are difficult to manage with utensils. May begin banging spoon on plate or use hand to sweep food off the table when no longer interested in eating.
- Shows good control of a cup (i.e., lifts it up, drinks from it, sets it down, and holds it with one hand); may set it down too hard or quickly at times, causing it to tip over.
- Helps to feed self; some toddlers can feed themselves independently, while others still require some help. Cultural beliefs strongly influence feeding practices and the encouragement of children's independence in feeding themselves at this age.

Toileting, Bathing, and Dressing

- Tries to wash self; plays with washcloth and soap.
- Helps with dressing (puts arms in sleeves, lifts feet to have socks put on). Likes to dress and undress self (takes off own shoes, socks, or mittens); often puts a shirt on upside down and backward or places both feet in one pant leg. Lacks the fine motor skills needed to manipulate button, snaps, and zippers; requires help with these.
- Lets an adult know when diaper or pants are soiled or wet.
- Begins to gain some control of bowels and bladder (intervals between wetting and soiling becoming longer, resulting in fewer accidents). Complete control is often not achieved until around age three (often takes longer for boys). Adults can prepare for this development by using consistent words to describe elimination (e.g., pee, poop, tinkle, shi, shi, wee-wee).

Sleeping

- Sleeps 10–12 hours at night. May fall asleep at dinner if the nap has been missed or if the day's activities have been vigorous. Adequate sleep is essential for children's optimum growth and cognitive and emotional development. Toddlers in Western cultures often are put to bed at an early and consistent time each night (7 to 8 p.m.), whereas evening bedtimes tend to be more flexible and occur later (10 or 11 p.m.) in many Asian and European cultures (Jeon, Dimitriou, & Halstead, 2021).
- Experiences occasional difficulty falling asleep; overflow of energy is shown in behaviors such as bouncing on the bed, calling for parent, demanding a drink or trip to the bathroom, singing, and making and remaking the bed—all of which seem to be ways of gradually "winding down." A short, consistent bedtime routine and quiet story often promotes relaxation and prepares toddlers for sleep.
- Makes many requests at bedtime for stuffed toys, a book or two, or a special blanket. Bedtime resistance is often an expression of the toddler's desire for control and independence.

Play and Social Activity

- Develops a strong sense of property rights; "mine" is heard frequently. Sharing is difficult; often hoards toys and other items.
- Enjoys helping but often gets into trouble when left alone (e.g., smears toothpaste, tries on lip gloss, empties dresser drawers, or unrolls toilet paper).

food jag A phase during which a child is willing to eat only certain foods.

neophobia Fearful of, or unwilling to try, something new such as a novel food.

1-year-old

DAILY ROUTINES *(continued)*

- Enjoys being read to; especially likes rhyming stories with repetition, such as *Llama Llama Red Pajama, One Duck Stuck, Five Little Monkeys, Bang! Bang! Toot! Toot!* and Dr. Seuss books; points to pictures and names objects.

- Likes to go on walks; stops frequently to look at things (like rocks, bits of paper, and insects); squats to pick up and examine objects; easily distracted; much dawdling, with no real interest in reaching any particular destination.

- Plays alone (solitary play) most of the time, although beginning to show some interest in other children; engages in a lot of watching. Participates in some occasional **parallel play** (play alongside but not with another child). Might offer play items to another child, but there is little cooperative (purposeful) play; the exception can be children who have spent considerable time in group care (Pursi & Lipponen, 2020).

- Seems to feel more secure and better able to settle down at bedtime if the door is left slightly ajar, with a light turned on in another room.

- Continues to nap; however, naps that are too long or too late can interfere with bedtime.

- Wakes up slowly from a nap; cannot be hurried or rushed into any activity.

learning activities to promote **brain development**

Toddlers learn primarily through play. They need to be given ample time and open-ended toys and objects to manipulate, experiment with, and explore in a safe environment. Simple, everyday objects and activities provide endless opportunities for learning about relationships and reactions and often prove to be the most interesting and appealing to toddlers (Figure 5-4).

Developmentally appropriate applications for families and teachers

- Respond to the toddler's jabbering and voice inflections, both in kind (playfully) and with simple words and questions; maintain conversational turn-taking; describe what you or the child are doing (this helps children to associate words with actions and objects).

- Encourage the toddler to point to familiar objects in picture books, catalogs, and magazines; name and count the objects and encourage (but do not force) the toddler to imitate you.

Figure 5-4 Simple objects stimulate toddlers' curiosity and imagination.

iStock.com/damircudic

parallel play Playing alongside or near another person, but not involved in that person's activity.

learning activities *(continued)*

- Hide a toy or other familiar object in an obvious place and encourage the toddler to find it (give clues as needed).

- Provide blocks, stacking rings, shape-sorting boxes, and nesting cups; such toys promote problem-solving and hand-eye coordination.

- Encourage frequent water play; the sink is always a favorite spot when an adult is working in the kitchen. (*Caution:* Use an absorbent towel or rug to catch spills and reduce the chance of slips or falls.) A plastic bowl or dishpan filled with an inch or so of water can be equally intriguing when set on the floor; adding a small amount of baby shampoo creates harmless bubbles; provide sponges, plastic cups, and small toys.

- Place favorite toys in different parts of the room so the toddler must crawl, cruise, or walk to reach them (thus practicing motor skills).

- Provide toys that can be pushed or pulled or a stable plastic or wooden riding toy to steer and propel with the feet; arrange safe, low places for climbing over, under, and on top of (label activities to help toddlers make connections). Avoid gender stereotypes when choosing toys (e.g., trucks are only for boys and dolls are only for girls). Offer toys that address a wide range of interests: boats, trucks, farm animals, books, art materials, dress-up clothes, garden tools, musical instruments, balls, plastic magnifying glass, play dishes, etc.

- Take short walks and talk about what you see (e.g., bugs, clouds, and colors); labeling objects along the way reinforces language development.

- Turn off the television. Young children learn from doing, not through passive activity.

- Encourage active play (e.g., running, pedaling, dancing) to promote healthy development, reduce the risk of obesity, and help toddlers release excess energy. Have them toss or kick a soft ball back and forth, blow and chase bubbles, or pick up and drop small objects (e.g., clothespins or blocks) into a bowl or bucket placed across the room.

TeachSource Digital Download

developmental **alerts**

Check with a health-care provider or early childhood specialist if, by twenty-four months of age, the child does *not*:

- Attempt to talk or repeat words.
- Understand some new words.
- Respond to own name or answer simple questions with "Yes" or "No."
- Walk alone (or with very little help).
- Exhibit a variety of emotions: anger, delight, fear, and surprise.
- Show interest in pictures; point to named objects when asked.
- Recognize self in a mirror (smile at, point to, or state own name).
- Make eye contact when responding to questions or making a request (unless this is a cultural taboo).
- Attempt self-feeding (hold own cup to mouth and drink from cup).
- Want any physical contact (i.e., to be held, touched, or picked up).

Note: Cultural differences may alter the timetable when some developmental skills are acquired. Expanded Developmental Alerts Checklists appear in Appendix A and also are available as digital downloads.

safety concerns

Continue to implement the safety practices described for the previous stages. Always be aware of new safety issues as the child continues to grow and develop.

Burns (Thermal and Electrical)

- Cover all electrical outlets with plastic caps.
- Prevent toddlers from touching hot objects such as oven doors, space heaters, water pipes, fireplace doors, outdoor grills, and toasters.
- Keep electrical appliance cords (e.g., computer, television, or curling iron) out of toddlers' reach.
- Apply sunscreen to prevent sunburns; dress toddlers in long sleeves and a hat if they are outdoors for long periods; protect their eyes against harmful ultraviolet rays with sunglasses.

Choking and Suffocation

- Remove objects and toys with small pieces (less than 1 1/2 inches [3.75 cm] in diameter) such as coins, watch or calculator batteries, marbles, pen tops, beads, buttons, magnets, gum and hard candies, paper clips, latex balloons, and plastic bags.
- Cut food into small pieces; insist that children sit down to eat; avoid foods such as popcorn, pretzels, hot dogs (unless cut crosswise and into small pieces), raw carrots, whole grapes, nuts, and hard candies.

Water Hazards

- Eliminate unsupervised water sources: swimming or wading pools, mop buckets, fish tanks, outdoor fountains, or other water features. Purchase and use locking devices on toilet seats; *children can drown in 2 inches (5 cm) of water.*
- Install a fence, gates, locks, and an alarm system to protect toddlers from wandering into unsupervised backyard pools or hot tubs.

Falls

- Place approved safety gates across stairwells; secure them properly to the door frame. Gates can also be used to confine toddlers to rooms where they can be supervised closely.
- Keep doors to the outside, garage, bathrooms, and stairwells locked.
- Pad sharp corners of tables and chairs.
- Eliminate tripping hazards: electrical cords, rugs, wet spills, and highly waxed floors; clear pathways of furniture and toys.

Poisons

- Store medications (e.g., vitamins, cough syrups, ointments, and prescription drugs), automotive and garden chemicals, cleaning and laundry supplies, cosmetics, and personal care products in a locked cabinet. (High shelves are not always safe from children who can climb.)
- Check for and remove poisonous plants from indoor and outdoor environments. (Contact a local county extension agent for more information.)

Strangulation

- Avoid clothing with drawstrings or ribbons around the head or neck.
- Limit strings on pull toys to no more than 14 inches (35 cm) in length; supervise their use closely. Remove toys, mobiles, or clothing with strings from the toddler's bed before sleeping.
- Fasten cords from curtains or window blinds so they are high and inaccessible to children.

The Two-Year-Old

This year can be terrific, but it can also be a challenge—for the child, family, and teachers. Exasperated adults often describe a two-year-old as impossible (or other words such as *demanding, unreasonable, defiant,* or *unpredictable* may come to mind). However, the two-year-old's fierce determination, impulsivity, and inability to accept limits are part of normal development and seldom under the child's control (Erdmann & Hertel, 2019) (Figure 5-5).

Two-year-olds face demands that can be overwhelming at times: new skills and behaviors to be learned and remembered, needs and feelings that are difficult to express, learned responses to be perfected, and puzzling adult expectations with which to comply. However, toddlers also are gaining an emerging sense of self-confidence as their developmental skills and awareness improve. This can result in moment-to-moment struggles as they try to resolve conflicting desires for independence (autonomy) or dependence (Erikson, 1959). Is it any wonder that two-year-olds are frustrated, have difficulty making choices, and say no, even to things they really want?

Most two-year-olds are able to identify themselves as either being a girl or a boy. However, they don't consider gender to be a permanent quality; they believe that it can be changed at any time simply by wearing different clothing or desiring it to happen. For example, wearing a dress makes you a girl, putting on a helmet or tie makes you a boy. Media exposure, adult expectations, and peer responses are continuously shaping the toddler's concept of gender and gender roles.

2-year-old

Although this year of transition may be somewhat trying for all, many positive things also happen. Two-year-olds are noted for their frequent and spontaneous outbursts of laughter and affection. They chatter nonstop, ask seemingly endless questions, and are on the go most of their waking hours. They are able to function more ably and amiably as newly acquired skills and earlier learning are consolidated.

New skills are learned quickly through trial and error, self-discovery, play, and hands-on-activities. However, the use of computers, child-oriented software, smart toys, electronic pads and game devices, DVDs, and television programming does not support this type of learning, nor does it give children any educational advantage at this age. Increased concerns have also been raised about obesity, sleep disturbances, inactivity, attention deficits, and language and motor delays associated with children's extensive media use during the early years (Gueron-Sela & Gordon-Hacker, 2020; Li et al., 2020; Supanitayanon, Trairatvorakul, & Chonchaiya, 2020). For these reasons, parents are advised to restrict children's use of all screen media (except for video chatting) before the age of two; screen time for children ages two to five should be limited to no more than one hour per day (AAP, 2019).

Figure 5-5 Toddlers often exhibit a strong sense of determination.

iStock.com/Sirichai Chitvises

Developmental Profiles and Growth Patterns

Growth and Physical Characteristics

- Gains an average of 2–2.5 pounds (0.9–1.1 kg) per year; weighs approximately 26–32 pounds (11.8–14.5 kg) or about four times their weight at birth.

- Grows approximately 3–5 inches (7.6–12.7 cm) per year; average height is 34–38 inches (86.3–96.5 cm) tall.

- Assumes a more erect posture; the abdomen is still large and protruding and the back somewhat swayed due to weak abdominal muscles that are not developed fully.

- Respirations are slow and regular (approximately 20–35 breaths per minute).

- Body temperature continues to fluctuate with activity, emotional state, and environment.

Did You Know ?

...most two-year-olds have now reached approximately 50 percent of their anticipated adult height?

2-year-old

Developmental Profiles and Growth Patterns *(continued)*

- The brain reaches about 80 percent of its adult size.
- Eruption of teeth is nearly complete; second molars appear, for a total of twenty deciduous (or *baby*) teeth.

Motor Development

- Walks with a more erect, heel-to-toe pattern; able to maneuver around obstacles in a pathway.
- Runs with greater confidence; has fewer falls.
- Squats for long periods while playing.
- Climbs stairs unassisted (but not with alternating feet), holding onto the railing for support.
- Balances on one foot (for a few moments), jumps up and down with both feet but might fall.
- Begins to achieve toilet training during this year (depending on the child's level of physical and neurological development), although accidents still should be expected; children will indicate readiness for toilet training (e.g., understands concepts of wet and dry, able to pull clothing up and down, communicates needs, and understands and follows directions).
- Throws a large ball underhand without losing balance.
- Holds a cup or glass (be sure it is unbreakable) in one hand.
- Unbuttons large buttons; unzips large zippers.
- Attempts to open doors by twisting the doorhandle.
- Grasps a large crayon with fist; scribbles enthusiastically on a large piece of paper or easel (Figure 5-6).
- Climbs up on a chair, turns around, and sits down.
- Enjoys pouring, filling, and dumping activities involving such materials as sand, water, small toys, or Styrofoam peanuts.
- Stacks four to six objects on top of one another.
- Uses feet to propel wheeled riding toys.

Figure 5-6 Two-year-olds hold chalk or markers in a fist when drawing.

alexxoral/Shutterstock.com

▶❚❚ **TeachSource Video Connections**

Assessing Motor Development

Toddlers become increasingly adept at controlling their body movements. They are able to manipulate objects with improving accuracy, assist with their personal care, walk and run with confidence, and draw with large, sweeping motions. These abilities serve as the foundation for more complex skills that the child will continue to develop. Respond to the following questions after you have watched the learning video *Observing and Monitoring Physical/Motor Development in Toddlers: The Importance of Assessment:*

1. Why is it important to assess the toddler's motor skill development in a naturalistic setting?

2. What is the purpose of asking parents to complete the same questionnaire that the teachers use for assessment?

3. Identify and describe three fine motor skills that the children performed in this video. What additional activities could you plan to reinforce a toddler's continued development of these skills?

Developmental Profiles and Growth Patterns *(continued)*

Perceptual-Cognitive Development

- Follows simple requests and directions: "Find your sweater," "Come here."

- Exhibits eye-hand movements that are better coordinated; puts objects together and takes them apart; fits large pegs into a pegboard, places large puzzle pieces in the approximate area where they should go. Children's vision should be checked if hand-eye skill development is delayed (Pinero-Pinto et al., 2020).

- Begins to use objects for purposes other than the intended ones (e.g., may push a block around as a pretend boat, use a box as a drum, or turn a bucket into a hat).

- Completes simple classification tasks based on a single dimension (e.g., separates toy dinosaurs from toy cars, crayons from markers, or red beads from blue beads, large blocks from small ones); this is an important development for learning future math skills.

Did You Know

...most toddlers are ambidextrous and use both hands equally well? Hand preference usually emerges between two and three years of age, with about 90–95 percent of children favoring their right hand.

2-year-old

- Stares for long moments; seems fascinated by, or engrossed in, figuring out a situation (where a tennis ball has rolled, where the dog went, what has caused a particular noise); however, often has a short attention span.

- Sits quietly and engages in self-selected activities for longer periods (Figure 5-7).

- Shows discovery of cause and effect (squeezing the cat makes her scratch or run away; moving the lever allows the patio door to open, rotating the faucet handle turns on the water).

- Knows where familiar persons should be; notes their absence; finds a hidden object by looking in the last hiding place first.

- Names objects in picture books; might pretend to pick something off the page and taste or smell it.

- Recognizes and expresses pain; can point to its location.

iStock.com/fizkes

Figure 5-7 Toddlers are able to focus on an activity for longer periods.

Speech and Language Development

- Enjoys being read to if allowed to participate by pointing, making relevant noises, and turning pages.

- Realizes that language is effective for getting others to respond to needs and preferences. Makes simple requests ("More cookies?"); refuses adult wishes, sometimes forcefully ("No!").

- Uses 50 to 300 words; vocabulary continuously increasing.

- Has broken the **linguistic code**; that is, much of a two-year-old's talk has meaning to them, but not always to adults (i.e., Lev Vygotsky's "self-talk").

- Understands significantly more language than is able to communicate verbally; most two-year-olds have receptive language that is far more advanced than their expressive language. Significant disparities in children's language development have been linked to mother's educational level and family socioeconomic status (i.e., fewer books, less verbal interaction) (Justice et al., 2020).

linguistic code Verbal expression that has meaning to the child.

2-year-old

Developmental Profiles and Growth Patterns *(continued)*

- Utters three- and four-word statements; uses conventional word order to form more complete sentences.
- Refers to self as "me" or sometimes "I" rather than by name ("Me go bye-bye"); has no trouble verbalizing "mine."
- Expresses negative statements by tacking on a negative word such as "no" or "not" ("Not more milk," "No bath").
- Asks repeatedly, "What's that?" "Why?"
- Uses some plurals, but not always correctly ("See the gooses"); often overgeneralizes grammatical rules. Talks about objects and events not immediately present, as in "We saw peoples." (This is both a cognitive and a linguistic advance.)
- Experiences occasional stammering and other common **dysfluencies**.
- Produces speech that is as much as 65–70 percent intelligible.

Social-Emotional Development

- Shows signs of empathy, caring, and helping behaviors (comforts another child who may be hurt or frightened); at times, can be overly affectionate in offering hugs and kisses to children (sociocultural differences and expectations may discourage or alter the nature of this behavior) (Corbit, Callaghan, & Svetlova, 2020; Stout et al., 2021).
- Continues to use physical aggression if frustrated or angry; this response is more exaggerated for some children than for others; physical aggression usually diminishes as verbal skills improve. Children's expressions of temperament are influenced through cultural socialization and, thus, are highly variable (Boziecevic et al., 2021; Senzaki, Shimizu, & Calma-Birling, 2021).
- Often expresses frustration through temper tantrums; frequency of tantrums typically peaks during this year; cannot be reasoned with while tantrum is in progress (Hughes et al., 2020). Adults can help toddlers begin to develop self-regulatory skills by providing positive attention and support when early signs of frustration become apparent.
- Finds it difficult to wait or take turns; often impatient.
- Eager to "help" with household chores; imitates everyday activities (might try to toilet a stuffed animal or feed and bathe a doll).
- Is bossy at times; orders peers and adults around; makes demands and expects immediate compliance.
- Watches and imitates the play of other children but seldom joins in; content to play alone.
- Offers toys to other children but is usually possessive of playthings; still tends to hoard toys.
- Finds it difficult to make choices; wants both options at the same time.
- Shows much defiance; shouting "No!" becomes almost automatic.
- Wants everything just so; is quite ritualistic; expects routines to be carried out exactly as before and belongings to be in their usual places.

dysfluency Repetition of whole words or phrases, uttered without frustration and often at the beginning of a statement, such as "Let's go, let's go get cookies."

What Do You See?

Perceptual-cognitive and social development. Toddlers are undergoing rapid and significant developmental changes. What typical perceptual-cognitive and social-emotional characteristics are the children in this photo exhibiting?

iStock.com/FatCamera

2-year-old

Spotlight on Neuroscience and Brain Development

Music and Brain Development

Music and music-related activities—dancing, singing, rituals, ceremonies—have played a central role in human cultures for millennia (Mehr et al., 2019). Music is often described as an expression of emotions that unites listeners and participants in a unique social bond.

Scientists have examined numerous aspects of music to determine if it has any noteworthy effect on the brain itself and/or expressed behavior. One conclusion is that exposure to music and formal musical training in childhood results in significantly better cognition and working memory (Saarikivi et al., 2019; Yurgil et al., 2020; Zhang 2020). Children who are exposed to music are also more likely to develop advanced language, math, and motor skills. Politimou and colleagues (2019) noted that even preschoolers who experienced informal and unstructured musical opportunities in their home showed better phonological awareness and grammar. They hypothesized that the rhythmic, melodic, and attention-getting features of music play an important role in facilitating children's early and continuous acquisition of complex language skills.

Imaging technologies have made it possible for neuroscientists to examine the human brain and determine what, if any, specific physiological effect(s) music may have on its structural and/or functional formation. Results indicate that music activates almost every region of the brain, including sensory, motor, auditory, emotional, and cognitive centers. Also, there is empirical evidence linking an individual's exposure to music and/or participation in musical activities with neurological differences. For example, Kim and colleagues (2020) noted that an individual's neural connections appear to change when they are presented with an altered melody of a familiar song. Habibi and colleagues (2018, 2020) reported that school-age children who were involved in formal musical training developed a thicker cortical layer (grey matter) and larger cortical volume in areas of the brain that respond to auditory stimuli. An increase in grey matter associated with musical training has been linked to improved memory and attention (Yahong & Wang, 2019).

Results from such studies have contributed to innovative and beneficial applications. For example, music is often used in neonatal intensive care units (NICU) to reduce stress and anxiety levels in premature infants and their parents. Background music therapy lowers heart and respiratory rates and improves infants' oral feeding (Akiyama et al., 2021; Standley & Gutierrez, 2020). Researchers have found that children who have autism spectrum disorder develop better communication, sensory, motor, and social interaction skills when they are involved in musical activities (Archontopoulou & Vaiouli, 2020; Mcgowan, Mcgregor & Laplatre, 2021; Pater, Spreen & van Yperen, 2021). Music and singing have also proven effective in supporting children's language learning processes and to be particularly beneficial with children who are dual-language learners (Busse et al., 2021; Nemeth, 2020). Music has also been used to stimulate and reestablish neural connections in individuals who have impaired consciousness (Shou et al., 2021).

Engagement with music and musical activities not only has positive effects on children's brain structure and functional development but is usually also an activity that children thoroughly enjoy.

What are the connections?

1. What aspects of development appear to benefit most from children's exposure to and involvement in musical activities?
2. What are some no- or low-cost ways that families can create a rich musical environment in their home?
3. What other applications might there be for using music to promote brain development?

DAILY ROUTINES

Eating

- Has fair appetite; requires only small amounts of food due to slower growth rate; interest in food fluctuates with fatigue and periods of growth (may cause children to be labeled as picky eaters); lunch often remains the preferred meal.

- Begins to develop strong food likes and dislikes (which should be respected); may go on temporary food jags, as discussed previously. Toddlers have a heightened sensitivity to textures and flavors, which may contribute to food refusal (Johnson et al., 2020).

- Prefers simple, recognizable foods; dislikes mixtures and often refuses new food items; wants familiar foods that are served in customary ways. Adult patience and repeated exposure to a novel food (8–10 times or more) often improve the toddler's likelihood of acceptance over time (Spill et al., 2019).

- Requires between-meal snacks, which should be of good nutritive value (fresh fruits and vegetables, cheese with whole-grain crackers, cereal, or yogurt), with junk foods limited.

- Feeds self with increasing skill; may be "too tired" or uninterested at times; gives up quickly when foods are difficult to manage or chew. Self-feeding and assisting with meal preparations often improve food acceptance (Moding et al., 2020).

- Has better control of a cup or glass, although frequent spills are likely to happen.

- Learns table manners through verbal instruction and by imitating those of adults and older children.

Toileting, Bathing, and Dressing

- Enjoys bath if allowed ample playtime (must *never* be left alone when bathing); tries to wash self; may object to being washed and squirm when being dried off.

- Dislikes, even resists, having hair shampooed.

- Wants to brush own teeth but isn't thorough (it is important that an adult always follow up the toddler's attempts). Provide a soft, child-sized toothbrush; apply only a pea-sized amount of fluoridated toothpaste to prevent toddler from swallowing too much fluoride (they are not yet able to rinse or spit effectively).

- Tries to help when being dressed but is not always successful; needs simple, manageable clothing; can usually undress self without much effort (Figure 5-8).

- Shows signs of readiness for bowel training (some children may have already mastered bowel control); uses appropriate words; becomes upset when pants are soiled and may run to the bathroom or hide behind furniture.

- Stays dry for longer periods of time, which is one sign of readiness for toilet training; other signs include interest in watching others use the toilet, holding a doll or stuffed animal over the toilet, clutching at diaper or pants, willingness to sit on potty for a few moments, expressing discomfort about being wet or soiled (Zero to Three, 2021).

Sleeping

- Sleeps between nine and twelve hours at nighttime.

- Still requires an afternoon nap; needs time to wake up slowly.

- Resists going to bed: however, is more likely to comply if given ample warning, maintains a consistent bedtime, and has a familiar prebedtime routine (with a bath, story, talk time, or a special toy) (Hoyniak et al., 2021).

- Takes a while to fall asleep, especially if overly tired; might sing, talk to themselves, bounce on the bed, call for parents, and make and remake the bed (again, these are ways of winding down).

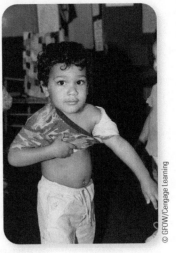

Figure 5-8 Toddlers often insist on dressing themselves, but they still need some adult help.

Play and Social Activity

- Enjoys dressing up and imitating family activities (wearing father's hat makes the child a "daddy"; putting on high-heeled shoes makes the child a "mommy").

- Likes to be around other children but does not always play well with them (observes intently, imitating other children's actions [parallel play] but is unlikely to join in).

- Displays extreme negativism toward parents and caregivers at times—an early step toward establishing independence; shouts "No!" or runs when asked to pick up toys, get ready for bed, or come to the dinner table.

- Pretends to have an imaginary friend as a constant companion; may carry around and talk to a favorite stuffed animal.

- Explores everything in the environment, including other children; might shove or push other children as if to test their reaction.

learning activities to promote **brain development**

Two-year-olds' interests are driven by movement, language, enthusiasm, and curiosity. Do things together and provide opportunities that strengthen existing skills and help children to develop new ones.

Developmentally appropriate applications for families and teachers

- Play games, such as large Lotto and picture dominoes, that encourage children to match colors, animals, facial expressions, and everyday objects.

- Offer manipulative materials to foster problem solving and hand–eye coordination: large beads for stringing; brightly colored cubes; puzzles; large, plastic, interlocking bricks; nesting toys.

- Provide toy replicas of farm and zoo animals, families, dishes and cooking and eating utensils, cars, trucks, and planes for sorting and imaginative play.

2-year-old

learning activities *(continued)*

- Read to the child regularly; provide colorful picture books for naming objects and animals, and describing everyday events; use simple, illustrated storybooks (one line per page) so the child can learn to "tell" the story; ask the child to turn the pages.

- Share nursery rhymes, simple finger plays, and action songs; respond to, imitate, and make up simple games based on the child's spontaneous rhyming or chanting.

- Set out (and keep a close eye on) washable paints, markers, chalk, large crayons, and large paper for the toddler's artistic expression.

- Encourage make-believe activities: save empty cereal and cracker boxes, plastic juice containers with intact labels, and recyclable bags for a pretend store; set out dress-up clothes and an unbreakable mirror; or provide plastic gardening tools and supplies.

- Provide wagons; large trucks and cars that can be loaded, pushed, or sat upon; a doll carriage or stroller; a rocking boat; or beanbags and rings for tossing.

- Create opportunities for musical enjoyment: encourage children to play musical instruments, invent and sing songs, dance, wave around scarves or paper streamers to musical rhythms, or pretend to be animals moving about.

- Play games that involve sorting simple objects: laundry (towels in one pile, socks in another); colored blocks (red in one stack, blue in the other).

- Let children help with household chores: dusting furniture, "washing" the car, sweeping the sidewalk, or "painting" with a brush and water.

- Go for walks; collect items to use for an art project; organize a parade; or play "I Spy" ("a brown dog," "a blue house," "something red").

TeachSource Digital Download

developmental **alerts**

Check with a health-care provider or early childhood specialist if, by the third birthday, the child does *not*:

- Eat a fairly well-rounded diet, even though amounts are limited.

- Walk confidently with few stumbles or falls; climb steps with help.

- Avoid bumping into objects.

- Carry out simple, two-step directions: "Come to Daddy and bring your book"; express desires; ask questions.

- Point to and name familiar objects; use two- or three-word sentences.

- Enjoy being read to; help to hold a book; name and point to objects.

- Show interest in playing with other children (watching, and perhaps imitating).

- Indicate a beginning interest in toilet training (runs to the bathroom, pulls pants down, and uses appropriate words).

- Sort familiar objects according to a single characteristic, such as type, color, shape, or size.

- Make eye contact when making a request or responding to questions (unless this is a cultural taboo). Failing to make eye contact may be an early sign of autism.

Note: Cultural differences may alter the timetable when some developmental skills are acquired. Expanded Developmental Alerts Checklists appear in Appendix A and are also available as digital downloads.

safety concerns

2-year-old

Continue to implement the safety practices described for previous stages. Always be aware of new safety issues as the child continues to grow and develop.

Burns

- Set the temperature of the hot water heater no higher than 120°F (49°C).
- Purchase and use protective devices on bathtub and sink faucets.
- Keep hot liquids and cooking tools out of reach.
- Check the temperature of metal surfaces on car seats and outdoor play equipment before allowing children to use.

Choking and Strangulation

- Continue to cut food (especially raw fruits and vegetables; hot dogs should always be sliced lengthwise first) into small pieces; insist that children sit down to eat; avoid popcorn, whole grapes, nuts, and hard candies.
- Avoid clothing with drawstrings or ribbons that could become entangled around a child's neck; do not provide neckties for dress-up clothing.
- Monitor and eliminate small magnets (e.g., refrigerator, dislodged from toys, stress-relieving adult desk toys or sculptures) from children's environment.

Water

- Supervise any accessible water source (e.g., wading pools, fish tanks, garden ponds or fountains, bathtubs). *Children can drown in 2 inches (5 cm) of water. Never leave children unattended.*

Play Environment

- Fasten bookcases, filing cabinets, dressers, and shelves securely to a wall or floor to prevent them from tipping over.
- Place toys and books on lower shelves so they are accessible to children.
- Keep the doors to the outside and stairwells locked.
- Cover electrical outlets and remove unnecessary electrical cords.

Poisons

- Store all medicines (including vitamins and nonprescription drugs), automotive and garden chemicals, cleaning supplies, cosmetics, and personal care products in a locked cabinet. (High shelves are not safe because young children are good climbers.)
- Check for and remove poisonous plants from indoor and outdoor environments.

Vehicles

- Never leave children alone in a car.
- Always securely fasten a child in a properly installed car safety seat.
- Insist that children hold an adult's hand when exiting a vehicle or walking where other cars are nearby.

positive behavior guidance

Adults are responsible for protecting toddlers from harm and teaching them about social and cultural expectations. Toddlers understand the world only from their own self-centered perspective, and they must learn gradually, through trial and error, how they are supposed to behave and fit in with society. This process requires ongoing adult guidance, patience, and nurturing support.

One-year-olds

- Acknowledge and encourage children's efforts, even if they aren't perfect: "I am proud of you for trying to put on your own shoe." "I know you tried hard to pick up all of the blocks."
- Minimize the need for rules by childproofing the environment.
- Maintain predictable routines and schedules so that children can anticipate what to expect.
- Set limits that are reasonable, developmentally appropriate, and necessary to protect children's safety.
- Provide short explanations and guide a child's actions: "Gentle touches" (take the child's hand and pet the dog); "No hitting" (pick the child up and move them to another area; distract or redirect the child's attention by offering another toy or activity).

- Enforce limits consistently so that the child understands your expectations.
- Ignore simple misbehaviors unless they are likely to cause someone harm.

Two-year-olds

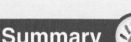

- Give children your undivided attention and let them know when they are behaving appropriately. Toddlers may misbehave to get adult attention.
- Recognize that children will forget and repeat undesirable behaviors.
- Accept the toddler's intense desire for autonomy. Whenever appropriate, offer a choice instead of insisting that they do things your way: for instance, ask "Do you want to wear the red shirt or the blue shirt?" or "Would you like to read a story or put a puzzle together after you put on your pajamas?"
- Choose your battles. Remember that toddlers may misbehave simply to get your attention. Ignore a negative behavior, so long as it doesn't cause harm to the child or to others. When the child is behaving appropriately, be sure to give them the attention that they are seeking.
- Set a positive example. Toddlers imitate the way that they see others behaving.
- Help toddlers to manage and defuse frustration by making a plan: "I know you want to keep on playing but it is dinnertime. What would you like to play after we eat?"
- Continue to set reasonable limits and consistently enforce them with care and compassion; focus on the behavior (not the child): "Blocks are for building, not throwing."

Summary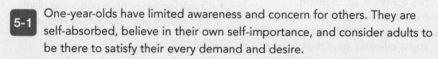

5-1 One-year-olds have limited awareness and concern for others. They are self-absorbed, believe in their own self-importance, and consider adults to be there to satisfy their every demand and desire.

5-2 Rapid changes occur in the motor development of one-year-olds. They learn how to walk unassisted, crawl up and down stairs, carry and manipulate objects, stack blocks, and help to feed themselves. Two-year-olds continue to perfect and elaborate on these skills: their locomotion is more deliberate and directional, they run and climb stairs unassisted, stack blocks higher, and learn to navigate riding toys.

- Toddlers' limited understanding of cause and effect, ability to judge size and distance, and grasp of functionality place them at high risk for unintentional injury.

5-3 Toddlers' language skills progress from using a single word to convey a complete thought to using two- or three-word sentences.

- Expressive language remains limited; receptive language is considerably more advanced.
- The toddler is beginning to grasp the concept of language and how it can be used for communication purposes: naming objects, making requests, and expressing wants and needs.

5-4 Two-year-olds are beginning to understand the concepts of size, shape, and position. They attempt simple puzzles, place objects in a container, begin to stack blocks and arrange items by size, etc.

5-5 Appetite wanes during the toddler years due to a slower rate of growth. Toddlers need less food (and fewer calories) per pound of body weight than they required as an infant.

Key Terms

autonomy **p. 113**

egocentricity **p. 114**

solitary play **p. 114**

holophrastic speech **p. 116**

telegraphic speech **p. 116**

receptive language **p. 116**

intelligible **p. 116**

expressive language **p. 117**

food jags **p. 119**

neophobia **p. 119**

parallel play **p. 120**

linguistic code **p. 125**

dysfluency **p. 126**

Apply What You Have Learned

A. Case Study Connections

Reread the developmental sketch about Darrius and his family presented at the beginning of this chapter and answer the following questions.

1. What language skills would you expect a typically developing two-year-old to have?

2. Do you consider Darrius's displays of anger and aggression to be typical or atypical of a toddler? Explain.

3. From a developmental perspective, explain why Darrius continues to get into his mother's kitchen cabinets and dresser drawers despite repeated warnings to stop.

4. Because Alandra sleeps in the morning while Darrius is playing, what special precautions should she take in their apartment to ensure his safety?

B. Review Questions

1. Describe two activities that would promote a two-year-old's developmental skills in each of the following areas: self-care, motor, and language.

2. Why do toddlers experience frequent tantrums or tantrum-like behaviors? In what ways would you expect to see a one-year-old begin to assert their autonomy?

3. Why are toddlers at high risk for unintentional injury? What steps must adults take to reduce this risk?

4. What is holophrastic speech? Provide three examples to illustrate this form of speech. At what age are children most likely to exhibit holophrastic speech?

5. Describe three activities designed to help two-year-olds learn about the concept of size.

C. Your Turn: Chapter to Practice

1. Visit the children's section of your local library. Select and briefly annotate ten to fifteen books that you would recommend for parents to read to their toddlers.

2. Make arrangements to observe an early intervention toddler classroom. Focus your observation on one toddler. Use the milestones in this chapter to assess the child's development in two different developmental domains. Prepare a summary of your observations. Provide two activities that would reinforce the child's skill acquisition in each of the two domains.

3. Observe a toddler classroom for approximately 30 minutes. Note how the teacher handles incidences of troublesome behavior. What strategies were used, and were they effective? What suggestions would you have for managing the situations differently based on the information in this chapter?

4. Develop a series of four or five activities that would reinforce and advance a toddler's manipulative and cognitive skills.

Online Resources

Centers for Disease Control and Prevention (CDC)

The Centers for Disease Control and Prevention (CDC) offers an extensive parent information site (enter "Parenting Information" into the search box) that addresses developmental milestones for children of all ages, safety tips, diseases and health promotion, parenting advice, videos for parents, and links to additional information resources.

Child Development Institute

Extensive coverage of child development topics, health and safety issues, current parenting topics, activities to reinforce learning, and behavior guidance tips can be accessed on this site.

National Autism Resource and Information Center

On this website, families, educators, health-care professionals, employers, and community workers will find information to help them work effectively with individuals of all ages who experience autism. The latest news, research, and resource library are provided.

Zero to Three

This national nonprofit organization has as its mission the promotion of infant and toddler health and development through funded research, advocacy for policies that benefit young children, and the dissemination of resource information for parents and educators. An extensive collection of video clips, podcasts, and articles on a wide range of topics can be accessed on this site.

References

Akiyama, A., Tsai, J-D., Tam, E. W., Y., Kamino, D., Hahn, C., Go, C. Y., Chau, V., Whyte, H., Wilson, D., McNair, C., Papaioannou, V., Hugh, S. C., Papsin, B. C., Nishijima, S., Yamazaki, T., Miller, S. P., & Ochi, A. (2021). The effect of music and white noise on electroencephalographic (EEG) functional connectivity in neonates in the neonatal intensive care unit. *Journal of Child Neurology, 36*(1), 3847.

American Academy of Pediatrics (AAP). (2019). *Health digital media use habits for babies, toddlers, & preschoolers.* Retrieved from https://www.healthychildren.org/English/family-life/Media/Pages/Healthy-Digital-Media-Use-Habits-for-Babies-Toddlers-Preschoolers.aspx.

Archontopoulou, A., & Vaiouli, P. (2020). Music and social skills for young children with autism: A survey of early childhood educators. *International Journal of Educational Research Review, 5*(3), 190–207.

Bastien, L., Tétreault, É., & Bernier, A. (2020). Disentangling the direction of associations between sleep and temperament in toddlers. *Behavioral Sleep Medicine, 18*(4), 523536.

Begum, A. J., Charman, T., Johnson, M. H., & Jones, E. J. (2020). Early motor differences in infants at elevated likelihood of autism spectrum disorder and/or attention deficit hyperactivity disorder. *Journal of Autism and Developmental Disorders, 50*(12), 4367–4384.

Boziecevic, L., De Pascalis, L., Montirosso, R., Ferrari, P. F., Giusti, L., Cooper, P. J., & Murray, L. (2021). Sculpting culture: Early maternal responsiveness and child emotion regulation – A UK-Italy comparison. *Journal of Cross-Cultural Psychology, 52*(1), 22–42.

Busse, V., Hennies, C., Kreutz, G., & Roden, I. (2021). Learning grammar through singing? An intervention with EFL primary school learners. *Learning and Instruction, 71,* 101372. https://doi.org/10.1016/j.learninstruc.2020.101372

Corbit, J., Callaghan, T., & Svetlova, M. (2020). Toddlers' costly helping in three societies. *Journal of Experimental Child Psychology, 195,* 104841. https://doi.org/10.1016/j.jecp.2020.104841

Diaz, V., Borjas, M., & Farrar, M. J. (2021). Is there an association between executive function and receptive vocabulary in bilingual children? A longitudinal examination. *Children, 8*(1), 44. https://doi.org/10.3390/children8010044

Erdmann, K. A., & Hertel, S. (2019). Self-regulation and co-regulation in early childhood – development, assessment and supporting factors. *Metacognition Learning, 14*(1), 229–238.

Erikson, E. (1959). Identity and the life cycle. *Psychological Issues, 1*(1), 1–171.

Florit, E., Barachetti, C., Majorano, M., & Lavelli, M. (2021). Home language activities and expressive vocabulary of toddlers from low-SES and monolingual families and bilingual immigrant families. *International Journal of Environmental Research and Public Health, 18*(1), 296. http://dx.doi.org/10.3390/ijerph18010296

Gandolfi, E., & Viterbori, P. (2020). Inhibitory control skills and language acquisition in toddlers and preschool children. *Language Learning, 70*(3), 604–642.

Gueron-Sela, N., & Gordon-Hacker, A. (2020). Longitudinal links between media use and focused attention through toddlerhood: A cumulative risk approach. *Frontiers in Psychology, 11*, 569222. https://doi.org/10.3389/fpsyg.2020.56922

Habibi, A., Damasio, A., Ilari, B., Veiga, R., Joshi, A. A., Leahy, R. M., Haldar, J. P., Varadarajan, D., Bhushan, C., & Damasio, H. (2018). Childhood music training induces change in micro and macroscopic brain structure: Results from a longitudinal study. *Cerebral Cortex, 28*(12), 4336–4347.

Habibi, A., Ilari, B., Heine, K., & Damasio, H. (2020). Changes in auditory cortical thickness following music training in children: Converging longitudinal and cross-sectional results. *Brain Structure and Function, 225*(8), 2463–2474.

Hadders-Algra, M. (2018). Early human motor development: From variation to the ability to vary and adapt. *Neuroscience & Biobehavioral Reviews, 90*, 411–427.

Hoyniak, C. P., Bates, J. E., McQuillan, M. E., Albert, L. E., Staples, A. D., Molfese, V. J., Rudasill, K. M., & Deater-Deckard, K. (2020, December). The family context of toddler sleep: Routines, sleep environment, and emotional security induction in the hour before bedtime. *Behavioral Sleep Medicine*, 1–19. https://doi.org/10.1080/15402002.2020.1865356

Hughes, C., Devine, R. T., Mesman, J., & Blair, C. (2020). Understanding the terrible twos: A longitudinal investigation of the impact of early executive function and parent–child interactions. *Developmental Science, 23*(6), e12979. https://doi.org/10.1111/desc.12979

Jeon, M., Dimitriou, D., & Halstead, E. J. (2021). A systematic review on cross-cultural comparative studies of sleep in young populations: The roles of cultural factors. *International Journal of Environmental Research and Public Health, 18*(4), 2005. https://doi.org/10.3390/ijerph18042005

Johnson, S. L., Davies, P. L., Boles, R. E., Gavin, W. J., & Bellows, L. L. (2020). Young children's food neophobia characteristics and sensory behaviors are related to their food intake. *The Journal of Nutrition, 145*(11), 2610–2616.

Johnson, S. L., & Moding, K. J. (2020). Introducing hard-to-like foods to infants and toddlers: Mothers' perspectives and children's experiences about learning to accept novel foods. *Nestle Nutrition Institute Workshop Series, 2020*(95), 88–99. https://doi.org/10.1159/000511515

Justice, L., M., Jiang, H., Bates, R., & Koury, A. (2020). Language disparities related to maternal education emerge by two years in a low-income sample. *Maternal and Child Health Journal, 24*(11), 1419–1427.

Kim, C. H., Seol, J, Jin, S-H., Kim, J. S., Kim, Y., Yi, S. W., & Chung, C. C. (2020). Increased fronto-temporal connectivity by modified melody in real music. *PLoS ONE, 15*(7), e0235770. https://doi.org/10.1371/journal.pone.0235770

Kim, S., Sodian, B., & Proust, J. (2020). 12- and 24-month-old infants search behavior under informational uncertainty. *Frontiers in Psychology, 11*, 566. https://doi.org/10.3389/fpsyg.2020.00566

Li, C., Cheng, G., Sha, T., Cheng, W., & Yan, Y. (2020). The relationship between screen use and health indicators among infants, toddlers, and preschoolers: A meta-analysis and systemic review. *International Journal of Environmental Research and Public Health, 17*(19), 7324. https://doi.org/10.3390/ijerph17197324

Marotz, L. R. (2020). *Health, safety, and nutrition for the young child* (10th ed.). Boston, MA: Cengage.

Mcgowan, J. J., Mcgregor, I., & Laplatre, G. (2021). Evaluation of the use of real-time 3D graphics to augment therapeutic music sessions for young people on the autism spectrum. *ACM Transactions on Accessible Computing, 12*(1), 1–41.

Mehr, S. A., Singh, M., Knox, D., Ketter, D. M., Pickens-Jones, D., Atwood, S., Lucas, C., Jacoby, N., Egner, A. A., Hopkins, E. J., Howard, R. M., Hartshorne, J. K., Jennings, M., & Si, J. (2019). Universality and diversity in human song. *Science, 366*(6468), eaax0868. https://science.sciencemag.org/content/366/6468/eaax0868?rss=1

Moding, K., Carney, E., Fisher, J., & Johnson, S. (2020). The role of self-feeding in food acceptance among toddlers. *Current Developments in Nutrition, 4*(Supplement 2), 1042. https://doi.org/10.1093/cdn/nzaa054_114

Morgan, L., Delehanty, A., Dillon, J. C., Schatschneider, C., & Wetherby, A. M. (2020). Measures of early social communication and vocabulary production to predict language outcomes at two and three years in late-talking toddlers. *Early Childhood Research Quarterly, 51*(2nd Quarter), 366–378.

Nemeth, K. (2020). Nurturing infants and toddlers with diverse language experiences. *Young Children, 75*(2), 90–93.

Pham, S., Lui, P. P., & Rollock, D. (2020). Intergenerational cultural conflict, assertiveness, and adjustment among Asian Americans. *Asian American Journal of Psychology, 11*(3), 168–178.

Piaget, J., & Inhelder, B. (1967). *The child's conception of space.* New York: Norton.

Pinero-Pinto, E., Pérez-Cabezas, V., De-Hita-Cantalejo, C., Ruiz-Molinero, C., Estanislao Gutiérrez-Sánchez, E., Jiménez-Rejano, J-J., Sánchez-González, J-M., & Sánchez-González, M. C. (2020). Vision development differences between slow and fast motor development in typical developing toddlers: A cross-sectional study. *International Journal of Environmental Research and Public Health, 17*, 3597. https://doi.org/10.3390/ijerph17103597

Pater, M., Spreen, M., & Yperen, T. (2021). The developmental progress in social behavior of children with autism spectrum disorder getting music therapy. A multiple case study. *Children and Youth Services Review, 120*(3–4), 105767. https://doi.org/10.1016/j.childyouth.2020.105767

Politimou, N., Bella, S. D., Farrugia, N., & Franco, F. (2019). Born to speak and sing: Musical predictors of language development in pre-schoolers. *Frontiers in Psychology, 10,* 948. https://doi.org/10.3389/fpsyg.2019.00948

Pursi A., & Lipponen, L. (2020). Creating and maintaining play connection in a toddler peer group. In A. Ridgway, G. Quiñones, & L. Li (Eds.), *Peer play and relationships in early childhood* (pp. 93–111). International Perspectives on Early Childhood Education and Development. Springer International.

Quinn, S., & Kidd, E. (2019). Symbolic play promotes non-verbal communicative exchange in infant–caregiver dyads. *British Journal of Developmental Psychology, 37*(1), 33–50.

Rantalainen, K., Paavola-Ruotsalainen, L., Alakortes, J., Carter, A. S., Ebeling, H. E., & Kunnari, S. (2021). Early vocabulary development: Relationships with prelinguistic skills and early social-emotional/behavioral problems and competencies. *Infant Behavior and Development, 62,* 101525. https://doi.org/10.1016/j.infbeh.2020,101525

Saarikivi, K. A., Huotilainen, M., Tervaniemi, M., & Putkinen, V. (2019). Selectively enhanced development of working memory in musically trained children and adolescents. *Frontiers in Integrative Neuroscience, 13,* 62. https://www.ncbi.nlm.nih.gov/pmc/articles/PMC6851266/

Senzaki, S., Shimizu, Y., & Calma-Birling, D. (2021). The development of temperament and maternal perception of child: A cross-cultural examination in the United States and Japan. *Personality and Individual Differences, 170*(1), 110407. https://doi.org/10.1016/j.paid.2020.110407

Shou, Z., Li, Z., Wang, X., Chen, M., Bai, Y., & Di, H. (2021). Non-invasive brain intervention techniques used in patients with disorders of consciousness. *International Journal of Neuroscience, 131*(4), 390–404.

Spill, M. K., Johns, K., Callahan, E. H., Shapiro, M. J., Wond, Y. P., Benjamin-Neelon, S. E., Birch, L., Black, M. M., Cook, J. T., Faith, M. S., Mennella, J. A., & Casavale, K. O. (2019). Repeated exposure to food and food acceptability in infants and toddlers: A systematic review. *The American Journal of Clinical Nutrition, 109*(Supplement 1), 978S–989S.

Standley, J. M., & Gutierrez, C. (2020). Benefits of a comprehensive evidence-based NICU-MT program: Family-centered neurodevelopmental music therapy for premature infants. *Pediatric Nursing, 46*(1), 40–46.

Stout, W., Karahuta, E., Laible, D., & Brandone, A. C. (2021). A longitudinal study of the differential social-cognitive foundations of early prosocial behaviors. *Infancy, 26*(2), 271–290.

Suizzo, M. A., Tedford, L.E., & McManus, M. (2019). Parental socialization beliefs and long-term goals for young children among three generations of Mexican American mothers. *Journal of Child and Family Studies, 28*(10), 2813–2825.

Supanitayanon, S., Trairatvorakul, P., & Chonchaiya, W. (2020). Screen media exposure in the first 2 years of life and preschool cognitive development: A longitudinal study. *Pediatric Research, 88*(6), 894–902.

Uhlenberg, J. M., & Geiken, R. (2021). Supporting young children's spatial understanding: Examining toddlers' experiences with contents and containers. *Early Childhood Education Journal, 49,* 49–60.

Watson, S., Costantini, C., & Clegg, M. E. (2020). The role of complementary feeding methods on early eating behaviors and food neophobia in toddlers. *Child Care in Practice, 26*(1), 94–106.

Yahong, C., & Wang, J. (2019). The effect of music training on pre-attentive processing of the brain. *Advances in Psychological Science, 27*(6), 1036–1043.

Yeary, J. (2020). Difficult goodbyes: Supporting toddlers who are coping with separation anxiety. *Young Children, 75*(3), 90–93.

Yurgil, K. A., Velasquez, M. A., Winston, J. L., Reichman, N. B., & Colombo, P. J. (2020). Music training, working memory, and neural oscillations: A review. *Frontiers in Psychology, 11,* 266. https://www.frontiersin.org/articles/10.3389/fpsyg.2020.00266/full

Zhang, S. (2020). The positive influence of music on the human brain. *Journal of Behavioral and Brain Science, 10*(1), 95–104.

Zero to Three. (2021). Potty training: Learning to use the toilet. Retrieved from https://www.zerotothree.org/resources/266-potty-training-learning-to-the-use-the-toilet.

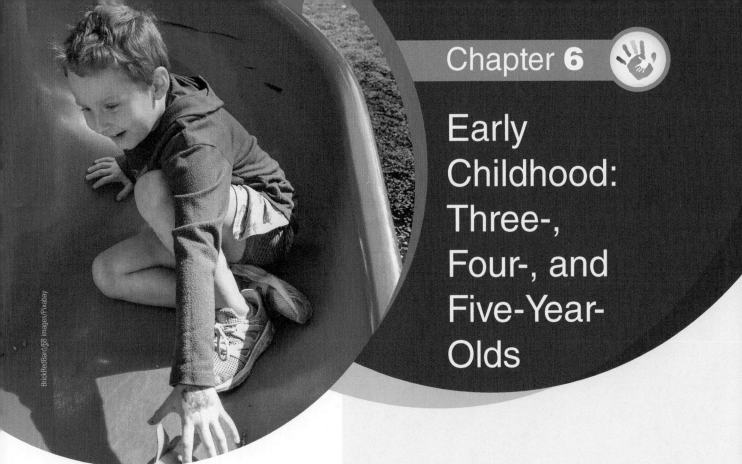

BrickRedBard98 images/Pixabay

Chapter 6

Early Childhood: Three-, Four-, and Five-Year-Olds

Learning Objectives

After reading this chapter, you will be able to:

6-1 Describe the changes that occur in children's cognitive development between three, four, and five years of age.

6-2 Discuss the preschooler's desire for adult attention and trace the ways that this need changes as children become more independent.

6-3 Identify at least eight ways that adults can support the preschool child's language development.

6-4 Describe the food preferences, eating habits, and caloric needs of typical three-, four-, and five-year-olds.

NAEYC NAEYC Professional Standards Linked to Chapter Content

1a, 1b, and 1c: Child development and learning in context
2a, 2b, and 2c: Family–teacher partnerships and community connections
3a, 3b, and 3c: Child observations, documentation, and assessment
4a, 4b, and 4c: Developmentally, culturally, and linguistically appropriate teaching practices
5a and 5b: Knowledge, application, and integration of academic content in the early curriculum

Hasina's interest in resuming her education was sparked after she attended a recruiting program sponsored by the local community college. When Hasina discovered there was space for her four-year-old daughter, Munisa, at the early childhood center on campus, she was even more determined. Hasina knows that Munisa's language and social development are delayed and believes that she will benefit from having more opportunities to interact with children her own age.

Each morning, Hasina drops Munisa off at the early childhood center while she attends classes and works in the school cafeteria. However, Munisa has been slow to adjust to her new school. She often prefers to play alone, seldom stays involved in any activity for more than a few minutes, and insists on carrying her security blanket wherever she goes.

It is important to Hasina and her husband that their daughter learns to speak Farsi as well as English. They know that Munisa is more comfortable and fluent conversing in Farsi and wonder if this may be contributing to her reluctance to interact with the other children.

Despite her busy schedule, Hasina sets aside time in the evenings to play with Munisa. They talk about things that she has done in school that day and sometimes work together on puzzles or art projects. Before Munisa heads to bed, they always sit quietly and read a story together. Hasina is becoming increasingly confident in her ability to encourage Munisa's development ever since attending a parent education class at the college. She now realizes how simple, everyday things she does with her daughter help to foster her brain development. Hasina thinks she would enjoy working with young children and is seriously considering becoming an early childhood teacher.

Ask Yourself

- Would you consider Munisa's personal-social development appropriate for her age?
- In what ways is Hasina encouraging Munisa's language and literacy development?
- What signs of stress is Munisa displaying as she adjusts to a new experience?
- What steps can Munisa's teachers take to support her transition and language development?

Three-, Four-, and Five-Year Olds

Three-, four-, and five-year-olds are typically full of energy, eagerness, and curiosity (Figure 6-1). They seem to be continuously on the move, engrossing themselves totally in whatever captures their interest at the moment. During these preschool years, children are perfecting their motor skills. They are becoming stronger, more purposeful, and precise in their actions as a result of increasing muscle mass and neurological maturation. These developments are essential preparations for the important fine motor tasks, such as writing, drawing, and manipulation, that lie ahead.

Creativity and imagination are evident in everything preschool-age children do, from their artwork and storytelling to intricate dramatic play. Vocabulary and intellectual skills are expanding rapidly, enabling children to express ideas, solve problems, and plan ahead. Grammatical errors and mispronunciations remain fairly common, especially among children who are dual-language learners (Pace et al., 2021; Troesch et al., 2021). For this reason, caution must be exercised when assessing a child who is bilingual for a potential language impairment or delay (Aikens et al., 2020).

The preschooler's vivid imagination also contributes to a heightened sense of fear and anxiety that often peaks during this stage (Bufferd, Dougherty, & Olino, 2019). Fear of the dark, of becoming lost, or of being left behind are relatively normal occurrences among children in all cultures. Nighttime fears or nightmares are often related to sounds (e.g., thunder, howling wind), concerns about intruders, or the presence of witches or imaginary monsters (under the bed or in a closet). Because preschool-age children are still in the preoperational stage of cognitive development, they attempt to self-explain things that are unknown. In other words, they are unable to think in abstract terms and, thus, create meaning based upon their limited experience and understanding.

Although children's reasoning may seem illogical to an adult, the anxiety they experience is real and must not be dismissed as non-existent fantasy. It is important that adults reassure children that they are safe and secure. They should also encourage children to talk about why they are afraid and involve them in identifying strategies (e.g., nightlight, door slightly open, a blanket or stuffed animal to hold) that may bring comfort. Most children will gradually grow out of this phase as their cognitive abilities become more sophisticated.

Figure 6-1 Children are exceptionally curious and inquisitive at this age.

The foundations of moral reasoning and moral judgment also begin to emerge during the preschool years. Advancing social-cognitive skills (**theory of the mind**) enable preschool-age children to develop empathy and to understand that other people have feelings, desires, fears, and expectations (Baker, D'Esterre, & Weaver, 2021; Paulus, Wörle, & Christner, 2020). Although they strongly believe in their own egocentric opinions, three-, four-, and five-year olds are becoming more adept at assessing a situation and forming a moral judgement about its fairness, honesty, and/or right or wrong. Their determinations are based upon social norms and values that are gradually being learned and internalized through a process of imitation, experience, and reinforcement (Huppert et al., 2019; Shimizu, Senzaki, & Cowell, 2021). Moral judgements, actions, and expressions also become more sophisticated with each year of advancing age. For example, Mammen, Köymen, and Tomasello (2018) noted that three-year-olds recognize and report when a rule or norm has been broken whereas five-year-olds provide an additional justification to support or defend their allegations.

Preschool-age children are also becoming more aware of concepts such as death and gender, but their immature cognitive abilities limit a comprehensive understanding. Children younger than five may acknowledge that someone or something has died but express hope that death can be reversed (Gutiérrez et al., 2020; Kronaizl, 2019; Longbottom & Slaughter, 2018; Schonfeld, 2019). They may feel some responsibility for having caused the death ("If I didn't open the door Rufus [pet dog] wouldn't have run away."). They also do not understand that all body functions cease upon death ("What if Rufus is cold at night?, "Who will feed him when he is hungry?"). By age seven, they understand death as universal and inevitable—that it happens to every living thing. Shortly thereafter, children can accept that all body processes end at the time of death.

Children's understanding of gender undergoes similar cognitive changes. Most three- and four-year-olds are able to identify themselves as being either a boy or girl. However, they also believe that gender can be changed temporarily by simply wearing different outfits or acting out different roles (Coyne et al., 2021; Hamlin et al., 2018). Researchers have noted that children's stereotyped ideas and behaviors are often reinforced through the types of play activities that teachers present and sanction (Alanazia, Alghamdib, & Alghamdic, 2020). Researchers have also found that young children tend to engage in activities they consider reflective of their own gender (e.g., girls feed dolls and cook food, boys fight fires and build houses) and to avoid those thought to be associated with the opposite gender. They are also more likely to establish friendships with gender-conforming peers, although girls exhibiting masculine behaviors are tolerated whereas boys who exhibit feminine-like behaviors tend to be ignored (Qian et al., 2020).

Preschool-age children continue to develop improved self-awareness, self-control, tolerance, and ability to make better choices. The degree of control and the age when these skills are likely to advance is highly variable and influenced by culturally-acquired norms and rules (Zhao et al., 2021). However, despite children's desire to gain independence, they continue to need reassurance that an adult is nearby to assist, comfort, mediate, and/or intervene if need be.

theory of the mind The ability to recognize and understand that other people have feelings, beliefs, emotions, and motives that may differ from one's own intentions.

3-year-old

The Three-Year-Old

Three-year-olds tend to be more peaceful, relaxed, and cooperative. Conflicts with adults that grew out of the two-year-old's struggle for independence are now fewer and less intense. Three-year-olds experience fewer emotional outbursts although temper tantrums may still occur when frustrations build. Children are more likely to comply with adult requests most of the time and to delay their need gratification longer than before. However, there are distinct gender and cultural differences in the expression of these behaviors and the importance given to developing compliance at a young age (Dong et al., 2021; Tan et al., 2020). For example, Silverman (2020) examined the results of studies conducted in ten countries. He found that universally, girls exhibit greater compliance than do boys. He also noted that girls tend to be internally motivated to comply, whereas boys are more likely to be motivated by external factors, such as disciplinary measures or the removal of a privilege.

Three-year-olds are also gaining better control of their body movements. This development enables them to attempt many new motor activities, such as walking across a balance beam, climbing ladders on play equipment, tossing and catching a ball, and pedaling a small tricycle. However, seldom do the three-year-old's limited motor skills and cognitive awareness match their level of enthusiasm. Thus, monitoring children's safety becomes paramount during this stage.

Three-year-olds are becoming more aware and accepting of others and, thus, are able to participate in group play for short periods of time. They willingly share and attempt to divide items equally among playmates (Decety, Steinbeis, & Cowell, 2021). They take obvious delight in themselves and life in general and show an irrepressible urge to discover everything they can about the world around them.

Developmental Profiles and Growth Patterns

Growth and Physical Characteristics

- Growth is steady, although it is slower than during the first two years.

- Height increases 2–3 inches (5–7.6 cm) per year; average height is 38–40 inches (96.5–101.6 cm), nearly double the child's birth length.

- Adult height can be predicted from measurements at three years of age; males are approximately 53 percent of their adult height; females are 57 percent.

- Gains an average of 3–5 pounds (1.4–2.3 kg) per year; weight averages 30–38 pounds (13.6–17.2 kg).

- Heart rate (pulse) averages 90–110 beats per minute.

- Respiratory rate is 20–30 breaths per minute, depending on activity level.

- Body temperature averages 96°F–99.4°F (35.5°C–37.4°C); temperature varies with exertion, illness, and stress.

- Legs grow more rapidly in length than do the arms, giving the three-year-old a taller, thinner, adultlike appearance.

- Head and chest circumference are nearly equal.

- Neck appears to lengthen as "baby fat" disappears.

- Posture is more erect; the abdomen no longer protrudes.

- Has a full set of baby teeth (20 teeth).

- Needs to consume approximately 1,500 calories daily.

Developmental Profiles and Growth Patterns (continued)

- Visual acuity is approximately 20/40, using the Snellen eye chart.

Motor Development

- Walks up and down stairs unassisted, using alternating feet; might jump from bottom step, landing on both feet.

- Balances momentarily on one foot.

- Kicks a large ball.

- Feeds self; needs minimal assistance.

- Jumps in place.

- Pedals a small tricycle or riding toy.

Figure 6-2 Three-year-olds now can hold a marker or pencil in a tripod grasp.

- Catches a large bouncing ball with both arms extended.

- Enjoys swinging on a swing (not too high or too fast); laughs and asks to be pushed.

- Shows improved control of crayons or markers; uses vertical, horizontal, and circular strokes; uses less pressure when drawing.

- Holds a crayon or marker between first two fingers and thumb (**tripod grasp**), not in a fist as earlier (Figure 6-2).

- Turns the pages of a book one at a time.

- Builds a tower of eight or more blocks.

- Completes simple puzzles with six to ten large pieces.

- Uses scissors to cut along a straight line although it may not be perfect. Plays with clay; pounds, rolls, and squeezes it with enthusiasm.

- Begins to show **hand dominance**.

- Carries a container of liquid, such as a cup of milk or bowl of water, without much spilling; pours liquid from a pitcher into another container.

- Manipulates large buttons and zippers on clothing.

- Washes and dries hands; brushes own teeth, but not thoroughly.

- Achieves complete bladder control, for the most part, during this time.

Perceptual-Cognitive Development

- Follows simple, two-step requests, "Find a book and come sit on my lap."

- Listens attentively to age-appropriate stories; makes relevant comments during stories, especially those that relate to home, family, and familiar events.

- Spends considerable time looking at books; may pretend to "read" to others by explaining the pictures.

- Requests stories with riddles, guessing, and suspense.

- Points with a fair degree of accuracy to correct pictures when given sound-alike words (*keys–cheese; fish–dish; sand–band; cat–bat*).

tripod grasp A hand position whereby an object, such as a pencil, is held between the thumb and first and second fingers.

hand dominance Preference for using one hand over the other; most individuals are said to be either right-handed or left-handed.

3-year-old

Developmental Profiles and Growth Patterns *(continued)*

- Plays realistically; feeds a doll, puts it down for a nap, and covers it up to stay warm; puts "gas" in the car (a chair) to take a trip (Figure 6-3). Hooks a truck and trailer together, loads the truck, and drives it away while making "motor" noises.

- Experiments with things to see how they work; takes objects apart and reassembles them into new "inventions."

- Places eight to ten pegs in a pegboard, or six round and six square blocks in a form board.

- Attempts to copy and draw circles, squares, and some letters, but imperfectly. Expresses interest in "writing" own name; produces markings and scribbles that are intended to represent letters.

- Identifies a triangle, a circle, and a square; can point to the correct shape when asked.

- Studies objects and sorts or orders them logically based on one dimension, such as color, shape, or size. Usually chooses color or size as a basis for classification (all red beads in one pile, green beads in another; arranges toy animals in a line from biggest to smallest).

- Shows understanding of basic size-shape comparisons most of the time; will indicate which is bigger when shown a tennis ball and a soccer ball; also understands the concept of *"smaller of the two."*

- Names and matches, at minimum, primary colors (red, yellow, and blue).

- Arranges cubes in a horizontal line; also positions cubes to form a bridge.

- Counts objects out loud; understands the concepts of *"more than," "less than,"* and *"same amount."* Holds up correct number of fingers when asked their age.

- Demonstrates understanding of prepositions (e.g., under, over, in, on, behind).

- Points to a picture that has *"more"* (cars, planes, or kittens) (Björklund & Palmér, 2020; van 't Noordende, 2020).

iStock.com/Mario De Moya F

Figure 6-3 **Preschool-age children are imaginative and engage in realistic make-believe play.**

▶❚❚ **TeachSource Video Connections**

The Preschooler's Motor Development

Three-year-olds have mastered most basic gross motor skills and now will concentrate their efforts on improving strength, accuracy, and coordination. Respond to the following questions after you have watched the learning video entitled *2–5 Years: Gross Motor Development for Early Childhood*:

1. What gross motor skills did the children display in the opening scenes of this video?

2. What gross motor skills would you expect a typically developing three-year-old to be capable of performing?

3. What indoor and outdoor activities could you plan to help three-year-olds practice and improve their gross motor skills?

Developmental Profiles and Growth Patterns *(continued)*

- Shows some understanding of duration of time by using phrases such as "all the time," "all day," or "for two days"; but some confusion remains: "I didn't take a nap tomorrow."
- Uses objects symbolically in play (a block of wood might be a truck, a ramp, or a bat (Bijvoet-van den Berg & Hoicka, 2019; Lee et al., 2019; Singh, 2021).

Speech and Language Development

- Recalls and talks about objects, events, and people that are not present: "Jasmine has a big dog at her house."
- Describes the actions of others: "Daddy's mowing the grass."
- Adds information to what has just been said: "Yeah, and then he grabbed it back."
- Answers simple questions appropriately.
- Asks many questions, particularly about the location and identity of objects and people (Figure 6-4).
- Uses an increasing number of speech forms that keep conversation going: "Why can't I?" "Where are we going now?" This characteristic is more common among children in Western cultures and less so in others (Liquin & Lombrozo, 2020; Rochanavibhata & Marian, 2020).
- Calls attention to self, objects, or events in the environment: "Watch me throw the ball far." "Look at my new shoes."
- Encourages the behavior of others: "Let's run in the sprinkler. You first."
- Joins in social interaction rituals: "Hi," "Bye," "Please," "Let's go."
- Comments about objects and ongoing events: "There's a horse"; "The truck's pulling a boat."
- Vocabulary has increased; now uses 300 to 1,000 words.
- Recites nursery rhymes; sings songs.
- Uses understandable speech more than 75 percent of the time.
- Produces expanded noun phrases: "big brown dog."
- Produces verbs with *ing* endings; uses *-s* to indicate more than one; often puts *-s* on already pluralized forms (*geeses, mices, deers*).
- Indicates negatives by inserting "no" or "not" before a simple noun or verb phrase ("Not baby").
- Answers "What are you doing?" "What is this?" and "Where?" questions dealing with familiar objects and events.

![Figure 6-4]

Figure 6-4   Children are inquisitive and ask many questions at this age.

iStock.com/kali9

Social-Emotional Development

- Seems to understand taking turns but is not always willing to do so (Figure 6-5).
- Laughs frequently; is friendly and eager to please.
- Has occasional nightmares and fears about the dark, monsters, fire, or being left behind.
- Joins in simple games and group activities, sometimes hesitantly.

3-year-old

Developmental Profiles and Growth Patterns *(continued)*

- Talks to self often.
- Identifies self as a "boy" or "girl"; often relies on physical appearance to make this determination about others (Hamlin et al., 2018).
- Observes other children playing; might join in for a short time; often imitates and plays parallel to other children.
- Defends toys and possessions; may be aggressive at times, grabbing a toy, hitting another child, or hiding toys.
- Engages in make-believe play alone and with other children (Chylińska & Gut, 2020; Thibodeau-Nielsen et al., 2020).
- Shows affection toward children who are younger or a child who is hurt.
- Sits and listens to stories up to 10 minutes at a time; does not bother other children who are listening to the story; becomes upset if disturbed or interrupted.
- May continue to have a special blanket, stuffed animal, or toy for comfort.

Figure 6-5 **Learning to play well with others takes time and practice.**

What Do You See?

Social inclusion. Learning to be part of a group requires special skills. What typical social-emotional behaviors are these three-year-olds exhibiting? What skills must young children develop in order to play and work together cooperatively?

DAILY ROUTINES

Eating

- Has fair appetite; prefers small servings. Dislikes many cooked vegetables; eats almost everything else; should not be forced to eat refused foods (Marotz, 2020).
- Feeds self independently if hungry. Uses spoon in semi-adult fashion; may spear food with a fork or occasionally resort to eating with hands.
- Eats slowly at times; plays with food when not hungry.

DAILY ROUTINES *(continued)*

- Pours milk and juice with fewer spills; serves individual portions from a serving dish with some adult prompting; "Fill it up to the line"; "Take only two spoonfuls."
- Drinks a great deal of milk. (However, be sure that children do not consume milk to the exclusion of other much-needed foods.)

Toileting, Bathing, and Dressing

- Helps to wash self in a bathtub but is not always thorough; often resists getting out of the tub.
- Brushes own teeth, but adults should continue to monitor and follow-up the child's brushing technique.
- Manages most of own toilet needs during the daytime. (Boys, especially, may continue to have daytime accidents, resulting in wet pants.)
- Some children sleep through the night without wetting the bed; others are in transition—they may stay dry at night for days or weeks, and then regress to night-wetting for several weeks.
- Is better at undressing than dressing, although is capable of putting on some articles of clothing, such as mittens, socks, and shoes.
- Manipulates zippers, large buttons, and snaps with increasing dexterity and skill but still requires some help.

Sleeping

- Sleeps 10–12 hours most nights; often wakes up early in the morning.
- Begins to give up afternoon naps; however, continues to benefit from a midday quiet time.
- Prepares for bed independently most of the time; has given up many bedtime rituals, but still needs a bedtime story or song and tucking-in.
- Has dreams that may cause the child to awaken; this is a common phase that usually passes. Maintain a consistent bedtime schedule and routine; read a story, play a quiet game, engage in storytelling; leave a hall light on.
- May occasionally get up and wander at night; quiet firmness may be needed to coax the child back into bed.

Play and Social Activity

- Wants to be included in everything; the "me too" age.
- Joins in spontaneous group play for short periods; very social; beginning to play cooperatively more often.
- Argues or quarrels with other children on occasion; adults should allow children an opportunity to try and settle their own disagreements before intervening, unless physical harm is threatened.
- Dresses up and participates in dramatic play activities that reflect everyday happenings (Taggart et al., 2020). Some children still maintain strong **gender** and role stereotypes: "Boys can't be nurses"; "Only girls can be dancers" (Hamlin et al., 2018).
- Responds well to options rather than to commands: "Do you want to put your pajamas on before or after we read a story?"
- Continues to find sharing difficult but seems to understand the concept.

Did You Know ?

…that you will spend approximately one-third of your lifetime sleeping if you get the recommended 8 hours of sleep each night? Your brain isn't taking a vacation during this time, though. It continues to work and process information while you sleep.

gender Reference to being either male or female.

3-year-old

learning activities to promote **brain development**

Three-year-olds are eager to learn, to be helpful, and to test their improving motor skills. Now is an ideal time to engage children in activities that foster language development, imagination, physical activity, and self-confidence.

Developmentally appropriate applications for families and teachers

- Limit children's video and television viewing to no more than two hours a day. All content should be developmentally appropriate; young children understand media as reality, not as fiction or entertainment. Active play promotes learning and decreases the risk of obesity.

- Encourage children to create new uses for safe household items and discards: a blanket stretched over a table to create a cave or tent; spoons for pretend cooking; discarded mail for playing post office or school; a hose with a trickle of water for washing a tricycle or wagon; a plastic milk carton for a floating boat; a paintbrush and water for "painting" outdoor structures; a cardboard box to turn into a rocketship.

- Provide more complex manipulative materials: parquetry blocks; pegboards with multicolored pegs; various items to count, sort, and match; construction sets with medium-size, interlocking pieces.

- Offer nontoxic art and craft materials that encourage experimentation: crayons, washable markers, chalk, play dough, round-tipped scissors, papers, glue, paints, and large brushes (supervision is required).

- Keep a plentiful supply of books about animals, families, everyday events, alphabet and counting activities, and poems and rhymes on hand; continue daily reading sessions. Ask children to retell stories using puppets, or have them create their own story ending.

- Make regular trips to the library; allow plenty of time for children to make their own book selections. Include some nonfiction books on topics that interest children, such as animals, the ocean, and planets.

- Spend time together outdoors: encourage active games—kick, hit, or throw balls; catch bugs; jump rope; fly kites, and play tag or hide-and-seek. Children should participate in at least 60 minutes of adult-led and 60 minutes of unstructured physical activity every day.

- Provide wheeled riding toys, wheelbarrow and garden tools, doll strollers, or shopping carts to build eye–hand–foot coordination (e.g., steering and maneuvering).

- Take children on walks, *at the child's pace;* allow ample time for children to explore, examine, and collect rocks, bugs, leaves, and seed pods; name and talk about things along the way. Plan walks around a theme: sounds, textures, colors, counting, etc. Have children display their found items: create a frame by painting the inside of a shoebox top; glue items to the cover and label (with help).

- Assign simple responsibilities for children to complete. Involve them in retrieving or putting away toys, classroom supplies, or clothing. Let them help to set the dinner table, put away groceries, wash the car, fill the dog's water bowl, or rake leaves.

TeachSource Digital Download

developmental **alerts**

Check with a health-care provider or early childhood specialist if, by the fourth birthday, the child does *not*:

- Have intelligible speech most of the time; have children's hearing checked if there is any reason for concern.
- Understand and follow simple commands and directions.
- State own name and age.
- Play near or with other children.
- Use three- to four-word sentences.
- Ask and answer "who," "what," and "where" questions.
- Stay with an activity for 3–4 minutes; play alone for several minutes at a time.
- Jump in place without falling.
- Balance on one foot, at least briefly.
- Help with dressing self.
- Engage in pretend play, using common objects for imaginative purposes.
- Maintain eye contact (unless this is a cultural taboo); the inability to do so may be a sign of an autism spectrum disorder.

Note: Cultural differences may alter the timetable when some developmental skills are acquired. Expanded Developmental Alerts Checklists appear in Appendix A and are also available as digital downloads.

safety **concerns**

Continue to implement the safety practices described for the previous stages. Always be aware of new safety issues as the child continues to grow and develop.

Burns
- Keep hot items out of children's reach.
- Place lighted candles, matches, and cigarette lighters where they are inaccessible.
- Monitor children carefully when outdoor grills, fireplaces, candles, or fireworks are lit.
- Turn water heater temperature down to no higher than 120°F (48.9°C).

Choking
- Avoid foods that can cause choking, such as popcorn, nuts, raw carrots, and hard candies; serve grapes and hot dogs only if they are cut into small pieces.
- Serve all foods in small, bite-size pieces and insist that children sit quietly while eating.
- Supervise children closely when they are eating items on a stick, such as a lollipop or popsicle.

Drowning
- Continue to supervise children closely when around any source of water; always empty wading pools when not in use.
- Fence in permanent pools; use pool alarm; keep gates closed and riding toys away from pool area.
- Learn cardiopulmonary resuscitation (CPR)!

Falls
- Insist that children wear sturdy, flat-soled shoes to prevent injuries when running and playing, especially outdoors. Shoes with hard or slippery soles and slip-on shoes or sandals increase the risk of tripping and falling.

3-year-old

Poisons

- Avoid the use of pesticides and chemicals on grass where children play; residues can get on hands and into sandboxes.
- Store hazardous substances, such as cleaning supplies, lawn chemicals, personal care items, and medications, in locked cabinets.

Traffic

- Insist on holding the child's hand when walking in parking lots or crossing streets.
- Always buckle the child securely into an appropriate car seat.

Spotlight on **Neuroscience** and **Brain Development**

The Gene-Brain-Autism Connection

Functional neuroimaging technologies, such as magnetic resonance imaging (MRI) and diffusion tensor imaging, are being used to study the brains of young children who have been diagnosed with autism or autism spectrum disorders (ASD) (Alvarez-Jimenez et al., 2020). The findings from these studies have consistently revealed abnormalities in the brain's structure, connectivity between brain cells, and neural network formation, including those involved in children's cognitive, sensorimotor, social, and language development (Cai et al., 2021; Fu et al., 2020).

Scientists in **genomics** and neuroscience are now focusing their efforts on identifying specific genes that may be involved in, and responsible for, these brain abnormalities (Hartig et al., 2021; Manoli & State, 2021; Quick, Wang, & State, 2021). Their ultimate goal is to determine the origins and cause(s) of autism and autism spectrum disorders and the effect that such alterations may have on behavior (Carroll et al., 2020). For example, why are boys diagnosed with autism earlier and at a significantly higher rate than are girls (Cariveau et al., 2021)? How robust or strong are the associations between abnormal neural connections and children's social behavior or language development? Are the observed neural alterations the cause or the result of abnormal connectivity? Why do children who appear to be on a typical developmental trajectory experience a sudden decline in language and social skills? What role might environmental factors play?

As is often the case, research findings raise more questions than they initially answer. What is becoming clearer is that autism and autism spectrum disorders are complex conditions that may not have a simple or singular answer. Additional studies are needed to pinpoint more specifically the underlying neurobiological causes. These findings, in turn, may contribute to the development of new diagnostic tools, earlier detection methods, and improved intervention strategies, such as the use of stem cells, non-invasive brain stimulation, new pharmaceuticals, and redesigned cognitive behavioral therapies, that are more effective than those currently in use (Carpita et al., 2020; Lamy et al., 2020; Liang et al., 2020).

What are the connections?

1. What behavioral signs of abnormal development might be observed in a toddler who is potentially autistic?
2. Why is early detection so important?

---

genomics The study of a person's genes, including their structure, function, environmental interactions, and role in health.

The Four-Year-Old

Tireless bundles of energy, brimming over ideas, overflowing with chatter and activity—these are the characteristics typical of most four-year-olds (Figure 6-6). Bouts of stubbornness and arguments between children and adults can be frequent as children test limits and work to once again achieve greater independence. Many are loud, boisterous, even belligerent at times. However, they are also better able to understand other peoples' perspectives and to express their frustrations with words rather than physical displays. They often try adults' patience with nonsense talk and silly jokes, constant chatter, and endless questions. At the same time, they have many lovable qualities. They are enthusiastic, eager to be helpful and to try new things, imaginative, and able to plan ahead to some extent: "When we get home, I'll make you a picture."

Figure 6-6 Four-year-olds are imaginative and busy much of the time.

iStock.com/PeopleImages

Although today's children are growing up in environments dominated by digital and electronic technologies—not just television, but also handheld games, computers, software, cell phones, Internet, videos, and "smart" toys—empirical evidence supporting their contribution to children's learning remains under investigation. There are also concerns about the amount of sedentary time that children are spending with these devices, especially with regard to obesity, and also their diminishing effect on imagination and creativity.

What we do know is that young children learn best through face-to-face social interaction and play with other children. During play, children develop critical verbal abilities, cognitive skills, and social-emotional competence. Hands-on opportunities to manipulate and experiment with real objects help children to build visual, spatial, and fine motor skills. However, scientists are finding that well-designed digital media can support some forms of learning when used in moderation and in conjunction with traditional educational experiences (Arnold et al., 2021; Griffith et al., 2020; Wang et al., 2021). Positive outcomes also have been demonstrated when children who have developmental delays, disabilities, or both use specially designed software and devices to reinforce learning (Grane & Crescenzi-Lanna, 2021; Whiteside et al., 2020).

Developmental Profiles and Growth Patterns

Growth and Physical Characteristics

- Gains approximately 4–5 pounds (1.8–2.3 kg) per year; weighs an average of 32–40 pounds (14.5–18.2 kg).
- Grows 2–2.5 inches (5.0–6.4 cm) in height per year; is approximately 40–45 inches (101.6–114 cm) tall.
- Heart rate (pulse) averages 90–110 beats per minute.
- Respiratory rate ranges from 20–30 breaths per minute, varying with activity and emotional state.
- Body temperature ranges from 98°F–99.4°F (36.6°C–37.4°C).
- Requires approximately 1,700 calories daily.
- Hears well; hearing acuity can be assessed by the child's correct usage of sounds and language, as well as by appropriate responses to questions and instructions.
- Visual acuity is approximately 20/30, as measured on the Snellen eye chart.

Developmental Profiles and Growth Patterns *(continued)*

4-year-old

Motor Development

- Walks a straight line (tape or chalk line on the floor).
- Hops on one foot.
- Pedals and steers a wheeled toy with confidence; turns corners and avoids obstacles and oncoming "traffic."
- Climbs ladders, trees, and playground equipment.
- Jumps over objects 5 or 6 inches (12.5 to 15 cm) high; lands with both feet together.
- Runs, starts, stops, and moves around obstacles with ease.
- Throws a ball overhand; distance and aim are improving.
- Builds a tower with ten or more blocks.
- Forms shapes and objects out of clay: cookies, snakes, simple animals, etc.
- Reproduces some shapes and letters.
- Holds a crayon or marker by using a tripod grasp.
- Paints and draws with purpose; might have an idea in mind but often has trouble implementing it, so calls the creation something else.
- Cuts along a straight line and six-inch circle with fair accuracy.
- Hammers nails and pegs with greater accuracy.
- Threads small wooden beads on a string.
- Transfers small objects with tongs or a spoon.

Perceptual-Cognitive Development

- Stacks at least five graduated cubes from largest to smallest; builds a pyramid of six blocks. Early spatial and assembly abilities have a positive correlation with future math skills.
- Indicates whether paired words sound the same (*sheet–feet, ball–wall*) or different (*ship–sheet, stop–start*).
- Names eighteen to twenty uppercase letters near the end of this year; some children may be able to print several letters and write their own name; may recognize some printed words (especially those that have a special meaning for them).
- Shows interest in reading; near the end of this period, a few children may begin to read simple words in books, such as alphabet books, with only a few words per page and many pictures (Benischek et al., 2020; Thomas, Colin, & Leybaert, 2020).
- Selects and enjoys stories about how things grow and operate.
- Delights in wordplay, creating silly language.
- Understands the concepts of "*tallest,*" "*biggest,*" "*same,*" and "*more*"; selects the picture that has the "most houses" or the "biggest dogs."
- Rote counts to twenty or more; has limited understanding of what numbers represent (Figure 6-7).

Figure 6-7 Children rote count but do not grasp the meaning of numbers.

iStock.com/SDI Productions

Developmental Profiles and Growth Patterns *(continued)*

- Understands the sequence of daily events: "When we get up in the morning, we get dressed, have breakfast, brush our teeth, and go to school."

- Begins to grasp the concepts of *"yesterday"* and *"tomorrow"* (Zhang & Hudson, 2018).

- Sorts, classifies, and patterns objects with various attributes, such as smallest to biggest; color and shape; or things that float or sink .

- Recognizes and identifies missing puzzle parts (of a person, car, or animal) when looking at the picture.

- Draws a person with three or more body parts.

Did You Know

...that children younger than four years have no long-term memory due to immature brain development? Their inability to recall early experiences is referred to as *infantile amnesia.*

4-year-old

Speech and Language Development

- Uses the prepositions *on, in,* and *under* correctly for the most part.

- Uses possessives consistently (*hers, theirs, baby's*) (Newkirk-Turner & Green, 2021).

- Answers "Whose?" "Who?" "Why?" and "How many?"

- Produces elaborate sentence structures: "The cat ran under the house before I could see what color it was" (Ronfard et al., 2018).

- Uses almost entirely intelligible speech.

- Begins to use the past tense of verbs correctly: "Mommy closed the door," "Daddy went to work."

- Refers to activities, events, objects, and people that are not present.

- Changes tone of voice and sentence structure to adapt to the listener's level of understanding: To baby brother, "Milk all gone?" To mother, "Did Ethan finish all of his milk?"

- States first and last name, gender, siblings' names, and sometimes home address correctly.

- Answers appropriately when asked what to do if tired, cold, or hungry.

- Recites and sings simple songs and rhymes.

What Do You See?

Concept and classification development. Four-year-olds are beginning to grasp the meaning of relationships or schema. What cognitive abilities are these children using to sort the objects by color? What additional types of learning could this activity be used to reinforce?

iStock.com/kali9

4-year-old

Developmental Profiles and Growth Patterns *(continued)*

Social-Emotional Development

- Is outgoing and friendly (cultural differences may reinforce or not encourage this behavior); can be overly enthusiastic at times.

- Changes moods rapidly and unpredictably; may laugh one minute, cry the next; tantrum over minor frustrations (e.g., a block structure that will not balance, difficulty tying a shoe); sulk over being left out or having a request denied.

- Holds conversations and shares strong emotions with imaginary playmates or companions; having an invisible friend is fairly common (Lev Vygotsky's self-talk) (Armah & Landers-Potts, 2021; Wigger, 2018).

- Establishes close relationships with playmates; beginning to have "best" friends (Figure 6-8).

- Boasts, exaggerates, and bends the truth with made-up stories or claims of boldness; tests the limits with "bathroom" or forbidden talk.

© GFOW/Cengage Learning

Figure 6-8 Four-year-olds often have a "best" friend.

▶❚❚ TeachSource **Video Connections**

Preschoolers and Language Development

Four-year-olds chatter endlessly and have much to say. They are learning how to use language for thinking, problem solving, and communicating their ideas to others. The ways in which children develop and use written and spoken language are highly influenced by cultural patterns. Respond to the following questions after you have watched the learning video *2–5 Years: Language Development for Early Childhood*:

1. What language development does the term *overregularization* describe?

2. What changes do most four-year-olds experience in language development?

3. What grammatical irregularities did you note in four-year-old Caroline's description of recent bowling and putt-putt golf experiences?

4. Would you consider her grammatical usage typical for a four-year-old? Explain.

Developmental Profiles and Growth Patterns *(continued)*

4-year-old

- Cooperates with others more often now; participates in group activities, role-playing, and make-believe activities (Jaggy et al., 2020).
- Shows pride in accomplishments; seeks frequent adult approval.
- May tattle on other children and appear selfish at times; still has difficulty understanding turn-taking in some situations (Marshall, Yudkin, & Crockett, 2021).
- Insists on trying to do things independently but can become so frustrated as to verge on tantrums when problems arise (paint that drips, paper airplane that will not fold correctly).
- Relies (most of the time) on verbal rather than physical aggression; may yell angrily rather than hit to make a point; threatens: "You can't come to my birthday party if I can't play with you."
- Uses name-calling and taunting as ways of excluding other children: "You're such a baby" or "You can't play with us."

DAILY ROUTINES

Eating

- Experiences periodic fluctuations in appetite; hungry and eager to eat at one meal, uninterested in eating at the next.
- Develops dislikes of certain foods and may refuse them to the point of tears if pushed (such pressure can cause serious adult–child conflict).
- Is able to use all eating utensils; quite skilled at spreading jelly or butter on bread or cutting soft foods such as bananas with a table knife.
- Talks while eating; eating and talking often get in each other's way; talking usually takes precedence over eating.
- Shows interest in helping with meal preparations (dumping premeasured ingredients, washing vegetables, setting the table).

Toileting, Bathing, and Dressing

- Takes care of own toileting needs; often demands privacy in the bathroom.
- Performs bathing and toothbrushing tasks with improved skill and attention; still needs some adult assistance and routine (subtle) inspection.
- Dresses self; can lace own shoes, fasten buttons, zip up jacket. Becomes frustrated if problems arise while getting dressed, yet stubbornly refuses adult help, even if it is needed.
- Likes to help with household tasks; is able to help sort and fold clean clothes, put clothes away, hang up towels, and pick up room; however, is easily distracted.

Sleeping

- Averages 10–12 hours of sleep at night, although the amount of sleep required varies from child to child; may still need an afternoon nap or quiet rest period.
- Bedtime is usually not a problem if cues, rather than orders, signal the time (when the story is finished, when the clock hands are in a certain position).
- Fear of the dark at night is relatively common for some children; a hallway light left on may be helpful.
- If children get up to use the bathroom, they may require help in settling back down to sleep.

DAILY ROUTINES *(continued)*

4-year-old

Play and Social Activities

- Playmates are important; plays cooperatively most of the time; can be bossy.
- Takes turns; shares (most of the time); wants to be with other children every waking moment.
- Needs (and seeks out) adult approval and attention; might comment, "Look what I did."; "See my boat."
- Understands and needs limits (but not too constraining); will abide by rules most of the time.
- Brags about possessions; shows off; boasts about family members. These behaviors are more typical in Western cultures and not always evident in others.

learning activities to promote **brain development**

Four-year-olds enjoy moving about, talking, engaging in make-believe, reading, and trying new things. Access to new learning experiences, a healthy diet, and ample opportunities to be physically active throughout the day are important for continued brain development.

Developmentally appropriate applications for families and teachers

- Join in simple board and card games (picture lotto, Candy Land, Red Light-Green Light!, The Ladybug Game) that depend on chance, not strategy; emphasis should be on attending, taking turns, and playing, not winning. (Learning to be a good sport does not come until much later.)
- Provide puzzles with five to twenty pieces (the number depends on the child), counting and alphabet games, matching games such as more detailed matching and dominos games.
- Offer a variety of basic science and math materials: ruler, compass, magnifying glass, small scales, plastic eyedroppers; encourage activities such as collecting leaves, raising worms, caring for ants or caterpillars, sprouting seeds, or measuring and recording the size of various food boxes.
- Appreciate (and sometimes join in) the child's spontaneous rhyming, chanting, silly name-calling, jokes, and riddles.
- Continue daily read-aloud times; encourage children to supply words or phrases, to guess what comes next, to retell the story (or parts of it) by telling what happened first, what happened last; introduce the idea of looking things up in a simple picture dictionary or online. Visit the library regularly, allowing the child ample time to choose books.
- Involve children in daily living activities: folding laundry, food preparation, selecting items in the grocery store, caring for a pet. Reinforce counting, language, and problem-solving skills while they participate.
- Encourage children's artistic interests: collect and paint rocks, turn household items into musical instruments, make a batch of homemade play dough, put on a puppet show, dance to music, or build structures from large cardboard boxes or an assortment of smaller food, shoe, or shipping boxes.
- Participate in 30–60 minutes of vigorous physical activity with your child each day: go for a walk; play in the park; ride bikes; provide balls for kicking, throwing, and hitting; enroll in swim, tumbling, or dance classes; play in the sprinkler or "swim" in an inflatable pool (*always requires an adult present*).

developmental **alerts**

Check with a health-care provider or early childhood specialist if, by the fifth birthday, the child does *not*:

- State own first and last name.
- Speak in three- and four-word sentences.
- Identify and draw simple shapes: circle, square, triangle.
- Catch a large ball when bounced (if children fail repeatedly, their vision should be checked).
- Speak and be understood by strangers (if there is a problem, have children's hearing checked to rule out a hearing loss).
- Have good control of posture and movement.
- Hop on one foot.
- Show interest in and respond to surroundings; ask questions, stop to look at and pick up small objects.
- Respond to statements without constantly asking to have them repeated.
- Dress self with minimal adult assistance; manage buttons and zippers.
- Take care of own toilet needs; have good bowel and bladder control with infrequent accidents.

Note: Cultural differences may alter the timetable when some developmental skills are acquired. Expanded Developmental Alerts Checklists appear in Appendix A and are also available as digital downloads.

4-year-old

safety **concerns**

Continue to implement the safety practices described for the previous stages. Always be aware of new safety issues as the child continues to grow and develop.

Burns

- Teach children the dangers of fire and hot items, such as outdoor grills/smokers, oven and fireplace doors, curling irons, and foods.
- Make sure smoke and carbon monoxide detectors are operational.
- Use cooking opportunities to help children learn appropriate safety practices.

Dangerous Objects

- Keep all chemicals, cleaning supplies, personal care products, medications, firearms, and dangerous tools in locked storage; curiosity peaks during this stage.
- Keep garage, storage shed, and basement doors locked until an

adult is nearby to monitor children's activity.

Falls

- Always insist that children wear a bike helmet and pads when biking or skating.
- Rethink the use of trampolines; many children sustain serious harm, including head and spinal cord injuries (Tileston & Raney, 2019).

Personal Safety

- Teach children their full name, address, what to do if they are approached by a stranger or become lost, and how to dial 911. Increased independence may cause children to wander too far from parents and teachers.

Toys

- When purchasing toys, evaluate their safety (e.g., rounded edges, not easily broken, nontoxic, nonflammable, no protruding wires, no electrical connections, and no loud noises).
- Avoid toys with small parts if there are younger children in the home or a school setting.

Suffocation

- Remove doors from an old freezer or refrigerator before disposing of it.
- Select toy boxes with removable lids or use open containers to prevent children from being trapped by a fallen top. Remove the lids from large plastic storage bins.

5-year-old

The Five-Year-Old

More in control of themselves, both physically and emotionally, most five-year-olds are in a period of relative calm and are becoming increasingly self-confident and reliable. However, their world is beginning to expand beyond home and family. Five-year-olds who attend kindergarten face a host of new challenges. For some, the transition is taken in stride and may be relatively smooth, especially if they have previously been enrolled in a high-quality early childhood program. Others may find the initial experience stressful but gradually adjust with parent and teacher support (Purtell et al., 2020). Jiang and colleagues (2021) noted that almost 70 percent of children, especially boys and children with disabilities, have difficulty transitioning to kindergarten.

Friends, friendships, and group activities involving both girls and boys are also becoming more important at this age (DelVecchio, 2021; Paulus, Christner, & Wörle, 2020). Lenz and colleagues (2021) noted that friendships begin to take on new meaning. Friends are selected on the basis of their trustworthiness and dependability in keeping secrets, sharing, and providing reliable information. The nature of these relationships is often reciprocal and may represent an important development in a child's ability to understand the social world. However, sharing and turn-taking continue to be difficult for some children. Five-year-olds expect others to share but are often unwilling to do so themselves; fairness is often seen only from the child's own perspective.

Five-year-olds devote much of their time and attention to the practice and mastery of skills across all developmental areas (Figure 6-9). They identify numbers and grasp their meaning, and enjoy tackling challenges and solving problems. They are beginning to use logical reasoning and evidence to form conclusions. For example, if a ball is hidden under one of three cups and it was not found under the first two, then it must be under the third cup. Most children begin learning how to read and write and are able to engage in fluent conversations. However, these skills may not be as advanced at this point for children who are dual language learners or from disadvantaged homes (Ansari et al., 2021).

Five-year-olds are exceedingly curious, energetic, and often fearless. They have a robust level of self-confidence but are unable to comprehend fully the inherent dangers or consequences of their actions. As a result, they experience a high rate of unintentional

© GROW/Cengage Learning

Figure 6-9 Practice leads to mastery.

injuries (Marotz, 2020). The risk is even greater for children who have developmental disorders (Agnafors et al., 2020; DiGuiseppi et al., 2018). Thus, safeguarding children's well-being continues to be of extreme importance. Adults must be on the alert, supervise children closely, anticipate their actions, and take measures to protect them from harm. However, it is also important not to create environments or situations that impose too many restrictions on children's play. Safe indoor and outdoor environments support children's active play and the mastery of important self-protection, language, social-emotional, and motor skills.

Developmental Profiles and Growth Patterns

5-year-old

Growth and Physical Characteristics

- Gains 4–5 pounds (1.8–2.3 kg) per year; weighs an average of 38–45 pounds (17.3–20.5 kg).
- Grows an average of 2–2.5 inches (5.1–6.4 cm) per year; is approximately 42–46 inches (106.7–116.8 cm) tall.
- Heart rate (pulse) is approximately 90–110 beats per minute.
- Respiratory rate ranges from 20–30 breaths per minute, depending on activity and emotional status.
- Body temperature is stabilized at 98°F–99.4°F.
- Head size is approximately that of an adult's.
- Begins to lose baby (deciduous) teeth (Figure 6-10).
- Body is adultlike in proportion.
- Requires approximately 1,800 calories daily.
- Visual acuity is approximately 20/20 on the Snellen eye chart.
- Visual tracking and **binocular vision** are well developed.

Figure 6-10 Five-year-olds may begin losing their "baby" teeth.

Motor Development

- Can walk backward, toe to heel; stands on tiptoes.
- Walks unassisted up and down stairs, alternating feet.
- Learns to turn somersaults (should be taught the right way to avoid injury).
- Touches toes without flexing the knees.
- Can walk the length of a balance beam.
- Learns to skip using alternate feet.
- Catches a bounced ball thrown from 3 feet (91.4 cm) away.
- Rides a tricycle or wheeled toy with speed and skillful steering; some children can learn to ride bicycles, usually with training wheels.
- Jumps or hops forward ten times in a row without falling.
- Balances on either foot for 10 seconds with good control.
- Builds three-dimensional structures with small cubes by copying from a picture or model.
- Reproduces many shapes and letters (square, triangle, *A, I, O, U, C, H, L, T*).

binocular vision Both eyes working together to send a single image to the brain.

Developmental Profiles and Growth Patterns *(continued)*

- Demonstrates fair control of a pencil or marker; begins to color within the lines; girls' fine motor skills are typically more advanced than boys at this age (Matarma, Lagström, & Löyttyniemi, 2020).

- Cuts on the line with scissors (but not perfectly) (Figure 6-11).

- Draws stick figure with six or more body parts.

- Establishes hand dominance for the most part.

5-year-old

Figure 6-11 Five-year-olds are able to cut fairly straight along a line.

Perceptual-Cognitive Development

- Follows three-step directions: "Pick up your toys, wash your hands, and put on your jacket so we can drive to grandma's house for dinner."

- Forms a rectangle from two triangular pieces.

- Builds steps with a set of small blocks.

- Understands and demonstrates the concept of "*same shape*," "*same size*."

- Sorts objects on the basis of two dimensions, such as color and form.

- Sorts a variety of objects so that all things in the group have a single common feature (classification skill: all are food items or boats or animals) (Lüken & Sauzet, 2021; Owen & Barnes, 2021). A child's conceptualization of categories may be highly influenced by cultural factors.

- Understands the concepts of "*smallest*" and "*shortest*"; places objects in order from shortest to tallest and smallest to largest.

- Identifies objects with specified serial positions: first, second, last.

- Rote counts to 20 and above; many children can count to 100 (Sella et al., 2020).

- Recognizes numerals from 1 to 10.

- Understands the concepts of "*more*" and "*less than*": "Which bowl has less water?"

- Understands the terms *dark, light,* and *early:* "I got up early before anyone else. It was still dark."

- Relates clock time to daily schedule: "Time to go to bed when the little hand points to 8."

- Shows interest in telling time; some children can tell time on the hour: five o'clock, two o'clock.

- Knows what a calendar is for; understands the concepts of "*today*," "*yesterday*," and "*tomorrow*."

- Recognizes and identifies a penny, nickel, and dime; beginning to count and show interest in saving money.

- Knows the alphabet; many children can name uppercase and lowercase letters and some letter sounds.

- Understands the concept of *half;* can say how many pieces an object has when it has been cut in half.

Did You Know

?

...that children will have heard between 3 and 11 million words by the time they enter kindergarten? Growing up in a literacy-rich environment increases word exposure and vocabulary size.

Developmental Profiles and Growth Patterns *(continued)*

- Asks innumerable questions: "Why?" "What?" "Where?" "When?"
- Eager to learn new things.

Speech and Language Development

- Has a vocabulary of 2,000 or more words.
- Tells a familiar story while looking at pictures in a book.
- Uses functional definitions (a ball is to bounce; a bed is to sleep in; a book is to read).
- States a fact and may include a justification: "Stop pushing, you are hurting me."
- Identifies and names four to eight colors.
- Recognizes the humor in simple jokes; makes up jokes and riddles.
- Produces sentences with five to seven words; much longer sentences are not unusual.
- States own birthday, name of hometown, and names of family members.
- Answers the telephone appropriately; calls an adult to the telephone or takes a brief message.
- Produces speech that is almost entirely intelligible and understandable to others.
- Uses *would, could,* and *should* appropriately.
- Uses the past tense of irregular verbs consistently (*went, caught, swam*).
- Uses past-tense inflection (*-ed*) appropriately to mark regular verbs (*jumped, rained, washed*).

▶❚❚ TeachSource Video Connections

Social Skill Development

Five-year-olds are imaginative, engaging, and social by nature. They usually get along well with other children, preferring to play with one or two friends at a time. However, they also can become bossy when things do not go their way. Respond to the following questions after you have watched the learning video *Preschool: Social Development, Cooperative Learning, and Play:*

1. What social skills must a child have to engage successfully in cooperative or constructive play groups?

2. In what ways can teachers encourage children's development of positive social skills?

3. What skills do children acquire as a result of group participation that cannot be gained from solitary play?

5-year-old

Social-Emotional Development

- Enjoys friendships; often has one or two special playmates (Wang et al., 2019).
- Shares toys, takes turns, and plays cooperatively (with occasional lapses); is often quite generous.
- Participates in group play and shared activities with other children; invents imaginative and elaborate play ideas (Chylińska, & Gut, 2020).
- Is usually affectionate and caring, especially toward younger or injured children and animals (Paulus, Wörle, & Christner, 2020).
- Follows directions and carries out assignments most of the time; usually does what the parent or teacher requests.

Developmental Profiles and Growth Patterns *(continued)*

- Continues to need adult comfort and reassurance but might be less open in seeking and accepting comfort.
- Has better self-control; experiences fewer dramatic swings of emotion.
- Likes to tell jokes, entertain, and make people laugh.
- Takes pride in accomplishments; boasts at times and seeks adult acknowledgment and approval.

5-year-old

What Do You See?

Friendships. Five-year-olds are quite sociable and enjoy spending time with friends. What social-emotional qualities have these boys developed to make this relationship possible? What other developmental skills are involved?

© GFOW/Cengage Learning

DAILY ROUTINES

Eating

- Has a good appetite, but not at every meal.
- Likes familiar foods; prefers most vegetables raw rather than cooked.
- Often adopts the food dislikes of family members, teachers, peers, or all three.
- Can "make" breakfast (pours cereal, gets out milk and juice) and lunch (spreads peanut butter and jam on bread).

Toileting, Bathing, and Dressing

- Takes full responsibility for own toileting needs; might put off going to the bathroom until an accident occurs or is barely avoided.
- Bathes fairly independently but may need some help getting started.
- Dresses self completely; learning to tie shoes; sometimes aware when clothing is on wrong side out or backward.
- Careless with clothes at times; leaves them scattered about and forgets where they were left; needs many reminders to pick them up.
- Blows nose with a tissue, but often does a careless or incomplete job; forgets to throw the tissue away; needs a reminder to wash hands afterward.

DAILY ROUTINES *(continued)*

Sleeping

- Manages all routines associated with getting ready for bed independently; can help with a younger brother's or sister's bedtime routine.
- Averages 10 or 11 hours of sleep per night. Some five-year-olds still may nap or rest quietly in the afternoon.
- Scary dreams and nightmares remain fairly common.
- Delays going to sleep if the day has been especially exciting or if long-anticipated events are scheduled for the next day.

Play and Social Activities

- Performs assigned chores and routines with few reminders; is usually helpful and cooperative.
- Knows the "right" way to do something and often has the "right" answers to questions; seems somewhat opinionated and rigid in beliefs at times.
- Remains attached to home and family; willing to have an adventure but wants it to begin and end at home; fearful that parents may leave or not return.
- Plays well with other children most times, but three might be a crowd: two five-year-olds often exclude the third.
- Shows affection and is protective toward younger siblings; may feel overburdened at times if the younger child demands too much attention.

5-year-old

learning activities to promote **brain development**

Five-year-olds are ready to take on more challenge and responsibility. They are drawn to activities that require problem solving, creative or artistic expression, or working with other children or adults.

Developmentally appropriate applications for families and teachers

- Provide inexpensive materials (newsprint, old magazines, wallpaper books, paint samples, or fabric scraps) for cutting, pasting, painting, coloring, and folding; turn a cardboard box into a loom for weaving or string instrument; offer easy sewing activities and smaller beads for stringing; gather wood scraps, glue, and tools for simple carpentry projects.
- Collect props and dress-up clothes that allow more detailed pretend play (e.g., family roles or occupations); visit and talk about community activities—house construction, post office and mail deliveries, a farmers' market; encourage play with puppets; assist in creating a stage. (A large cardboard box works well.)
- Continue to read aloud regularly and frequently; expose children to books on a wide variety of topics.
- Encourage children's increasing interest in paper-and-pencil, number-, letter-, and word-recognition games that they often invent, but may need adult help to play.
- Plan cooking experiences that involve children: washing and peeling vegetables; cutting out cookies; measuring, mixing, and stirring.

learning activities *(continued)*

- Set up improvised target games that promote eye–hand coordination (beanbag toss, bowling, ring toss, horseshoes, or basketball with a low hoop); ensure opportunities for vigorous play (with wheeled toys; jungle gyms and parallel bars; digging, raking, sweeping, and hauling).

- Create an indoor or outdoor treasure hunt. Write the names of common objects on a piece of paper (e.g., stone, leaf, bug, paper, toy, brush, and book) for children to find; alternatively, draw or cut pictures from a magazine. Talk about the characteristics of "treasures" that children have found: sizes, textures, colors, and function.

Developmental Alerts Box Here

5-year-old

developmental **alerts**

Check with a health-care provider or early childhood specialist if, by the sixth birthday, the child does *not*:

- Alternate feet when walking up and down stairs.
- Speak in a moderate voice—not too loud, too soft, too high, or too low.
- Follow simple three-step directions in stated order: "Please go to the cupboard, get a cup, and bring it to me."
- Use four to five words in acceptable sentence structure.
- Cut along a line with scissors.
- Sit still and listen to an entire short story (5–7 minutes).
- Maintain eye contact when spoken to (unless this is a cultural taboo).
- Play well with other children; listen, take turns, and offer assistance.
- Perform most self-grooming tasks independently (brush teeth, wash hands and face).

Note: Cultural differences may alter the timetable when some developmental skills are acquired. Expanded Developmental Alerts Checklists appear in Appendix A and are also available as digital downloads.

safety **concerns**

Continue to implement the safety practices described for the previous stages. Always be aware of new safety issues as the child continues to grow and develop.

Falls
- Monitor parks and play areas for potential hazards—broken glass, sharp objects, defective structures, holes, inadequate cushioning material under play equipment, etc.

Toys
- Refrain from purchasing toys that make loud noises, involve projectiles, or require electricity; battery-operated toys provide a safer alternative.

Traffic
- Teach street safety, especially to children who walk to and from school; review safety practices often.
- Use recommended car seats and safety restraints appropriate for the child's increasing weight and height.

safety concerns *(continued)*

Personal Safety

- *Never* leave children alone in a vehicle for any length of time; temperatures (hot or cold) inside a closed vehicle can become deadly in a matter of minutes. Unattended children also may be targeted by potential kidnappers.
- Teach children to run away and seek adult help if approached by a stranger. Tell them to yell, "You're not my mommy (daddy)." Establish a code word to help children recognize a trusted adult.

- Teach children water safety rules and how to swim.

Poisoning

- Use only nontoxic art supplies; check product labels carefully (see the Consumer Product Safety Commission website for product information and safety recalls).
- Remind children to always check with an adult before putting items possibly not meant for eating (such as pills or berries found growing on plants) in their mouth.

5-year-old

positive behavior guidance

Adults play an essential role in helping preschool-age children develop self-control. They must set behavioral expectations that are developmentally realistic for children, state them in positive terms, and enforce them consistently. It is also important that adults provide unconditional love and serve as positive role models for children.

Three-year-olds

- Set limits and use short, simple statements to explain why they are necessary.
- Acknowledge children when they are behaving appropriately. "That was nice of you to share your crayons."
- Remain calm and patient; keep your own anger and frustration under control.
- Redirect the child's activity: if the child is throwing sand, ask them to help you sweep the sand back into the sandbox.

Four-year-olds

- Offer choices: "Do you want to wear your sandals or sneakers?"
- Explain natural consequences to help children understand the outcomes of their actions: "If you spill the paint, there won't be any left for our picture." "If you bump into the other children with your bike, you will need to leave the area."
- Provide simple directions and warnings so that children know what to expect next: "Lunch will be served in a few minutes, so we need to begin picking up the toys now."

Five-year-olds

- Involve children in problem solving: "Which toy do you think your brother would like?" "Where should we look for your jacket?"
- Remove children from an activity if inappropriate behavior continues and give them time alone to think about their actions.
- Include children in setting rules to increase compliance: "What should we do if someone pushes another child?"

Summary

6-1 Preschoolers undergo remarkable advancements in their cognitive abilities:
- Three-year-olds listen, imitate, and understand basic concepts (e.g., bigger, smaller, more, less, etc.).
- Four-year-olds recognize letters and numbers and begin to understand their meaning, classify objects, answer questions correctly, and create imaginative stories.
- Five-year-olds have grasped more advanced concepts such as telling time, understanding a calendar, expressing complex thoughts, and classifying objects based on more than one dimension.

6-2 Preschool-age children want and continue to need a great deal of adult support, reassurance, and approval, although this becomes less significant as they move out of the preschool and into the primary school years.

6-3 Adults serve an important role in promoting children's early language skills through interactive conversation, reading stories, singing songs, asking questions, and encouraging storytelling.

6-4 Eating patterns change during the preschool years. Three-year-olds are learning to use utensils and require some adult assistance during meals; four-year-olds are able to manage most eating skills with minimal help, are easily distracted, and enjoy helping with food preparations; five-year-olds typically have a good appetite and have developed an awareness and interest in food options.

Key Terms

theory of the mind **p. 139**   hand dominance **p. 141**   genomics **p. 148**

tripod grasp **p. 141**   gender **p. 145**   binocular vision **p. 157**

Apply What You Have Learned

A. Case Study Connections

Reread the developmental sketch about Hasina and Munisa presented at the beginning of this chapter and answer the following questions.

1. Assuming that Munisa's motor development is progressing typically, what skills would you expect to observe?

2. What social behaviors would be characteristic of a four-year-old?

3. How would you respond to Hasina if she asked, "How much responsibility can I expect Munisa to assume for her own personal care at this age?"

4. What activities, in addition to reading bedtime stories, might Hasina engage in to further Munisa's language development?

B. Review Questions

1. Compare and contrast the motor skills of a three- and five-year-old child.

2. Describe three major speech and language skills that emerge between three and five years of age (in the order in which they should develop).

3. What self-help skills would you expect a typically developing four-year-old to be capable of performing?

4. Should a teacher be concerned about a four-year-old who exhibits frequent mood swings or often tattles? Why or why not?

5. Describe how a teacher might use a cooking activity to promote five-year-olds' perceptual-cognitive development.

6. Why are preschool-age children more likely than younger children to experience fears and nightmares?

C. Your Turn: Chapter to Practice

1. Interview the parent of a preschool-age child. Find out what behavior(s) the child's parent(s) finds most challenging or troublesome. What seems to trigger the behavior(s)? How does the parent manage the behavior(s), and is the approach effective in achieving the parent's desired outcome?

2. Develop an activity that teaches a three-year-old the concepts of *small*, *smaller*, and *smallest*, and present it to several children. Were you successful in teaching the concepts? What would you change if you were to repeat the learning activity at another time?

3. Interview the parent of a preschool-age child who has special developmental needs. What specific concerns does the parent have about the child's developmental progress? What short- and long-term goals does the parent hope the child can achieve? Conduct a second interview with a parent of a preschool-age child who is developmentally advanced for their age and ask the same questions. In what ways are the parents' objectives similar and different?

Online Resources

Canadian Paediatric Society

The Canadian Paediatric Society is a national advocacy association comprised of pediatricians. Their website, *Caring for Kids*, provides access to a wealth of information for parents on topics related to children's development, behavior and behavior management, safety, mental health, nutrition, health conditions, etc. Their goal is to promote children's healthy development and lifestyle behaviors.

Council for Exceptional Children (CEC)

The Council for Exceptional Children (CEC) is the largest international professional organization dedicated to advocating and improving educational outcomes for persons with exceptionalities, disabilities, or giftedness. Extensive resources, including podcasts, videos, curriculum resources, and practical tools to help educators improve their practice, are accessible on this website.

National Association for Bilingual Education (NABE)

This organization advocates for the "educational equity and excellence of bilingual/ multilingual students." It currently has more than twenty special interest groups devoted to children from early childhood through higher education, educators, policy makers, parents, and researchers. The Weekly eNews page includes articles of general interest and developing trends.

Society for Research on Child Development (SRCD)

The Society for Research on Child Development (SRCD) has a longstanding history of supporting and disseminating interdisciplinary child development research. It publishes three journals that are distributed worldwide: *Child Development, Child Development Perspectives,* and *Monographs in addition to Social Policy Reports.*

U.S. Consumer Product Safety Commission (CPSC) (*Safety Education: Safety Guides*)

The CPSC provides excellent safety guidelines that address a variety of topics especially relevant for young children—from toys and furniture to clothing and pool safety. Up-to-date product recalls are also provided.

References

Agnafors, S., Torgerson, J., Rusner, M., & Kjellström, A. N. (2020). Injuries in children and adolescents with psychiatric disorders. *BMC Public Health, 20*(1), 1273. https://doi.org/10.1186/s12889-020-09283-3

Aikens, N., West, J., McKee, K., Moiduddin, E., Atkins-Burnett, S., & Xue, Y. (2020). Screening approaches for determining the language of assessment for dual language learners: Evidence from Head Start and a universal preschool initiative. *Early Childhood Research Quarterly, 51* (2nd quarter), 39–54.

Alanazia, D., Alghamdib, R., & Alghamdic, A. (2020). Teacher perceptions of gender roles, socialization, and culture during children's physical play. *International Journal of the Whole Child, 5*(1), 28–38.

Alvarez-Jimenez C., Múnera-Garzón, N., Zuluaga, M. A., Velasco, N. F., & Romero, E. (2020). Autism spectrum disorder characterization in children by capturing local-regional brain changes in MRI. *Medical Physics, 47*(1), 119131. https://doi.org/10.1002/mp.13901

Ansari, A., Pianta, R. C., Whittaker, J. E., Vitiello, V., & Ruzek, E. (2021). Enrollment in public-prekindergarten and school readiness skills at kindergarten entry: Differential associations by home language, income, and program characteristics. *Early Childhood Research Quarterly, 54*, 60–71.

Armah, A., & Landers-Potts, M. (2021). A review of imaginary companions and their implications for development. *Imagination, Cognition and Personality.* https://doi.org/10.1177/0276236621999324

Arnold, D. H., Chary, M., Gair, S. L., Helm, A. F., Herman, R., Kang, S., & Lokhandwala, S. (2021). A randomized controlled trial of an educational app to improve preschoolers' emergent literacy skills. *Journal of Children and Media, 15*(1), 1–19.

Baker, E. R., D'Esterre, A. P., & Weaver, J. P. (2021). Executive function and Theory of Mind in explaining young children's moral reasoning: A test of the Hierarchical Competing Systems Model. *Cognitive Development, 58*(1), 101035. https://doi.org/10.1016/j.cogdev.2021.101035

Benischek, A., Long, X., Rohr, C. S., Bray, S., Dewey, D., & Lebel, C. (2020). Pre-reading language abilities and the brain's functional reading network in young children. *NeuroImage, 217*, 116903. https://doi.org/10.1016/j.neuroimage.2020.116903

Bijvoet-van den Berg, S., & Hoicka, E. (2019). Preschoolers understand and generate pretend actions using object substitution. *Journal of Experimental Child Psychology, 177*, 313–334.

Björklund, C., & Palmér, H. (2020). Preschoolers' reasoning about numbers in picture books. *Mathematical Thinking and Learning, 22*(3), 195–213.

Bufferd, S. J., Dougherty, L. R., & Olino, T. M. (2019). Mapping the frequency and severity of anxiety behaviors in preschool-aged children. *Journal of Anxiety Disorders, 63*, 9–17.

Cai, S., Wang, X., Yang, F., Chen, D., & Huang, L. (2021). Differences in brain structural covariance network characteristics in children and adults with autism spectrum disorder. *Autism Research, 14*(2), 265–275.

Cariveau, T., McCracken, C. E., Bradshaw, J., Postorino, V., Shillingsburg, M. A., McDougle, C. J., Aman, M. G., McCracken, J. T., Tierney, E., Johnson, C., Lecavalier, L., Smith, T., Swiezy, N. B., King, B. H., Hollander, E., Sikich, L., Vitiello, B., & Scahill, L. (2021). Gender differences in treatment-seeking youth with autism and autism-spectrum disorder. *Journal of Child and Family Studies, 30*, 784–792.

Carpita, B., Marazziti, D., Palego, L., Giannaccini, G., Betti, L., & Dell'Osso, L. (2020). Microbiota, immune system and autism spectrum disorders: An integrative model towards novel treatment options. *Current Medicinal Chemistry, 27*(31), 5119–5136.

Carroll, L., Braeutigam, S., Dawes, J. M., Krsnik, Z., Kostovic, I., Coutinho, E., Dewing, J. M., Horton, C. A., Gomez-Nicola, D., & Menassa, D. A. (2020). Autism spectrum disorders: Multiple routes to, and multiple consequences of, abnormal synaptic function and connectivity. *The Neuroscientist, 27*(1), 10–29.

Chylińska, M., & Gut, A. (2020). Pretend play as a creative action: On the exploratory and evaluative features of children's pretense. *Theory & Psychology, 30*(4), 548–566.

Coyne, S. M., Rogers, A., Shawcroft, J., & Hurst, J. L. (2021). Dressing up with Disney and make-believe with Marvel: The impact of gendered costumes on gender typing, prosocial behavior and perseverance during early childhood. *Sex Roles*, 1–13. https://doi.org/10.1007/s11199-020-01217-y

Decety, J., Steinbeis, N., & Cowell, J. M. (2021). The neurodevelopment of social preferences in early childhood. *Current Opinion in Neurobiology, 68*, 23–28.

DelVecchio, B. L. (2021). We're not all friends here (and that's okay). *Young Children, 76*(1), 73–77.

DiGuiseppi, C., Levy, S. E., Sabourin, K. R., Soke, G. N., Rosenberg, S., Lee, L-C., Moody, E., & Schieve, L. A. (2018). Injuries in children with autism spectrum disorder: Study to explore early development (SEED). *Journal of Autism and Developmental Disorders, 48*(2), 461–472.

Dong, S., Dubas, J. S., Deković, M., Wand, Z., van Aken, M. A., & Wu, M. (2021). Committed compliance and maternal parenting behaviors predict internalization of rules and externalizing behaviors in Chinese preschool children. *Early Education and Development, 32*(3). https://doi.org/10.1080/10409289.2020.1857168

Fu, L., Wang, Y., Fang, H., Xiao, X., Xiao, T., Li, Y., Li, C., Wu, Q., Chu, K., Xiao, C., & Ke, X. (2020). Longitudinal study of brain asymmetries in autism and developmental delays aged 2–5 years. *Neuroscience, 432,* 137–149.

Grane, M., & Crescenzi-Lanna, L. (2021). Improving the interaction design of apps for children with special educational needs. *Journal of Educational Multimedia and Hypermedia, 30*(2), 139–164.

Griffith, S. F., Hagan, M. B., Heymann, P., Heflin, B., & Bagner, D. M. (2020). Apps as learning tools: A systematic review. *Pediatrics, 145*(1), e20191579. https://doi.org/10.1542/peds.2019-1579

Gutiérrez, I. T., Menendez, D., Jiang, M. J., Hernandez, I. G., Miller, P., & Rosengren, K. S. (2020). Embracing death: Mexican parent and child perspectives on death. *Child Development, 91*(2), e491–e511. https://doi.org/10.1111/cdev.13263

Hamlin, M. L. D., Gutierrez, B. C., Bryant, D. N., Arredondo, M., & Takesako, K. (2018). Gender is what you look like: Emerging gender identities in young children and preoccupation with appearance. *Self and Identity, 17*(4), 455–466.

Hartig, R., Wolf, D., Schmeisser, M. J., & Kelsch, W. (2021). Genetic influences of autism candidate genes on circuit wiring and olfactory decoding. *Cell and Tissue Research, 383*(1), 581–595.

Huppert, E., Cowell, J. M., Cheng, Y., Contreras-Ibáñez, C., Gomez-Sicard, N., Gonzalez-Gadea, M. L., Huepe, D., Ibanez, A., Lee, K., Mahasneh, R., Malcolm-Smith, S., Salas, N., Selcuk, B., Tungodden, B., Wong, A., Zhou, X., & Decety, J. (2019). The development of children's preferences for equality and equity across 13 individualistic and collectivist cultures. *Developmental Science, 22*(2), e12729. https://doi.org/10.1111/desc.12729

Jaggy, A., Mainhard, T., Sticca, F., & Perren, S. (2020). The emergence of dyadic pretend play quality during peer play: The role of child competence, play partner competence and dyadic constellation. *Social Development, 29*(4), 976–994.

Jiang, H., Justice, L., Purtell, K. M., Lin, T-J., & Logan, J. (2021). Prevalence and prediction of kindergarten-transition difficulties. *Early Childhood Research Quarterly, 55*(2nd Quarter), 15–23.

Kronaizl, S. G. (2019). Discussing death with children: A developmental approach. *Pediatric Nursing, 45*(1), 47–50.

Lamy, M., Pedapati, E. V., Dominick, K. L., Wink, L. K., & Erickson, C. A. (2020). Recent advances in the pharmacological management of behavioral disturbances associated with autism spectrum disorder in children and adolescents. *Pediatric Drugs 22*(5), 473–483.

Lee, G. T., Xu, S., Guo, S., Gilic, L., Pu, Y., & Xu, J. (2019). Teaching "imaginary objects" symbolic play to young children with autism. *Journal of Autism and Developmental Disorders, 49*(10), 4109–4122.

Lenz, S., Essler, S., Wörle, M., & Paulus, M. (2021). "Who will share with me?": Preschoolers rely on their friends more than on nonfriends to share with them. *Journal of Experimental Child Psychology, 203*(3), 105037. https://doi.org/10.1016/j.jecp.2020.105037

Lenz, S., & Paulus, M. (2021). Friendship is more than strategic reciprocity: Preschoolers' selective sharing with friends cannot be reduced to strategic concerns. *Journal of Experimental Child Psychology, 206*(2), 105101. https://doi.org/10.1016/j.jecp.2021.105101

Liang, Y., Duan, L., Xu, X., Li, X., Liu, M., Chen, H., Lu, J., & Xia, J. (2020). Mesenchymal stem cell-derived exosomes for treatment of autism spectrum disorder. *ACS Applied Bio Materials, 3*(9), 6384–6393.

Liquin, E. G., & Lombrozo, T. (2020). Explanation-seeking curiosity in childhood. *Current Opinion in Behavioral Sciences, 35,* 14–20.

Longbottom, S., & Slaughter, V. (2018). Source of children's knowledge about death and dying. *Philosophical Transactions of the Royal Society B: Biological Sciences, 373*(1754), 20170267. https://doi.org/10.1098/rstb.2017.0267

Lüken, M. M., & Sauzet, O. (2021). Patterning strategies in early childhood: A mixed methods study examining 3- to 5-year-old children's patterning competencies. *Mathematical Thinking and Learning, 23*(1), 28–48.

Mammen, M., Köymen, B., & Tomasello, M. (2018). The reasons young children give to peers when explaining their judgments of moral and conventional rules. *Developmental Psychology, 54*(2), 254–262.

Marotz, L. R. (2020). *Health, safety, and nutrition for the young child* (10th ed.). Boston, MA: Cengage.

Marshall, J., Yudkin, D. A. & Crockett, M. J. (2021). Children punish third parties to satisfy both consequentialist and retributive motives. *Nature Human Behaviour, 5,* 361–368.

Matarma, T., Lagström, H., & Löyttyniemi, E. (2020). Motor skills of 5-year-old children: Gender differences and activity and family correlates. *Perceptual and Motor Skills, 127*(2), 367–385.

Manoli, D. S., & State, M. W. (2021). Autism spectrum disorder genetics and the search for pathological mechanisms. *The American Journal of Psychiatry, 178*(1), 30–38.

Newkirk-Turner, B. L., & Green, L. (2021). Language use and development of third-person singular contexts: Assessment implications. *Language, Speech, and Hearing Services in Schools, 52*(1), 16–30.

Owen, K., & Barnes, C. (2021). The development of categorization in early childhood: A review. *Early Child Development and Care, 191*(1), 13–20.

Pace, A., Luo, R., Levine, D., Iglesias, A., de Villiers, J., Golinkoff, R. M., Wilson, M. S., & Hirsh-Pasek, K. (2021). Within and across language predictors of word learning processes in dual language learners. *Child Development, 92*(1), 35–53.

Paulus, M., Christner, N., & Wörle, M. (2020). The normative status of friendship: Do young children enforce sharing with friends and appreciate reasonable partiality? *Journal of Experimental Child Psychology, 194,* 104826. https://doi.org/10.1016/j.jecp.2020.10482

Paulus, M., Wörle, M., & Christner, N. (2020). The emergence of human altruism: Preschool children develop a norm for empathy-based comforting. *Journal of Cognition and Development, 21*(1), 104–124.

Purtell, K. M., Valauri, A., Rhoad-Drogalis, A., Jiang, H., Justice, L. M., Lin, T-J., & Logan, J. A. (2020). Understanding policies and practices that support successful transitions to kindergarten. *Early Childhood Research Quarterly, 52* (Part B, 3rd Quarter), 5–14.

Qian, M., Wang, Y., Wong, W. I., Fu, G., Zuo, B., & VanderLaan, D. P. (2020). The effects of race, gender, and gender-typed behavior of children's friendship appraisals. *Archives of Sexual Behavior, 50*(3). https://doi.org/10.1007/s10508-020-01825-5

Quick, V. B. S., Wang, B., & State, M. W. (2021). Leveraging large genomic datasets to illuminate the pathobiology of autism spectrum disorders. *Neuropsychopharmacology, 46*(1), 55–69. http://doi.org/10.1038/s41386-020-0768-y

Rochanavibhata, S., & Marian, V. (2020). Maternal scaffolding styles and children's developing narrative skills: A cross-cultural comparison of autobiographical conversations in the US and Thailand. *Learning, Culture and Social Interaction, 26,* 100413. https://doi.org/10.1016/j.lcsi.2020.100413

Ronfard, S., Zambrana, I. M., Hermansen, T. K., & Kelemen, D. (2018). Question-asking in childhood: A review of the literature and a framework for understanding its development. *Developmental Review, 49,* 101–120.

Schonfeld, D. J. (2019). Helping young children grieve and understand death. (2019). *Young Children, 74*(2), 74–75.

Sella, F., Lucangeli, D., Kadosh, R. C., & Zorzi, M. (2020). Making sense of number words and Arabic digits: Does order count more? *Child Development, 91*(5), 1456–1470.

Shimizu, Y., Senzaki, S., & Cowell, J. M. (2021). Cultural similarities and differences in the development of sociomoral judgments: An eye-tracking study. *Cognitive Development, 57*(4), 100974. http://doi.org/10.1016/j.cogdev.2020.100974

Silverman, I. W. (2020). Gender differences in young children's compliance to maternal directives: A meta-analysis. *International Journal of Behavioral Development, 44*(2), 146–156.

Singh, P. (2021). Affordance-based framework of object perception in children's pretend play: A nonrepresentational alternative. *International Journal of Play, 10*(1), 109–123.

Taggart, J., Becker, I., Rauen, J., Kallas, H. A., & Lillard, A. S. (2020). What shall we do: Pretend or real? Preschoolers' choices and parents' perceptions. *Journal of Cognition and Development, 21*(2), 261–281.

Tan, P. Z., Oppenheimer, C. W., Ladouceur, C. D., Butterfield, R. D., & Silk, J. S. (2020). A review of associations between parental emotion socialization behaviors and the neural substrates of emotional reactivity and regulation in youth. *Developmental Psychology, 56*(3), 516–527.

Thibodeau-Nielsen, R. B., Gilpin, A. T., Palermo, F., Nancarrow, A. F., Farrell, C. B., Turley, D., DeCaro, J. A., Lochman, J. E., & Boxmeyer, C. L. (2020). Pretend play as a protective factor for developing executive functions among children living in poverty. *Cognitive Development, 56,* 100964. https://doi.org/10.1016/j.cogdev.2020.100964

Thomas, N., Colin, C. & Leybaert, J. (2020). Interactive reading to improve language and emergent literacy skills of preschool children from low socioeconomic and language-minority backgrounds. *Early Childhood Education Journal, 48*(5), 549–560.

Tileston, K., & Raney, E. M. (2019). Trampolines can cause serious injuries; Use should be discouraged. *AAP News.* Retrieved from https://www.aappublications.org/news/2019/09/10/focus091019.

Troesch, L. M., Segerer, R., Claus-Pröstler, N., & Grob, A. (2021). Parental acculturation attitudes: Direct and indirect impacts on children's second language acquisition. *Early Education and Development, 32*(2), 272–290.

van 't Noordende, J. E., Kroesbergen, E. H., Leseman, P. P., & Volman, M. J. M. (2020). The role of non-symbolic and symbolic skills in the development of early numerical cognition from preschool to kindergarten age. *Journal of Cognition and Development, 22*(1), 68–83.

Wang, F., Gao, C., Kaufman, J., Tong, Y., & Chen, J. (2021). Watching versus touching: The effectiveness of a touchscreen app to teach children to tell time. *Computers & Education, 160,* 104021. https://doi.org/10.1016/J.COMPEDU.2020.104021

Wang, Y., Palonen, T., Hurme, T-R., & Kinos, J. (2019). Do you want to play with me today? Friendship stability among preschool children. *European Early Childhood Education Research Journal, 27*(2), 170–184.

Whiteside, E. E., Ayres, K. M., Ledford, J. R., & Trump, C. (2020). Evaluating the use of video- and computer-based technology supports to facilitate small group instruction. *Education and Training in Autism and Developmental Disabilities, 55*(4), 438–450.

Wigger, J. B. (2018). Invisible friends across four countries: Kenya, Malawi, Nepal and the Dominican Republic. *International Journal of Psychology, 53*(S1), 46–52.

Zhang, M., & Hudson, J. A. (2018). Children's understanding of *yesterday* and *tomorrow. Journal of Experimental Child Psychology, 170,* 107–133.

Zhao, X., Wente, A., Flecha, M. F., Galvan, D. S., Gopnik, A., & Kushnir, T. (2021). Culture moderates the relationship between self-control ability and free will beliefs in childhood. *Cognition, 210,* 104609. https://doi.org/0.1016/j.cognition.2021.104609

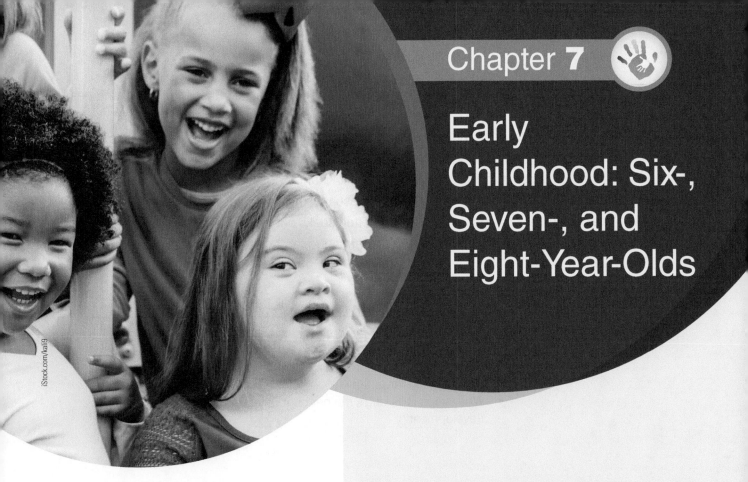

iStock.com/kali9

Chapter 7

Early Childhood: Six-, Seven-, and Eight-Year-Olds

Learning Objectives

After reading this chapter, you will be able to:

7-1 Describe at least two sensory learning experiences that would be developmentally appropriate for six-, seven-, and eight-year-olds.

7-2 Explain why behavior problems and emotional outbursts may reappear during this developmental stage.

7-3 Compare and contrast the speech and language skills of six- and eight-year-olds.

7-4 Explain and demonstrate Piaget's concept of conservation.

7-5 Discuss the role of friendships in children's development.

NAEYC NAEYC Professional Standards Linked to Chapter Content

1a, 1b, and 1c: Child development and learning in context

2a and 2c: Family–teacher partnerships and community connections

3a and 3b: Child observations, documentation, and assessment

4a, 4b, and 4c: Developmentally, culturally, and linguistically appropriate teaching practices

5a and 5b: Knowledge, application, and integration of academic content in the early childhood curriculum

6b: Professionalism as an early childhood educator

For weeks, Huang has asked his mother repeatedly when school will begin. Soon to turn seven, he is eagerly anticipating the start of first grade, riding on a school bus, and eating lunch in the school cafeteria. Huang recently met his new teacher, Mr. Chen, during an open house held at the school and is excited about having a "man teacher." His mother, Bao-yu, has been concerned about Huang since his father's death and thinks that he will benefit from having a male role model back into his life.

Huang is happy that his best friend, Lin, will be in the same class this year. Unlike Huang, who is an only child, Lin is the youngest of four siblings. Lin's parents work long hours and seldom show any interest in his school activities or homework. They view their primary role to be that of caretakers and believe that teachers are responsible for helping their son to learn. Lin struggles to read, reproduce spelling words, and grasp simple addition and subtraction concepts. The kindergarten teacher was reluctant to advance Lin to the first grade, but Mr. Chen assured her that he would devote extra time to help the boy succeed. Mr. Chen is aware that Lin's family speaks little English at home and has limited resources.

Huang thinks it is "pretty neat" that he will go to school all day like his mother, who plans to finish her associates degree in accounting this spring. She is proud of her son's progress in school and works with him at home so that he continues to do well. Huang's advanced reading and writing skills are apparent in the imaginative stories that he composes on the computer when he and his mother visit their local library. When he is finished, Huang often seeks out his "favorite" librarian so he can read his story to her. Huang also is excited about learning to tell time and repeatedly wants his mother to ask him what time it is.

Ask Yourself

- What environmental factors may explain, in part, why Huang and Lin are performing differently in school?
- How may Lin benefit from Mr. Chen's recommendation rather than repeating kindergarten?
- What steps is Huang's mother currently taking to support his literacy development?

Did You Know ?

...that more than half of all low-income families have no books for children in their homes? Children who are read to and have access to books develop better reading, math, and communication skills.

emerging literacy Early experiences, such as being read and talked to, naming objects, and identifying letters, that prepare a child for later reading, writing, and language development.

sensory Refers to the five senses: hearing, seeing, touching, smelling, and tasting.

Six-, Seven-, and Eight-Year-Olds

The period following the preschool years is especially remarkable. Children are in a stage of developmental integration—organizing and combining various developmental skills to accomplish increasingly complex tasks. Short- and long-term memory and the ability to recall details improve significantly at this age. This is an important development because it enables children to learn and retain new information and to integrate it with prior knowledge.

Above all, most six-, seven-, and eight-year-olds are ready and eager to attend school, even though they may be somewhat apprehensive when the time actually arrives. Going to school creates stress and anxieties about things such as arriving on time, remembering to bring back assigned homework, having a new teacher, being accepted and making new friends, taking tests, or walking home alone (Groeneveld et al., 2020; Marcus & Tomasi, 2020).

Learning to read is one of the most complex perceptual tasks children will encounter during this developmental stage (Gordon & Browne, 2016; Piaget, 1926) (Figure 7-1). Recognizing visual letter symbols and associating them with their spoken sounds is an important component of **emerging literacy**. It also means that children must learn to combine letters to form words and to put these words together to form intelligible thoughts that can be read or spoken (Cunningham et al., 2021). Complex as the task is, most children become relatively adept at reading between six and eight years of age; for some, the skill soon is taken for granted.

Sensory activities continue to be an effective method for promoting children's learning. This approach encourages children to manipulate a variety of materials—blocks; puzzles; paints, glue, paper, and found materials; sand, water, leaves, and dirt; musical instruments; and, measurement devices. It can also include project-based activities that reinforce learning across all developmental domains and actively engage children in experiences such as cooking, gardening, carpentry, science, and dramatic play. The National Association for the Education of Young Children (NAEYC) strongly endorses a play-based, **hands-on learning** approach with six-, seven-, and eight-year-olds, as well as with younger children. This philosophy is clearly stated in the organization's position statement, *Developmentally Appropriate Practice* (NAEYC, 2020). Particularly noteworthy are the subsections entitled "Principles of Child Development and Learning and Implications that Inform Practice" and "Guidelines for Developmentally Appropriate Practice in Action" that outline the rationale for individualizing children's educational opportunities. Above all, this position statement acknowledges that each child is a unique individual whose developmental abilities, family and cultural and linguistic heritage, needs, and learning style differ from those of other children. Similar recommendations that emphasize the importance of individualizing learning have been adopted by other early childhood professional organizations, including family child care and school-age programs.

Figure 7-1 Learning to read is one of the most complex perceptual tasks that children will undertake during this developmental stage.

Play-based learning remains an important instructional method for fostering children's cognitive and social skill development in the early primary grades (Taylor & Boyer, 2020). However, Allee-Herndon and Roberts (2021) note that this approach has been replaced by intentional and test-driven learning in many classrooms. The authors suggest that a high standard of learning and developmental outcomes is achievable, especially for children living in poverty, when teachers implement a combination of purposeful play and instruction. DeLuca and colleagues (2020) similarly argue that a play-based pedagogy can effectively promote children's independent learning while also meeting state assessment-based learning standards.

For the most part, six-, seven-, and eight-year-olds play well with other children, especially if the group is not too large. There is keen interest in making friends, being a friend, and having friends. Friends are often defined as someone who is "fun," "pretty," "strong," or "nice." They are usually playmates whom the child has ready access to in the neighborhood and at school. Researchers have also found that social friendships are more commonly established among children who speak with a similar accent, dialect, or language (Spence, Hornsey, & Imuta, 2021). Children who have a disability, such as autism, language impairment, or conduct disorder are more likely to be excluded from friendships and to experience discrimination and bullying (Lloyd-Esenkaya et al., 2021; Woodgate et al., 2020).

Friendships at this age are established easily and abandoned readily; few are stable or long-lasting (Afshordi & Liberman, 2021). Frequent quarreling and bossing among friends are common: "If you play with Jamal, then you're not *my* friend." Some children show considerable aggression, but it tends to be verbal, aimed at hurting feelings rather than at causing physical harm. Negative friendship quality (e.g., lack of trust, loyalty, intimacy), not the number of friends, is closely associated with children's feelings of loneliness and low self-esteem (Schwartz-Mette et al., 2020).

Both boys and girls are becoming more competent at managing their own personal needs—washing, dressing, toileting, eating, getting up, and getting ready for school. They observe family rules regarding mealtimes, television, chores, and the need for privacy. They can be trusted to run errands and carry out simple responsibilities at home and school without frequent reminders. In other words, children are in control of themselves and their immediate world.

Did You Know   **?**

…that kindergarten attendance is not mandatory in the majority of U.S. states? Many states do not require compulsory school enrollment until a child reaches age seven; a few do not require attendance until age eight.

hands-on learning A curriculum approach that involves children as active participants, encouraging them to manipulate, investigate, experiment, and solve problems.

6-year-old

Throughout the primary school years, many children seem almost driven by the need to do everything right, yet they enjoy being challenged and completing tasks. They are able to focus and concentrate on projects for longer periods at a time. They enjoy building models, working on crafts, playing computer and board games, and participating in organized activities. Most children like school and become increasingly comfortable with themselves, their families, and their teachers.

The Six-Year-Old

Exciting adventures begin to open up to six-year-olds as their coordination improves and their size and strength increase. Children need ample opportunities for vigorous play each day to promote their physical development, decrease the risk for obesity, and channel excess energy. However, new challenges often are met with a mixture of enthusiasm and frustration. Six-year-olds typically have difficulty making choices and, at times, are overwhelmed by unfamiliar situations. At the same time, changes in their cognitive abilities enable them to see rules as useful for understanding everyday events and the behavior of others. They are also becoming increasingly able to control and express their emotions in positive ways.

For many children, this period also marks the beginning of formal, subject- oriented schooling. It should be noted that many early childhood educators, researchers, and professional organizations consider highly structured academic activities (e.g., worksheets, drills, memorization, tests) developmentally inappropriate at this age (Brown, Ku, & Barry, 2021; Haslip & Gullo, 2018; Hui, Forbes, & Yang, 2021). Behavior problems and signs of stress or tension such as tics, nail-biting, hair-twisting, bed-wetting, or sleeping difficulties may flare up as children encounter new challenges and struggles. Generally, these pass as children become familiar with expectations and the responsibilities associated with going to school.

Despite the turmoil and trying times, most six-year-olds experience an abundance of happy times marked by a lively curiosity, an eagerness to learn, an endearing sense of humor, and exuberant outbursts of affection and good will (Figure 7-2).

iStock.com/SDI Productions

Figure 7-2 Six-year-olds are curious and eager to learn.

Developmental Profiles and Growth Patterns

Growth and Physical Characteristics

- Continues to grow slowly but steadily.
- Gains 2–3 inches (5–7.5 cm) in height each year: girls are an average of 42–46 inches (105–115 cm) tall; boys are an average of 44–47 inches (110–117.5 cm).
- Adds 5–7 pounds (2.3–3.2 kg) in weight per year: girls weigh approximately 38–47 pounds (19.1–22.3 kg); boys weigh approximately 42–49 pounds (17.3–21.4 kg). Increased muscle mass accounts for a significant portion of weight gain.

Developmental Profiles and Growth Patterns *(continued)*

- Heart rate (80 beats per minute) and respiratory rates (18–28 breaths per minute) are similar to those of adults; both rates vary with activity.
- Appears lanky as the long bones in arms and legs begin a phase of rapid growth.
- Loses "baby" (**deciduous**) **teeth**; permanent (secondary) teeth erupt, beginning with the two upper front teeth; girls tend to lose teeth at an earlier age than do boys.
- Has a visual acuity of approximately 20/20; children testing 20/40 or less should have a comprehensive professional evaluation (Leske et al., 2021; Musch et al., 2020).
- Farsightedness is not uncommon and may be outgrown as children mature.
- Develops more adultlike facial features and overall physical appearance.
- Requires approximately 1,600 to 1,700 calories per day.

Motor Development

- Has increased muscle strength; boys are typically stronger than girls of a similar size.
- Gains greater control over large and fine motor skills; movements are becoming more precise and deliberate, although some clumsiness persists.
- Enjoys vigorous physical activity (running, jumping, climbing, and throwing).
- Moves constantly, even when trying to sit still.
- Has increased dexterity and eye–hand coordination along with improved motor functioning, which make it easier for children to learn how to ride a bicycle (without training wheels), swim, swing a bat, or kick a ball.
- Enjoys art projects (likes to paint, model with clay, "make things," draw and color, put things together, and work with wood).
- Writes numbers and letters with varying degrees of precision and interest; may reverse or confuse certain letters (such as *b/d, p/g, g/q, or t/f*).

What Do You See?

Physical activity. Active play is natural for most children. What motor skills are these children using? In what ways do children benefit from being physically active each day? How could the activity in this picture be modified for a child who has limited physical mobility?

iStock.com/SolStock

---

deciduous teeth The initial set of teeth that eventually fall out; often referred to as "baby teeth."

Developmental Profiles and Growth Patterns *(continued)*

- Traces around hand and other objects.
- Folds and cuts paper into simple shapes.
- Ties own shoes (but this task is still a struggle for some children).

Perceptual-Cognitive Development

- Shows increased attention span; works at tasks for longer periods of time, although concentrated effort is not always consistent.
- Understands concepts such as simple time markers (e.g., today, tomorrow, and yesterday) or uncomplicated concepts of motion (cars go faster than bicycles).
- Tells time correctly most of the time; may not always get the minutes right (Hamanouche & Cordes, 2020).
- Identifies seasons and major holidays and the activities associated with each.
- Enjoys challenges: puzzles, counting and sorting activities, paper-and-pencil mazes, and games that involve counting or matching letters and words with pictures.
- Recognizes some words by sight; attempts to sound out words (some children may be reading well by this time).
- Understands the concept of numbers; can repeat three numbers backward.
- Identifies familiar coins (i.e., pennies, nickels, dimes, and quarters).
- Includes at least six body parts when drawing a person.

▶❚❚ TeachSource Video Connections

Cognitive Development

Children's advanced speech-language and perceptual-cognitive skills, including improved memory capacity, information processing, and abstract thinking, begin to open new opportunities for complex learning. Respond to the following questions after you have watched the learning video *Beginning Reading Instruction/Learning Vocabulary in Meaningful Context:*

1. What instructional strategies did the teacher use to help children grasp the meaning of new vocabulary words?
2. What cognitive-perceptual and speech-language skills were the children using in their efforts to define new vocabulary words?
3. In what ways did the teacher use his understanding of the six-year-old's typical development to create a literacy rich classroom environment?

Speech and Language Development

- Talks nonstop (this behavior may not be encouraged in all cultures); sometimes described as a "chatterbox."
- Acquires language pattern reflective of their cultural background.
- Carries on adultlike conversations; asks many questions.
- Learns as many as 5 to 10 new words each day; vocabulary consists of approximately 10,000 to 14,000 words.

Developmental Profiles and Growth Patterns *(continued)*

- Uses appropriate verb tenses, word order, and sentence structure.

- Uses language rather than tantrums or physical aggression to express displeasure: "That's mine! Give it back, or I'm telling."

- Talks self through the required steps in simple problem-solving situations (although the logic may be irregular and unclear to adults).

- Imitates slang and profanity; finds "bathroom" or "forbidden" talk extremely funny.

Figure 7-3 Six-year-olds find humor in almost everything.

- Delights in telling jokes and riddles; often the humor is far from subtle (Figure 7-3).

- Begins to read simple stories; still enjoys being read to and making up stories.

- Is capable of learning more than one language; does so spontaneously in a bilingual or multilingual family (Torregrossa et al., 2021; Wallin & Cheevakumjorn, 2020). Neuroscientists have identified structural and functional changes in the brains of dual language learners (Luk, Pliatsikas, & Rossi, 2020).

- Names and correctly holds up the right and left hands fairly consistently; identifies the smallest of two shapes and the longer of two lines.

- Clings to certain beliefs involving magic or fantasy (the Tooth Fairy swapping a coin for a tooth; the Easter Bunny hiding eggs; blowing out birthday candles and making a wish).

- Has limited cognitive understanding of death and dying (children believe that it can be reversed or that they may have caused it to happen; often express fear that parents might die, especially their mother). Children's ideas about death and responses to a death are also highly influenced by cultural beliefs (Gutiérrez et al., 2020; Panagiotaki et al., 2018; Watson-Jones et al., 2017).

Social-Emotional Development

- Experiences sudden mood swings: can be "best friends" with someone one minute and "worst of enemies" the next; loving one day, uncooperative and irritable the next; especially unpredictable toward the mother or primary caregiver.

- Becomes less dependent on family members as their friendship circle begins to expand; still needs familial closeness, security, and nurturing, yet has urges to break away and "grow up" (Piaget, 1929).

- Craves and seeks adult approval, reassurance, and praise; anxious to please; may complain excessively about minor hurts or other children's behavior to gain attention.

- Continues to be self-centered (egocentric); still sees and interprets events almost entirely from own perspective (i.e., views everything and everyone as existing for the child's own benefit).

- Easily disappointed and frustrated by self-perceived failure.

- Has difficulty composing and soothing self at times; dislikes being corrected or losing at games; might sulk, cry, refuse to play, or reinvent rules to suit own purposes.

- Is enthusiastic and inquisitive about surroundings and everyday events.

6-year-old

Developmental Profiles and Growth Patterns *(continued)*

- Shows little or no understanding of ethical behavior or moral standards; often fibs, cheats, or takes items belonging to others without meaning to cause harm.
- Recognize when they have been "bad"; values of "good" and "bad" are based on school, family, and cultural expectations and rules.
- May become increasingly fearful of thunderstorms, the dark, unidentified noises, dogs, and other animals (Burnham et al., 2018).

DAILY ROUTINES

Eating

- Has a healthy appetite most of the time; often takes helpings larger than can finish. May skip an occasional meal; however, usually makes up for it later on.
- Has strong food preferences and definite dislikes; willingness to try new foods is unpredictable.
- Uses table manners that often do not meet adult standards; may revert to eating with fingers on occasion; stuffs mouth with too much food at times; continues to spill milk or drop food in their lap.
- Continues to have some difficulty using a table knife for cutting and a fork for anything but spearing food.
- Finds it difficult to sit quietly through an entire meal; wiggles and squirms, gets off (or "falls" off) a chair, drops utensils, or needs to go to the bathroom.

Personal Care and Dressing

- Balks at having to take a bath; finds many excuses for delaying or avoiding a bath entirely.
- Manages toileting routines without much adult help; sometimes is in a hurry or waits too long so that "accidents" happen.
- Reverts to occasional accidental soiling or wetting of pants, especially during new experiences, such as in the first weeks of school or when under stress.
- Sleeps through most nights without having to get up to use the bathroom. *Note:* Some children, especially boys, may not maintain a dry bed for another year or so.
- Performs self-care routines such as handwashing, bathing, and toothbrushing in a hurry; not always careful or thorough; still needs frequent supervision and demonstrations to make sure that routines are carried out properly.
- Expresses interest in selecting own clothes; still needs some guidance in determining occasion and seasonal appropriateness.
- Drops clothing on the floor or bed, loses shoes around the house, and flings jacket down; often forgets where items were left (Figure 7-4).

Sleeping

- Requires 9–11 hours of uninterrupted sleep.
- Sleeps through most nights; some children, particularly boys, continue to experience nightmares and sleep disturbances (Lewien et al., 2021).

6-year-old

DAILY ROUTINES *(continued)*

- Sometimes requests a night-light, special blanket, or favorite stuffed toy (may want all three).

- Finds numerous ways to avoid bedtime; when finally in bed, falls asleep quickly.

- Amuses self with books, toys, television, or coloring if awake before the rest of the family.

Play and Social Activities

- Has strong sense of self, which is evident in terms of preferences and dislikes; uncompromising about wants and needs. (These often do not coincide with adult plans or requests.)

- Is possessive about toys, books, family, and friends, but is able to share on some occasions.

- Forms a close, friendly relationship with one or two other children (often slightly older); play involves working together toward specific goals.

- Becomes intolerant of being told what to do; may revert to tantrums on occasion.

- Seeks teachers' attention, praise, and reassurance; now views the teacher (rather than the parent) as the ultimate source of "truth."

Figure 7-4 Six-year-olds are often forgetful when it comes to caring for their clothes.

learning activities to promote **brain development**

Six-year-olds are naturally curious and eager to learn. They enjoy imaginative play, art, math, science, outdoor activities, and projects that involve building, sorting, and matching. Learning to read and write is also of special interest.

Developmentally appropriate applications for families and teachers

- Provide materials for drawing, cutting, pasting, and painting.

- Offer paper-and-pencil games (dot-to-dot, number-to-number, word search, hidden objects, copying and tracing activities).

- Provide (and frequently join in) simple card games (such as Hearts, Uno, and Flinch) and board games (e.g., Scrabble Junior, Candy Land, checkers, and dominos), especially those in which competitiveness is minimal.

- Keep a plentiful supply of books and magazines on hand for children to look at, as well as for adults to read with children; encourage children to make up and tell their own stories. Make weekly trips to the library or access digital books on the Internet.

- Share children's interest in collecting objects (e.g., seashells, colored stones, or bugs); help them to group, label, and display objects.

6-year-old

learning activities *(continued)*

- Teach children what to do if they become lost or are approached by a stranger.

- Provide an assortment of dress-up clothes for boys and girls; use children's interests and familiar community workers as a guide for role-playing.

- Encourage simple carpentry and construction activities; provide wood scraps (along with hammer, glue, and small nails), blocks, empty boxes, cars, trucks, planes, and plastic zoo and farm animals. Avoid battery-driven and mechanical toys that offer little involvement (hence limited learning) once their novelty has worn off.

- Encourage at least 60 minutes a day of vigorous physical activity (e.g., bicycling; skating; swimming; gardening; throwing, catching, batting, and kicking balls; and walking). Limit time spent on computer and electronic games, which encourage sedentary behavior and reduce children's active play (a major cause of obesity).

- Involve children in cooking activities; use these opportunities to build language, math, science, and problem-solving skills, and to teach about healthy eating.

TeachSource Digital Download

developmental **alerts**

Check with a health-care provider or early childhood specialist if, by the seventh birthday, the child does *not*:

- Show signs of ongoing growth (increases in height and weight)

- Continue to display improved mastery of motor skills, such as running, jumping, climbing, balancing, and throwing or catching a ball.

- Show some interest in reading and trying to reproduce letters, especially own name.

- Follow simple, multiple-step directions: "Finish your book, put it on the shelf, and then put on your coat."

- Understand basic concepts, such as *largest*, *larger*, *biggest*, *next*, *first*, and *before*.

- Follow through with instructions and complete simple tasks (putting dishes in the sink, picking up clothes, or finishing a puzzle). *Note:* All children forget. Task incompletion is not a problem unless a child *repeatedly* leaves tasks unfinished.

- Begin to develop alternatives to the excessive use of aggression and inappropriate behavior to get their way.

- Develop a steady decrease in tension-type behavior that may be associated with the start of school or participation in an organized activity (repeated grimacing or facial tics, eye twitching, grinding of teeth, nail-biting, regressive soiling or wetting, aggression, frequent stomachaches, difficulty sleeping, or refusing to go to school).

Note: Cultural differences may alter the timetable when some developmental skills are acquired. Expanded Developmental Alerts Checklists appear in Appendix A and are also available as digital downloads.

▶❚❚ TeachSource **Video Connections**

Learning About Responsibility

When children are involved in classroom and household responsibilities, they learn important things about themselves and group involvement. They also develop skills that will help them to be successful as they grow up. Respond to the following questions after you have watched the learning video *School Age: Guidance:*

1. Why is it important to assign children tasks to complete on a one-time or routine basis?

2. What do children learn from being assigned responsibilities?

3. What challenges might a child who has never had any responsibilities be likely to experience in school?

safety concerns

Continue to implement the safety practices described for the previous stages. Always be aware of new safety issues as the child continues to grow and develop.

Burns
- Keep matches and lighters in locked storage.

Falls
- Make sure that clothing fits properly; skirts and pants that are too long can cause a child to trip or become entangled in play equipment. Remind children to keep shoes tied or Velcro straps fastened.
- Require children to wear a helmet and other appropriate protective gear whenever they ride bikes, skateboards, or scooters.

Equipment
- Store machinery and sharp instruments in a safe place, out of children's reach.

- Teach children proper use of scissors, knives, hammers, and kitchen equipment.
- Set parental controls on televisions and computers to protect children from undesirable or unwanted content.

Personal
- Teach children that it is inappropriate for anyone to touch their private parts without permission. Talk with them about how to get help if this occurs, and whom they should tell.
- Let children know that they always should tell an adult if they are being bullied.
- Reinforce children's resilience skills (e.g., communication, problem-solving, and conflict resolution).

6-year-old

safety concerns (continued)

Traffic
- Review the safety rules to follow in and around motor vehicles, such as when crossing streets or riding a bicycle. Teach children to dismount and walk their bike across the street only at an intersection.
- Discuss appropriate behavior to follow on a bus if your child rides one to school: wait until the bus comes to a complete stop before entering or disembarking; always remain seated; keep head and arms inside of the bus.

- Insist that children always wear a seatbelt when riding in any motor vehicle.

Water
- Enroll children in swimming lessons and teach them the correct safety rules to follow around pools. Have proper rescue equipment accessible.
- Never leave children unattended near water.

Spotlight on Neuroscience and Brain Development

Sleep and Children's Brain Development

Why do humans and animals sleep? What purpose does sleep serve? Scientists have long been intrigued by these questions but have had few answers until recently. What they are learning is that sleep offers surprising health benefits, whereas insufficient sleep can have detrimental consequences, especially for young children. Sleep deprivation in children is associated with a higher risk of obesity, in addition to behavior and cognitive problems (Miller et al., 2021; Simon et al., 2020; Williamson et al., 2020). Agathão and colleagues (2020) noted a higher incidence of chronic mental health disorders, including depression, anxiety, substance use, and excessive health-related concerns, among school-age children and adolescents who failed to get adequate sleep. Boys were particularly affected by these conditions.

Sleep disorders, including difficulty going to sleep, nightmares, and remaining asleep, are common among children. An estimated 25–30 percent of young children and adolescents experience some form of temporary sleep disturbance. However, behaviors that parents perceive as being problematic are often influenced by cultural differences in sleep patterns and practices (Jeon, Dimitriou, & Halstead, 2021).

Children's hectic and sometimes over-scheduled lifestyles and worries about school and friends may contribute to late bedtimes and disrupted sleep patterns. Television viewing, use of computers and electronic media especially in the hours prior to bedtime, and lack of physical activity are factors also known to compromise the sleep quality of older children and adolescents. Children who have autism spectrum disorder, developmental syndromes (e.g., Asperger's, Down, and Williams), and certain medical conditions (e.g., anemia, eczema, obesity, and snoring) may experience serious, prolonged sleep disorders that require medical treatment (Johnson & Zarrinnegar, 2021; Torun et al., 2020).

Parenting practices have also been identified as playing a central role in children's disordered sleep. Inconsistent bedtimes and routines, co-sleeping, and household chaos often contribute to disturbed sleep patterns (Daniel et al., 2020; Newton, Honaker, & Reid, 2020; Ordway et al., 2020). These findings underline the need to help parents understand the importance of establishing consistent bedtime routines that promote children's quality sleep.

Although empirical studies have contributed to an understanding of the health benefits associated with high-quality sleep, it may be the effects on children's brain development that prove to be of even greater significance. Numerous studies have documented sleep's physiological impact on neurocognitive processing and memory (Galván, 2020; Peiffer et al., 2020). Researchers have shown that sleep improves memory by enabling the brain to consolidate and organize the information it has received throughout the day. Chronic sleep deprivation interferes with this process (neural plasticity) and limits short-term memory, which, in turn, impedes cognitive function and lowers IQ scores (Qian et al., 2020; Ujam, Bódizs, & Dresler, 2020). Furthermore, scientists have identified a positive association between adequate sleep and an increase in gray matter volume in children's brains (Migueles et al., 2021). Gray matter is responsible for processing and transmitting sensory impulses involved in emotions, memory, vision and hearing, muscle control, thought, and decision-making.

The findings of these and similar studies reinforce the critical importance of assuring that children obtain adequate sleep for good health, optimal brain development, learning, and behavior regulation. Most young children eventually outgrow occasional periods of troubled sleep and go on to establish healthy sleep habits. However, concerns about a child's prolonged sleep disturbances should always be discussed with a health-care provider.

What are the connections?

1. What factors may interfere with children's ability to get sufficient sleep?
2. What potential effects does sleep deficiency have on a child's health and cognitive function?
3. What strategies can parents implement to improve the quality of children's sleep?

The Seven-Year-Old

Seven-year-olds have many positive traits. They are becoming more reasonable to deal with, cooperative, and willing to share. They are better listeners and are able to understand and follow through with requests for the most part. They stay on task longer and strive mightily to do everything perfectly (which only increases their worry load). They move with considerable ease and confidence, have good hand-eye coordination, and continue to perfect their fine motor skills.

Seven-year-olds work hard at being responsible, being "good," and doing things "right" (Figure 7-5). They tend to take themselves seriously—too seriously at times. When they fail to live up to their own self-imposed expectations, they may sulk, become overly frustrated, lose self-esteem, and/or withdraw. It is as if children at this age are trying to think things through and to integrate what they already know with the flood of new experiences coming their way.

Worrying about what might or might not come to pass is also typical. For example, anticipating yet dreading second grade can create significant anxiety. Maybe the work will be too hard; maybe the teacher won't be nice; or maybe the other kids won't be friendly. Overwhelming efforts to cope with these conflicts may lead to unpredictable outbursts and mood swings. These complicated emotions require parents and teachers to exercise considerable patience and tolerance with seven-year-olds and to help them set expectations that are realistic and achievable.

© GFOW/Cengage Learning

Figure 7-5 Seven-year-olds take pride in doing everything right.

Developmental Profiles and Growth Patterns

Growth and Physical Characteristics

- Grows slowly and steadily during this year; some girls may overtake boys in height.

- Increases in weight tend to be relatively small; a gain of 6 pounds (2.7 kg) per year is typical. Seven-year-olds weigh approximately 50–55 pounds (22.7–25 kg).

- Adds an average of 2.5 inches (6.25 cm) in height per year. Girls are approximately 44–44.5 inches (110–116.3 cm) tall; boys are approximately 46–49.5 inches (115–124 cm) tall.

- Muscle mass is nearly equal for boys and girls.

- Develops a longer, leaner, adultlike appearance; posture is more erect; the arms and legs continue to lengthen.

- Experiences fluctuations in energy level; spurts of high energy are often followed by temporary periods of fatigue.

- Continues to develop frequent respiratory infections and other minor illnesses; however, these episodes occur less often than at age six.

- Eyeballs continue to change shape and size; as a result, children become less farsighted and develop better near vision; periodic eye exams are important for monitoring children's ability to see.

- Hair often grows darker in color.

- Loses four or five teeth; permanent teeth continue to replace baby teeth.

Motor Development

- Exhibits large and fine motor control that is more precisely tuned: balances on either foot; runs up and down stairs with alternating feet; throws and catches smaller balls; practices batting balls; manipulates a computer mouse, knitting needles, or paintbrush with greater accuracy (Figure 7-6).

- Approaches more challenging physical activities, such as climbing up or jumping down from high places, with caution.

- Practices a new motor skill over and over until mastered, and then abandons it to work on something else.

Figure 7-6 Seven-year-olds can manipulate objects with skill and accuracy.

iStock.com/nd3000

- Finds the floor more comfortable than furniture when reading, playing games, or watching television; legs are often in constant motion.

- Uses a knife and fork appropriately, but inconsistently.

- Holds a pencil in a tight grasp near the tip; rests head on forearm, lowers head almost to the tabletop when doing pencil-and-paper tasks.

- Produces letters and numbers in a deliberate and confident fashion (characters are increasingly precise and uniform in size and shape; may run out of room on the line or page when writing).

- Prints own name with a pencil.

Developmental Profiles and Growth Patterns *(continued)*

Perceptual-Cognitive Development

- Uses logical thinking and reasoning to solve complex problems.

- Understands the concepts of space and time in ways that are logical, symbolic, and more practical (a year is "a long time"; 100 miles is "far away"; a minute is longer than a second; an hour is longer than a minute). Children's grasp of abstract number and spatial concepts is correlated with better mathematical achievement in school (Hawes & Ansari, 2020; Soylu & Newman, 2020).

7-year-old

- Begins to grasp Jean Piaget's concepts of **conservation**; for example, the shape of a container does not necessarily reflect the quantity that it can hold (Figure 7-7). (Children now are entering Piaget's stage of *concrete operations.*)

Figure 7-7 **Children are beginning to understand that two differently shaped containers can hold the same amount of liquid.**

- Gains a better understanding of cause and effect: "If I'm late for school again, I'll be in big trouble"; "Ice cubes will melt if they get too warm."

- Tells time by the clock and understands calendar time—days, months, years, and seasons; children who have difficulty grasping these concepts may also struggle to learn math.

- Plans ahead: "I'm saving this cookie for later tonight."

- Shows marked fascination with magic tricks; enjoys putting on shows for family and friends.

- Finds reading easier; many seven-year-olds read for their own enjoyment and delight in retelling story details.

- Has better reading than spelling skills.

- Continues to reverse some letters and substitute sounds on occasion; this is typical development and does not indicate a reading or learning disability.

- Understands numbers and estimation; can do simple addition and subtraction computations and begin to conceptualize and solve number and word problems mentally.

- Enjoys counting and saving money.

- Includes more detail in drawings; draws a person with ten or twelve parts.

Did You Know **?**

...many studies have shown that children who are physically active each day perform better academically, have higher grades, and experience fewer behavior problems?

Speech and Language Development

- Engages in storytelling; likes to write short stories and tell imaginative tales.

- Has an expansive vocabulary consisting of several thousand words.

conservation The stage in children's cognitive development in which they understand that an object's physical qualities (e.g., weight and mass) remain the same despite changes in its appearance; for example, flattening a ball of play-dough does not affect its weight or amount.

7-year-old

Developmental Profiles and Growth Patterns *(continued)*

- Uses adultlike sentence structure and language in conversation; patterns reflect cultural, linguistic, and geographical differences as well as early literacy exposure.

- Becomes more precise and elaborate in the use of language; includes more descriptive adjectives and adverbs in conversation and written stories.

- Uses gestures to illustrate conversations.

- Criticizes own performance: "I didn't draw that right," "Her picture is better than mine."

- Engages in verbal exaggeration: "I ate ten hot dogs at the picnic."

- Explains events in terms of own preferences or needs: "It didn't rain yesterday because I was going on a picnic."

- Describes personal experiences in great detail: "First we parked the car, then we hiked up this long trail, then we sat down on a broken tree near a lake and ate...."

- Understands and carries out multiple-step instructions (with up to five steps); may need to have directions repeated because they didn't listen to the entire request the first time.

- Enjoys writing email messages and simple notes to friends.

Social-Emotional Development

- Is cooperative and affectionate toward adults and less frequently annoyed with their requests and expectations.

- Sees humor in everyday happenings and is more outgoing.

- Likes to be the "teacher's helper"; is eager for the teacher's attention and approval, but less obvious about seeking it than when they were younger.

- Seeks out friendships; friends are important, but the child can find plenty to do if no one is available.

- Is beginning to develop empathy for others' feelings, motives, and actions.

▶❚❚ **TeachSource Video Connections**

Cognitive Development and Concrete Operations

Children are developing an increasingly sophisticated understanding of how things work, their causes and effects, and how various manipulations can alter the outcome. These cognitive advances pique children's curiosity and interest in undertaking new activities. Respond to the following questions after you have watched the learning video entitled *5–11 Years: Piaget's Concrete Operational Stage:*

1. Which cognitive abilities make it possible for seven-year-olds to understand the concepts of size and volume as described in Piaget's theory of conservation?

2. Which changes in children's cognitive skills are evident during Piaget's concrete operational stage?

3. In what ways do these newly emerging cognitive abilities influence children's development in other domains, such as motor, speech and language, and social-emotional?

4. Do all children experience this stage of cognitive development? How might cultural or developmental differences influence this process?

Developmental Profiles and Growth Patterns *(continued)*

- Quarrels less often, although squabbles and tattling continue to occur in both one-on-one and group play; may decide to play or work alone if frustrated.

- Complains that family decisions are unjust; perceives that a particular sibling receives more attention or privileges.

- Has better self-control but may exhibit strong emotional reactions when frustrated or in a situation they consider to be unfair.

- Blames others for own mistakes; makes up alibis for personal shortcomings: "I could have made a better one, but my teacher didn't give me enough time."

- Prefers same-gender playmates; more likely to play in groups.

- Worries about not being liked; feelings easily hurt; might cry, be embarrassed, or state adamantly, "I will never play with you again," when criticized.

- Takes responsibilities seriously; can be trusted to carry out directions and commitments; worries about being late for school or not getting work done on time.

7-year-old

DAILY ROUTINES

Eating

- Eats most foods; is better about sampling unfamiliar foods or taking small tastes of disliked foods, but still may refuse a few strong "hates."

- Shows interest in food; likes to help with grocery shopping and meal preparation.

- Eats with improved table manners, although adults may consider them far from perfect; spills milk less often and has fewer other accidents due to silliness, impulse, or haste to finish.

- Uses eating utensils with relative ease; seldom eats with fingers; some children still have trouble cutting meat.

- Is easily distracted during mealtimes by conversations and things going on elsewhere; at other times, is focused on eating and finishing quickly.

Personal Care and Dressing

- Manages own bath or shower with minimal assistance; is often reluctant to begin bathing; however, once started, seems to relax and enjoy the experience.

- Dresses self, although slow and distracted at times; can speed up the process when time becomes critical or there is something else that they want to do.

- Buttons and zips own clothes; ties own shoes; not always careful or precise (i.e., buttons askew, zipper undone, or shoelaces soon dragging).

- Shows little interest in clothes; wears whatever is laid out or available.

- Shows more interest in combing or brushing own hair.

- Has achieved complete bowel and bladder control; individual rhythm is well established; may resist having bowel movements at school.

- Less likely to get up during the night to use the toilet.

7-year-old

DAILY ROUTINES *(continued)*

Sleeping

- Averages 10–11 hours of sleep at night; insufficient sleep makes it difficult to get up in the morning and contributes to poor academic performance and behavior problems (Hershner, 2020; Simon et al., 2020).

- Sleeps soundly, with few if any bad dreams; instead, often dreams about participating in exploits and adventures.

- May have difficulty sleeping during periods of increased stress and anxiety (Fehr, Chambers, & Ramasami, 2021).

- Gets ready for bed independently most nights, but still enjoys being tucked in or read to.

- Wakes up early most mornings by self; may remain in bed and occupy time with toys, counting savings in a piggy bank, looking at a baseball card collection, reading, and so forth.

Play and Social Activities

- Participates in organized group activities (such as Boys' and Girls' Clubs, Cub Scouts and Brownies, 4-H, or swim and soccer teams).

- Dislikes missing school or social events; wants to keep up with friends and classmates.

- Has interest in creative arts, music, dancing, or drama; prefers to participate with a friend but will go alone if no one is available.

- Engages in favorite play activities such as bicycle riding, climbing activities, basketball, soccer, skating, jumping rope, and computer games.

- Likes to play competitive board and card games but may bend the rules when losing.

- Turns activities into challenges. "Let's see who can throw rocks the farthest." "I can run to the corner faster than you can."

learning activities to promote **brain development**

Seven-year-olds use their basic skills and understanding to tackle new challenges. They enjoy reading complex stories, sharing what they know with others, and using their creativity to compose stories and plays. Active games and outdoor play provide opportunities for releasing excess energy, practicing motor skills, and learning how to interact cooperatively with other children.

Developmentally appropriate applications for families and teachers

- Take trips to the library for children's story time and dramatic play activities, as well as for checking out books; many children's digital books can be accessed online.

- Sign up for free or low-cost community offerings of interest to the child (e.g., art, theater, science, swimming, T-ball, tumbling, yoga, or zoo and museum programs).

- Utilize the outdoors for learning; take family "collecting walks" in a park, on the beach, or around the neighborhood; support children's interests in photographing, collecting, and organizing found treasures (Figure 7-8).

learning activities *(continued)*

7-year-old

Figure 7-8 The outdoors provides a wealth of learning opportunities.

- Provide several small tools and equipment (such as for carpentry or gardening implements; science materials for growing a potato vine or maintaining an ant farm; creating a small aquarium; composting food scraps to make soil; building a weather vane).

- Gather materials for art projects, building models, or conducting science experiments (e.g., pieces of wood, Styrofoam, various weights and textures of cardboard and paper, beads, fabric, ribbon, yarn, and so forth).

- Offer dress-up clothes and props for planning and staging "original" shows; encourage children to write their own stories or songs and be sure to attend their "performances."

- Assemble a box of discarded small appliances (such as a clock, hair dryer, radio, food mixer, power drill—with *cords removed*) and tools for taking them apart.

- Provide a dollhouse, farm or zoo set, space station, or airport, complete with small-scale people, animals, and equipment.

- Set out different-sized containers (plastic, metal, or glass [if closely supervised]). Add water to each container and encourage children to create musical notes by tapping on the various containers.

TeachSource Digital Download

developmental **alerts**

Check with a health-care provider or early childhood specialist if, by the eighth birthday, the child does *not*:

- Attend to the task at hand; show longer periods of sitting quietly, listening, and responding appropriately.

- Follow through on simple instructions.

7-year-old

developmental **alerts** (continued)

- Go to school willingly most days (of concern are excessive complaints about stomachaches, headaches, or other "ills" when getting ready for school).

- Make friends (observe closely to see whether the child plays alone most of the time or withdraws consistently from contact with other children).

- Sleep soundly most nights. (Frequent or recurring nightmares are usually rare at this age.)

- See or hear well most of the time; frequent squinting, excessive rubbing of the eyes, or asking to have statements repeated requires professional evaluation.

- Handle stressful situations without undue emotional upset (i.e., excessive crying, sleeping or eating disturbances, withdrawal, and frequent anxiety).

- Assume responsibility for personal care (e.g., dressing, bathing, and feeding self) most of the time.

- Show improved fine motor skills: draw basic shapes, reproduce letters and numbers, cut along straight and curved lines.

Note: Cultural differences may alter the timetable when some developmental skills are acquired. Expanded Developmental Alerts Checklists appear in Appendix A and are also available as digital downloads.

safety **concerns**

Continue to implement the safety practices described for the previous stages. Be aware of new safety issues as the child continues to grow and develop.

Firearms

- Store unloaded guns in a locked cabinet, with ammunition kept in a different locked location.
- Teach children never to pick up or even touch a gun and to report immediately to an adult if they find one. Check with the families of your children's friends to determine whether guns are present and properly stored in their house.

Play Environments

- Review rules for safe play and the use of playground equipment when away from home. Know who your child's friends are and the types of play in which they typically engage.
- Remind children to always wash their hands after playing, especially if they have touched any animals, play equipment, or sand (beach or sandbox).

Tools/Equipment

- Do not let children use power mowers or other motorized yard equipment (e.g., weed eaters or hedge trimmers); keep children away when equipment is in use.

Water

- Continue to supervise children whenever they are in a pool, lake, or around any body of water.
- Teach children to swim and to follow water safety rules. Insist that they wear approved flotation vests when in or around large bodies of water (while fishing, boating, or skiing).

The Eight-Year-Old

Eight-year-olds display a great enthusiasm for life. Energy is concentrated on improving skills that they already possess and enhancing what they already know. Eight-year-olds, once again, experience strong feelings of independence and are eager to make decisions about their own plans and friends. Interests and attention are increasingly devoted to peers and team or group activities rather than to family, teachers, or siblings. However, eight-year-olds continue to need adult guidance and to feel the love and security of family despite their increased reliance on peers for gratification. Sometime near midyear, boys and girls begin to go their separate ways and to form new interests in same-gender groups.

A small percentage of children may begin to engage in aggressive, intimidating, or **bullying** behaviors. Their targets are often peers who are perceived as loners, lacking in self-confidence, having a disability, unable to defend themselves, or are more likely to react or retaliate to taunting (Armitage, 2021; Hamel, Schwab, & Wahl, 2021). Gage and colleagues (2021) reported that Black and Hispanic children and those with a disability are victimized at significantly higher rates than their White typically developing peers.

Occasional incidences of name-calling, threatening, or hitting are not uncommon at this age, but it is important that they be addressed. However, a pattern of intentional, repetitive, and hurtful behavior that escalates as children approach adolescence distinguishes bullying from typical developmental expectations.

Researchers continue to study why some children have more difficulty controlling aggressive behavior than do others. Their findings suggest that bullies typically fall into two categories. The first group includes children who use their physical strength to intimidate others. They tend to be self-assured, impulsive, angry, and lacking in empathy and moral engagement (Mapes et al., 2020; Pan et al., 2020). In addition, these children often live in an economically-disadvantaged household, are exposed to an authoritarian parenting style, and/or experience frequent family violence and parent-child conflict (Baiden et al., 2020; Hong et al., 2020; Tatiani, 2021). The second group consists of children who tend to be passive and are less likely to initiate bullying but are willing to join in after it has begun. These children often possess poor social skills and low self-esteem and may themselves be victims of abuse or neglect. They also have difficulty knowing how to initiate appropriate social interaction and how to control their own impulsive behaviors.

Schools and communities have implemented anti-bullying programs to reduce intimidating behaviors, increase empathy and kindness, and prevent the immediate and long-term effects of bullying on children's development. These initiatives are aimed at increasing children's resilience by promoting positive social, communication, and anger management skills; boosting self-esteem; and reducing harassing behaviors (Gaffney, Ttofi, & Farrington, 2021). Prevention efforts are also focusing on bystanders and victims of bullying, helping them to develop empowering behaviors such as walking away, avoiding bullies, problem solving, informing an adult, and using peaceful conflict resolution strategies (CDC, 2021; Taliaferro et al., 2020).

8-year-old

Did You Know ?

...that approximately 40–80 percent of school-age children report being bullied at some point? Children who are bullied experience a range of serious psychological disorders including depression, anxiety, and suicide.

bullying Verbal and physical behavior that is hurtful, intentional, and repeatedly directed toward a person or child who is viewed as being weaker.

Developmental Profiles and Growth Patterns

8-year-old

Growth and Physical Characteristics

- Continues to gain 5–7 pounds (2.3–3.2 kg) per year; an eight-year-old weighs approximately 55–61 pounds (25–27.7 kg). Girls typically weigh less than boys.

- Grows slowly and steadily in height, averaging 2.5 inches (6.25 cm) per year; girls are generally taller [46–49 inches (115–122.5 cm)] than boys [48–52 inches (120–130 cm)].

- Develops a more mature body shape and appearance; arms and legs grow longer, creating an image that is tall and lanky.

- Has nearly 20/20 vision (normal); periodic vision checks are necessary to assure that children's visual acuity is developing properly.

- Some girls may begin to develop breasts and pubic hair and experience menses; early puberty onset is often linked to childhood obesity (Brix et al., 2020).

- May have mood swings associated with early hormonal changes.

- Is generally healthy and experiences fewer illnesses than when younger.

Motor Development

- Enjoys vigorous activity; likes to dance, inline skate, swim, wrestle, ride bikes, play basketball, jump rope, and fly kites (Figure 7-9).

- Seeks out opportunities to participate in team activities and games such as soccer, baseball, softball, tennis, and kickball.

- Exhibits significant improvement in agility, balance, speed, and strength.

- Develops improved eye–hand coordination; copies words and numbers from a blackboard with increasing speed and accuracy; is able to learn cursive writing and to play a musical instrument.

- Possesses seemingly endless energy.

Figure 7-9 Eight-year-olds enjoy good health and vigorous activity.

Perceptual-Cognitive Development

- Collects objects; classifies, organizes, and displays items according to more complex systems; bargains and trades with friends to obtain additional pieces.

- Saves money for small purchases; eagerly develops plans to earn cash from odd jobs; studies catalogs and magazines for ideas of items to purchase.

- Begins taking an interest in what others think and do; understands that there are distant countries and different customs, languages, and cultures.

Developmental Profiles and Growth Patterns (continued)

- Accepts challenges and responsibilities with enthusiasm; delights in being asked to perform tasks, both at home and in school; is interested in being acknowledged or rewarded for their efforts.
- Likes to read and work independently; spends considerable time planning and making lists.
- Reads with improved fluency (speed, accuracy, understanding, and expression).
- Understands perspective (i.e., shadow, distance, and shape); drawings reflect greater detail and more realistic portrayal of objects.
- Grasps the basic principles of conservation. (A tall, narrow jar might look different from one that is short and wide, but they both can hold the same amount of liquid.)
- Uses more sophisticated logic to understand everyday events; for example, is systematic in looking for a misplaced jacket, backpack, or toy.
- Adds and subtracts multiple-digit numbers; learning simple multiplication and division.
- Looks forward to school and is disappointed when ill or unable to attend.

8-year-old

Speech and Language Development

- Delights in telling jokes and riddles.
- Understands and carries out multiple-step instructions (with up to five steps); may need to have directions repeated because they did not listen to the entire request.
- Reads with ease and understanding.
- Composes and sends imaginative and detailed messages to friends and family via email, texting, or video chat (Figure 7-10).
- Uses language to criticize and compliment others; repeats slang and curse words.
- Understands and follows the rules of grammar in conversation and written form.
- Is intrigued with learning secret word codes and using code language.
- Converses fluently with adults; able to think and talk about the past and future: "What time is my swim meet next week?" "Where did we go on vacation last summer?"

Figure 7-10 **Eight-year-olds compose messages and tell stories with imaginative detail.**

© GFOW/Cengage Learning

Social-Emotional Development

- Is more self-assured and confident in own abilities; less likely to be self-critical even when a mistake has been made.
- Begins to form opinions about moral values and attitudes; declares things either right or wrong (based on family and cultural principles) (Lim et al., 2020). Peer group membership also begins to exert a stronger influence on children's moral attitudes and choices (Misch & Dunham, 2021).

Developmental Profiles and Growth Patterns *(continued)*

8-year-old

What Do You See?

Friendships. Having a few "best friends" is important for eight-year-olds. What social-emotional qualities have these boys now developed that make it possible to establish mutual friendships?

iStock.com/monkeybusinessimages

- Plays with two or three "best friends," most often of the same age and gender; makes friends easily; expects and trusts friends to not disclose shared secrets (Liberman, 2020).

- Enjoys spending some time alone; may begin to desire more privacy, which should be respected.

- Seems less critical of own performance but is easily frustrated and upset when unable to complete a task or when the product does not meet expectations.

- Participates in team games and activities; group membership and peer acceptance are becoming more important.

- Shows increased interest in establishing and following rules.

- Continues to blame others or makes up alibis to explain own shortcomings or mistakes.

- Enjoys talking on the telephone or communicating with friends and family via email, texting, Zoom, or a host of social network apps (e.g., Instagram, Snapchat, Spotlite, Kidzworld).

▶❚❚ TeachSource Video Connections

Moral Development

As children mature, they begin to develop a greater understanding of social expectations, the consequences of their choices, and the ability to "know better." Respond to the following questions after you have watched the learning video *5–11 Years: Moral Development in Middle Childhood:*

1. Why are six-, seven-, and eight-year-olds only able to view a person's behavior as being either "right" or "wrong"?

2. What is guilt?

3. How would a child in the preconventional stage of moral development respond to another child who takes an extra cookie at lunchtime and hides it in their pocket? How might the response differ if the child were in the conventional stage?

Developmental Profiles and Growth Patterns *(continued)*

- Understands and respects the fact that some children are more talented in certain areas such as drawing, sports, reading, art, or music.

- Enjoys performing for adults and challenging them in games; is proud of accomplishments and eager for adult recognition and approval. This behavior is less likely to be displayed in cultures where attention to self is discouraged; parental acknowledgment may be expressed quietly or nonverbally through eye contact or a smile.

- Exhibits spur-of-the-moment mood swings, happy one minute, obstinate and rude the next; can be overly sensitive and dramatic.

8-year-old

DAILY ROUTINES

Eating

- Looks forward to meals; boys are often hungry and will consume more food than girls. Serving nutrient-dense foods (such as fruits, vegetables, whole grains, low-fat dairy, and lean meat) and limiting calorie-dense items (candy, cookies, chips, soft drinks, French fries) meets critical growth requirements and reduces the risk of **obesity** (Marotz, 2020). Calorie intake needs to be balanced with physical activity to prevent excessive weight gain.

- Is willing to try new foods and some of those previously refused; likes to make some decisions about foods to be served and eaten.

- Expresses an interest in cooking and assisting with meal preparations.

- Takes pride in using good table manners, especially when eating out or when company is present; at home, manners are of less concern.

- Finishes meals quickly to resume previous activities; may stuff mouth with too much food or not chew food thoroughly in order to hurry through a meal.

Personal Care and Dressing

- Develops a pattern for bowel and bladder functions; usually has good control but may need to urinate more frequently when under stress.

- Hurries through handwashing; dirt often ends up on the towel rather than washed down the drain.

- Enjoys bath and playing in water; easily sidetracked when supposed to be getting ready to bathe; some children are able to prepare their own bath or shower.

- Takes greater interest in appearance, selecting and coordinating own outfits, brushing hair, and looking good.

- Helps to care for own clothes; hangs clothes up most times, assists with laundry by folding and returning items to dresser.

- Ties own shoes skillfully, but often too busy to be bothered.

---

obesity Although no uniform definition exists, experts usually consider a child whose height-weight ratio (otherwise known as body mass index, or BMI) exceeds the 85th percentile for their age to be overweight, and obese if it is greater than the 95th percentile.

8-year-old

DAILY ROUTINES *(continued)*

Sleeping

- Sleeps soundly through the night (requires 10–11 hours); efforts to delay bedtime might suggest that less sleep is needed.

- Begins to question the established bedtime; wants to stay up later; becomes easily distracted and involved in other activities while getting ready for bed.

- Sometimes wakes early and gets dressed while family members are still sleeping.

Play and Social Activities

- Enjoys competitive activities and sports (e.g., soccer, baseball, swimming, or gymnastics); eager to join a team, but just as eager to quit if discouraged or there is too much forced competition.

- Begins to adopt a know-it-all attitude toward the end of the eighth year; becomes bossy or argumentative with peers (and adults) at times; this behavior is more commonly noted not only in Western cultures, but it also may be observed in others.

- Likes to play board, electronic, computer, and card games; often interprets rules to improve their chances of winning.

- Seeks acceptance from peers; begins to imitate the clothing fads, hairstyles, behavior, and language of admired peers.

learning activities to promote **brain development**

Eight-year-olds need many independent opportunities to explore their unique interests—writing, math, science, technology, music, art, sports, dance, and theater—and to practice and advance the knowledge and skills that they already have acquired. They enjoy helping adults and take pride in completing assigned tasks.

Developmentally appropriate applications for families and teachers

- Provide (and join in) games that require a moderate degree of strategy (e.g., chess, checkers, dominoes, card games, magic sets, and educational computer games).

- Encourage creativity; provide materials for painting, crafts, cooking, gardening, science, or building projects.

- Make frequent trips to the library; provide books to read, as well as stories on CDs; many children's books and reading activities are free to download or read online.

- Arrange opportunities for children to participate in noncompetitive activities—swimming, dancing, tumbling, skating, basketball, karate, bowling, or playing a musical instrument; this is a time for exploring many interests and developing new skills; seldom is there a long-term commitment to any particular activity.

- Assign routine household tasks, such as feeding the dog, folding laundry, dusting furniture, bringing in the mail, watering plants, or setting the dinner table, to foster a sense of responsibility and self-esteem.

- Create a family-tree photo album. Have children take pictures of family members with a cell phone or still camera; create an album (in digital or print format), and encourage children to compose a few sentences about each person.

learning activities *(continued)*

- Have fun with music. Help children make instruments from common household objects or discarded items: a cereal-box guitar (with rubber-band "strings"), shakers (a margarine container filled with small pebbles or cereal that can be eaten later), coffee can drums, paper-towel kazoos, etc.

- Provide children with sentence starters and ask them to complete the thought: "When it rains outside I like to…"; "If I could be any animal I would be a…"; "The color blue makes me think about…."; "If I could take a trip anywhere I would go to…"

- Invite children to write and illustrate their own book. Alternatively, read the first few pages of a book together and have children create their own ending to the story.

TeachSource Digital Download

8-year-old

developmental **alerts**

Check with a health-care provider or early childhood specialist if, by the ninth birthday, the child does *not*:

- Exhibit a good appetite and continue to grow (height and weight). (Some children, especially girls, may begin to show early signs of an eating disorder at this point.) Medical evaluation should be sought for excessive weight gains or losses.

- Experience fewer illnesses and sleep well.

- Show improved motor skills in terms of agility, speed, and balance.

- Control strong emotions and physical aggression on most occasions.

- Understand abstract concepts and use complex thought processes to solve problems.

- Look forward to school and the challenge of learning on most days.

- Follow through on multiple-step instructions.

- Express ideas clearly and fluently.

- Form friendships with other children and participate in group activities.

Note: Cultural differences may alter the timetable when some developmental skills are acquired. Expanded Developmental Alerts Checklists appear in Appendix A and are also available as digital downloads.

safety **concerns**

Continue to implement the safety practices described for the previous stages. Be aware of new safety issues as the child continues to grow and develop.

Animals

- Remind children to respect animals (not to approach unfamiliar animals and to refrain from yelling or making sudden movements).
- Teach children to recognize poisonous snakes and to leave them alone.

- Insist on thorough handwashing after touching any animal to avoid illness.

Backpacks

- Provide backpacks with dual shoulder straps to prevent injury; load the heaviest items against the child's

8-year-old

back; packs should weigh less than 20 percent of the child's body weight. Wheeled backpacks are preferable.

Media

- Monitor children's computer use; remove electronic equipment (e.g., computers and video game consoles) from children's bedrooms and place them within view; set parental controls (security) to block access to unwanted Internet sites; establish a family email account for children to use and monitor it closely.
- Talk to children about not giving out personal information to protect their online safety; have them use a nickname when online.
- Know what television programs and movies children are watching, what music they are listening to, and what video games they are playing (both at home and at friends' houses).

Toys

- Supervise the use of more advanced toys, such as chemistry or woodworking sets and those that involve motors, electricity, or propellants.
- Require children to wear a helmet and appropriate protective gear when biking, skating, roller-blading, skateboarding, or playing baseball or softball.

Water and Sport Activities

- Require children to wear a life jacket whenever fishing, boating, skiing, or participating in other water sports.
- Make sure children wear appropriate protective gear (e.g., helmet, knee/elbow pads, mouthguard, eye protection) when participating in sport activities.

positive behavior guidance

Although six-, seven-, and eight-year-olds begin to question and test limits, they also need and want rules that are easy to understand, provide structure, and are enforced consistently. They must be allowed to develop increasing independence, but only with continued adult supervision.

Six-, seven-, and eight-year-olds

- Adults serve as role models for children by displaying positive behavioral responses and self-control. Set a good example: take a deep breath, maintain eye contact, and respond in a calm, nonthreatening manner. If necessary, remove yourself from a stressful situation momentarily until you regain your composure.

- State expectations clearly and in terms that children can understand; enforce them consistently.

- Establish rules in positive terms so that they teach children how to behave appropriately rather than emphasizing behaviors that are deemed unacceptable: "We always go down the slide on our bottoms, feet first," "Hands must be washed before we can eat."

- Acknowledge the child's feelings and frustrations. Listen to their explanations, even though you may not agree with what is said.

- Help children learn effective problem solving, communication, and conflict resolution skills.

- Use logical consequences or withhold privileges when rules have been broken: "I can't let you go to Laura's house because you didn't clean up your room when I asked."

- Acknowledge children's appropriate behavior, such as saying, "You really were a big help by putting away the groceries."

- Avoid the use of time out unless it is necessary to help children regain their composure. Briefly explain why this action is being taken and send children to their room or a quiet area; this allows them time to think about their behavior and to regain emotional control.

- Ignore behaviors that, while inappropriate, are not likely to cause harm to the child or to others. When children end the undesirable behavior, be sure to give them some form of attention or acknowledgment.

Summary

7-1 The transition to formal schooling marks a distinctive change for many children. New experiences and opportunities generally are met with a combination of enthusiasm and improving abilities, as well as periodic reluctance and frustration.

- Children continue to learn best through hands-on experiences with actual materials. They are eager to learn and able to accomplish many complex skills, including reading, writing, telling time, counting money, and following detailed instructions during this stage.

7-2 Children often set high expectations for themselves and then falter when they find that they cannot meet these standards.

- Frustration may be vented through mood swings, unpredictable outbursts, complaints, alibis, and physical aggression on occasion.
- These behaviors tend to decrease in frequency and intensity as children mature and develop better self-control.

7-3 Children's vocabulary expands rapidly during this stage, and their ability to articulate ideas becomes more complex.

7-4 Cognitive maturation enables children to grasp and understand the meaning of increasingly complex concepts, such as numbers, volume, money, distance, space, and time.

7-5 Friends and friendships gradually assume a greater importance for children as they approach age eight. They make friends easily, establish friendships that are longer lasting, and become less dependent on family members to meet their social needs. However, family remains important.

Key Terms

emerging literacy **p. 170**   deciduous teeth **p. 173**   obesity **p. 193**

sensory **p. 170**   conservation **p. 183**

hands-on learning **p. 171**   bullying **p. 189**

Apply What You Have Learned

A. Case Study Connections

Reread the developmental sketch about Huang and Lin presented at the beginning of this chapter and answer the following questions:

1. Which initial forms of screening would you arrange for Lin to ensure that his learning delays were not being caused by a health-related condition?

2. What motor skills would you expect Huang to exhibit if his development was typical for a seven-year-old?

3. Is it appropriate for Huang's mother to encourage his participation in a local youth soccer league? Explain your answer from a developmental perspective.

B. Review Questions

1. Compare and contrast the cognitive skills of the typical six-year-old and eight-year-old.

2. Should you be concerned about a seven-year-old who weighs 75 pounds? Explain.

3. What classroom activities can a teacher plan to reinforce eight-year-olds' interest in reading and writing?

4. Describe three perceptual skills that indicate a readiness to begin reading.

5. Identify three reasonable expectations for a six-year-old in terms of family routines.

C. Your Turn: Chapter to Practice

1. Interview at least five children who are seven or eight years old. Find out if they ever feel afraid at school. How often do they feel this way? What makes them afraid? Do they tell anyone about what they are experiencing? Summarize and comment on your findings.

2. Make arrangements to observe a first- or second-grade classroom. Describe what steps the teacher has taken to address ethnic and cultural diversity. What additional suggestions would you offer?

3. Visit a local retail store where children's toys are sold. Identify two toys that you think would appeal to a six-year-old. Briefly describe each toy and explain what qualities make it a safe and developmentally appropriate choice.

4. Conduct a 15-minute observation of a kindergarten class during their outdoor recess period. What types of behavior problems did you note during this time? How did the supervising teacher handle each situation, and was the approach effective? Would you have responded differently? If so, explain how.

Online Resources

Healthy Youth
This CDC site offers comprehensive information on a range of topics that include children's well-being, school health, nutrition, physical activity, statistics, funding opportunities, and media resources.

National Center for Cultural Competence
This award-winning site is sponsored by the Georgetown University Center for Child and Human Development. Extensive self-assessment and resource materials on cultural, linguistic, and family diversity are provided (also available in Spanish).

National Center for Families Learning (NCFL)
The organization's mission is to "eradicate poverty through education solutions for families." Numerous culturally-relevant literacy resources that "support multigenerational learning for families from early childhood through adulthood" can be accessed on this website. Be sure to explore all areas of the *Professional Development* and *Free Resources* (see, *Wonderopolos*® for kids and their *Circles*® curriculum for Native American children) sections for materials that are offered in many languages.

Stopbullying.gov
The U.S. Department of Health and Human Services has posted information about bullying and cyberbullying at this website, including definitions, access to state bullying laws and policies, and prevention resource materials for families, children, educators, and community organizations.

References

Afshordi, N., & Liberman, Z. (2021). Keeping friends in mind: Development of friendship concepts in early childhood. *Social Development, 30*(2), 331–342.

Agathão, B. R., Lopes, C. S., Cunha, D. B., & Sichieri, R. (2020). Gender differences in the impact of sleep duration on common mental disorders in school students. *BMC Public Health, 20*, 148. https://doi.org/10.1186/s12889-020-8260-5

Allee-Herndon, K. A., & Roberts, S. K. (2021). The power of purposeful play in primary grades: Adjusting pedagogy for children's needs and academic gains. *Journal of Education, 201*(1), 54–63.

Armitage, R. (2021). Bullying in children: Impact on child health. *BMJ Paediatric Open, 5*(1), e000939. https://doi.org/10.1136/bmjpo-2020-000939

Baiden, P., LaBrenz, C. A., Okine, L., Thrasher, S., & Asiedua-Baiden, G. (2020). The toxic duo: Bullying involvement and adverse childhood experiences as factors associated with school disengagement among children. *Children and Youth Services Review, 119*, 105383. https://doi.org/10.1016/j.childyouth.2020.105383

Brix, N., Ernst, A., Lauridsen, L. L. B., Parner, E. T., Arah, O. A., Olsen, J., Henriksen, T. B., & Ramlau-Hansena, C. H. (2020). Childhood overweight and obesity and timing of puberty in boys and girls: Cohort and sibling-matched analyses. *International Journal of Epidemiology, 49*(3), 834–844.

Brown, C. P., Ku, D. H., & Barry, D. P. (2021). Making sense of instruction within the changed kindergarten: Perspectives from preservice early childhood educators and teacher educators. *Journal of Early Childhood Teacher Education, 42*(1), 20–52.

Burnham, J. J., Mutua, K., Tallent, D. A., Robinson, O. P., Bledsoe, K. G., & Davis, A. P. (2018). Comparing the fears of children with and without significant disabilities. *Canadian Journal of Counselling and Psychotherapy, 52*(3). Retrieved from https://cjc-rcc.ucalgary.ca/article/view/61187.

Centers for Disease Control and Prevention (CDC). (2021). Bystanders to bullying. Retrieved from https://www.stopbullying.gov/prevention/bystanders-to-bullying.

Cunningham, A. J., Burgess, A. P., Witton, C., Talcott, J. B., & Shapiro, L. R. (2021). Dynamic relationships between phonological memory and reading: A five year longitudinal study from age 4 to 9. *Developmental Science, 24*(1), e12986. Retrieved from https://doi.org/10.1111/desc.12986.

Daniel, L. C., Childress, J. L., Flannery, J. L., Weaver-Rogers, S., Garcia, W. I., Bonilla-Santiago, G., & Williamson, A. A. (2020). Identifying modifiable factors linking parenting and sleep in racial/ethnic minority children. *Journal of Pediatric Psychology, 45*(8), 867–876.

DeLuca, C., Pyle, A., Braund, H., & Faith, L. (2020). Leveraging assessment to promote kindergarten learners' independence and self-regulation within play-based classrooms. *Assessment in Education: Principles, Policy & Practice, 27*(4), 394–415.

Fehr, K. K., Chambers, D. E., & Ramasami, J. (2021). The impact of anxiety on behavioral sleep difficulties and treatment in young children: A review of the literature. *Journal of Clinical Psychology in Medical Settings, 28*, 102–112.

Gaffney, H., Ttofi, M. M., & Farrington, D. P. (2021). What works in anti-bullying programs? Analysis of effective intervention components. *Journal of School Psychology, 85*, 37–56.

Gage, N. A., Katsiyannis, A., Rose, C., & Adams, S. E. (2021, March 24). Disproportionate bullying victimization and perpetration by disability status, race, and gender: A national analysis. *Advances in Neurodevelopmental Disorders.* https://doi.org/10.1007/s41252-021-00200-2

Galván, A. (2020). The need for sleep in the adolescent brain. *Trends in Cognitive Sciences, 24*(1), 70–89.

Gordon, A., & Browne, K. (2016). *Beginnings and beyond: Foundations in early childhood education* (10th ed.). Boston, MA: Cengage Learning.

Groeneveld, M. G., Savas, M., van Rossum, E. F. C., & Vermeer, H. J. (2020). Children's hair cortisol as a biomarker of stress at school: A follow-up study. *Stress, 23*(5), 590–596.

Gutiérrez, I. T., Menendez, D., Jiang, M. J., Hernandez, I. G., Miller, P., & Rosengren, K. S. (2020). Embracing death: Mexican parent and child perspectives on death. *Child Development, 91*(2), e491–e511.

Hamanouche, K., & Cordes, S. (2020). Learning about time: Knowledge of formal timing symbols is related to individual differences in temporal precision. *Journal of Experimental Psychology: Learning, Memory, and Cognition, 46*(1), 117–126.

Hamel, N., Schwab, S., & Wahl, S. (2021). Bullying: Group differences of being victim and being bully and the influence of social relations. *Studies in Educational Evaluation, 68*, 100964. https://doi.org/10.1016/j.stueduc.2020.100964

Haslip, M. J., & Gullo, D. F. (2018). The changing landscape of early childhood education: Implications for policy and practice. *Early Childhood Education Journal, 46*, 249–264.

Hawes, Z., & Ansari, D. (2020). What explains the relationship between spatial and mathematical skills? A review of evidence from brain and behavior. *Psychonomic Bulletin & Review, 27*, 465–482.

Hershner, S. (2020). Sleep and academic performance: Measuring the impact of sleep. *Current Opinion in Behavioral Sciences, 22*, 51–56.

Hong, J. S., Kim, D. H., Narvey, C., Piquero, A. R., deLara, E., & Padilla, Y. C. (2020 June). Understanding the link between family economic hardship and children's bullying behavior. *Youth & Society.* https://doi.org/10.1177/0044118X20932594

Hui, L., Forbes, A., & Yang, W. (2021). Developing culturally and developmentally appropriate early STEM learning experiences. *Early Education and Development, 32*(1), 1–6.

Jeon, M., Dimitriou, D., & Halstead, E. J. (2021). Comparative studies of sleep in young populations: The roles of cultural factors. *International Journal of Environmental Research and Public Health, 18*(4), 1–45.

Johnson, K. P., & Zarrinnegar, P. (2021). Autism spectrum disorder and sleep. *Child & Adolescent Psychiatric Clinics, 30*(1), 195–208.

Leske, D. A., Hatt, S. R., Wernimont, S. M., Castañeda, Y. S., Cheng-Patel, C. S., Liebermann, L., Birch, E. E., & Holmes, J. M. (2021). Association of visual acuity with eye-related quality of life and functional vision across childhood eye conditions. *American Journal of Ophthalmology, 223,* 220–228.

Lewien, C., Genuneit, J., Meigen, C., Kiess, W., & Poulain, T. (2021). Sleep-related difficulties in healthy children and adolescents. *BMC Pediatrics, 21,* 82. https://doi.org/10.1186/s12887-021-02529-y

Liberman, Z. (2020). Keep the cat in the bag: Children understand that telling a friend's secret can harm the friendship. *Developmental Psychology, 56*(7), 1290–1304.

Lim, J., Peterson, C. C., De Rosnay, M., & Slaughter, V. (2020). Children's moral evaluations of prosocial and self-interested lying in relation to age, ToM, cognitive empathy and culture. *European Journal of Developmental Psychology, 17*(4), 504–526.

Lloyd-Esenkaya, V., Forrest, C. L., Jordan, A., Russell, A. J., & St Clair, M. C. (2021). What is the nature of peer interactions in children with language disorders? A qualitative study of parent and practitioner views. *Autism and Developmental Language Impairments, 6.* Retrieved from https://doi.org/10.1177/23969415211005307.

Luk, G., Pliatsikas, C., & Rossi, E. (2020). Brain changes associated with language development and learning: A primer on methodology and applications. *System, 89,* 102209. https://doi.org/10.1016/j.system.2020.102209

Mapes, A. R., Scafe, M., Mutignani, L. M., Rodriguez, J. H., Pastrana, F. A., Gregus, S., Craig, J. T., & Cavell, T. A. (2020). Liked by peers or liked by teachers: Differential patterns of bullying over time. *Journal of School Violence, 19*(4), 470–484.

Marcus, M., & Tomasi, D. (2020). Emotional and cognitive responses to academic performance and grade anxiety. *Journal of Medical Research and Health Sciences, 3*(4), 919–925.

Marotz, L. R. (2020). *Health, safety, and nutrition for the young child* (10th ed.). Boston, MA: Cengage.

Migueles, J. H., Cadenas-Sanchez, C., Esteban-Cornejo, I., Mora-Gonzalez, J., Rodriguez-Ayllon, M., Solis-Urra, P., Erickson, K. I., Kramer, A. F., Hillman, C. H., Catena, A., & Ortega, C. A. (2021). Associations of sleep with gray matter volume and their implications for academic achievement, executive function and intelligence in children with overweight/obesity. *Pediatric Obesity, 16*(2), e12707. https://doi.org/10.1111/ijpo.12707

Miller, M. A., Bates, S., Ji, C., & Cappuccio, F. P. (2021). Systematic review and meta-analyses of the relationship between short sleep and incidence of obesity and effectiveness of sleep interventions on weight gain in preschool children. *Obesity Reviews, 22*(2), e13113. https://doi.org/10.1111/obr.13113

Misch, A., & Dunham, Y. (2021). (Peer) Group influence on children's prosocial and antisocial behavior. *Journal of Experimental Child Psychology, 201,* 104994. https://doi.org/10.1016/j.jecp.2020.104994

Musch, D. C., Andrews, C., Schumann, R., & Baker, J. (2020). A community-based effort to increase the rate of follow-up eye examinations of school-age children who fail vision screening: A randomized clinical trial. *Journal of American Association for Pediatric Ophthalmology and Strabismus, 24*(2), 98. e1–98.e4. https://doi.org/10.1016/j.jaapos.2019.12.012

National Association for the Education of Young Children (NAEYC). (2020). *Developmentally Appropriate Practice.* Retrieved from https://www.naeyc.org/resources/position-statements/dap/contents.

Newton, A. T., Honaker, S. M., & Reid, G. J. (2020). Risk and protective factors and processes for behavioral sleep problems among preschool and early school-aged children: A systematic review. *Sleep Medicine Reviews, 52,* 101303. https://doi.org/10.1016/j.smrv.2020.101303

Ordway, M. R., Sadler, L., S., Jeon, S., O'Connell, M., Banasiak, N., Fenick, A. M., Crowley, A. A., Canapari, C., & Redeker, N. S. (2020). Sleep health in young children living with socioeconomic adversity. *Research in Nursing & Health, 43*(4), 329–340.

Pan, B., Zhang, L., Ji, L., Garandeau, C. F., Salmivalli, C., & Zhang, W. (2020). Classroom status hierarchy moderates association between social dominance goals and bullying behavior in middle childhood and early adolescence. *Journal of Youth and Adolescence, 49,* 2285–2297. https://doi.org/10.1007/s10964-020-01285-z

Panagiotaki, G., Hopkins, M., Nobes, G., Ward, E., & Griffiths, D. (2018). Children's and adults' understanding of death: Cognitive, parental, and experiential influences. *Journal of Experimental Child Psychology, 166,* 96–115.

Peiffer, A., Brichet, M., De Tiège, X., Peigneux, P., & Urbain, C. (2020). The power of children's sleep - Improved declarative memory consolidation in children compared with adults. *Scientific Reports, 10*(1), 9979. https://doi.org/10.1038/s41598-020-66880-3

Piaget, J. (1926). *The language and thought of the child.* New York: Harcourt, Brace, & World.

Piaget, J. (1929). *The child's conception of the world.* New York: Harcourt Brace.

Qian, L., Taotao, R., Xue, L., Jiaxing, N., Yongjun, M., & Zhou, G. (2020). Effect of sleep restriction on cognitive function and its underlying mechanism. *Advances in Psychological Science, 28*(9), 1493–1507.

Schwartz-Mette, R. A., Shankman, J., Dueweke, A. R., Borowski, S., & Rose, A. J. (2020). Relations of friendship experiences with depressive symptoms and loneliness in childhood and adolescence: A meta-analytic review. *Psychological Bulletin, 146*(8), 664–700.

Simon, E. B., Vallat, R., Barnes, C. M., & Walker, M. P. (2020). Sleep loss and the socio-emotional brain. *Trends in Cognitive Sciences, 24*(6), 435–450.

Soylu, F., & Newman, S. D. (2020). Editorial: Towards an understanding of the relationship between spatial processing ability and numerical and mathematical cognition. *Frontiers in Psychology, 11*, 14. https://doi.org/10.3389/fpsyg.2020.00014

Spence, J. L., Hornsey, M. J., & Imuta, K. (2021). Something about the way you speak: A meta-analysis on children's linguistic-based social preferences. *Child Development, 92*(2), 517–535.

Taliaferro, L. A., Doty, J. L., Gower, A. L., Querna, K., & Rovito, M. J. (2020). Profiles of risk and protection for violence and bullying perpetration among adolescent boys. *Journal of School Health, 90*(3), 212–223.

Tatiani, G. (2021). The influence of parental style and socioeconomic circumstances on school bullying: A systematic review. *Journal of Educational Research and Reviews, 9*(1), 1–5.

Taylor, M. E., & Boyer, W. (2020). Play-based learning: Evidence-based research to improve children's learning experiences in the kindergarten classroom. *Early Childhood Education Journal, 48*, 127–133.

Torregrossa, J., Andreou, M., Bongartz, C., & Tsimpli, I. M. (2021). Bilingual acquisition of reference: The role of language experience, executive functions and cross-linguistic effects. *Bilingualism: Language and Cognition*, 1–13. https://doi.org/10.1017/S1366728920000826

Torun, E. G., Ertugrul, A., Tekguc, & Bostanci, I. (2020). Sleep patterns and development of children with atopic dermatitis. *International Archives of Allergy and Immunology, 181*(11), 871–878.

Ujma, P. P., Bódizs, R., & Dresler, M. (2020). Sleep and intelligence: Critical review and future directions. *Current Opinion in Behavioral Sciences, 33*, 109–117.

Wallin, J., & Cheevakumjorn, B. (2020). Learning English as a second language: Earlier is better. *Journal of English Educators Society, 5*(1), 1–8.

Watson-Jones, R. E., Busch, J. T., Harris, P. L., & Legare, C. H. (2017). Does the body survive death? Cultural variation in beliefs about life everlasting. *Cognitive Science, 41*(S3), 455–476.

Williamson, A. A., Mindell, J. A., Hiscock, H., & Quach, J. (2020). Longitudinal sleep problem trajectories are associated with multiple impairments in child well-being. *The Journal of Child Psychology & Psychiatry, 61*(10), 1092–1103.

Woodgate, R. L., Gonzalez, M., Demczuk, L., Snow, W. M., Barriage, S., & Kirk, S. (2020). How do peers promote social inclusion of children with disabilities? A mixed-methods systematic review. *Disability & Rehabilitation, 42*(18), 2553–2579.

iStock.com/Inside Creative House

Chapter 8

Middle Childhood: Nine-, Ten-, Eleven-, and Twelve-Year-Olds

Learning Objectives

After reading this chapter, you will be able to:

8-1 Provide examples of the physical changes that occur during early puberty.

8-2 Define the concept of friendship from a nine- and a ten-year-old's perspective.

8-3 Plan developmentally appropriate activities for nine- to ten-year-olds and eleven- to twelve-year-olds.

8-4 Compare and contrast the language development of nine- and ten-year-olds with that of eleven- and twelve-year-olds.

NAEYC NAEYC Professional Standards Linked to Chapter Content

1a, 1b, and 1c: Child development and learning in context

2a and 2c: Family–teacher partnerships and community connections

3a, 3c, and 3d: Child observations, documentation, and assessment

4a and 4b: Developmentally, culturally, and linguistically appropriate teaching practices

6c: Professionalism as an early childhood educator

Jacob's mother has been a single parent for several years and is soon to be remarried. Jacob, who will soon turn twelve, thinks it is "awesome to finally have a father again." He and his new stepfather have already spent many hours together, attending sporting events, camping in the mountains, going on long bike rides, and building model airplanes. Jacob enjoys school, especially his math and computer classes, and has many "best friends." His teacher considers Jacob a model student and appreciates his hard work and offers to help around the classroom.

Jacob has been adjusting slowly to the idea of having a stepsister. Madie, a caring and talkative nine-year-old, is somewhat less enthusiastic than Jacob about school. During the last parent–teacher conference, Madie's teachers expressed concern about her inability to remain seated and focused on assignments for longer than five or ten minutes at a time. Her stepmother has made similar observations at home. Madie has difficulty following multistep directions and is often quite disorganized. She "forgets" to feed the dog, that she was asked to set the dinner table, and when her homework assignments are due. She has few friends and prefers to play alone in her room, or with her new stepbrother and his friends. However, Jacob finds it annoying when Madie tags along and frequently begs his mother to make her stop.

Ask Yourself

- How would you describe a typical eleven-year-old's development based on this scenario?
- Would you refer Madie to an early childhood specialist for evaluation if you were her teacher? Why? Why not?

Nine-, Ten-, Eleven-, and Twelve-Year Olds

The stretch of years from age eight to twelve is usually an enjoyable and relatively peaceful time for the most part. Children are able to plan ahead and to delay their immediate desires. Spontaneous behavior is gradually channeled into more goal-directed efforts as children begin making the transition from a state of dependence to one of greater independence. Although they are no longer young children, preteens are also not yet capable adults. This tension can lead to increased doubts, loss of self-esteem, and questions about how they should fit in.

The middle years are also marked by a hunger for knowledge and understanding. Most children have adjusted to being at school for six or more hours each day. The stresses, strains, and frustrations of learning to read, write, do basic arithmetic, and follow directions are long forgotten. Language usage becomes more sophisticated and adultlike. During this period, children also develop an increasingly complex ability to think in the abstract, understand cause and effect, and use **logic** to solve problems and figure out how things work. They comprehend that some items can serve different purposes—a shovel can be used not only for digging, but also for prying the lid off of a paint can; a broom can be used for sweeping or playing hockey; a mixing bowl can be used to draw a perfect circle.

Near the end of this stage, many children begin to undergo early physical and developmental changes associated with puberty. The onset and extent of these changes vary from child to child and also reflect the influence of genetic, ethnic, and cultural differences (Figure 8-1). Early hormonal changes, noted in some girls and boys who are as young as eight or nine years of age, have raised questions about the effects this may have on children's social and emotional development. Children who experience precocious puberty are often subjected to bullying, teasing, and social isolation (Skoog & Kapetanovi, 2021). They are also more likely to develop depression and other psychiatric disorders as they struggle with these changes (Coban et al., 2021). Researchers are trying to determine why puberty is occurring earlier and have identified several major risk factors, including genetics, environment, and childhood obesity (Canton et al., 2021; Loochi et al., 2021).

iStock.com/FatCamera

Figure 8-1 Children grow and develop at very different rates.

logic A process of reasoning based on a series of facts or events.

It is important that parents prepare children for the changes that they will begin to experience as they approach puberty (e.g., enlarging breasts, menstruation, facial and pubic hair, spontaneous erections, deepening voice, moodiness, and modesty) so that they are not confused or frightened by what is occurring. These discussions should include information about physical and emotional changes that both genders undergo to help children understand that puberty is universal. The American Academy of Pediatrics (AAP), Canadian Paediatric Society (CPS), and similar health organizations have posted information on their websites to help parents address the topic of puberty with children. Although sex education is taught in some schools, children may find the information intimidating and be uncomfortable asking questions in the presence of their peers. Reassuring children that these developmental changes are normal and that they can count on parents or other trusted adult to answer their questions is crucial in achieving a healthy transition.

Middle childhood is also a time when some children may begin to experiment with new behaviors, such as wearing alternative clothing and hairstyles, quitting a longtime sport or favorite musical instrument, forming associations with a "different crowd," or dieting. Families may find these changes distressing, but they are part of an important developmental process that shapes self-identity and helps children determine what ultimately is right for them. A small percentage of children may also begin to experiment with substances such as legal or illegal drugs, tobacco, alcohol, e-cigarettes, or inhalants, which can pose a serious threat to their well-being and may require professional intervention and treatment. Low self-esteem, peer victimization, exposure to neighborhood crime and drugs, and family conflict increase the likelihood that children will engage in these behaviors (Sigal et al., 2021; Wang et al., 2021b).

Although children's ideas about gender identity and behavior are relatively set by middle childhood, some male–female contrasts become more evident during this stage (Klaczynski, Felmban, & Kole, 2020). Boys' ideas about what is masculine remain quite rigid and tend to follow a more stereotypical path (e.g., football, baseball, or competitive video games). In contrast, girls may be completely at ease with their femininity and also begin to branch out and explore a broad range of activities, such as hunting, fishing, carpentry, cross-country running, and team sports. However, there is limited tolerance for crossing gender lines, especially when it comes to boys who hang around with girls, exhibit "unmanly" behavior, or dress in feminine-type clothing (Masters, Hixson, & Hayes, 2021; Smith et al., 2018). It must be remembered that a child's ethnic and cultural heritage continues to be a strong determinant in shaping gender behavior and role expectations.

Despite frequent protests and rejections, children still want and need their family's continued trust and support. It is important that families and teachers maintain an ongoing dialogue with children about subjects such as personal health, substance abuse (i.e., drugs, alcohol, and smoking), online safety, and sex education (i.e., typical development, pregnancy, and protection from sexually transmitted diseases) because many of these decisions have serious, long-term consequences. When adults treat these issues in an open and nonthreatening manner and continue to monitor children's behavior, they convey a sense of understanding and compassion. In turn, parental caring fosters children's self-esteem and reduces the likelihood that they will engage in risky behaviors (Orihuela et al., 2020; Sigal et al., 2021; Wang et al., 2021a).

Nine- and Ten-Year-Olds

Most nine- and ten-year-olds have entered a phase of relative contentment—sometimes described as the calm before the storm of adolescence. Although nine-year-olds may still display some emotional highs and lows, these outbursts gradually mellow by age 10. Home and family continue to provide a source of security and comfort for most children. Hugs and kisses are still offered as signs of affection for family members.

Most nine- and ten-year-olds also find school enjoyable. They eagerly anticipate classes and meeting with friends and are disappointed if they must miss out on school activities. Teachers are respected and their attention is highly coveted. Small homemade gifts and offers of assistance are made in the hope of pleasing one's teachers. Although children's attention span is longer, they still have considerable restless energy that must be released. Frequent opportunities to move about in the classroom and to play outdoors are essential for reducing undesirable behavior (Dodd & Lester, 2021; Fedewa et al., 2021).

What Do You See?

Physical development. Nine- and ten-year-olds enjoy and seek out challenge. What developmental advancements make it possible for this girl to do what she is doing?

© GFOW/Cengage Learning

Developmental Profiles and Growth Patterns

Growth and Physical Characteristics

- Grows at a slow and irregular rate; girls begin to experience growth spurts that are far more dramatic than those of boys; boys are more alike in size and smaller than most girls.
- Assumes a slimmer shape as fat accumulations begin to shift.
- Appears awkward as various body parts grow at different rates; the lower half of body grows faster; the arms and legs appear long and out of proportion to the rest of the body.
- Brain increases significantly in size, almost reaching adult proportions by age 10.
- Gains approximately 2 inches (5 cm) in height each year; increases are usually greater during growth spurts.
- Adds approximately 6 1/2 pounds (14.3 kg) per year.

9 and 10 year olds

Developmental Profiles and Growth Patterns *(continued)*

- Loses remaining "baby" teeth; overcrowding might occur when larger, permanent teeth erupt into a still-small jaw.
- Begins to experience early prepubertal changes. Some girls may begin to develop budding breasts, appearance of pubic hair, rounding of hips, accentuated waistline; darkening of hair color; boys are less likely to undergo any observable sexual changes for another year or two.

Motor Development

- Throws a ball with accuracy; writes, sketches, and performs other fine motor skills with improved coordination. This period is marked by continued refinement of fine motor skills, especially notable among girls (Liutsko et al., 2020).
- Uses arms, legs, hands, and feet with ease and improved precision; boys tend to excel in large motor activities that require strength and speed (Adriyani, Iskandar, & Camelia, 2020; Gillen et al., 2019).
- Runs, climbs, skips rope, swims, rides bikes, and skates with skill and confidence.
- Enjoys team sports, but still may need to develop some of the necessary complex skills.
- Likes to use hands for arts and crafts, cooking, woodworking, needlework, painting, building models, or taking apart objects such as a clock or telephone.
- Includes considerable detail in drawings.
- Takes great joy and pride in writing and perfecting handwriting skills.

Perceptual-Cognitive Development

- Develops the ability to reason based more on experience and logic than on **intuition** (Piaget's stage of **concrete operational thought**): "If I hurry and walk the dog, I will have time to play with my friends." Still sees some situations as either/or, with "yes" or "no" answers, but is beginning to think in less concrete, more creative ways (Anil & Bhat, 2020; Piaget, 1928). Understands abstract concepts if real (concrete) objects can be seen and manipulated: "If I eat one cookie now, only two will be left for later."

iStock.com/fstop123

Figure 8-2 Hands-on involvement continues to support optimal learning.

- Likes challenges in arithmetic, but does not always understand mathematical relationships involved in complex operations such as multiplication or division (Clark, Hudnall, & Pérez-González, 2020; Grenier et al., 2020).
- Learns best through hands-on learning; prefers to research information in books or online, conduct science experiments, build models, or put on a play rather than listen to teachers' lectures that produce the same information (Figure 8-2).

intuition A thought or idea based on a feeling or hunch.

concrete operational thought Piaget's third stage of cognitive development; the period when conservation and classification concepts are understood.

Developmental Profiles and Growth Patterns *(continued)*

- Enjoys time at school; finds it difficult to sit still for periods longer than 30 minutes; forgets all about school as soon as it is over.

- Uses reading and writing skills for activities outside of school (e.g., compiling shopping lists, composing scripts for puppet shows, drawing and labeling neighborhood maps, texting or sending email).

- Shows improved understanding of cause and effect.

- Continues to master concepts of time, weight, volume, and distance.

- Traces events based on recall; is able to think in reverse, following a series of occurrences back to their beginnings.

- Prefers reading books that are longer, contain greater detail and description, and provide complex plots.

- Looks for ways to earn money; plans and saves money for a special purchase.

Speech and Language Development

- Talks, often nonstop and for no specific reason; sometimes talks simply to gain attention; may be reserved in the classroom, but boisterous and talkative at other times.

- Expresses feelings and emotions effectively through words.

- Understands and uses language as a system for communicating with others.

- Uses slang expressions commonly expressed by peers in conversation (e.g., "sweet," "seriously," "awesome," "hey dude").

- Recognizes that some words have double meanings (e.g., "far out," "cool haircut," "wicked," or "chill").

- Finds humor in using illogical metaphors (plays on words) in jokes and riddles; being funny appears to increase children's popularity among peers (Halfpenny & James, 2020; Laursen et al., 2020) (Figure 8-3).

- Shows advanced understanding of grammatical sequences; recognizes when a sentence is not grammatically correct.

> **Did You Know** ?
>
> ...that researchers have identified cultural differences in the timing and methods used to teach children about numerical concepts, values, and manipulations (e.g., adding, subtracting, multiplying, and division) that appear to give Asian children an advantage in mathematics over their Western counterparts?

© Creatista/Shutterstock.com

Figure 8-3 Nine- and ten-year-olds delight in telling jokes and riddles.

Developmental Profiles and Growth Patterns *(continued)*

Social-Emotional Development

- Enjoys being with friends; seeks out friendships based on mutual interests, gender, and proximity (neighborhood children, classmates, online contacts); may rely heavily on social media (TikTok, Instagram, Snapchat) for self-expression, entertainment, acknowledgement ("likes"), and "friend" networks. Has several "good" friends and an "enemy" or two; friends and friendships may change from day to day; is often verbally critical of another gender ("Boys are too rough," "Girls are sissies") (Bukowski & DeLay, 2020; Kitts, & Leal, 2021).

- Begins to show more interest in rules and basing games on realistic play; rules should be kept simple so that everyone enjoys playing (Figure 8-4). Likes to win and is not always a good loser.

Figure 8-4 Children begin to develop the concepts of fairness, honesty, and distinguishing right from wrong during this stage.

- Responds with name-calling and teasing when provoked; less likely to use physical aggression than previously; also understands that such behavior can affect others' feelings (Wang et al., 2020b). Still relies on adults occasionally to settle some disputes.

- Begins to develop moral reasoning and perspective taking; adopts social customs and moral values of one's culture; understands honesty, right from wrong, fairness, good and bad, tolerance, and respect but the evidence may not always be apparent in their behavior (Booker et al., 2021; Verkuyten & Killen, 2021).

- Develops strong attachments to teachers, coaches, and club leaders; may see them as heroes; often makes an extra effort to please them and gain their attention.

- Acts with considerable confidence; often believe that they know everything and can do no wrong.

- Takes criticism as a personal attack; feelings are easily hurt; has difficulty at times dealing with failure and frustration.

- Worries about daily experiences (e.g., school performance, peer relationships, family expectations, victimization, bodily changes); such occurrences are not uncommon and may cause considerable distress (Bacter et al., 2021; CDC, 2021a; Pickering, Hadwin, & Kovshoff, 2020); persistent signs of anxiety, stress, or depression require medical attention.

▶❚❚ TeachSource **Video Connections**

Emotional Development and Bullying

Although most grade-school children achieve reasonable control of their emotions, a small percentage may engage in aggressive, antisocial behavior that is intentional. Respond to the following questions after you have watched the learning video *School Age: Emotional Development*:

1. What consequences may children experience if they are being bullied?

2. Why might some children who are bullied be reluctant to tell an adult?

3. What should children be taught about how to respond to bullying?

DAILY ROUTINES

Eating

- Experiences fluctuating appetite depending upon the amount and vigor of activity; consumes more food with increased activity; prefers to eat when hungry rather than at prescribed times.

- Eats at any time of day, yet often is still hungry at mealtime; is more receptive to trying new foods. Many children also enjoy cooking and helping with meal preparations. Prefers certain favorite foods, usually pizza, French fries, tacos, burgers, ice cream, and cookies; has few dislikes, but is less fond of cooked vegetables (tends to prefer them raw).

- Battles over posture and table manners (e.g., elbows on the table; slouched in chair; or a fisted grasp of forks and spoons) but usually displays good manners when eating out or at a friend's house.

- Overeating may occur when children are feeling stressed or anxious; may develop into an eating disorder if the behavior persists (Thomas, Williams, & Vanderwert, 2021).

Personal Care and Dressing

- Shows limited interest in personal hygiene; often needs reminders to bathe, wash hair, brush teeth, and put on clean clothes.

- Requires coaxing to bathe but, after a bath is started, may not want to get out of the tub or shower.

- Takes some interest in appearance; wants to dress and look like friends; school clothes take on an important role in self-identification.

- Manages own toileting needs without reminders; seldom gets up at night unless too much liquid is consumed before bedtime.

9 and 10 year olds

DAILY ROUTINES *(continued)*

Sleeping

- Seems unaware of fatigue and the need for sleep.

- Requires 9–10 hours of sleep to function throughout the day. Wakes up in time for school without much coaxing if getting enough sleep. Sleep is essential for the consolidation of information and long-term memory. Insufficient sleep interferes with learning and has also been linked to increased weight gain (Leong et al., 2019; Schroeder et al., 2020).

- Girls may have more bedtime rituals and take longer to fall asleep than do boys.

- Nightmares and fear of the dark may redevelop; some children experience sleepwalking, waking up in the middle of the night, or bed-wetting. Parents should not criticize children who develop these problems, and seek professional help if they persist.

Play and Social Activities

- Maintains activity level that fluctuates between extremes of high intensity and almost nonexistent activity; may virtually collapse following periods of intense play. Strong positive associations have been established between children's engagement in physical activity and enhanced cognitive functioning and mental health (Getu, 2020; Zeng et al., 2021).

- Spends free time reading magazines, playing computer games, watching videos, listening to music, texting, and talking with friends.

- Forms and joins clubs with secret codes, languages, and signs.

- Offers to help with simple household chores such as dusting and sweeping, vacuuming, putting away groceries, and washing the car.

- Develops new hobbies or collections based on special interests.

learning activities to promote **brain development**

Nine- and ten-year-olds are ready and eager for new challenges that involve learning and applying developmental skills. Reading, writing, experimenting, adventure, and competitive games are among their favorite activities. They also enjoy crafts and doing things with their hands, such as building, drawing, and assembling collections.

Developmentally appropriate applications for families and teachers

- Take advantage of educational opportunities in the community. Plan outings to the beach, farmers' market, library, museums, zoo, park, aquarium, garden center, cabinet-maker, pet shop, arboretum or nature center, or grocery store.

- Encourage children to appreciate diversity by learning about the customs and celebrations of other cultures. Obtain library books, visit websites, invite guests, locate musical instruments, attend celebrations, and prepare ethnic foods for children to taste. Teach children to be respectful and to avoid prejudicial actions and language.

- Gather sports equipment such as balls, bats, nets, and rackets; encourage children to organize and participate in group activities. Know the signs of concussion and monitor children closely.

- Provide space, seeds, and tools for planting and maintaining a garden.

9 and 10 year olds

learning activities *(continued)*

- Assemble materials and provide basic instructions for conducting science experiments; science activity suggestions can be found in many good books at the public library or on child-oriented websites.

- Nurture children's interest in reading, writing, and friendships by locating pen pals in another state or country: encourage children to correspond (via letter, email, Zoom, or Duo); read books about where a pen pal lives; locate the state or country on a map.

- Encourage children to participate in at least 60 minutes of vigorous physical activity daily for healthy development; plan some activities that all family members can do together.

- Maintain open communication with children. Spend time together, talk about their interests and friends, and be caring, respectful, and supportive.

TeachSource Digital Download

developmental **alerts**

Check with a health-care provider or early childhood specialist if, by the eleventh birthday, the child does *not*:

- Continue to grow at a rate appropriate for the child's gender.

- Show continued improvement of fine motor skills.

- Make or keep friends.

- Enjoy going to school and show interest in learning most days. (If this does not happen, have children's hearing and vision tested; vision and hearing problems affect children's ability to learn and maintain their interest in learning. Also observe children for signs of anxiety, undue stress, or depression; seek medical care if the behaviors persist.)

- Approach new situations with reasonable confidence; show a willingness to try.

- Handle failure and frustration in a constructive manner; learn from mistakes.

- Sleep through the night or experiences prolonged problems with bed-wetting, nightmares, or sleepwalking.

Note: Cultural differences may alter the timetable when some developmental skills are acquired. Expanded Developmental Alerts Checklists appear in Appendix A and are also available as digital downloads.

safety **concerns**

Continue to implement the safety practices described for the previous stages. Always be aware of new safety issues as the child continues to grow and develop.

Media Exposure

- Be aware of websites (and content) that children visit. Teach them Internet safety rules and the importance of not giving out personal information (e.g., name, address, telephone number, or birth date) online. Set security controls to block websites that you don't want children to access.

safety **concerns** (continued)

- Know what music children listen to, what video games they play, and what movies they watch, to determine whether they are being exposed to violence, sex, or the drug culture.

Firearms

- Educate children about the dangers of guns and other weapons. Stress the importance of not handling firearms and always alerting an adult if one is found.
- Store firearms and ammunition separately and keep in locked storage; never leave loaded firearms unattended.

Traffic

- Insist that children wear seat belts on every motor trip.

- Review safe practices for crossing streets, getting in and out of parked cars, riding a bicycle, skateboarding, and otherwise acting responsibly around traffic.
- Make sure that children always wear helmets and appropriate protective gear when engaged in sport activities.

Water

- Provide and require children to wear approved flotation devices whenever fishing, skiing, or boating.
- Teach basic water safety and continue to supervise water-related activities.

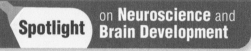

Spotlight on **Neuroscience** and **Brain Development**

Physical Activity and Children's Neurocognitive Functioning

Sedentary lifestyles have been identified as a primary cause of overweight and obesity. The World Health Organization (WHO) estimates that more than 1.9 billion adults over the age of 18, 340 million children between 5 and 18 years, and 38.2 million children under 5 years of age are overweight or obese (WHO, 2019). Estimates for the United States place more than 170 million adults and 14.4 million children and adolescents in these same categories (CDC, 2021b). Individuals belonging to some minority groups and those with less education experience the highest obesity incidence.

Scientists have identified structural differences in the brains of young children who are overweight or obese (Zavala-Crichton et al., 2020). They typically develop a thinner cortical layer in areas of the brain that affect **executive function**, cognition, academic performance, and motor activity (Gill et al., 2021; Ronan, Alexander-Bloch, & Fletcher, 2020). Neural connectivity pattern differences have also been reported. These and similar findings raise serious concerns about the short- and long-term effects that obesity may have on children's health, learning, and social-emotional development.

Interventions that increase children's physical activity have achieved a slowing and reversal of some negative health outcomes associated with obesity. Scientists have also determined that physical activity has a positive effect on brain plasticity and neurocognition. New neural connections form in response to increased blood flow and chemical changes associated with reduced stress.

Empirical data from longitudinal studies have established statistically significant correlations between children's engagement in vigorous physical fitness activities and improved academic achievement (McLoughlin, Bai, & Welk, 2020). Esteban-Cornejo and colleagues (2019) and Meijer and colleagues (2020) also noted a positive relationship between children's cardiovascular fitness and better working memory, attention, written expression, and intelligence. Additional studies have demonstrated that

executive function The cognitive processes that control working memory (planning, organizing, problem-solving), thinking (ability to focus and shift attention), and behavioral regulation (self-control).

measurable improvements in children's physical and academic well-being can be achieved through the development and implementation of low-cost exercise programs.

Researchers have conducted similar studies with children who experience **neurodevelopmental disorders** to determine if exercise has comparable effects. Because these children are at high risk for becoming overweight or obese, it is important that they engage in regular physical activity. Wang and colleagues (2020a) conducted a mini-basketball training program with preschool-age children who had been diagnosed with autism spectrum disorder. Children showed modest gains in executive functions, social communication, and a reduction in repetitive behaviors by the end of the twelve-week session. Other researchers have reported similar improvements in children's cognitive and motor skills after they participated in moderately intense physical activity over a longer time period (Milajerdi et al., 2021; Sung et al., 2021; Veldman et al., 2021). They also exhibited better concentration, recall, and decision-making abilities and were less likely to repeat a grade level (Burns, Bai, & Brusseau, 2020).

The beneficial effects of exercise are important for children's health, brain development, and brain functioning. Improvements are especially significant for children who experience neurodevelopmental disorders, obesity, and socioeconomic disadvantage. Physical activities can be incorporated easily throughout the school curriculum. Modifications to some activities may be necessary to assure that children of all abilities can participate.

What are the connections?

1. Why do you think child and adult populations have become more sedentary?
2. In what ways can teachers integrate more physical activity across the curriculum?
3. Why is it important that children learn to enjoy and engage in physical activity while they are young?
4. What additional health benefits are associated with being physically active and fit?

Eleven- and Twelve-Year-Olds

Eleven- and twelve-year-olds are saying goodbye to childhood and entering their preteen years. For the most part, they are endearing individuals. They are curious, helpful, and usually happy (Figure 8-5). They assist with chores around the house, sometimes even volunteering before being asked, especially if compensation is provided. Their language, motor, and cognitive skills are reaching adult levels of sophistication. By age twelve, children have developed a sense of confidence in their capabilities and approach tasks with renewed interest.

Children's emotional stability is becoming less predictable at this age. Moodiness and occasional disagreements can be expected. The nature of parental responses and attachment strength continue to play an influential role in shaping children's emotional regulation (Wang et al., 2021a; Waters et al., 2019).

Eleven- and twelve-year-olds are energetic and enjoy participating in organized sports and physical activities. In general, their health is good, and they begin to understand that a healthy lifestyle is not only important but also requires dedicated awareness and effort. However, eleven- and twelve-year-olds also see themselves as invincible.

iStock.com/monkeybusinessimages

Figure 8-5 Eleven- and twelve-year-olds are curious, energetic, and self-confident.

neurodevelopmental disorders Conditions that affect how the brain functions, including autism spectrum disorder, learning and intellectual disabilities, attention deficit hyperactivity disorder (ADHD), and conduct disorders.

Few children think about or believe they will ever experience serious health conditions such as sexually transmitted diseases (STDs), lung cancer, diabetes, or heart disease, despite engaging in risky behaviors (e.g., drug and alcohol use, inactivity, unhealthy dietary patterns) (Liu et al., 2020; Tripathi & Mishra, 2020).

11 and 12 year olds

Developmental Profiles and Growth Patterns

Growth and Physical Characteristics

- Triples birth length by the end of this period. Height and weight vary significantly from child to child; body shape and proportion are influenced by heredity and environment.

- Girls are first to experience a prepuberty growth spurt, growing taller and weighing more than boys at this age; may add as much as 3.5 inches (8.75 cm) and 20 pounds (44 kg) in one year. This period of rapid growth ends around age twelve to thirteen for girls; boys' growth rate is much slower and doesn't begin to accelerate until the early teens.

- Bodily changes mark approaching puberty (e.g., widening hips and budding breasts [girls], enlarging testes and penis [boys], appearance of underarm, facial, and pubic hair) (Laube & Fuhrmann, 2020).

- Menstruation begins if it has not already started; some girls have vaginal discharge sooner; some may be upset if not progressing at the same rate as other girls.

- Spontaneous erections are common among eleven- and twelve-year-old boys; pictures, physical activity, talk, and daydreams can trigger these events; some begin to have nocturnal emissions (involuntary discharge of seminal fluid at night).

- Gains in muscle mass and strength, especially boys; girls often reach their maximum muscle strength by age twelve.

- Stands more erect; increases in bone size and length cause shoulders, collarbone, rib cage, and shoulder blades to appear more prominent.

- Complaints of headaches and blurred vision are not uncommon if children are experiencing vision problems; the added strain of schoolwork (smaller print, computer use, longer periods of reading and writing) may cause some children to request an eye examination.

Motor Development

- Displays movements that are smoother and more coordinated; however, rapid growth spurts can cause temporary clumsiness.

- Enjoys participating in activities such as dancing, karate, soccer, yoga, gymnastics, swimming, and organized games in which improved skills can be used and tested.

- Concentrates efforts on continued refinement of fine motor abilities through a variety of activities (e.g., model-building, rocket construction,

Figure 8-6 Improved fine motor skills enable children to attempt and be successful at new activities.

drawing, woodworking, cooking, sewing, arts and crafts, writing letters, or playing a musical instrument); now has perfected most fundamental gross motor skills (Figure 8-6).

Developmental Profiles and Growth Patterns *(continued)*

- Writes with greater ease, legibility, and speed. Requires outlets for release of excess energy that builds during the school day; enjoys team sports, riding bikes, playing in the park, taking dance lessons, going for a walk with friends, shooting hoops, playing soccer.

- Has an abundance of energy but also fatigues quickly.

- Uses improved strength to run faster, throw balls farther, jump higher, kick or bat balls more accurately, and wrestle with friends.

Perceptual-Cognitive Development

- Begins thinking in more **abstract** terms; expanded memory ability enables improved long-term recall; now remembers stored information, so no longer needs to rely solely on experiencing an event to understand it.

- Succeeds in sequencing, ordering, and classifying objects as a result of improved long-term memory capacity; these skills are essential for solving complex science and mathematical problems (Caviola et al., 2020; Vernucci et al., 2021).

> **Did You Know** ?
>
> ...that school-aged girls typically show more advanced literacy skills than do boys? This early advantage has been attributed to gender-based motivational differences. Long-term differences in literacy skills often are linked to socioeconomic background for both genders.

- Accepts the idea that problems can have multiple solutions; often works through problems by talking aloud to oneself. Develops solutions or responses based on logic.

- Enjoys challenges, problem solving, researching, and testing possible solutions; researches the Internet and books for information (Figure 8-7).

- Exhibits a longer attention span; is generally able to remain focused and complete school assignments and other tasks in a timely fashion.

- Develops detailed plans and lists to reach a desired goal.

- Performs many routine tasks without having to give them much thought; increased memory sophistication makes automatic responses possible.

- Shows more complex understanding of cause and effect; learns from

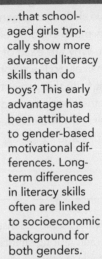

iStock.com/Ableimages

Figure 8-7 Children enjoy the challenge of researching and solving problems at this age.

mistakes; identifies factors that may have contributed to or caused an event (e.g., combining baking soda with vinegar releases a gas; attaching a longer tail helps a kite to fly higher in strong winds).

Speech and Language Development

- Completes the majority of language development by the end of this stage; only subtle refinements are still necessary during the next few years.

abstract The ability to think and use concepts; an idea or theory.

Developmental Profiles and Growth Patterns *(continued)*

11 and 12
year olds

What Do You See?

Interest in learning. Advanced cognitive skills and expanding interests make children eager to learn. Why are each of these children likely to learn something different from this project, even though they have worked on it together? How do children learn best at this age?

iStock.com/Memedozaslan

- Talks and argues, often nonstop, with anyone who will listen; this behavior is more apparent in Western cultures (and among children who are acculturated into Western cultures), whereas it is considered unacceptable in others.

- Uses longer and more complex sentence structures in written and oral communications.

- Masters increasingly complex vocabulary; adds 4,000–5,000 new words each year; uses vocabulary skillfully to weave elaborate stories and precise descriptions.

- Becomes a thoughtful listener.

- Understands that word statements can have implied (intended) meanings. (When your mother asks, "Is your homework done?" she might really mean that you had better stop playing, gather up your books, and get started.)

- Grasps concepts of irony and sarcasm; has a good sense of humor and enjoys telling jokes, riddles, and rhymes to entertain others (Rothermich et al., 2019).

- Masters several language styles, shifting back and forth based on the occasion: uses a more formal style when talking with teachers, a more casual style with parents, and a style that often includes slang and code words when conversing with friends or peers (Firmansyah, 2018).

Social-Emotional Development

- Organizes group games and activities but may modify rules while the game is in progress; has strong opinions about what is right versus wrong.

- Views self-image as very important; typically defines self in terms of appearance, possessions, friends, or activities; may also make comparisons to much admired adults (Magson et al., 2019; Timeo, Riva, & Paladino, 2020).

- Becomes increasingly self-conscious and self-critical; vacillates between feeling confident and lacking self-confidence (Griffith et al., 2021).

- Understands the need to assume responsibility for own behavior and that there are consequences associated with one's choices and actions.

- Forms complex relationships with same-gendered friends who have similar interests and intellectual abilities; boys and girls begin to go their separate ways during this point in development (Boutwell, Meldrum, & Petkovsek, 2017).

- Engages in playful and humorous teasing.

Developmental Profiles and Growth Patterns *(continued)*

- Begins to think and talk about occupational interests and career plans; daydreams and fantasizes about the future.

- Develops a critical and idealistic view of the world; realizes that the world is larger than one's own neighborhood; expresses interest in other cultures, foods, languages, and customs.

- Adopts the dress, hairstyles, and mannerisms of peers, sports figures, and celebrities; researches and reads about popular personalities online.

- Recognizes that loyalty, honesty, trustworthiness, and being a considerate listener are prerequisites to becoming a good friend; may spend more time now with peers than with family members.

- Handles frustration with fewer emotional outbursts; is able to express what is emotionally troubling; accompanies words with facial expressions and gestures for emphasis.

11 and 12 year olds

▶ǁ TeachSource Video Connections

Middle Childhood and Cognitive Development

Most of the developmental skills that children will need as they approach adolescence are now in place. Eleven- and twelve-year-olds are able to think abstractly, make judgments based on logic, and face challenges with a reasonable degree of competence and self-confidence. Respond to the following questions after you have watched the learning video *5–11 Years: Observation Module for Middle Childhood:*

1. What cognitive skills are the children using to arrive at their responses to the conservation demonstration and to the question, "What did you do last night?"

2. What qualities did the first two children in the video clip use to describe themselves? Were they consistent with gender expectations?

3. Were you surprised by the responses of the first two children in the video clip to the questions about gender differences? What do you think accounted for the contrast in their answers?

4. What signs of stress or tension did you note while the first two children were being interviewed? If you were a teacher, how might you use this feedback?

DAILY ROUTINES

Eating

- Eats nonstop and is always hungry; boys in particular may consume astonishing amounts and combinations of foods (Figure 8-8). Boys require approximately 2,500 calories daily; girls need 2,200 calories daily.

- Has few dislikes; is willing to eat less preferred foods now and then; shows interest in trying foods from other cultures.

- Desires a large snack upon arriving home from school; searches the cabinets and refrigerator for anything to eat. Having access to nutritious foods encourages healthy eating habits.

- Makes some connection between eating (calories) and gaining or losing weight, especially girls. Boys and girls may begin talking about dieting and weight control to address concerns about body image, ways to improve athletic abilities, or both. Preadolescents should be monitored closely for signs of a developing eating disorder (Thomas, Williams, & Vanderwert, 2021).

Personal Care and Dressing

- Cares for most personal needs without any adult assistance.

- Bathes often and willingly; keeps clean; often prefers showers.

- Still needs the occasional reminder to wash hands.

Figure 8-8 Eleven- and twelve-year-old children seem to be constantly hungry and able to eat at almost any time.

iStock.com/SDI Productions

- Brushes and flosses teeth regularly; believes that a bright smile is important for appearance. Dental checkups are recommended every six months to monitor rapidly erupting permanent teeth and to treat existing cavities. Children who have developmental disorders are at high risk for dental cavities and deformed teeth and may require more frequent monitoring (Andreeva & Atanasova, 2020; Jamali et al., 2021).

- Takes pride in appearance; likes to wear what is fashionable or what friends are wearing.

Sleeping

- Requires plenty of uninterrupted sleep (8 ½ to 9 hours); growth spurts and active play often leave children feeling tired. Growth and appetite-regulating hormones are released while children are sleeping.

- Heads to bed without much resistance, but now wants to stay up longer on weeknights and even later on weekends and nonschool days.

- Sleeps less soundly than previously; may wake up early and read or finish homework before getting up.

- Bad dreams may still be problematic for some eleven- and twelve-year-olds. Daily activities should be monitored for events that may trigger disrupted sleep (e.g., overactivity, involvement in undesirable behavior, exposure to violence).

Play and Social Activities

- Shows less interest in frivolous play; prefers goal-directed activities (e.g., money-making schemes, competing on a swim team, creating newsletters, and attending summer camp).

- Gets involved in organized youth groups such as sports teams, 4-H, or Scouts, or just spends time alone with a friend or two; never without something to do.

DAILY ROUTINES *(continued)*

- Likes animals; offers to care for and train pets.
- Reads enthusiastically; enjoys listening to music, attending movies, watching the news, surfing the Internet, and playing video games.
- Enjoys and participates in outdoor activities such as skateboarding, inline skating, basketball, tennis, hockey, riding bikes, or walking with friends.
- Prefers to attend movies, theater, or sport performances with friends (and without parents) on occasion.

11 and 12 year olds

learning activities to promote **brain development**

Eleven- and twelve-year-olds are notoriously high-energy and curious. They seem interested in trying everything and often need guidance in focusing their attention on one activity at a time. They thrive on activities that lead to a sense of accomplishment, including competitive sports, complex board games, crafts, collecting items, building models, and earning money. They are intrigued with technology and electronic gadgets and can easily spend hours on the Internet or playing video games unless an adult limits their involvement.

Developmentally appropriate applications for families and teachers

- Continue to maintain open communication with children. Spend time together, know what is going on in their lives, and be supportive (not judgmental). Provide children with information about their personal health (on topics such as sexuality, drugs and alcohol, pregnancy, and sexually transmitted diseases) and the importance of making sound decisions. Encourage them to come to you with their questions and problems.
- Encourage children's interest in reading; take them to the library or bookstore or access content on your library's website.
- Read and discuss newspaper and magazine articles together; suggest that children create their own newsletter.
- Help children develop a sense of responsibility by assigning tasks that they can perform on a regular basis (e.g., caring for a pet, reading stories to a younger sibling, folding laundry, loading the dishwasher, or sweeping the garage).
- Gather a variety of large cardboard boxes, paints, and other materials; challenge children to design a structure (e.g., a store, library, train, castle, farm, or space station).
- Help children stage a play; invite them to write the script, design scenery, construct simple props, and rehearse.
- Offer to help children plan and organize a pet show, bike parade, scavenger hunt, or neighborhood fundraiser.
- Locate free or low-cost opportunities to join organized group or sporting activities; these are often available through local parks and recreation departments, YMCA/ YWCAs, church youth groups, and after-school programs.
- Provide children with a variety of art materials (e.g., paints, crayons, markers, paper, old magazines and catalogs, cloth scraps); encourage children to collect natural materials such as leaves, pebbles, interesting twigs, seed pods, feathers, and grasses to use for collages.

11 and 12
year olds

developmental **alerts**

Check with a health-care provider or early childhood specialist if, by the thirteenth birthday, the child does *not*:

- Have movements that are smooth and coordinated.

- Have energy sufficient for playing, riding bikes, or engaging in other desired activities.

- Stay focused on tasks at hand.

- Understand basic cause-and-effect relationships.

- Handle criticism and frustration with a reasonable response (physical aggression and excessive crying could be an indication of underlying problems).

- Exhibit a healthy appetite. (Frequent skipping of meals is not typical for this age group and may be an early sign of an eating disorder; excessive eating also should be monitored.)

- Make and keep friends.

Note: Cultural differences may alter the timetable when some developmental skills are acquired. Expanded Developmental Alerts Checklists appear in Appendix A and are also available as digital downloads.

safety **concerns**

Continue to implement the safety practices described for the previous stages. Always be aware of new safety issues as the child continues to grow and develop.

Machinery
- Teach children how to operate small appliances and equipment safely.
- Provide basic first aid instruction or enroll children in a local first aid training course.

Media Exposure
- Monitor children's online activities (e.g., websites, social networking, and chat rooms) for inappropriate content and correspondence. A teen craze known as the choking game, space monkey, funky chicken, space cowboy, rush, airplaning, suffocation roulette, and a host of other names involves temporarily cutting off one's oxygen supply through self-strangulation (Chater, 2021). The purpose is to experience a momentary high before losing consciousness. Peer pressure and online videos continue to encourage this addictive and dangerous practice which can lead to death, stroke, brain damage, seizures, and/or memory loss. Visible marks or bruises on the child's neck, headache, temporary confusion, bloodshot eyes, behavior changes, or possession of items such as rope, scarves, or belts may be warning signs. Parents should discuss the risks of playing this game with their children and seek professional care if they engage in this practice.
- Reinforce the importance of online safety: not giving out personal information, not responding to marketers, and setting browsers to delete cookies automatically.
- Talk with children about **cyberbullying** and **sexting**; let them know it is inappropriate (and illegal in some states) to engage in this activity and to inform you if they ever receive these types of messages, whether or not they are about themselves.
- Limit the amount of time children spend online (unless related to

cyberbullying Sending hurtful, threatening, or harassing messages via the Internet or cell phone.

sexting Sending sexually explicit messages or pictures of yourself or friends via a cell phone.

safety concerns *(continued)*

schoolwork) or playing video games. Children need to be active; too much sedentary activity increases the risk of obesity and interferes with other learning opportunities.

Sports

- Make sure that proper protective equipment is available and worn; check its condition periodically. Sunscreen should be applied regularly if children are involved in outdoor activities.
- Make sure that an adult is supervising any athletic competition; check the safety of area, equipment, and practices.
- Meet and talk with team coaches; know what they expect of children,

how they interact with children, and steps that they take to protect children's safety.

Substance Abuse

- Be aware of warning signs associated with "huffing" or "dusting" (inhaling) hazardous vapors from common household products such as hair spray, polish remover, aerosol paints, ammonia, butane lighters, aerosol computer cleaners, and gasoline. Note any unusual odor on the child's breath or clothing, slurred speech, jitteriness, poor appetite, bloodshot eyes, or reddened areas around the nose or mouth.
- Discuss the hazards of prescription and nonprescription drug abuse and underage drinking.

11 and 12 year olds

positive behavior guidance

The years between nine and twelve mark the end of childhood and the approach of adolescence. It is during these years that adults need to change their disciplinary style so that children begin to assume gradual responsibility for their own behavior and parents become less controlling.

Nine-, ten-, eleven-, and twelve-year-olds

- Focus on children's positive behaviors and let them know often that you respect and appreciate their efforts to behave in a responsible manner.
- Involve children in setting appropriate limits and expectations and enforce them consistently. Children are more likely to abide by rules if they have helped to develop them.
- Take time to hear children's side of the story before passing judgment. Let children know that you understand how they feel; however, doing so doesn't necessarily suggest that you accept their behavior.
- Provide unconditional love. Everyone makes mistakes from time to time, and children are still in the process of learning to make sound decisions.
- Maintain an open dialogue with children and encourage them to talk about their concerns and feelings.
- Help children develop and use problem-solving and conflict-resolution skills to make responsible choices.
- Use consequences to reinforce compliance with behavioral expectations: performing poorly on a math test because the child "forgot" to bring their book home the night before (**natural consequence**); not being allowed to attend a movie with friends because they were late coming home the previous time (**logical consequence**).

natural consequence An outcome that occurs as a result of a certain behavior.

logical consequence A planned response that is implemented in response to misbehavior.

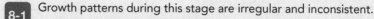

Summary

8-1 Growth patterns during this stage are irregular and inconsistent.

- Girls tend to grow more than do boys, although there are significant differences among children of the same gender. Some girls begin to experience prepubertal changes.

8-2 Friendships are becoming increasingly important.

- Peers begin to serve as important role models and information sources, although family ties are still needed and valued.

- Boys and girls begin to go their separate ways and to establish friendships with same-gendered peers.

8-3 Nine- to twelve-year-olds possess many advanced skills that enable them to engage in more complex activities. They are industrious, eager to learn, and able to follow detailed instructions. They enjoy physical challenges, sports-related activities, projects that involve designing and building objects, and artistic adventures.

8-4 Nine- and ten-year-olds have a reasonable grasp of language and understand its power for expressing ideas, concerns, and desires. They are quite talkative and able to carry on meaningful conversations. Eleven- and twelve-year-olds have achieved adultlike fluency and conversational skills. They are good listeners, express convincing opinions, and are able to adapt their language style to the setting.

Key Terms

logic **p. 203**

intuition **p. 206**

concrete operational thought **p. 206**

executive function **p. 212**

neurodevelopmental disorders **p. 213**

abstract **p. 215**

cyberbullying **p. 220**

sexting **p. 220**

natural consequence **p. 221**

logical consequence **p. 221**

Apply What You Have Learned

A. Case Study Connections

Reread the developmental sketch about Jacob and Madie presented at the beginning of this chapter and answer the following questions:

1. What physical characteristics would you expect to observe in the typical eleven-year-old?

2. Would it be developmentally appropriate to expect most eleven-year-olds to like school? Why do you agree or disagree with this statement?

3. From a developmental perspective, do you think Jacob's reactions to having his sister tag along are typical or atypical? Explain.

4. Would you consider Madie's development to be normal for a nine-year-old? Explain.

B. Review Questions

1. What gender differences are nine-year-olds likely to exhibit in their social-emotional development?
2. How do nine- and eleven-year-olds differ in their ability to think abstractly?
3. What physical changes are ten-year-olds likely to experience?
4. Describe the cognitive abilities typical of most eleven- and twelve-year-olds.
5. Identify three qualities that are needed to make and keep friends.

C. Your Turn: Chapter to Practice

1. Volunteer to mentor children (between 9 and 11 years old) in an after-school program. What strengths and limitations did the children bring to the program? What aspects did you find most challenging?
2. Watch several television programs designed for the preteen audience. Describe the language, behavior, and themes portrayed in each show. What was your overall reaction to the type of shows that preteens are likely to watch? Would you recommend them to families? Explain why or why not.
3. Arrange to observe children (between 9 and 12 years old) during their school lunch hour. Describe the nature of their interactions and conversation topics. How closely did their behaviors follow the developmental milestones described in this chapter?
4. Interview four or five children between the ages of 9 and 10 or 11 and 12 years. Ask them to name their favorite popular songs. Locate and listen to the lyrics of several of these songs, and comment on your findings.

Online Resources

American Psychological Association
Easy-to-understand explanations and guidelines for building children's resilience can be found at the American Psychological Association's website. The *Psychology Help Center* features resource information relevant to children's social-emotional wellness, family relationships, racism, school related stress, and coping with natural disasters.

Child and Adolescent Mental Health
This section of the National Institute of Mental Health site includes an overview of child mental health and warning signs, a video section, resource listing, and articles on current topics. Information on clinical trials and links to educational resources and hotlines are also provided.

ConnectSafely
Extensive safety information and resources that address a range of children's safety issues (e.g., social media, identity theft, video-gaming, sexual exploitation, mobile safety) are provided at this site for parents, teens, children, and educators. Numerous podcasts and webcasts are available in English and Spanish.

YourChild
This award-winning website, sponsored by the University of Michigan Health System, provides evidence-based information and media resources on a comprehensive list of child development, safety, nutrition, illness, and behavioral topics. Explore the

"Parenting Resource" link for information on important subjects that parents will find beneficial for understanding and supporting children as they grow and develop.

KidsHealth in the Classroom
This website is supported by the Nemours Foundation. Teachers will appreciate the expansive list of lesson plans (e.g., learning objectives, materials, activity, extension ideas), handouts, and quizzes that address numerous developmental topics. Materials are organized by grade level; each level includes sections labeled "human body," "health problems," and "personal health." Although the information is designed for educators, parents may also find the information and lesson plans beneficial, especially for home-schooling purposes.

References

Adriyani, R., Iskandar, D., & Camelia, L. S. (2020). Gender differences in motor coordination and physical activity. *Advances in Health Sciences Research, 21*, 122–126. https://doi.org/10.2991/ahsr.k.200214.034

Andreeva, R., & Atanasova, S. (2020). Prevalence of periodontal diseases in children with Down syndrome. *Journal of IMAB, 26*(4), 3383–3386.

Anil, M. A., & Bhat, J. (2020). Transitional changes in cognitive-communicative abilities in adolescents: A literature review. *Journal of Natural Science, Biology, and Medicine, 11*(2), 85–92.

Bacter, C., Bălțătescu, S., Marc, C., Săveanu, S., & Buhas, R. (2021). Correlates of preadolescent emotional health in 18 countries. A study using children's words data. *Child Indicators Research, 14*, 1703–1722. https://doi.org/10.1007/s12187-021-09819-y

Booker, J. A., Ispa, J. M., Im, J., Maiya, S., Roos, J., & Carlo, G. (2021). African American mothers talk to their preadolescents about honesty and lying. *Cultural Diversity and Ethnic Minority Psychology*. Advance online publication. https://doi.org/10.1037/cdp0000396

Boutwell, B. B., Meldrum, R. C., & Petkovsek, M. A. (2017). General intelligence in friendship selection: A study of preadolescent best friend dyads. *Intelligence, 64*, 30–35.

Bukowski, W. M., & DeLay, D. (2020). Studying same-gender preference as a defining feature of cultural contexts. *Frontiers in Psychology, 11*, 1863. https://doi.org/10.3389/fpsyg.2020.01863

Burns, R. D., Bai, Y., & Brusseau, T. A. (2020). Physical activity and sports participation associates with cognitive functioning and academic progression: An analysis using the combined 2017-2018 National Survey of Children's Health. *Journal of Physical Activity and Health, 17*(12), 1197–1204.

Canton, A. P. M., Krepischi, A. C. V., Montenegro, L. R., Costa. S., Rosenberg, C., Steunou, V., Sobrier, M-L., Santana, L., Honjo, R. S., Kim, C. A., de Zegher, F., Idkowiak, J. Gillingan, L. C., Arlt, W., Funari, M. F., Jorge, A. A., Mendonca, B. B., Netchine, I., Brito, V. N. & Latronico, A. C. (2021). Insights from the genetic characterization of central precocious puberty associated with multiple anomalies. *Human Reproduction, 36*(2), 506–518.

Caviola, S., Colling, L. J., Mammarella, I. C., & Szücs, D. (2020). Predictors of mathematics in primary school: Magnitude comparison, verbal and spatial working memory measures. *Developmental Science, 23*(6), e12957. https://doi.org/10.1111/desc.12957

Centers for Disease Control and Prevention (CDC). (2021a). *Data and statistics on children's mental health*. Retrieved from https://www.cdc.gov/childrensmentalhealth/data.html.

Centers for Disease Control and Prevention (CDC). (2021b). *Prevalence of childhood obesity in the United States*. Retrieved from https://www.cdc.gov/obesity/data/childhood.html.

Chater, A. M. (2021). Does intentional asphyxiation by strangulation have addictive properties? *Addiction, 116*(4), 718–724.

Clark, C. A. C., Hudnall, R. H., & Pérez-González, S. (2020). Children's neural responses to a novel mathematics concept. *Trends in Neuroscience and Education, 20*, 100128. https://doi.org/10.1016/j.tine.2020.100128

Coban, O. G., Bedel, A., Önde, A., Adanir, A. S., Tuhan, H., & Parlak, M. (2021). Psychiatric disorders, peer-victimization, and quality of life in girls with central precocious puberty. *Journal of Psychosomatic Research, 143*, 110401. https://doi.org/10.1016/j.jpsychores.2021.110401

Dodd, H. F., & Lester, K. J. (2021). Adventurous play as a mechanism for reducing risk for childhood anxiety: A conceptual model. *Clinical Child and Family Psychology Review, 24*(1), 164–181.

Esteban-Cornejo, I., Mora-Gonzalez, J., Cadenas-Sanchez, C., Contreras-Rodriguez, O., Verdejo-Romane, J., Henriksson, P., Migueles, J. H., Rodriguez-Ayllon, M., Molina-García, P., Suo, C., Hillman, C. H., Kramer, A. F., Erickson, K. I., Catena, A., Verdejo-García, A., & Ortega, F. B. (2019). Fitness, cortical thickness and surface area in overweight/obese children: The mediating role of body composition and relationship with intelligence. *Neuroimage, 186*, 771–781.

Fedewa, A., Erwin, H., Wilson, J., & Ahn, S. (2021). Relationship between the timing of recess breaks and discipline referrals among elementary children. *Children, Youth and Environments, 31*(1), 165–177.

Firmansyah, D. (2018). Analysis of language skills in primary school children (Study development of child psychology of language). *Journal of Primary Education, 2*(1), 35. https://doi.org/10.22460/pej.v1i1.668

Getu, T. (2020). The effect of physical activity on academic performance and mental health: Systematic review. *American Journal of Science, Engineering and Technology, 5*(3), 131–136.

Gill, N., Gjelsvik, A., Mercurio, L. Y., & Amanullah, S. (2021). Childhood obesity is associated with poor academic skills and coping mechanisms. *The Journal of Pediatrics, 228*, 278–284.

Gillen, Z. M., Shoemaker, M. E., McKay, B. D., Bohannon, N. A., Gibson, S. M., & Cramer, J. T. (2019). Muscle strength, size, and neuromuscular function before and during adolescence. *European Journal of Applied Physiology, 119*, 1619–1632.

Grenier, A. E., Dickson, D. S., Sparks, C. S., & Wicha, N. Y. Y. (2020). Meaning to multiply: Electrophysiological evidence that children and adults treat multiplication facts differently. *Developmental Cognitive Neuroscience, 46*, 100873. https://doi.org/10.1016/j.dcn.2020.100873

Griffith, J. M., Clark, H. M., Haraden, D.A., Young, J. F., & Hankin, B. L. (2021). Affective development from middle childhood to late adolescence: Trajectories of mean-level change in negative and positive affect. *Journal of Youth and Adolescence*. Advance online publication. https://doi.org/10.1007/s10964-021-01425-z

Halfpenny, C. C., & James, L. A. (2020). Humor styles and empathy in junior-school children. *Europe's Journal of Psychology, 16* (1), 148–166.

Masters, S. L., Hixson, K., & Hayes, A. R. (2021). Perceptions of gender norm violations among middle school students: An experimental study of the effects of violation type on exclusion expectations. *The Journal of Early Adolescence, 41*(4), 527–549.

Jamali, Z., Ghaffari, P., Aminabadi, N. A., Norouzi, S., & Shirazi, S. (2021). Oral health status and oral health-related quality of life in children with attention-deficit hyperactivity disorder and oppositional defiant disorder. *Special Care in Dentistry, 41*(2), 178–186.

Kitts, J. A., & Leal, D. F. (2021). What is(n't) a friend? Dimensions of the friendship concept among adolescents. *Social Networks, 66*, 161–170.

Klaczynski, P. A., Felmban, W. S., & Kole, J. (2020). Gender intensification and gender generalization biases in pre-adolescents, adolescents, and emerging adults. *British Journal of Developmental Psychology, 38*(3), 415–433.

Laube, C., & Fuhrmann, D. (2020). Is early good or bad? Early puberty onset and its consequences for learning. *Current Opinion in Behavioral Science, 36*, 150–156.

Laursen, B., Altman, R. L., Bukowski, W. M., & Wei, L. (2020). Being fun: An overlooked indicator of childhood social status. *Personality, 88*(5), 993–1006.

Leong, R. L. F., van Rijn, E., Koh, S. Y. J., Chee, M. W. L., & Lo, J. C. (2019). Sleep improves memory for the content but not execution of intentions in adolescents. *Sleep Medicine, 56*, 111–116.

Liu, Y., Smith, N. D. L., Lloyd, S. L., Striley, C. W., & Cottler, L. B. (2020). Prescription stimulant use and associated risk factors for non-oral use among 10 to 18 year olds. *Journal of Psychoactive Drugs, 52*(5), 421–432.

Liutsko, L., Muiños, R., Ral, J. M. T., & Contreras, M. J. (2020). Fine motor precision tasks: Sex differences in performance with and without visual guidance across different age groups. *Behavioral Sciences, 10*(1), 36. https://doi.org/10.3390/bs10010036

Loochi, S. A., Demol, S., Nagelberg, N., Lebenthal, Y., Phillip, M., & Yackobovitch-Gavan, M. (2021). Gonadotropin releasing hormone analogue therapy in girls with idiopathic precocious puberty/early-fast puberty: Dynamics in adiposity indices, eating habits and quality of life. *Journal of Pediatric Endocrinology and Metabolism, 34*(3), 373–383.

Magson, N. R., Oar, E. L., Fardouly, J., Johnco, C. J., & Rapee, R. M. (2019). The preteen perfectionist: An evaluation of the perfectionism social disconnection model. *Child Psychiatry and Human Development, 50*, 960–974.

McLoughlin, G. M., Bai, Y., & Welk, G. J. (2020). Longitudinal associations between physical fitness and academic achievement in youth. *Medicine & Science in Sports & Exercise, 52*(3), 616–622.

Milajerdi, H. R., Sheikh, M., Najafabadi, M. G., Safhaei, B., Naghdi, N., & Dewey, D. (2021). The effects of physical activity and exergaming on motor skills and executive functions in children with autism spectrum disorder. *Games for Health, 10*(1), 33–42. Retrieved from https://www.liebertpub.com/doi/full/10.1089/g4h.2019.0180.

Meijer, A., Königs, M., Vermeulen, G. T., Visscher, C., Bosker, R. J., Hartman, E., & Oosterlaan, J. (2020). The effects of physical activity on brain structure and neurophysiological functioning in children: A systematic review and meta-analysis. *Developmental Cognitive Neuroscience, 45*, 100828. https://doi.org/10.1016/j.dcn.2020.100828

Orihuela, C. A., Mrug, S., Davies, S., Elliott, M. N., Emery, S. T., Peskin, M. F., Reisner, S., & Schuster, M. A. (2020). Neighborhood disorder, family functioning, and risky sexual behaviors in adolescence. *Journal of Youth and Adolescence, 49*(5), 991–1004.

Piaget, J. (1928). *Judgment and reasoning in the child*. New York: Harcourt, Brace, and Co.

Pickering, L., Hadwin, J. A., & Kovshoff, H. (2020). The role of peers in the development of social anxiety in adolescent girls: A systematic review. *Adolescent Research Review 5*, 341–362.

Ronan, L., Alexander-Bloch, A., & Fletcher, P. C. (2020). Childhood obesity, cortical structure, and executive function in health children. *Cerebral Cortex, 30*(4), 2519–2528.

Rothermich, K., Caivano, O., Knoll, L. J., & Talwar, V. (2019). Do they really mean it? Children's inference of speaker intentions and the role of age and gender. *Language and Speech, 63*(4), 689–712.

Schroeder, K., Kubik, M. Y., Sirard, J. R., Lee, J., & Fulkerson, J. A. (2020). Sleep is inversely associated with sedentary time among youth with obesity. *American Journal of Health Behavior, 44*(6), 756–764(9).

Sigal, M., Ross, B. J., Behnke, A. O., & Plunkett, S. W. (2021). Neighborhood, peer, and parental influences on minor and major substance use of Latino and Black adolescents. *Children, 8*(4), 267. Retrieved from http://dx.doi.org/10.3390/children8040267.

Skoog, T., & Kapetanovi, S. (2021). The role of pubertal timing in the development of peer victimization and offending from early- to mid-adolescence. *Journal of Early Adolescence,* 1–28. https://journals.sagepub.com/doi/10.1177/02724316211002265

Smith, D. S., Schacter, H. L., Enders, C., & Juvonen, J. (2018). Gender norm salience across middle schools: Contextual variations in associations between gender typicality and socioemotional distress. *Journal of Youth and Adolescence, 47*, 947–960.

Sung, M-C., Ku, B., Leung, W., & MacDonald, M. (2021). The effect of physical activity interventions on executive function among people with neurodevelopmental disorders: A meta-analysis. *Journal of Autism and Developmental Disorders* (2021). Advance online publication. https://doi.org/10.1007/s10803-021-05009-5

Thomas, K. S., Williams, M. O., & Vanderwert, R. E. (2021). Disordered eating and internalizing symptoms in preadolescence. *Brain and Behavior, 11*(1), e01904. https://doi.org/10.1002/brb3.1904

Timeo, S., Riva, P., & Paladino, M. P. (2020). Being liked or not being liked: A study of social-media exclusion in a preadolescent population. *Journal of Adolescence, 80*, 173–181.

Tripathi, M., & Mishra, S. K. (2020). Screen time and adiposity among children and adolescents: A systematic review. *Journal of Public Health, 28*, 227–244.

Veldman, S. L. C., Chin, A., Paw, M. J. M., & Altenburg, T. M. (2021). Physical activity and prospective associations with indicators of health and development in children aged <5 years: A systematic review. *International Journal of Behavioral Nutrition and Physical Activity, 18*, 6. https://doi.org/10.1186/s12966-020-01072-w

Verkuyten, M., & Killen, M. (2021). Tolerance, dissenting beliefs, and cultural diversity. *Child Development Perspectives, 15*(1), 51–56.

Vernucci, S., Canet-Juric, L., Zamora, E. V., & Richard's, M. M. (2021). The structure of working memory during childhood: A systematic review. *Journal of Cognitive Psychology, 33*(2), 103–118.

Wang, J., Yang, Y., Tang, Y., Wu, M., Jiang, S., & Zou, H. (2021a). Longitudinal links among parent-child attachment, emotion parenting, and problem behaviors of preadolescents. *Children and Youth Services Review, 121*, 105797. https://doi.org/10.1016/j.childyouth.2020.105797

Wang, J-G., Cai, K-L., Liu, Z-M., Herold, F., Zou, L., Zhu, L-N., Xiong, Z., & Chen, A-G. (2020a). Effects of mini-basketball training program on executive functions and core symptoms among preschool children with autism spectrum disorders. *Brain Sciences, 10*, 263. Retrieved from https://res.mdpi.com/brainsci/brainsci-10-00263/article_deploy/brainsci-10-00263.pdf.

Wang, J. H., Kiefer, S. M., Smith, N. D. W., Huang, L., Gilfix, H. L., & Brennan, E. M. (2020b). Associations of early adolescents' best friendships, peer groups, and coolness with overt and relational aggression. *The Journal of Early Adolescence, 40*(6), 828–856.

Wang, Z., Buu, A., Lohrmann, D. K., Shih, P. C., & Lin, H-C. (2021b). The role of family conflict in mediating impulsivity to early substance exposure among preteens. *Addictive Behaviors, 115*, 106779. https://doi.org/10.1016/j.addbeh.2020.106779

Waters, L., Loton, D. J., Grace, D., Jacques-Hamilton, R., & Zyphur, M. J. (2019, October 10). Observing change over time in strength-based parenting and subjective wellbeing for pre-teens and teens. *Frontiers in Psychology, 10*, 2273. https://doi.org/10.3389/fpsyg.2019.02273

World Health Organization (WHO). (2019). *Obesity and overweight.* Retrieved from https://www.who.int/news-room/fact-sheets/detail/obesity-and-overweight.

Zavala-Crichton, J. P., Esteban-Cornejo, I., Solis-Urra, P., Mora-Gonzalez, J., Cadenas-Sanchez, C., Rodriguez-Ayllon, M., Migueles, J. H., Molina-Garcia, P., Verdejo-Roman, J., Kramer, A. F., Hillman, C. H., Erickson, K. I., Catena, A., & Oretga, F. B. (2020). Association of sedentary behavior with brain structure and intelligence in children with overweight or obesity: The ActiveBrains Project. *Journal of Clinical Medicine, 9*(4), 1101. https://doi.org/10.3390/jcm9041101

Zeng, X., Cai, L., Wong, S. H., Lai, L., Lv, Y., Tan, W., Jing, J., & Chen, Y. (2021). Association of sedentary time and physical activity with executive function among children. *Academic Pediatrics, 21*(1), 63–69.

Chapter 9

Adolescence: Thirteen- to Nineteen-Year-Olds

Learning Objectives

After reading this chapter, you will be able to:

9-1 Identify changes that occur in the adolescent brain and explain how they affect behavior.

9-2 Explain why thirteen- and fourteen-year-olds often experience a loss of self-confidence.

9-3 Describe the role that friends and friendships play during middle adolescence.

9-4 Discuss the nature of social-emotional development in late adolescence.

NAEYC NAEYC Professional Standards Linked to Chapter Content

1a, 1b, and 1c: Child development and learning in context

2a: Family–teacher partnerships and community connections

3a, 3b, and 3c: Child observations, documentation, and assessment

4a and 4b: Developmentally, culturally, and linguistically appropriate teaching practices

6b: Professionalism as an early childhood educator

Maria and Sophia Acosta moved from Costa Rica to the United States with their parents several months before the beginning of the current school year. Both girls had attended private schools and speak relatively fluent English, which made their transition into the middle and high schools here somewhat easier. Maria, soon to be sixteen, is sociable, outgoing, and an exceptional soccer player who makes friends quickly. She enjoys learning about her new culture and participating in things that teenagers in this country typically do at her age, such as watching movies with friends, texting, shopping at the mall, talking about boys, and dating.

Maria's thirteen-year-old sister, Sophia, is an accomplished pianist and honor student. She is small for her age, soft-spoken, and not as outgoing. Sophia has met several friends through her involvement on the school newspaper and governance councils, but she spends little time with them outside of these activities.

Although the girls' parents are pleased with their adjustment to a new culture and schools, they also have several concerns. Their family always has been very close and deeply religious. They believe that Maria is spending far too much time with her friends and not enough time at home with her family or devoted to her studies. They know little about her new friends and worry that Maria could easily be pressured into doing things of which they disapprove, such as drinking or experimenting with drugs, because she is eager to be accepted. In addition, her parents have been surprised by some of the recent changes that they have observed in Maria's clothing and music choices, as well as her impulsive decisions. Although they have fewer concerns about Sophia's progress, they worry that she has become more self-conscious, moody, and withdrawn lately. She often retreats to her bedroom in the evening and seems to have only one close friend with whom she spends time.

Ask Yourself

- What developmental behaviors are each of the girls exhibiting that may be cause for concern?
- What steps would you encourage the girls' parents to take if they have concerns about their development?
- In what ways may differences in cultural expectations be contributing to the parents' worries?

Thirteen- to Nineteen-Year-Olds

Adolescence marks a period of dramatic transitions, confusion, and uncertainty for children, their families, and teachers alike. Bodily changes and emerging feelings of sexuality can lead to increased self-consciousness, self-doubt, and a readjustment of self-identity. Children who were once spontaneous, cooperative, and fun-loving may become moody, questioning, and, at times, rebellious teenagers. They resent being treated as children, yet they are not ready to assume full responsibility for decisions governing their own behavior until near the end of this stage. Although they may challenge adult authority and demand independence, adolescents truly want and need their families to care and to set reasonable limits that help to protect them from harmful consequences (e.g., substance abuse, sexually transmitted diseases, pregnancy, or crime). Is it any wonder that few adults want to relive their adolescence, or that parents have mixed emotions as their children enter their teenage years?

Although it is easy to dwell on the negative aspects of adolescence, it is more important to remember that most children are "good kids," even those who may be obstinate or difficult to manage at times (Figure 9-1). They possess many positive intellectual and personal qualities: They are eager to learn, curious, capable, industrious, inventive, and interested in making a difference. They are able to think in abstract terms, use logic to solve problems, and communicate complex thoughts with adultlike sophistication (Anil & Bhat, 2020; Demetriou et al., 2020). They begin to dream about career options during the early adolescent years, and later pursue the training opportunities that ultimately will help to achieve their goals. They embrace technology, are active participants in social networking, and rely on instant messaging to stay connected with friends and family (Campos et al., 2021; Webster, Dunne, & Hunter, 2021).

Why does the adolescent show such a contrast in personalities? Recent neurobiological and medical research have provided some clues. It has long been thought that brain

Did You Know ?

...that adolescents make up 20 percent of the world's population, and approximately 85 percent of them live in developing countries?

Figure 9-1 Most adolescents are "good kids" who have many positive qualities.

13 and 14 year olds

development was complete by the time children reached their teen years. However, continued analyses of brain images reveal that significant structural changes in the cerebral cortex (i.e., increased white matter, thinning of gray matter, and sensitivity to brain chemicals) and functional reorganization of **neural connections** and networks continue well into the early twenties (Edde et al., 2021). Scientists have noted that these developments typically occur earlier in girls and are associated with puberty (Brouwer et al., 2021).

The brain centers most affected by these developmental changes include those that regulate emotion, decision making, memory, social and sexual behavior, and impulsivity, which may help to explain the adolescent's often unpredictable and questionable behavior choices (Figure 9-2). These responses should not be viewed as negative qualities, but rather as behaviors that eventually enable adolescents to understand themselves better, determine how they fit into a society, make sound decisions, and, ultimately, to achieve adult maturity. What adolescents need most during these turbulent years are caring adults who provide patience, understanding, consistency, and nurturing support.

Temporal Lobe   Frontal Lobe

Figure 9-2 Structural and functional changes occur in the temporal and frontal lobes of the adolescent brain.

Thirteen- and Fourteen-Year-Olds (Early Adolescence)

Thirteen- and fourteen-year-olds are confronted with countless new feelings, experiences, and expectations which, at times, may prove to be overwhelming. They often face a host of fears and uncertainties as they transition to junior high or middle school: "Will I have any friends?" "What if the classes are too hard?" "What if the teachers don't like me?"

The adolescent's perception of, and response to, such events is influenced by their unique cultural, social, and religious beliefs and family circumstances (Anniko, Boersma, & Tillfors, 2019; Kim, 2021). Although most children are able to successfully cope with adolescent challenges, some will experience unmanageable psychological distress. This can elevate their risk for developing serious mental health problems, including anxiety and eating disorders, depression, and suicide (CDC, 2021). These conditions tend to peak during early adolescence unless troubling behaviors are identified and treated

neural connections Organized linkages formed between brain cells as a result of learning.

early. Efforts to help adolescents set realistic goals, regulate their emotions, pursue new interests, build positive social relationships, and strengthen resilience skills are important preventive measures.

Despite these challenges, young adolescents have many positive qualities. They are extremely curious, able to think hypothetically, and readily accepting of intellectual challenge. They begin to discover a multitude of new interests and activities—organized sports, arts, academic subjects, etc.—and want to try them all, but they must make tough choices due to time constraints. However, concerns about physical appearance begin to raise feelings of insecurity as hormones trigger troublesome weight gain, acne, facial hair, menstruation, voice changes, and extremities that grow at uneven rates. These changes signal an important transition from childhood to adulthood and are celebrated as a "coming of age" in some cultures. Even though thirteen-year-olds may consider themselves to be grown up and perceive rules and limits as overly confining and restrictive, they need consistent nurturing and guidance now more than ever.

Although thirteen-year-olds experience some loss of self-confidence as they adjust to the many physical and psychological changes occurring in their lives, their sense of self-identity quickly returns the following year. Fourteen-year-olds conduct themselves with greater self-assurance and emotional control, become more outgoing, have an improved (positive) outlook on life, and consider friendships more important. Their time outside of classes is often spent with same-gender peers—participating in extracurricular activities of mutual interest (e.g., school council, chess or glee club, theater, organized athletics, church groups, 4-H, computer gaming, etc.), gathering at a local hangout, talking on cell phones, texting, blogging, or engaging in other social networking platforms. Advancements in social and moral development are evident in the fourteen-year-olds' emerging interests in civic responsibility (giving back) and participation in community service or volunteer projects. In other words, fourteen-year-olds are beginning to show significant signs of maturing.

Developmental Profiles and Growth Patterns

Growth and Physical Characteristics

- Weight gain varies by individual, based on food intake, physical activity, and genetics.

- Continues to grow taller; boys, especially, begin to experience rapid growth spurts. Girls may experience small increases, but most have already reached their adult height by this time.

- Head size and facial features are adultlike; the arms, legs, and feet often appear large and out of proportion to the rest of the body.

- Has a full set of permanent teeth, except for the second and third molars (wisdom teeth).

- Tires easily, especially after vigorous activity, but quickly regains energy following a brief rest.

- Has blood pressure that approximates adult values (approximately 110/80); varies with the child's weight, activity, emotional state, and ethnicity (some racial groups are prone to higher blood pressure) (Hardy & Urbina, 2021). Inadequate sleep, increased sodium intake, obesity, and inactivity are factors that are contributing to an increase in hypertension (high blood pressure) among today's adolescents.

- Develops facial blemishes due to hormonal changes.

- Continues to experience bodily changes associated with puberty; girls begin having regular monthly periods; boys develop facial hair, voice changes, and nocturnal emissions.

- Complains of blurred vision or fatigue while reading; should have eyes examined to rule out any acuity problem if complaints persist.

Developmental Profiles and Growth Patterns *(continued)*

Motor Development

- Has movements that are often awkward and uncoordinated due to irregular and rapid growth.

- Engages in purposeful activity; spends less time "just fooling around."

- Is able to sit quietly for longer periods, but still needs frequent outlets to relieve excess energy.

- Exhibits greater speed and agility, especially girls; girls reach their peak strength at around age fourteen; boys experience rapid gains in strength and endurance once puberty is reached (approximately two years later than girls).

- Develops new interests in individual sports (e.g., swimming, golf, track, gymnastics) and team athletics (e.g., softball, soccer, basketball, football, hockey) (Figure 9-3).

Lynn Marotz

Figure 9-3 New interests in sports reflect the adolescent's improved motor abilities.

Perceptual-Cognitive Development

- Uses more advanced thought processes (e.g., theoretical, rational, and logical) to formulate opinions.

- Begins to analyze problems from multiple perspectives before arriving at a solution; first makes a prediction (hypothesis) and then considers multiple variables or options one at a time before arriving at a conclusion. (Piaget referred to this process as **formal operational thinking**.)

- Is able to understand and learn advanced material; thinks abstractly about complex issues, but still lacks the experience necessary to make sound decisions at all times.

- Likes school and academic challenge: arrives early; is eager to meet up with friends and to explore new academic subjects and extracurricular activities.

- Feels overwhelmed at times by schoolwork, tests, and expectations.

- Fascinated with technology; uses the Internet for homework, entertainment, and communication purposes; has difficulty determining if media content is truthful and reliable and, thus, is easily mislead (Fomby et al., 2021).

- Spends considerable time in self-reflection; often retreats to the bedroom to think and to communicate online with friends (Hipson et al., 2021).

- Plans and organizes activities without adult assistance.

- Begins to make some future plans, but most attention is focused on the present.

Speech and Language Development

- Is articulate in expressing ideas and thoughts; word comprehension and fluency have nearly reached adult levels.

- Pauses and thinks before responding.

formal operational thinking Piaget's fourth stage of cognitive development; the period when children are capable of using abstract thought to predict, test, and reason to arrive at a logical conclusion.

Developmental Profiles and Growth Patterns *(continued)*

- Answers questions in a direct and concise manner; is less likely to engage in spontaneous conversation with family members than during earlier years.

- Spends endless time texting, emailing, and talking on the phone with friends (Lieberman & Schroeder, 2021).

- Understands irony, sarcasm, and metaphors when used in conversation.

Social-Emotional Development

- Has unpredictable periods of moodiness (usually related to hormonal changes); may be rude or act out when frustrated or faced with new or stressful challenges.

- Develops firm moral viewpoints about what is right and wrong.

- Is often opinionated and questions parental decisions; although this may result in hurt feelings, it is an important step in becoming independent.

- Embarrassed by displays of adult affection in public (e.g., father putting his arm around son's shoulder, mother hugging daughter good-bye).

- Begins to display signs of adolescent **egocentrism**; becomes increasingly self-conscious and sensitive to criticism; compares self to an **imaginary audience** (e.g., friends, movie stars, rock musicians, and fashion models in magazines) and attempts to mimic their image; often expresses dissatisfaction with own body appearance (especially girls) and personal achievements. Some cultural differences in the importance of appearance-related social approval and self-esteem have been reported (Prieler, Choi, & Lee, 2021).

- Spends increasing time with friends rather than family (Figure 9-4).

- Has strong desire for peer acceptance; makes an effort to fit in through choice of clothes, behavior, music, and mutual-interest activities (Andrews, Ahmed, & Blakemore, 2021).

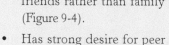

Figure 9-4 Friends and friendships become more important than time spent with family.

- Has mixed feelings about sexual relationships, although may begin to engage in exploratory behaviors and discussions with peers. Family dysfunction, minority affiliation, drug and alcohol use, and low self-esteem increase the risk for early sexual activity (Gazendam et al., 2020; Inanc et al., 2020).

- Is developing a stronger sense of self-identity, but still wavers between feeling confident and independent one moment and insecure and needing reassurance the next.

---

egocentrism Adolescents' belief in their own self-importance.

imaginary audience A component of egocentrism whereby adolescents believe that others care about and notice their behavior and appearance.

▶❚❚ TeachSource **Video Connections**

Understanding Adolescent Emotions

New experiences, conflicts, and challenges can be intimidating and some-times lead to emotions that adolescents find difficult to understand and con-trol. Respond to the following questions after you have watched the learning video *Social-Emotional Development: Understanding Adolescents:*

1. Why would holding a group meeting with these adolescent boys be an effective way to help them address their anger?

2. What positive strategies were the boys able to identify that allowed them to deal with their anger and stress?

3. Why is it important that adults take time to establish rapport with adoles-cents and listen to their side of the story?

DAILY ROUTINES

Eating

- Continues to have a hearty appetite (especially boys); increased food consumption often precedes an impending growth spurt.

- Arrives home from school in need of a snack; often eats while studying, watching television, and before bedtime; food choices are not always the most nutritious.

- Concerns about weight may lead to self-imposed food restriction and unhealthy diets, especially among girls; nutritious, well-balanced meals should be provided and children's food intake observed carefully. (*Note:* Avoid drawing too much attention to eating behaviors or making negative comments about weight; doing so may increase the teen's determination and resistance to change).

- May show an increased interest in cooking and preparing meals for themselves and others.

Personal Care and Dressing

- Manages own bathing and care routines but may need gentle reminders at times.

- Begins to shave or trim facial hair (boys); girls may shave legs and underarms.

- Takes pride in appearance; has definite clothing preferences.

- Prefers to select and may help purchase some of own clothing items; choices often reflect what is considered to be "in style" with peers.

Sleeping

- Stays up later at night: studies, finishes homework, watches television, or plays computer games; often has difficulty waking up in the morning. Changes in the adolescent's wake-sleep cycle (associated with puberty) create a preference for going to bed later and getting up later thin the morning (Coch, 2021).

DAILY ROUTINES *(continued)*

- Insufficient sleep has been linked to depression, poor academic performance, and substance abuse in adolescents (Karan et al., 2021).

Social Activities

- Relies on friends for companionship. Girls form a close social bond with one or two same-gender friends and confide in them about personal matters. Boys prefer doing things together with several friends or as a group but are less likely to share personal information.

- Shows some interest in casual dating; attends school dances, parties, and other social events; goes to the movies as a couple or with other couples in a group.

- Meets and communicates often with friends through texting and social networking sites; staying connected with friends may reduce feelings of loneliness; however, hurtful comments posted online can be detrimental to children's self-esteem (Webster, Dunne, & Hunter, 2021).

learning activities to promote **brain development**

The world of possibilities is beginning to open up for thirteen- and fourteen-year-olds. They need continued support and encouragement to explore new opportunities and activities. This is also an important time to emphasize and reinforce healthy lifestyle habits, personal safety, and wise decision making.

Developmentally appropriate applications for families and teachers

- Encourage children to explore a variety of academic subjects and extracurricular activities; refrain from criticizing or making children feel guilty if they decide to opt out after giving it their best effort.

- Support children's interest in civic responsibility; help them to identify opportunities for volunteering (e.g., animal shelter, local library, neighborhood or school garden, and mentoring younger children), fund-raising for a local cause, or participating in community service projects.

- Designate one evening each week as a "family night." Plan and cook a meal together, make popcorn and watch a movie, play box or electronic games, take a walk, ride bikes, swim, or engage in some other activity together. Time spent with one another strengthens communication and family ties.

- Promote children's interests in the environment and social responsibility: challenge them to design alternative energy devices, such as a solar stove, wind generator, or water heater.

- Foster adolescents' creative literacy: help them to compose a short novel, write and produce a play, film and edit a movie, or initiate a neighborhood newsletter.

- Interest children in researching and organizing a collection: coins, shells, baseball cards, bumper stickers, pencils, maps, insects, or travel souvenirs.

- Challenge children to try a new sport (e.g., track, Frisbee golf, swimming, basketball, table tennis, lacrosse, soccer, handball, bowling, or volleyball). Reinforce the importance of being physically active every day to maintain fitness and health (physical and mental).

- Assign tasks that children are responsible for completing on a regular basis (e.g., feeding and walking the dog, folding and putting away laundry, setting out the recycling containers, vacuuming, or mowing the lawn).

TeachSource Digital Download

developmental **alerts**

Check with a health-care provider or child development specialist if, by the fifteenth birthday, the child does *not*:

- Make friends and socialize with them; show interest in activities that were once enjoyable; maintain reasonable eating and sleeping habits. Sudden or prolonged behavioral changes may indicate an emotional problem that needs to be addressed.
- Continue to grow or experience physical changes associated with puberty.
- Demonstrate an ability to think in the abstract; consider more than one solution when solving a problem.
- Read with understanding; express ideas so they are meaningful to others.
- Look forward to school and attend on a regular basis (e.g., makes frequent excuses to stay home or skips school without parents' knowledge).
- Abide by family rules and expectations on most occasions, even if it is under protest.
- Demonstrate moral reasoning or the ability to distinguish right from wrong (e.g., engages in risky behaviors such as drinking, drugs, sexting, or petty crime).

Note: Cultural differences may alter the timetable when some developmental skills are acquired. Expanded Developmental Alerts Checklists appear in Appendix A and are also available as digital downloads.

safety **concerns**

Continue to implement the safety practices described for the previous stages. Always be aware of new safety issues as the child continues to grow and develop.

Sports

- Make sure that children are healthy and have medical clearance to play organized sports.
- Insist that appropriate safety equipment be worn at all times, even during practice. Check the condition of any equipment periodically to make sure it is intact, the correct size for the child using it, and is adjusted properly.
- Be familiar with the quality of supervision or coaching that children receive. Are children positively reinforced to perform? Are injuries handled properly? Are rest and hydration breaks offered? Are adults trained to administer cardiopulmonary resuscitation (CPR) and first aid?

Suicide/Depression

- Note sudden or significant changes in children's moods (e.g., increased or unusual irritability, aggression, withdrawal, or sadness), eating routines, sleep patterns, or any combination of the three. Depression and suicidal thoughts often peak during early adolescence; professional help should be sought if any signs are observed (Ali et al., 2021; Gijzen et al., 2021).
- Monitor adolescents' social networking and Internet use; let them know to alert an adult if they are ever the target of cyberbullying, sexting, solicitation, or identity theft.
- Maintain an open, nonjudgmental dialogue with teens; encourage them to discuss their concerns with a trusted adult (e.g., parent, family friend, teacher, or coach) (Figure 9-5).

Media Exposure

- Talk with children about online safety: chat-room guidelines; adult-content sites; data-mining by marketers; not

13 and 14 year olds

safety **concerns** *(continued)*

accepting messages from unknown persons; telling an adult if they receive inappropriate content; not posting personal information.

- Locate computers in a public area where the child's online activity can be monitored more easily, not in the child's bedroom.
- Limit the amount of time that children spend online, on a tablet, computer, cell phone, or other handheld device.

Risky Behaviors

- Provide adolescents with information to help them make sound decisions regarding sexual activity,

alcohol consumption, illicit drugs, prescription medication abuse, tattoos, body piercings, etc.
- Note early behavioral and emotional signs of a potential eating disorder: consuming less food, skipping meals, weight loss, prolonged dissatisfaction with body image, vomiting, excessive exercising, depression, or any combination of these.
- Establish a plan to know where adolescents are at all times: when to call, where they are going, and when they can be expected to return. They may protest but also find comfort in knowing that someone cares.

Did You Know ❓

...that more than half of all premature adult deaths are related to high-risk adolescent behaviors, such as smoking, violence, unprotected sex, and a sedentary lifestyle?

Figure 9-5 Adolescents should feel comfortable talking to a trusted adult.

iStock.com/SDI Productions

Spotlight on **Neuroscience** and **Brain Development**

The Adolescent Brain and Psychoactive Stimulants

Parents often describe the process of raising teenagers as one of their most significant challenges. They find children's mood swings and irrational behaviors puzzling at times. They wonder how the morals and values they have instilled to this point seem to vanish when adolescents are making important and often life-altering decisions. Such apparent contradictions in behavior cause many parents to question if, how, or should they have taken a different approach.

Throughout adolescence, children seem to be more easily tempted, impulsive, and less likely to control their desires in situations that require them to think before they act. Scientists have linked these risky behaviors to structural and functional changes in the prefrontal cortex of the adolescent's brain (Edde et al., 2021; Kryza-Lacombe et al., 2021; McIlvain et al., 2020). This particular region is responsible for regulating emotional control, planning, and sensitivity to pleasurable rewards. As a result, adolescents are more likely to exercise poor self-control and participate in thrill-seeking activities until new neural connections are formed and fully established (LaSpada et al, 2021).

Alcohol consumption and drug use—particularly marijuana (cannabis)—are among the most common high-risk behaviors that adolescents engage in. Both are problematic because these substances are known to have detrimental short- and long-term effects on neurocognitive development. Research results indicate that the adolescent brain is especially sensitive to the effects of **psychoactive stimulants** (Blest-Hopley et al., 2020; Morie & Potenza, 2021). As a result, teens may experience enhanced pleasurable sensations and are more likely to become addicted. Knowing this has raised serious concerns about adolescents' access to cannabis as more states take steps to legalize these products (Korn et al., 2021; Yu et al., 2020).

Cannabis exposure during adolescence is known to alter neural connections in regions of the brain that affect cognition and inhibitory control. Ellingson and colleagues (2021) noted a significant association between adolescents' cannabis use and impaired verbal learning and short-term memory. Students who engaged in casual use experienced decreased motivation and academic performance and an increase in behaviors that required disciplinary action (Schaefer et al., 2021). Increased impulsivity and impaired driving ability are also confirmed by results from numerous studies. On-going efforts to determine if early cannabis use predisposes individuals to mental health problems and disorders in adulthood suggest that there may be a positive relationship (Hudson & Hudson, 2021).

For some adolescents, the act of engaging in risky behaviors produces significant excitement and pleasurable feelings. However, most adolescents are able to exercise relative self-control and to make reasonable decisions. Individual differences in temperament, biological makeup, family expectations and support, social and cultural values, and religious beliefs exert a strong influence on the way these behaviors are ultimately expressed. Although these developments occur during a period when more time is spent with friends than with family, parents continue to play a critical role in helping adolescents successfully navigate this critical path to adulthood.

What are the connections?

1. What brain-based explanation could you offer to a distraught parent of a fifteen-year-old who was caught drinking at a friend's house?
2. Are fourteen-year-olds mature enough to begin driving a vehicle? Explain your response from a brain development perspective.
3. Why do so many drug prevention programs that are implemented in secondary schools often fail? How might they use the current knowledge about adolescent brain development to design effective programs?

Fifteen and Sixteen-Year-Olds (Middle Adolescence)

Behavioral contrasts continue to be evident during middle adolescence. However, the ways in which they are experienced and expressed often vary due to differences in family, social, religious, and cultural values. Typical fifteen-year-olds exhibit many developmental traits that are similar to those of thirteen-year-olds. Once again, they become more introspective, indifferent, rebellious, and intent on gaining autonomy. Friends (one on one and in groups) gradually replace family as a source of comfort, security, and personal information. Fifteen-year-olds either like school and work hard to achieve good grades, or they become disengaged and uninterested. They find convenient reasons (e.g., school activities, errands, and social events) not to stay home and, when they are at home, often retreat to their room and immerse

psychoactive stimulants This category of drugs includes antidepressants, stimulants, narcotics, hallucinogens, and marijuana (cannabis).

themselves in computer games, online chatting, listening to music, daydreaming, or watching television. Although most fifteen-year-olds enjoy excellent health, they may experience considerable stress and tension from daily occurrences (e.g., test taking, team tryouts, feelings of sexuality, friendships, bullying and discrimination) (Kim, 2021; Vos et al., 2021).

Many positive qualities begin to return as adolescents approach their sixteenth birthday. They develop a renewed sense of self-confidence, respect, emotional control, tolerance, and self-determination. Friends are important and continue to play a vital role. Relationships are formed based on common interests, are relatively stable, and are intimate in some cases.

Sexual identity is well established, although some adolescents are reluctant to acknowledge or to discuss concerns about homosexual tendencies or gender nonconformity (Simon et al., 2020; Xu, Norton, & Rahman, 2021). This can interfere with the adolescent's sense of acceptance or belonging and lead to significant peer victimization and depression (van Beusekon et al., 2020). Perceived pressures to conform to gender expectations are typically stronger for adolescent males than they are for adolescent females. Jackson, Bussey, and Myers (2021) noted that the pressure to exhibit gender conforming behaviors is typically self- and parent-generated for adolescent males whereas it is primarily self-generated for adolescent females.

Sixteen-year-olds have developed more advanced cognitive and analytical skills that enable **deductive reasoning**, improved decision making, and planning for the future (de Blas, Gómez-Veiga, & García-Madruga, 2021; Demetriou et al., 2020). They continue to explore and experiment with everything from clothing styles and interpersonal relationships to technology, political and philosophical ideas, and vocational interests (Figure 9-6). In other words, sixteen-year-olds are well on their way to becoming independent thinkers and doers.

15 and 16 year olds

Figure 9-6 Adolescents continue to refine their self-identity by exploring and experimenting with everything from technology to interpersonal relationships.

iStock.com/monkeybusinessimages

deductive reasoning A process of considering hypothetical alternatives before reaching a conclusion.

Developmental Profiles and Growth Patterns

Growth and Physical Characteristics

- Weight gain varies by individual and depends on food intake, physical activity, and genetics.
- Continues to grow taller; boys, especially, experience rapid growth spurts. Girls have reached their approximate adult height; males will not do so until their early twenties.
- Wisdom teeth (third molars) may erupt.
- Still tires easily, especially following vigorous activity.
- Experiences fewer skin eruptions (acne) as hormone levels stabilize.
- Continues to undergo gradual body changes associated with puberty.
- The arms, legs, hands, and feet still may appear large and out of proportion to the rest of the body.
- Continues to add muscle mass, especially for boys, but also for girls who are athletically active.

Motor Development

- Motor coordination, speed, and endurance have reached their peak in girls; boys begin to surpass girls in these abilities and continue to improve until age twenty.
- Hand–eye coordination becomes more precise and controlled.
- Appears awkward and uncoordinated (clumsy) during periods of rapid growth; prone to more injuries during these times.

Perceptual-Cognitive Development

- Solves abstract problems using deductive reasoning; is able to visualize or recall a concept, place, or thing without actually seeing or experiencing it at the time.
- Plans ahead: considers the pros and cons of several weekend activities before deciding on a final choice; makes hypothetical plans for the summer break; thinks about future career options.
- Uses **scientific reasoning** to solve increasingly complex problems; combines knowledge, experience, and logic to arrive at a solution or outcome.
- Becomes aware of a much larger world; is curious, eager for academic challenge, and interested in trying new things.

15 and 16 year olds

▶❚❚ TeachSource **Video Connections**

Technology and Learning

Technology has revolutionized our daily lives and changed the way that students learn. Innovative instructional programs offer enriched opportunities for exploring and understanding complex information. Respond to the following questions as you watch the learning video *Integrating Technology to Improve Student Learning: A High School Science Simulation:*

1. What perceptual-cognitive skills are fifteen- and sixteen-year-olds developing that enable them to grasp complex ideas, such as technology and genetics?

2. In what ways are the students using scientific reasoning to explain genetic differences?

3. Why would the use of instructional technology appeal to adolescents?

4. What examples of the adolescent's ability to focus attention on multiple activities at the same time can be observed in this video?

scientific reasoning Critical thinking skills (identify, analyze, and conclude) used to achieve a solution.

Developmental Profiles and Growth Patterns *(continued)*

15 and 16 year olds

- Is able to focus attention on several activities at the same time: listens to music on headphones or watches television while doing homework.
- Recognizes that not all information is trustworthy; is becoming better at evaluating an information source before accepting it as reliable.

Speech and Language Development

- Experiences modest gains in vocabulary; girls continue to score higher than boys on tests of verbal ability.
- Is capable of learning additional languages, but requires more time and effort than when they were younger (an important consideration for schools given the increasing numbers of non-English-speaking children).
- Adjusts language and communication style according to the situation: conversing on the phone with friends, discussing a project with teachers, or texting in cyber slang.
- Uses increasingly complex grammar and sentence constructions to express ideas.
- Spends considerable time engaged in social networking and communicating with friends (e.g., texting, "tweeting," taking and posting "selfies").
- Understands and engages in adult humor.

Did You Know ?

...that teens send approximately 50 text messages a day (1,500 per month)? Girls send and receive an average of 80 messages per day, boys approximately 30, and most messages focus on friends or school-related activities.

Social-Emotional Development

- Establishes friendships with peers of both genders; having friends and being "popular" are important (Pouwels et al., 2021; Wang et al., 2021) (Figure 9-7). Friendships are valued in all cultures worldwide, although their importance and significance vary (Lu et al., 2021).
- Continues to struggle with self-identity issues, especially if there are real or perceived differences from one's peers (e.g., religious beliefs, biracial, sexual orientation, adopted, ethnicity, or special needs); is sensitive to peer comments.

Figure 9-7 Adolescents begin to take an interest in forming romantic relationships.

- Develops an interest in forming serious romantic relationships. This is an important step in refining one's self-identity and self-image, determining sexual orientation, establishing personal values related to intimacy and sexual behavior, and learning about the qualities desired in a partner.
- Has a strong drive to achieve autonomy from the family; dislikes parental authority and limits placed on activities.
- Is caring, cooperative, and responsible much of the time; temperamental, moody, and rebellious on occasion, especially when wishes are not granted.
- Adopts clothing styles and behavior of peer group; may also experiment with risky behaviors (e.g., illicit drugs, tattoos, body piercings, sexual activity, tobacco, and alcohol) to make a statement or to gain acceptance.
- Recognizes right from wrong, but makes some irresponsible decisions that may contradict this understanding (Bajovic & Rizzo, 2021; Introzzi et al., 2021).

DAILY ROUTINES

Eating

- Continues to have a healthy appetite, but is less likely to participate in family meals; often eats when hungry or convenient due to time conflicts with school or extracurricular activities.

- Shows interest in food-weight-health connections. Teasing, stress, depression, concerns about body image, and parent comments about weight or body shape can lead to disordered eating, especially among girls (Dahill et al., 2021). Severe dieting and disordered eating behaviors (e.g., anorexia, binge eating) are more common among both genders during this age period and can lead to serious health consequences (Hornberger & Lane, 2021; Williamson et al., 2021).

- Explores new foods and alternative dietary practices (e.g., eating vegetarian meals or organic foods, restricting carbohydrates, eliminating processed foods, and lowering fat intake), but may have less interest in cooking.

Personal Care and Dressing

- Takes pride in personal grooming and appearance; girls often apply makeup; boys shave facial hair.

- Bathes or showers daily; washes hair frequently.

- Usually quite particular about clothing choices; prefers items that reflect current styles and fashion trends.

Sleeping

- Requires approximately nine hours of uninterrupted nighttime sleep to maintain health and attention. Sleep deprivation can interfere with learning, diminish alertness, and contribute to moodiness, irritability, and behavior problems (Galván, 2020; Karan et al., 2021).

- Stays up late at night; biological changes during adolescence cause a shift in wake/sleep rhythms (toward a later bedtime and later morning awake time); may fail to get adequate sleep due to school activities, employment, homework, socializing with friends, or all of these.

Social Activities

- Prefers spending time alone when home; often goes to own bedroom, closes the door, and listens to music, reads, or spends time looking at websites on a cell phone or computer. Solitude provides adolescents with important time to deescalate from a busy day, think about things that have occurred, make plans, and pursue information of interest (Coplan, Hipson, & Bowker, 2021; Hipson et al., 2021).

- Develops new friendships; may spend more time with friends than with family; friends provide an important source of companionship, feedback, and emotional support, especially among girls.

- Enjoys challenge and competition; explores and participates in a variety of social and extracurricular activities; some adolescents may also hold down part-time jobs.

15 and 16 year olds

learning activities to promote **brain development**

Although fifteen- and sixteen-year-olds are becoming more independent, they also want reassurance that adults care and are available if needed. Times spent together provide opportunities for adolescents to talk about subjects that are important to them. Continue to do activities together, have family meals, and guide children's evolving interests.

Developmentally appropriate applications for families and teachers

- Provide opportunities for privacy; respect adolescents' need and preference for spending time alone; knock before entering their room.

15 and 16 year olds

learning activities *(continued)*

- Encourage and support children's interest in developing leadership skills and assuming leadership roles at school or in local organizations.

- Offer to help arrange small social gatherings where teens can mingle in a safe setting (e.g., pool or deck party, sleepover, watching a movie or playing games at home with friends, or hosting youth group meetings).

- Support interests in new activities (e.g., singing, theater, art, playing a musical instrument, hunting, robotics, golf, yoga, astronomy, cooking, or hiking).

- Assist teens in locating volunteer opportunities or occasional part-time work (e.g., babysitting, mowing lawns, shoveling snow, pet sitting, or raking leaves).

- Plan trips centered on a learning theme (e.g., space museum, aquarium, national park, working ranch, adventure camp, historical place, snorkeling, or an exposure to a different cultural experience).

- Organize a book club; have teens take turns selecting a book for the group to read and discuss.

- Interest teens in learning about genealogy, researching their family background, and developing a family tree.

- Continue to discuss high-risk behaviors and preventive measures; provide educational reading materials and encourage teens to ask questions.

- Teach time management and organizational skills; encourage teens to set up a digital calendar where due dates for homework, tests, and activities can be noted; create a quiet area for studying and storing school materials.

- Prepare teens to handle difficult situations (e.g., being offered drugs or alcohol, being pressured to have sex, etc.); role-play strategies for avoiding involvement.

- Establish a bank account or credit card (with limited funds) to help teens learn how to manage their money.

TeachSource Digital Download

developmental **alerts**

Check with a health-care provider or child development specialist if, by the seventeenth birthday, the child does *not:*

- Have or keep friends; is not included in group activities.

- Remember or plan ahead on most occasions.

- Maintain reasonable interest in personal hygiene and daily activities, including school; sudden apathy or failing grades may be signs of depression or other mental health disorders.

- Use language correctly to express thoughts and requests; interpret or respond appropriately to nonverbal behavior.

- Grasp humor, jokes, or puns.

- Confront new situations with a relative degree of self-confidence.

- Avoid involvement in harmful behaviors (e.g., drugs, alcohol abuse, bullying, promiscuous sex, crime, and truancy).

Note: Cultural differences may alter the timetable when some developmental skills are acquired. Expanded Developmental Alerts Checklists appear in Appendix A and are also available as digital downloads.

safety concerns

Continue to implement the safety practices described for the previous stages. Always be aware of new safety issues as the child continues to grow and develop.

Sporting Activities

- Insist that proper protective gear be worn when participating in sporting activities: paintball (goggles); biking (helmet); skateboarding (helmet, protective knee and elbow pads); hunting (earplugs, goggles, reflective vest); baseball and softball (helmet, mouth and shin guards); boating (life jacket), etc.
- Seek medical evaluation for any head injury; prevent teens from returning to the sporting activity until given medical clearance.

Media Exposure

- Monitor adolescents' Internet use (e.g., social networking sites, movies, computer games, and music) at home; make it a point to know what teens are accessing when alone or spending time with friends.
- Educate teens about potential risks involved in an online presence: urge caution about giving out or posting personal information; report cyberbullying, solicitation, or "sexting" to an adult; never agree to meet an online "friend" unless in a public area, with a trusted friend, and after informing an adult.

Dating

- Educate teens about dating, setting personal limits, and maintaining healthy relationships.
- Discuss dating violence; talk about the warning signs and what to do if teens find themselves in an abusive relationship.
- Provide teens with information about pregnancy and sexually transmitted disease (STD) prevention to help them make informed decisions.

Travel

- Insist that seat belts be worn when riding in a vehicle with family or friends.
- Educate teens about refusing to ride with a drunk or reckless driver and to report the individual.
- Have teens call when they leave and arrive at their destination; let them know that this rule isn't about trust—rather, it has to do with your concerns about their safety.
- Make sure that teens have emergency contact information along with them, such as parents' cell phone numbers.

17 and 18 year olds

Seventeen- and Eighteen-Year-Olds (Late Adolescence)

The remaining years of adolescence are characterized by minimal developmental changes that are either dramatic or significant in number. Girls have completed their physical and reproductive growth, whereas boys will continue to experience small gains in height and muscle mass well into their early twenties. Cognition, social-emotional capacity, speech and language, and motor abilities are well established by now and undergo only minor refinement during late adolescence.

Seventeen- and eighteen-year-olds have established a clear sexual identity and are usually comfortable with themselves, self-reliant, more emotionally stable, and philosophical about life. They are now able to shift their interests and energies from skill acquisition and peer acceptance to contemplating the future (Figure 9-8): "What plans do I have following high school?" "What are my long-range career goals, and what must I do to achieve them?" "Am I interested in an intimate relationship or long-term commitment?" "How do I plan on supporting myself financially?" How adolescents

Figure 9-8 Adolescents devote much thought to researching career options and making future plans.

iStock.com/SDI Productions

ultimately make these decisions is strongly influenced by their cultural, economic, social, and family values (Iovu, Hărăgus, & Roth, 2018; Ulrich, Helker, & Losekamm, 2021). In some cultural and social groups, for example, adolescents are expected to continue living with their family and to contribute financially until they marry. By contrast, it is presumed that adolescents in many Western societies will leave home and establish their independence once they have completed school.

And so, the journey through childhood nears an end as adolescents approach their nineteenth birthday. Most are ready and eager to begin the next chapter of life and to face a host of new challenges, decisions, and opportunities as they become young adults.

Developmental Profiles and Growth Patterns

Growth and Physical Characteristics

- Undergoes few changes in basic physical development; has almost reached adult maturity.
- Experiences small increases in height, weight, and bone mass; males continue to add muscle mass and grow taller until their early twenties; girls have achieved their full adult height.
- Enjoys good health and few illnesses in most cases.
- Experiences a relatively high rate of injury, death, and disability due to irrational decisions, impulsive behavior, and carelessness.

Motor Development

- Continues to develop muscular strength and agility into the early twenties, especially males; girls typically do not experience these changes after reaching puberty.
- Achieves precise finger dexterity and hand–eye coordination; draws, builds, plays an instrument, and manipulates computer and video games with skill.
- Has movements that are now coordinated and controlled.

Developmental Profiles and Growth Patterns *(continued)*

Perceptual-Cognitive Development

- Uses recall, logic, and abstract thinking to solve complex problems.

- Begins to rely on **analytical thinking** when planning and problem solving more often than in the past; identifies and evaluates potential solutions, although does not always reach a rational decision (Figure 9-9).

- Shows some gender differences in cognitive abilities: girls tend to achieve greater verbal skills; boys may excel in nonverbal areas such as science, technology, and mathematics. However, these differences have become less significant as more equitable opportunities and support are equalizing skill acquisition across genders (Reilly, Neumann, & Andrews, 2019).

Figure 9-9 On the brink of adulthood, older adolescents now are capable of solving complex problems based on analytical thinking processes.

17 and 18 year olds

- Continues to make impulsive decisions and illogical choices that sometimes make adults wonder. Remember that adolescent brains still are undergoing development, pruning, and maturation in the areas responsible for emotional control and decision making (Kray, Kreis, & Lorenz, 2021).

Speech and Language Development

- Uses correct grammar and more elaborate sentence structure; is able to critique own written work.

- Articulates complex ideas, varying the style according to the situation.

- Continues to expand vocabulary; adds words that are more advanced, sophisticated, and abstract.

- Participates heavily in social networking; uses Internet slang and shortcuts masterfully to converse (text) with friends ("b/c,"

Figure 9-10 Teens spend considerable time engaged in social networking and staying in touch with friends.

because; "g2g," got to go; "sbrd," so bored; "meh," whatever; "PAW," parents are watching; "fr," for real) (Figure 9-10).

- Forms strong opinions and enjoys debating opposing views.

- Understands and uses **figurative language**: "He jumped as high as the sky," "She was as quiet as a mouse," "They are like two peas in a pod."

analytical thinking A cognitive process used when attempting to solve problems or make plans; identifying and evaluating the pros and cons of alternative solutions.

figurative language Words or statements that have meanings other than their literal definitions.

Developmental Profiles and Growth Patterns *(continued)*

Social-Emotional Development

17 and 18 year olds

- Is becoming more open and receptive to adult advice; may actually request it on occasion (Billingsley, Rivens, & Hurd, 2021; Koestner et al., 2020).

- Continues to refine a self-identity based more on realistic goals and cultural ideals and less on idealistic notions ("I want to be a famous musician, but it's going to take a lot of hard work and dedication.")

- Has more self-confidence; is less likely to be influenced by peers or to rely on them for approval.

- Sees oneself as part of a much larger global world; is less self-centered. Continues to redefine personal values and beliefs about social roles and civic responsibilities; seeks out opportunities to become involved in community, church, or political programs (Osman, Miranda, & Jourde, 2020; Wray-Lake & Abrams, 2020).

- Has better emotional control, but still exhibits a range of moods and occasional impulsive behavior.

- Shows greater empathy and ability to perceive others' emotions; girls are somewhat more perceptive than are boys (Portt et al., 2020).

- Seeks intimate relationships based more on shared interests than pure romantic desire.

- Understands and is more likely to accept responsibility for own behavior.

Did You Know ?

...that many high school students give back to their communities by volunteering? They account for more than 25 percent of all volunteers and most often participate in civic events that address home-lessness, hunger, fund-raising, community cleanup, animal care, and mentoring children in recreation-al activities.

▶❚❚ TeachSource **Video Connections**

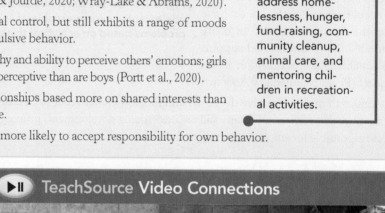

Peer Influence

Friendships and peers play an essential role in adolescent development. However, the nature of these relationships changes over time. Respond to the following questions as you watch the learning video *12–18 Years: Peers and Domain Influences in Development*:

1. What is meant by "domain-specific peer influence"?
2. What developmental areas are parents most likely to influence?
3. Why do seventeen- and eighteen-year-olds value the input of peers and parents differently?
4. Why do they appear to be more receptive to adult advice at this point in their development?

DAILY ROUTINES

Eating

- Continues to have important nutritional needs (e.g., calories, protein, calcium, vitamins, iron, zinc, etc.) that must be satisfied to assure optimum growth, health, and performance.
- Eating patterns may become more erratic as activities and schedules compete with mealtimes; skips occasional meals, overeats following vigorous workouts or during stressful periods.
- Makes independent decisions about food choices; eats with friends and away from home more often.
- Weight concerns and emotional problems may lead to unhealthy diets, eating disorders, or both (Shriver et al., 2021). Has difficulty distinguishing accurate information from misinformation and myth; easily swayed by health and nutrition misinformation posted online.

Personal Care and Dressing

- Is self-sufficient in managing personal care responsibilities.
- Chooses clothes that are "popular" with peers or that express individuality.

Sleeping

- Requires approximately nine hours of uninterrupted nighttime sleep.
- May nap following vigorous activity or if up late the night before; napping too long can delay falling asleep at night.
- Stress, medications, and mental health disorders such as depression may interfere with sleep patterns (sleeping too much or too little).

Social Activities

- Has learned to drive and may transport self to school activities and events.
- Juggles school, homework, and employment so that there is still time to take in a movie with friends, attend a sporting event or party, go out on a date, or simply join friends for something to eat.
- Has more friends of another gender, some of whom the adolescent may be dating; friendships are formed on the basis of personalities and common interests, with fewer concerns about popularity.
- Spends considerable time staying in touch with friends through social networks, instant messaging, or phone calls.
- Continues to develop and experiment with new interests and activities, such as surfing, skiing, or bowling; learning another language; playing a musical instrument; discovering religion; taking up yoga; repairing cars; practicing martial arts.

17 and 18 year olds

learning activities to promote **brain development**

Maintaining a respectful relationship with teens is important at this stage. Encourage healthy eating and sleep habits, set realistic expectations, and support their interests in planning for the future.

Developmentally appropriate applications for families and teachers

- Continue to discuss risky behaviors and safety considerations; role-play strategies for resisting negative peer pressure.
- Offer guidance with experiences that may be new to the adolescent, such as opening a checking account, applying for admission to college, purchasing a first car, or obtaining employment.

17 and 18 year olds

learning activities *(continued)*

- Help adolescents to learn healthy stress and anger management techniques.
- Encourage and support the adolescent's interest in volunteering or becoming involved in community politics or service activities.
- Motivate adolescents to follow a healthy diet and engage in physical activity.
- Create opportunities that give adolescents greater responsibility and acknowledge their efforts and contributions.
- Talk about and practice time management skills (these will be helpful as they continue their education and seek employment).
- Locate first aid and CPR classes and urge adolescents to complete the training.

TeachSource Digital Download

developmental **alerts**

Check with a health-care provider or child development specialist if, by the nineteenth birthday, the child does *not*:

- Maintain usual eating and sleeping routines; sudden or prolonged changes may signal substance abuse or mental health problems.
- Show interest and initiative in achieving independence from family.
- Link moral reasoning to behavioral choices; take responsibility for own behavior and learn from experience.
- Exhibit self-confidence and positive self-esteem in most daily activities.
- Attend school on a regular basis.
- Use reasonable judgment in regulating emotions.
- Grasp and process information when making decisions.
- Achieve functional literacy (reading and writing skills).
- Make and keep friends that have a positive influence on behavior.

Note: Cultural differences may alter the timetable when some developmental skills are acquired. Expanded Developmental Alerts Checklists appear in Appendix A and are also available as digital downloads.

safety **concerns**

Continue to implement the safety practices described for the previous stages. Always be aware of new safety issues as the child continues to grow and develop.

Health and Well-being
- Reinforce the importance of consuming a healthy diet and maintaining an active lifestyle.
- Continue to talk with adolescents about the risks of pregnancy and sexually transmitted infections.
- Recognize the signs of undue stress; encourage teens to talk about things that are making them feel anxious; be a patient listener and provide nonjudgmental support; reinforce healthy coping skills (e.g., tackling challenges in small steps; seeing the positive side of a problem; and, making time for fun and relaxation by listening to music, exercising, taking a

walk, talking with friends, or reading a book).

Unintentional Injury

- Continue to emphasize safe driving; motor vehicle accident and fatality rates are highest among older teens, especially males (Yellman et al., 2020) (Figure 9-11). Teens tend to believe that they are invincible!
- Prohibit the use of cell phones and texting while driving or driving under the influence of drugs or alcohol (a legal offense). Many states have passed laws banning texting or talking on a cell phone while driving.
- Urge caution when participating in recreational activities such as weight lifting, hunting, riding all-terrain vehicles (ATVs), boating, jogging, and swimming. Make sure that proper equipment, training, and supervision are provided.
- Educate adolescents about the risk and warning signs of concussions (traumatic brain injury, or TBI) that may be sustained during athletic activity. Stress the importance of seeking medical attention and clearance before the activity is resumed.
- Ensure that adolescents complete appropriate safety training if they use firearms for hunting or target practice.

Violence (Suicide, Homicide)

- Recognize the early warning signs of depression, mood disorders, sexual abuse, and potential suicide; sexual nonconformity, racism, and disability status increase the likelihood of malicious harassment and bullying (Fox et al., 2020;

Adolescent (15- to 20-year-olds) Motor Vehicle Fatalities, 2019

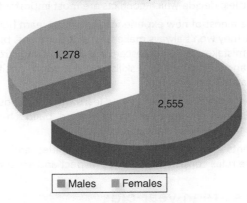

■ Males ■ Females

Figure 9-11 Adolescent motor vehicle fatalities.

Source: National Highway Traffic Safety Administration (NHTSA). Fatality analysis reporting system encyclopedia (FARS): 2019 Annual Report File (ARF). Retrieved from http://www.nhtsa.gov/FARS.

17 and 18 year olds

Goldbach, Raymond, & Burgess, 2021; Gordon, 2020).
- Educate adolescents about their increased vulnerability to the effects of drugs and alcohol; maturational changes in brain structure and function can interfere with rational thought, intensify sensitivity to substances, and increase the probability of addiction.
- Know who the adolescent's friends are, where they hang out, and what they do when they are together.
- Foster resilience and empower teens to resist peer pressure; continue to strengthen the adolescent's communication skills, self-esteem, and healthy mentoring relationships with caring adults.

positive behavior **guidance**

Behavioral guidance and limit-setting remain important adult responsibilities. However, the expectations and way in which these roles are performed are highly influenced by a person's values and social and cultural background. Adolescents who are raised in societies where parent–child relationships demand respect and obedience are less likely to experience conflict than are their peers who live in countries where autonomy is strongly encouraged. Teens need and want continued adult support, protection, respect, and guidance in making sound decisions (even if they seem to object) (Marotz & Kupzyk, 2017). At the same time, adults can promote adolescents' quest for autonomy by gradually relinquishing parental control and involving them in responsible decision making.

Thirteen- and fourteen-year-olds

- Let teens know that you are available to talk (in a nonjudgmental manner); encourage them to discuss concerns with family or a trusted adult; make a point to spend time together as a family.

- Choose your battles; decide which conflicts are most important to address.

- Adolescents face a host of new experiences and must learn how to make responsible choices. Understand that they won't always make the right decisions, but the hope is that they will learn from their mistakes. Help adolescents to develop and strengthen resilience skills (e.g., communication and problem-solving skills, social support, positive self-esteem, stress reduction, emotional regulation, goal-setting).

- Listen to the adolescent's side of the story; learn why they chose to violate a rule. It isn't necessary to agree, but it is important to respect their opinion, build a healthy relationship, and help them to understand why the rule was necessary.

- Involve adolescents in establishing rules, responsibilities, and consequences for unacceptable behavior. Enforce rules consistently to build respect and accountability.

Fifteen- and sixteen-year-olds

- Make an effort to know the adolescent's friends and the values they share; meet them at school functions; invite them over to hang out. Friends can be a source of positive social-emotional support or the basis for negative peer pressure.

- Never hit, humiliate, or call the adolescent sarcastic names. Overreacting, disciplining when you are angry, being verbally abusive, or using physical force sets a poor example and teaches negative ways of handling a difficult situation.

- Negotiate to reduce frequent disagreements and help adolescents understand the rationale for establishing a rule; involve your teen in defining the behavior in question, identifying reasonable solutions, arriving at a mutual decision, implementing, enforcing, and monitoring how well the solution is working.

- Use logical consequences: take their cell phone away if too much time is spent talking or texting with friends or if homework is ignored; set a curfew thirty minutes earlier if the teen was thirty minutes late.

- Acknowledge and reinforce responsible behavior; teens want adults to notice and to be proud of their accomplishments.

- Address harmful or risky behaviors in a direct, firm, and consistent manner. Let adolescents know that their poor choices indicate a lack of readiness to make mature decisions.

Seventeen- and eighteen-year-olds

- Continue to provide a safe, structured environment; maintain and enforce reasonable limits.

- Convey a sense of trust and respect, even though teens may make occasional mistakes in judgment. Encourage them to talk about and learn from mistakes.

- Give adolescents increased responsibility for handling their own affairs (e.g., bank account, laundry, scheduling, bill payments, or making clothing purchases) and acknowledge their efforts. Take time to help adolescents learn from their mistakes.

- Let adolescents know that you are available to talk; they continue to need support and reassurance as they encounter new and challenging experiences.

Summary

9-1   Changes associated with puberty and brain development require periods of major reorganization and readjustment.

- Structural modifications that occur in the brain's cortex region during adolescence require new neural connections to be formed.

- Emotion, decision making, and memory are regulated by the cortex.

continued on following page

Summary ✋

9-2 Thirteen- and fourteen-year-olds begin to experience numerous physical and psychological changes associated with puberty. These hormone-driven changes can cause children to lose self-confidence while they gradually comprehend, reexamine, and adjust to a new identity.

9-3 Fifteen- and sixteen-year-olds continue to value friendships and consider them to be important for companionship, emotional support, information, and an opportunity for sharing common interests. Friendships also provide a forum for learning about oneself and feelings toward others.

9-4 Seventeen- and eighteen-year-olds have achieved a level of relative maturity and independent thought. They generally understand who they are, how and where they fit in, and what they want in life. They begin to accept responsibility for their behavior and are less likely to act on impulse.

Key Terms

neural connections **p. 229**

formal operational thinking
  p. 231

egocentrism **p. 232**

imaginary audience **p. 232**

psychoactive stimulants **p. 237**

deductive reasoning **p. 238**

scientific reasoning **p. 239**

analytical thinking **p. 245**

figurative language **p. 245**

Apply What You Have Learned

A. Case Study Connections

Reread the developmental sketch about Maria and Sophia presented at the beginning of this chapter and answer the following questions:

1. What social-emotional behaviors are characteristic of most typical thirteen- and fourteen-year-olds?

2. How do friendships and the nature of their importance differ for thirteen-year-olds and sixteen-year-olds? Would you consider Maria's and Sophia's relationships with friends to be typical for their age?

3. What factors may account for the differences in the girls' personalities?

4. What age-appropriate issues should Maria's and Sophia's parents be discussing with them to protect their safety and well-being?

B. Review Questions

1. What physical changes are thirteen- and fourteen-year-olds likely to experience?

2. What cognitive advantages does formal operational thinking give the adolescent?

3. Describe the nature of peer relationships and the role they play in the lives of fifteen- and sixteen-year-olds.

4. How would you respond to parents who ask why their once-well-behaved child is now acting impulsively and making questionable choices as an adolescent?

5. Why do adolescents prefer to stay up late at night? What are the consequences of sleep deprivation?

6. Explain, from a developmental standpoint, why adolescents seem to devote so much time to instant messaging and social networking.

7. What is egocentrism? What adolescent behaviors would illustrate this concept?

C. Your Turn: Chapter to Practice

1. Interview a teen from each of the age divisions described in this chapter (13–14, 15–16, 17–18 years). Ask them to identify two or three concerns that they find particularly challenging at this time. In what ways are the concerns similar and different among the age groups? What conclusions can you draw from these findings?

2. Visit with a school truancy officer. What is the school's policy regarding truancy? What reasons are cited most often for student truancy? In what ways does the school work with students and families to prevent repeat truancy?

3. Develop a rationale based on the information in this chapter to explain why the legal drinking age in most countries is set at eighteen years.

4. Social networking platforms (e.g., Twitter, TikTok, YouTube, Instagram, Snapchat) have become important tools for marketing to adolescents. Explore several sites. Describe the type of products that are advertised and media features used to capture and hold adolescents' attention. Discuss why these methods are successful based on your understanding of adolescents' developmental characteristics.

Online Resources

American Institutes for Research (AIR)
This international organization is one of the largest nonprofit research groups to focus on behavioral and social science. Explore the "Education" section for access to an extensive list of resource information for teachers across all grade levels and in specialty areas (e.g., English-language learners [ELL], reading and literacy, STEM, mathematics, technology, after-school programs, special education, equity, child development, and LGBTQ youth).

Learning for Justice
An abundance of free resource material is provided for educators who work with children K–12. Topics address various social injustice forms related to religion, ability, race and ethnicity, class, immigration, gender and sexual identity, bullying and bias, and rights and activism. Explore the "Build a Learning Plan" feature.

Talking with Kids About Tough Issues
The Henry J. Kaiser Family Foundation and Children Now have partnered to encourage and support families in their effort to discuss challenging issues (e.g., alcohol, sex, violence, HIV/AIDS, and drug abuse) with children. Research-based information, pamphlets, and links to additional resource sites are provided.

WiredSafety
This site is dedicated to the promotion of online safety education and the elimination of harassment and cybercrime. Numerous topics for educators, children, and families are addressed.

References

Ali, B., Rockett, I. R. H., Miller, T. R., & Leonardo, J. B. (2021). Racial/ethnic differences in preceding circumstances of suicide and potential suicide. *Journal of Racial and Ethnic Health Disparities*. Advance online publication. https://doi.org/10.1007/s40615-020-00957-7

Andrews, J. L., Ahmed, S. P., & Blakemore, S-J. (2021). Navigating the social environment in adolescence: The role of social brain development. *Biological Psychiatry, 89*(2), 109–118.

Anil, M. A., & Bhat, J. S. (2020). Transitional changes in cognitive-communicative abilities in adolescents: A literature review. *Journal of Natural Science, Biology and Medicine, 11*(2), 85–92. Retrieved from http://www.jnsbm.org/text.asp?2020/11/2/85/290484.

Anniko, M. K., Boersma, K., & Tillfors, M. (2019). Sources of stress and worry in the development of stress-related mental health problems: A longitudinal investigation from early- to mid-adolescence. *Anxiety, Stress, and Coping 32*(2), 155–167.

Bajovic, M., & Rizzo, K. (2021). Meta-moral cognition: Bridging the gap among adolescents' moral thinking, moral emotions and moral actions. *International Journal of Adolescence and Youth, 26*(1), 1–11.

Billingsley, J. T., Rivens, A. J., & Hurd, N. M. (2021). Family closeness and mentor formation among Black youth. *Journal of Child and Family Studies, 30*, 793–807. https://doi.org/10.1007/s10826-020-01895-y

Blest-Hopley, G., Colizzi, M., Giampietro, V., & Bhattacharyya, S. (2020). Is the adolescent brain at greater vulnerability to the effects of cannabis? A narrative review of the evidence. *Frontiers in Psychology, 11*, 859. https://doi.org/10.3389/fpsyt.2020.00859

Brouwer, R. M., Schutte, J., Janssen, R., Boomsma, D. I., Pol, H. E. H., & Schnack, H. G. (2021). The speed of development of adolescent brain age depends on sex and is genetically determined. *Cerebral Cortex, 31*(2), 1296–1306.

Campos, L., Veríssimo, L., Nobre, B., Morais, C., & Dias, P. (2021). Protective factors in the use of electronic media according to youth and their parents: An exploratory study. *International Journal of Environmental Research and Public Health, 18*(7), 3573. https://doi.org/10.3390/ijerph18073573

Centers for Disease Control and Prevention (CDC). (2021). Data and statistics on children's mental health. Retrieved from https://www.cdc.gov/childrensmentalhealth/data.html.

Coch, D. (2021). Sleep, learning, and school start times in adolescence. Retrieved from https://solportal.ibe-unesco.org/articles/sleep-learning-and-school-start-times-in-adolescence/.

Coplan, R. J., Hipson, W. E., & Bowker, J. C. (2021). Social withdrawal and aloneliness in adolescence: Examining the implications of too much and not enough solitude. *Journal of Youth and Adolescence, 50*(6), 1219–1233.

Dahill, L., Mitchison, D., Morrison, N. M. V., Touyz, S., Bussey, K., Trompeter, N., Lonergan, A., & Hay, P. (2021). Prevalence of parental comments on weight/shape/eating amongst sons and daughters in an adolescent sample. *Nutrients, 13*(1), 158. https://doi.org/10.3390/nu13010158

de Blas, G. D., Gómez-Veiga, I., & García-Madruga, J. (2021). Arithmetic word problems revisited: Cognitive processes and academic performance in secondary school. *Education Sciences, 11*(4), 155. https://doi.org/10.3390/educsci11040155

Demetriou, A., Kazi, S., Makris, N., & Spanoudis, G. (2020). Cognitive ability, cognitive self-awareness, and school performance: From childhood to adolescence. *Intelligence, 79*(1), 101432. https://doi.org/10.1016/j.intell.2020.101432

Edde, M., Leroux, G., Altena, E., & Chanraud, S. (2021). Functional brain connectivity changes across the human life span: From fetal development to old age. *Journal of Neuroscience Research, 99*(1), 236–262.

Ellingson, J. M., Ross, J. M., Winiger, E., Stallings, M. C., Corley, R. P., Friedman, N. P., Hewitt, J. K., Tapert, S. F., Brown, S. A., Wall, T. L., & Hopfer, C. J. (2021). Familial factors may not explain the effect of moderate-to-heavy cannabis use on cognitive functioning in adolescents: A sibling-comparison study. *Addiction, 116*(4), 833–844.

Fomby, P., Goode, J. A., Truong-Vu, K-P., & Mollborn, S. (2021). Adolescent technology, sleep, and physical activity time in two U.S. cohorts. *Youth & Society, 53*(4), 585–609.

Fox, K. R., Choukas-Bradley, S., Salk, R. H., Marshal, M. P., & Thoma, B. C. (2020). Mental health among sexual and gender minority adolescents: Examining interactions with race and ethnicity. *Journal of Consulting and Clinical Psychology, 88*(5), 402–415.

Galván, A. (2020). The need for sleep in the adolescent brain. *Trends in Cognitive Sciences, 24*(1), 79–89.

Gazendam, N., Cleverley, K., King, N., Pickett, W., & Phillips, S. P. (2020). Individual and social determinants of early sexual activity: A study of gender-based differences using the 2018 Canadian Health Behaviour in School-aged Children Study (HBSC). *PLoS ONE 15*(9), e0238515. https://doi.org/10.1371/journal.pone.0238515

Gijzen, M. W. M., Rasing, S. P. A., Creemers, D. H. M., Smit, F., Engels, R. C. M., & De Beurs, D. (2021). Suicide ideation as a symptom of adolescent depression: A network analysis. *Journal of Affective Disorders, 278*, 68–77. https://doi.org/10.1016/j.jad.2020.09.029

Goldbach, J. T., Raymond, H. F., & Burgess, C. M. (2021). Patterns of bullying behavior by sexual orientation. *Journal of Interpersonal Violence, 36*(3-4), 1189–1207.

Gordon, J. (2020). Addressing the crisis of Black youth suicide. Retrieved from https://www.nimh.nih.gov/about/director/messages/2020/addressing-the-crisis-of-black-youth-suicide.shtml.

Hardy, S. T., & Urbina, E. M. (2021). Blood pressure in childhood and adolescence. *American Journal of Hypertension, 34*(3), 242–249.

Hipson, W. E., Coplan, R. J., Dufour, M., Wood, K. R., & Bo, J. C. (2021). Time alone well spent? A person-centered analysis of adolescents' solitary activities. *Social Development.* Advance online publication. https://doi.org/10.1111/sode.12518

Hornberger, L. L., & Lane, M. A. (2021). Identification and management of eating disorders in children and adolescents. *Pediatrics, 147*(1), e2020040279. https://doi.org/10.1542/peds.2020-040279

Hudson, A., & Hudson, P. (2021). Risk factors for cannabis-related mental health harms in older adults: A review. *Clinical Gerontologist, 44*(1), 3–15.

Inanc, H., Meckstroth, A., Keating, B., Adamek, K., Zaveri, H., O'Neil, S., McDonald, K., & Ochoa, L. (2020). Factors influencing youth sexual activity: Conceptual models for sexual risk avoidance and cessation. OPRE Research Brief #2020-153. Washington, DC: Office of Planning, Research, and Evaluation, Administration for Children and Families, U.S. Department of Health and Human Services. Retrieved from https://www.acf.hhs.gov/sites/default/files/documents/opre/factors-influencing-youth-sexual-activity-dec-2020_0.pdf.

Introzzi, I. M., Richard's, M. M., Aydmune, Y., Zamora, E. V., Stelzer, F., Coni, A. G., Lopez-Ramon, M. F., & Navarro-Pardo, E. (2021). Development of perceptual inhibition in adolescents – A critical period? *Symmetry, 13*(3), 457. https://doi.org/10.3390/sym13030457

Iovu, M-B., Hărăgus, P-T., & Roth, M. (2018). Constructing future expectations in adolescence: Relation to individual characteristics and ecological assets in family and friends. *International Journal of Adolescence and Youth, 23*(1), 110. https://doi.org/10.1080/02673843.2016.1247007

Jackson, E. F., Bussey, K., & Myers, E. (2021). Encouraging gender conformity or sanctioning nonconformity? Felt pressure from parents, peers, and the self. *Journal of Youth and Adolescence, 50*(4), 613–627.

Karan, M., Bai, S., Almeida, D. M., Irwin, M. R., McCreath, H., & Fuligni, A. J. (2021). Sleep-wake timings in adolescence: Chronotype development and associations with adjustment. *Journal of Youth and Adolescence, 50*(4), 628–640.

Kim, K. M. (2021). What makes adolescents psychologically distressed? Life events as risk factors for depression and suicide. *European Child & Adolescent Psychiatry, 30*(3), 359–367.

Koestner, R., Powers, T. A., Holding, A., Hope, N., & Milyavskaya, M. (2020). The relation of parental support of emerging adults' goals to well-being over time: The mediating roles of goal progress and autonomy need satisfaction. *Motivation Science, 6*(4), 374–385.

Korn, L., Haynie, D. L., Luk, J. W., Sita, K., & Simons-Morton, B. G. (2021). Attitudes, subjective norms, and perceived behavioral control associated with age of first use of cannabis among adolescents. *Journal of School Health, 91*(1), 50–58.

Kray, J., Kreis, B. K., & Lorenz, C. (2021). Age differences in decision making under known risk: The role of working memory and impulsivity. *Developmental Psychology, 57*(2), 241–252.

Kryza-Lacombe, M., Christian, I. R., Liuzzi, M. T., Owen, C., Hernandez, B., Dougherty, L. R., & Wiggins, J. L. (2021). Executive functioning moderates neural reward processing in youth. *Cognitive, Affective, and Behavioral Neuroscience, 21*(1), 105–118.

LaSpada, N., Delker, E., East, P., Blanco, E., Delva, J., Burrows, R., Lozoff, B., & Gahagan, S. (2021). Risk taking, sensation seeking and personality as related to changes in substance use from adolescence to young adulthood. *Journal of Adolescence, 82*, 23–31. https://doi.org/10.1016/j.adolescence.2020.04.011

Lieberman, A., & Schroeder, J. (2021). Two social lives: How differences between online and offline interaction influence social outcomes. *Current Opinion in Psychology, 41*, 16–21. https://doi.org/10.1016/j.copsyc.2019.06.022

Lu, P., Oh, J., Leahy, K. E., & Chopik, W. J. (2021, January 18). Friendship importance around the world: Links to cultural factors, health, and well-being. *Frontiers in Psychology.* https://doi.org/10.3389/fpsyg.2020.570839

Marotz, L. R., & Kupzyk, S. (2017). *Parenting today's children: A developmental perspective.* Boston, MA: Cengage Learning.

McIlvain, G., Clements, R. G., Magoon, E. M., Spielberg, J. M., Telzer, E. H., & Johnson, C. L. (2020). Viscoelasticity of reward and control systems in adolescent risk taking. *NeuroImage, 215*, 116850. https://doi.org/10.1016/j.neuroimage.2020.116850

Morie, K. P., & Potenza, M. N. (2021). A mini-review of relationships between cannabis use and neural foundations of reward processing, inhibitory control and working memory. *Frontiers in Psychiatry.* Retrieved from| https://www.frontiersin.org/articles/10.3389/fpsyt.2021.657371/full.

Osman, M., Miranda, D., & Jourde, C. (2020). Youth political engagement in adolescence. *Canadian Psychology/Psychologie canadienne, 61*(1), 1–21.

Portt, E., Person, S., Person, B., Rawana, E., & Brownlee, K. (2020). Empathy and positive aspects of adolescent peer relationships: A scoping review. *Journal of Child and Family Studies, 29*(1), 2416–2433.

Pouwels, J. L., Valkenburg, P. M., Beyens, I., van Driel, I. I., & Keijsers, L. (2021). Social media use and friendship closeness in adolescents' daily lives: An experience sampling study. *Developmental Psychology, 57*(2), 309–323.

Prieler, M., Choi, J., & Lee, H. E. (2021). The relationships among self-worth contingency on others' approval, appearance comparisons on Facebook, and adolescent girls' body esteem: A cross-cultural study. *International Journal of Environmental Research and Public Health, 18*(3), 901. https://doi.org/10.3390/ijerph18030901

Reilly, D., Neumann, D. L., & Andrews, G. (2019). Investigating gender differences in mathematics and science: Results from the 2011 Trends in Mathematics and Science Survey. *Research in Science Education, 49*, 25–50.

Schaefer, J. D., Hamdi, N. R., Malone, S. M., Vrieze, S., Wilson, S., McGue, M., & Iacono, W. G. (2021). Associations between adolescent cannabis use and young-adult functioning in three longitudinal twin studies. *Proceedings of the National Academy of Sciences of the United States of America, 118*(14), e2013180118. https://doi.org/10.1073/pnas.2013180118

Shriver, L. H., Dollar, J. M., Calkins, S. D., Keane, S. P., Shanahan, L., & Wiedman, L. (2021). Emotional eating in adolescence: Effects of emotion regulation, weight status and negative body image. *Nutrients, 13*(1), 79. https://doi.org/10.3390/nu13010079

Simon, K. A., Vázquez, C. P., Bruun, S. T., & Farr, R. H. (2020). Retrospective feelings of difference based on gender and sexuality among emerging adults. *Psychology of Sexual Orientation and Gender Diversity, 7*(1), 26–39.

Ulrich, A., Helker, K., & Losekamm, K. (2021). "What can I be when I grow up?"– The influence of own and others' career expectations on adolescents' perception of stress in their career orientation phase. *Sustainability, 13*(2), 912. https://doi.org/10.3390/su13020912

van Beusekon, G., Collier, K. L., Bos, H. M. W., Sandfort, T. G. M., & Overbeek, G. (2020). Gender non-conformity and peer victimization: Sex and sexual attraction differences by age. *The Journal of Sex Research, 57*(2), 234–246.

Vos, S. R., Shrader, C. H., Alvarez, V. C., Meca, A., Under, J. B., Brown, E. C., Zeledon, I., Soto, D., & Schwartz, S. J. (2021). Cultural stress in the age of mass xenophobia: Perspectives from Latin/o adolescents. *International Journal of Intercultural Relations, 80*, 217–230.

Wang, L., Liang, L., Liu, Z., Yuan, K., Ju, J., & Bian, Y. (2021, January 28). The developmental process of peer support networks: The role of friendship. *Frontiers in Psychology, 12*, 615148. https://doi.org/10.3389/fpsyg.2021.615148

Webster, D., Dunne, L., & Hunter, R. (2021). Association between social networks and subjective well-being in adolescents: A systematic review. *Youth & Society, 53*(2), 175–210.

Williamson, G., Osa, M. L., Budd, E., & Kelly, N. R. (2021). Weight-related teasing is associated with body concerns, disordered eating, and health diagnoses in racially and ethnically diverse young men. *Body Image, 38*, 37–48.

Wray-Lake, L., & Abrams, L. S. (2020). Pathways to civic engagement among urban youth of color. *Monographs of the Society for Research in Child Development, 85*(2), 7–154.

Xu, Y., Norton, S., & Rahman, Q. (2021). Childhood gender nonconformity and the stability of self-reported sexual orientation from adolescence to young adulthood in a birth cohort. *Developmental Psychology, 57*(4), 557–569.

Yellman, M. A., Bryan, L., Sauber-Schatz, E. K., & Brener, N. (2020). Transportation risk behaviors among high school students—Youth Risk Behavior Survey, United States, 2019. *MMWR, 69*(Suppl-1), 77–83.

Yu, B., Chen, X., Chen, X., & Yan, H. (2020). Marijuana legalization and historical trends in marijuana use among US residents aged 12–25: Results from the 1979–2016 National Survey on Drug Use and Health. *BMC Public Health, 20*(1), 156. https://doi.org/10.1186/s12889-020-8253-4

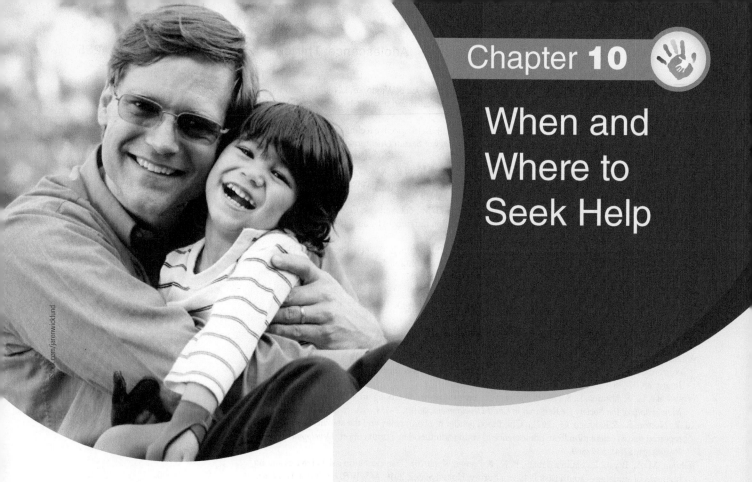

When and Where to Seek Help

Learning Objectives

After reading this chapter, you will be able to:

10-1 Discuss at least five legislative acts passed on behalf of children with exceptionalities and their families.

10-2 Describe several factors that can complicate the process of determining if a child is or is not developing typically.

10-3 Defend this statement: Observing and recording a child's behavior is an essential first step in determining if there is a developmental problem.

10-4 Discuss the developmental team's role in the assessment and intervention process.

NAEYC NAEYC Professional Standards Linked to Chapter Content

1a, 1b, and 1c: Child development and learning in context

2a, 2b, and 2c: Family–teacher partnerships and community connections

3a, 3b, and 3c: Child observations, documentation, and assessment

4c: Developmentally, culturally, and linguistically appropriate teaching practices

6a and 6b: Professionalism as an early childhood educator

Amita's parents recently moved to a new community where her father would begin working on a graduate degree at the local university. Her family's initial concern was to find a suitable child care program for four-year-old Amita, who is bilingual but speaks only limited English. A neighbor suggested they contact the Head Start program located on campus to see if they had an opening. Amita and her parents were fortunate that the Head Start director was able to offer a space that had been vacated just days before.

The teachers' supportive attention helped ease Amita's transition into the program. They quickly discovered that she understood more English words than she was able to speak. However, Amita's teachers became concerned about her overall development in the weeks and months that followed. She seemed to have difficulty acquiring additional words, frequently looked puzzled when spoken to, and often failed to respond appropriately when given directions. Amita seldom interacted with the other children despite their urgings, instead choosing simply to stand and observe. The teachers also expressed concern about her inability to stay engaged in an activity for more than two or three minutes at a time. There was one exception: Amita enjoyed painting and would remain at the easel until the teachers gently guided her to another activity.

When asked about Amita's health history, her mother spoke vaguely of earaches and "runny ears," "hot spells," and "twitches." Amita's mother, who recently celebrated her twenty-first birthday, is a thin, pale woman, midway into her second pregnancy. She works full time in the university cafeteria and is the family's sole breadwinner.

Amita's mother displays genuine warmth and concern for her daughter but apparently does not understand the importance of seeking medical care for herself or her family. The Head Start teachers have recommended that Amita be evaluated by a physician and have her hearing tested. However, Amita's parents have no family doctor or health insurance to help cover expenses. They also seem reluctant to accept that there may be anything wrong with Amita, believing instead that "she is only four and will eventually grow out of these problems."

Ask Yourself

- What behaviors have caused Amita's teachers to be concerned about her developmental progress?
- What environmental factors may have contributed to Amita's developmental delays?

Is my child all right? Most parents, at one time or another, have asked this question during their children's early and growing-up years (Figure 10-1) (Broski & Dunn, 2020; Mackie et al., 2021). Many caregivers and teachers ask a similar question about a child who seems "different" from other children with whom they work. Such questions are a positive sign because they indicate awareness and concern about behaviors they are observing. Children, as emphasized in Chapters 1 and 2, are unique and can vary greatly in their development. Many factors, including genetics, culture, family structure and values, nutrition, health, and poverty influence the rate and nature of children's developmental progress. It is the rare child who is truly typical in every way. Some children who have developmental irregularities of one kind or another do not experience any long-term negative effects. Other children who have irregularities that do not appear significant may be at considerable developmental risk. In both instances, it is important that the child be seen by a health-care professional or child development specialist and perhaps referred for evaluation and intervention services.

Public Policy and Social Attitudes

Supporting children's optimal development has become a major social and legislative focus. Much of the initial impetus came in the 1960s as part of the antipoverty movement (often referred to as the "war on poverty"). Many precedent-setting research studies provided conclusive evidence that developmental disabilities in infants and young children could be reduced significantly through early intervention.

Figure 10-1 Families often wonder if their child is developing "normally."

Several major policy decisions have evolved as a result of this philosophical shift. One is based on the prevention of development disorders through improved maternal access to prenatal care, nutritious food, and knowledge of healthy lifestyle practices. Another is the early identification of children with, or at risk for, developmental disorders. Years of research results have confirmed that intervention strategies are more effective when they are initiated early. Significant advancements have also been made in the development of new intervention strategies, expansion of services and resources, and adoption of a family systems approach (Casagrande & Ingersoll, 2021; Pierce et al., 2021).

Legislation Supporting Optimum Development

The passage of legislation in the 1960s established several precedent-setting programs that supported child and family health. These developments marked one of the first large-scale efforts aimed at reducing developmental risks and disabilities:

- **PL 88-452 Head Start (1965)** This act, part of the antipoverty movement, established the Head Start program and its supplemental services, including developmental screening, medical and dental care, nutrition, parent training, and early education for income-eligible children three to five years of age. Amendments in 1972 and 1974 mandated Head Start to serve children with disabilities as well. Reauthorization in 1994 created Early Head Start programs, which extended services to infants and toddlers from income-eligible families.
- **PL 101-239 Early and Periodic Screening, Diagnosis, and Treatment Act (EPSDT) (1967)** This national program was added to Medicaid and continues to serve the health and developmental needs (diagnosis and treatment) of income-eligible children who are deemed to be at risk.
- **PL 94-105 Supplemental Nutrition Program for Women, Infants, and Children (WIC) (1975)** The primary goal of this program is aimed at improving the health of at-risk mothers during their pregnancy in order to promote full-term fetal development and increase newborn birth weight. Medical supervision, food vouchers, and nutrition education are provided to income-eligible pregnant and nursing women and their children under age five to ensure a healthy start.

Legislation that specifically addressed the needs of children who have developmental differences has also been enacted, including the following:

- **PL 89-10 Elementary and Secondary Education Act (ESEA) (1965)** This act established federal requirements and funding for U.S. public schools (K–12). Additional funds and resources were authorized for schools and districts (preschool through high school) serving a high proportion of children from low-income families; these programs are designated as Title I programs.
- **PL 90-538 Handicapped Children's Early Education and Assistance Act (HCEEAA) (1968)** This law provided funding for the establishment of model classrooms to serve preschool children who had confirmed disabilities.
- **Section 504 of the Rehabilitation Act (1973; 2008)** Schools and programs that receive funding from the U.S. Department of Education are required to provide

educational services and accommodations to meet the needs of any child who has a disability that interferes with their learning. The intent of this law is to remove barriers, prevent discrimination, and protect a child's rights to services and a free and appropriate public education.

- **PL 94-142 Education for All Handicapped Children Act (EHA) (1975)** This landmark law required states to provide comprehensive evaluation, "free and appropriate" education, and intervention services for all children ages three to five years who have, or are at risk for, developmental disabilities. The law was amended in 1990 and 1997 and renamed the Individuals with Disabilities Education Act (IDEA) (PL 101-476), described below.
- **PL 99-457 Education of the Handicapped Act Amendments (1986)** Because the original initiative (PL 94-142) had proven to be so successful, it was amended to extend early intervention services to infants, toddlers, and their families through the Individualized Family Service Plan (IFSP). This portion of the bill (now known as Part C of IDEA) establishes grant-supported programs that may not be available in all communities. Additional features of this act include an emphasis on multidisciplinary assessment, a designated service coordinator, a family-focused approach, and a system of service coordination.
- **PL 101-336 Americans with Disabilities Act (ADA) (1990)** This national civil rights law protects persons of all ages against discrimination because of a disability. The intent is to remove barriers that interfere with full inclusion in education, employment, and public services. The law's implications for children and their families are clear. Early childhood programs and schools cannot refuse to enroll children who have a disability unless they present a danger to others. Reasonable modifications must be made to school settings, policies, and programs to accommodate all children and their parents. (See http://www.ada.gov/childqanda .htm.)
- **PL 101-476 Individuals with Disabilities Education Act (IDEA) (1990)** This law amended the original Education for All Handicapped Children Act (PL 94-142) and updated the language and service provisions. It established Part B special education services for children 3–21 years old and Part C services for infants, toddlers, and their families. The law also requires schools to develop an Individual Transition Plan (ITP) for students who have had an IEP and will be graduating from high school. The law was again amended in 1997 (as PL 105-17) and emphasized the role of students and their families in the educational process and improved children's access to a general education curriculum.
- **PL 108-446 Individuals with Disabilities Education Improvement Act of 2004** This law increased accountability for children's educational outcomes, improved identification methods,

▶❚❚ TeachSource **Video Connections**

Including Children with Exceptionalities

Children bring a rich diversity of abilities, interests, talents, languages, needs, and backgrounds to today's classrooms. Their commonalities and differences present teachers with unlimited opportunities to individualize learning so that each student succeeds. All children, not only those with exceptionalities, benefit from participation in inclusive classroom settings. Respond to the following questions after you have watched the learning video *Human Exceptionalities: An Introduction by a Special Education Teacher:*

1. Define and explain the term "human exceptionality."
2. Identify and describe three disability categories that are covered by the Individuals with Disabilities Education Act (IDEA).
3. What are the advantages of using a multidisciplinary approach with children who have exceptionalities?
4. Explain why a child's family should be included on their multidisciplinary team?
5. In what ways do all children benefit from participation in an inclusive classroom?

established preparation standards for special education teachers, enhanced family involvement, and reduced the amount of required paperwork. It also established guidelines for the appropriate discipline of students with disabilities.

- **PL 107-110 No Child Left Behind Act (NCLB) (2002)** This legislation, a reauthorization of the ESEA, attempted to address the problems of academic inequity and failure in this country. The intended goal was to hold schools and teachers accountable for quality improvements in educational opportunities for *all* children and, in turn, increase academic success rates or lose federal funding. Although many positive changes resulted, the law also triggered several unintended consequences (e.g., undue emphasis on standardized testing and test scores, unethical testing practices, incompatible goals of IDEA and NCLB, and school budgetary crises). In 2012, the Obama administration began granting waivers to states that requested exemption from having to meet all NCLB regulations if they agreed to establish high grade-level standards, invest in teachers to improve their effectiveness, and be held more accountable.
- **PL 110-325 Americans with Disabilities Act Amendments Act (2008)** This amendment expanded the definition of disability to include impairments that significantly restricted an individual's activity.
- **PL 114-95 The Every Student Succeeds Act (ESSA) (2015)** This law replaced the No Child Left Behind Act. The major difference between the two laws is that states are now responsible for administering standardized tests (reading and math tests for grades 3 through 8 and once in high school), setting proficiency goals, establishing penalties if goals are not met, and reporting to the U.S. Department of Education. Each state must also develop a plan for evaluating schools and implementing improvement strategies if they are needed. The goal is to reduce government involvement and shift the responsibility for providing quality education to individual states.

Early Identification and Intervention Programs

Legislative and public policy changes have established several avenues for getting children with suspected developmental problems into appropriate evaluation and early intervention programs.

Infants and Children at Medical Risk

Family physicians and pediatricians have become increasingly aware of the importance of evaluating infants and young children for developmental and behavioral problems (Lipkin & Macias, 2020) (Figure 10-2). Many pediatric practices today ask families to complete a developmental screening tool such as the Abbreviated Denver Developmental Screening Test, the Revised Parent Developmental Questionnaire, or the Ages and Stages Questionnaire® during each office visit so that children's progress can be monitored closely (Camp & Bonnell, 2020; Zuckerman et al., 2021). Physicians are also beginning to note deviations in infants' neurological development that could indicate an irregularity and are referring families to genetic, neurological, and child development specialists for evaluation. These trends have contributed to the earlier detection of high-risk conditions, such as autism, vision and hearing impairments, and delayed language and/or motor skills, that are often associated with a failure to achieve important developmental milestones.

Infants who are discharged from premature nurseries and neonatal intensive care units, including those from multiple births, comprise another group of children known to experience a high rate of developmental problems. Many communities in urban areas now have follow-up clinics where the developmental progress of these children can be monitored on a regular basis. Appropriate intervention services can be secured when disabilities or delays are identified in their earliest stages and, thus, lessen the potentially harmful effects that they otherwise may have on children's developmental progress.

Medical conditions such as diabetes, hearing loss, communicable diseases, cancer, and arthritis can also have a negative effect on a child's development. Children's energy and interest in learning may be affected negatively by the unpleasant side effects of medications and/or medical procedures. For this reason, it is important to monitor these children closely and note any behavioral changes. Patience, caring support, and appropriate intervention services can help children continue to learn and make developmental progress during difficult times.

Figure 10-2 Developmental delays associated with certain medical conditions and syndromes are better understood today.

Community Screening

The majority of young children who will benefit from early identification and intervention do not always come from medically high-risk groups. These children may be located most effectively through a variety of community screening services.

Screening programs are designed to identify children who have or might be at risk for developmental problems. The primary emphasis is focused on evaluating a child's hearing and vision, general health, speech and language, cognition, motor skills, and overall developmental progress. Most screening tests are easily administered locally to large numbers of children. Often, these evaluations can be accessed through local public health departments, Head Start programs, community colleges and universities, clinics, public schools, and early childhood programs. Teachers and volunteers can be trained to conduct certain types of screenings, such as measurements of children's height, weight, and vision. Advanced training usually is required to administer other forms of assessment such as hearing, speech and language, and developmental progress.

Careful consideration should always be given to obtaining data from multiple assessment sources. This approach yields a comprehensive and unbiased understanding of the child's developmental status before any conclusions are reached. It also ensures that children will receive the appropriate intervention services. Delays in providing needed therapies and educational services can reduce the chances of successfully improving or overcoming some conditions.

Child Find is a nationwide system of screening programs mandated by IDEA and administered by individual states (Barger et al., 2018). Its purpose is twofold. One is to raise public awareness about developmental disabilities and to locate eligible infants and young children who have undiagnosed developmental disorders or are at risk for the onset of such problems. The second purpose is to help families locate appropriate diagnostic screenings and intervention programs and services. The IDEA law requires all states to establish a Child Find system, identify eligibility criteria, and develop intervention service guidelines.

Child Find A screening program designed to locate children who have developmental problems through improved public awareness.

Spotlight on Neuroscience and Brain Development

Premature Birth and Neurocognitive Development

Each year, one in every ten infants in the United States is born prematurely; the rate is significantly higher among African American mothers (CDC, 2020). Premature infants (less than 37 gestation weeks) experience an increased incidence of vision and hearing problems, impaired motor development, cognitive and language deficiencies, behavioral problems, and respiratory conditions (Bisiacchi & Cainelli, 2021; Nagy et al., 2021). Complications associated with premature birth are also responsible for the leading cause of infant death in the United States and worldwide.

Fetal organs, particularly the brain, undergo rapid growth and maturation during the final weeks of a mother's pregnancy. Premature birth interrupts this process and is a major cause of the sensory, cognitive, and neurological complications that often occur. Kostović and colleagues (2021) and other scientists have noted that many premature infants experience some degree of cognitive impairment due to the incomplete development of critical neural pathway connections in the fetal brain.

Scientists and medical personnel have been able to pinpoint specific areas in the brain that are adversely affected by an infant's premature birth. Magnetic resonance imaging (MRI) has revealed a smaller cerebral volume (white matter) and other neural structure abnormalities (connectivity) that can lead to various neurodevelopmental impairments (de Almeida et al., 2021; Wu et al., 2020). Fenton and colleagues (2021) have suggested that these differences may be less predictive of cognitive impairment than are the brain injuries associated with premature birth. Brain injuries are relatively common in very preterm infants (28–32 gestation weeks) and are often caused by hemorrhaging of fragile blood vessels (Ballabh & de Vries, 2021). Early and exclusive breast feeding has been shown to be somewhat effective in reducing the incidence of brain hemorrhages associated with premature birth (Carome, Rahman, & Parvez, 2021).

Children who are born prematurely often have difficulty with planning, changing focus, maintaining attention, inhibition, and short-term memory (Cainelli et al., 2021; Wheelock et al., 2021). Deficits may become more apparent during the school-age years as academic demands increase (Martínez-Nadal & Bosch, 2021). Some children with mild impairments will improve with adaptive learning strategies. Others will experience significant lifelong cognitive and behavioral struggles because of altered brain structures and functional development.

Efforts to better understand the causes of premature birth and options for its prevention remain a national and international priority. Although the survival rate of preterm infants has improved, the prevention of neurodevelopmental complications remains a challenge. At present, early identification and targeted intervention services show the most promise for improvement in the developmental outcomes of children who are born prematurely.

What are the connections?

1. Why should countries be concerned about their premature birth rates?
2. What are the potential effects that premature birth can have on a child's development?
3. Why are executive function impairments common in preterm births?

Is There a Problem?

Deciding whether a developmental delay or irregularity is of serious concern is not always easy. The signs can be so subtle, so hard to pinpoint, that it is often difficult to distinguish clearly between children who have a definite problem (the definite *yeses*), and those who definitely do not have a problem (the definite *nos*). Identifying the *maybes*—is there a problem or not?—can be an even more complex issue.

In determining whether a delay or deviation is of real concern, several factors may complicate the matter, such as the following:

- Children who exhibit signs of developmental problems in certain areas often continue to develop like a typical child in every other way; such children present a confusing developmental profile. (See the Developmental Checklists in Appendix A.)

- The range of an individual child's achievements within developmental areas can vary greatly because of different maturation rates and environmental conditions. Both factors are interacting continuously to exert a strong influence on every aspect of a child's development.

Figure 10-3 Diversity of family and community values, beliefs, and cultural differences must be considered and treated with respect and dignity.

- Family beliefs, values, and cultural background exert a direct influence on child-rearing practices (Trawick-Smith, 2018). Developmental milestones are not predetermined, nor are they universal. The way they are perceived varies from culture to culture and from family to family. Thus, respect for diverse family and community beliefs and practices always must be considered when gathering and interpreting information about a child's development (Figure 10-3).

- Developmental delays or disorders may not be immediately apparent. Many children learn to compensate for a deficiency. For example, children who have a mild to moderate hearing loss might position themselves closer to the teacher during story time so they can hear. Children who have difficulty learning to read might depend on other cognitive strategies to overcome their limitations. Sometimes deficiencies are not apparent until the child is placed in structured situations that demand a certain level of performance (as in a first-grade reading or mathematics class) (Allen & Cowdery, 2022).

- Intermittent health problems can affect children's performance. For example, a child may have severe and recurring bouts of **otitis media** (middle-ear infection) that improve temporarily or completely resolve between episodes. A hearing test administered when the child is free of infection may reveal no hearing loss, although the same child may experience significant deafness during an acute infection. Periods of intermittent hearing loss, sometimes lasting a week or more, can cause some children to develop considerable language and cognitive delays, as well as troublesome behaviors (Brennan-Jones et al., 2020). Misbehavior or the apparent disregard of requests or instructions may occur simply because children cannot hear. Too often, these behaviors are misinterpreted as defiance or willfulness instead of recognizing them as a medical problem that is interfering with a child's ability to learn and function.

When to Seek Help

At what point should a hunch or an uncomfortable feeling about a child's development or behavior necessitate a call for action? The answer is clear: whenever families or teachers have a concern! Any uneasiness needs to be discussed with a pediatrician, health-care provider, or child development specialist sooner rather than later.

Concern about a developmental irregularity also demands immediate investigation anytime that it interferes with a child's participation in everyday activities. Repeated occurrences or repetitions of a troublesome behavior are often a reliable sign that professional help should be sought. However, seldom is a single incidence of a questionable behavior cause for concern. What is of concern is a child's *continuing* reluctance to attempt a new skill or to fully acquire a basic developmental skill. For

otitis media An infection of the middle ear.

▶️ TeachSource Video Connections

Children with Developmental Disabilities in the Classroom

The importance of identifying children's developmental disabilities early and arranging appropriate intervention services has been stressed throughout the book. The lives of many children have benefitted because of the improved awareness, knowledge, and dedication of families, teachers, and clinicians. Respond to the following questions after you have watched the learning video *5–11 Years: Developmental Disabilities in Middle Childhood:*

1. Why must person-first language always be used when referring to children who have a disability?

2. How would you justify the importance of early identification, early intervention, and inclusionary practices after watching this video?

3. What social skills does each child in the video have that are similar to their typically developing peers? How do they differ?

example, a ten-month-old who attempts to sit alone but still must use both hands for support may or may not have a problem. On the other hand, clusters of developmental differences are always significant—a ten-month-old who is not sitting without support, not smiling, and not babbling in response to others is likely to be at developmental risk.

What should teachers and caregivers do when a family fails to express concern or denies the possibility of a problem? Although it may be difficult, it is the teacher's responsibility to discuss any concerns about a child's development in a straightforward, compassionate, and objective manner with the family. It is important that teachers report only what has been observed and what they would expect to see based upon the child's developmental stage. They must refrain from making a diagnosis or labeling the child's behavior. For example, a teacher should say, "Danesha avoids eye contact, has a limited vocabulary, and often responds inappropriately to questions," rather than "Danesha is probably autistic." Once this information has been shared, teachers should work closely with the family to help them understand and accept the child's need for further evaluation. *Under no circumstances should a teacher or administrator bypass family members and make referrals without their permission.* When families are offered support and assistance in making the necessary arrangements, they are more likely to follow through with recommendations.

Information Gathering

A comprehensive developmental evaluation requires that information be obtained from multiple sources: observation and recording, screening, and diagnostic assessment. Diagnostic assessment includes in-depth testing and clinical interpretation of all results. Clinicians from various disciplines should participate in the diagnostic process. It is their responsibility to provide detailed information about the specific nature of the child's problems, as well as recommended treatments. For example, a four-year-old's delayed speech might be observed by family members and noted during routine screening procedures. Subsequent diagnostic testing by clinicians may pinpoint several other conditions: a moderate, **bilateral** hearing loss, poor production of many letter sounds, and an expressive vocabulary typical of a three-year-old. These clinical findings can be translated into specific educational strategies and intervention procedures that ultimately will benefit the child's overall development.

Observing and Recording

The evaluation process always begins with systematic observation (see Chapter 1). Noting and recording various aspects of a child's behavior enables the evaluator—whether a family member, a teacher, or a clinician—to focus on what is actually occurring. In other words, observations yield objective information about what the child can and cannot do at the time of the observation.

An effective evaluation is also based on multiple observations, conducted over a period of days and in a variety of natural settings that are familiar to the child (NAEYC,

bilateral Affecting both sides, as in loss of hearing in both ears.

Figure 10-4 Families often contribute information that adds insight and meaning to the evaluation process.

iStock.com/Jovanmandic

2021; U.S. HHS, 2021). Direct observation often confirms or rules out impressions or suspicions regarding a child's abilities. For example, a child might not count to five when asked to do so in a testing situation. However, that same child, may be overheard correctly counting teddy bears on the pages of a book that he is "reading" to himself. A child thought to have attention-deficit hyperactivity disorder (ADHD) might be observed sitting quietly for five to ten minutes when given activities that she finds interesting and challenging, thereby ruling out concerns about hyperactivity. *Note:* The term *hyperactive* is greatly overused and misused. A child should not be so labeled unless specifically diagnosed by a multidisciplinary team. Focusing on a child at play, alone or with other children, can be particularly revealing. Again, no evaluation is valid without direct and objective observations of a child in familiar surroundings.

A family's observations are an especially valuable component of the assessment process (Figure 10-4). Family members often can provide information that is not available from other sources. Their observations also provide insight into unique family attitudes, perceptions, and expectations concerning the child. Involving families in the observation phase of evaluation can also be beneficial in terms of reducing their anxieties. Furthermore, direct observation often reveals a child's previously unrecognized abilities. When family members have an opportunity to see their children engaged in appropriate activities, they may be encouraged to focus more on the children's strengths and positive qualities than on their limitations.

Screening Tests

Screening tests are useful for gathering general information about children's developmental disorders and determining whether more comprehensive evaluation is needed. They are designed to assess a child's current abilities, as well as potential delays in fine and large motor skills, cognition, speech and language development, and personal and social responsiveness.

If problems or suspected problems are noted during an initial screening, further in-depth clinical assessment by a child development specialist is needed before a final diagnosis can be reached. *Note:* Results obtained from screening tests are neither conclusive nor diagnostic. They do not predict a child's future abilities or achievement potential and should not be used as a basis for planning intervention programs.

Several questions should be asked when choosing or interpreting a screening instrument:

- Is it appropriate for the child's age?
- Is it free of bias related to the child's economic, geographic, cultural, or linguistic background (DeCandia et al., 2020)?
- Can it be administered in the child's native language (Bevan et al., 2020)? If not, is a skilled interpreter available to assist the child and family if needed?
- Is it reliable for identifying children who should be referred for additional testing from those who do not require additional evaluation at this time?

A sample of widely used screening tests and assessment instruments is provided in Appendix B. Included are also examples of ecological tools for evaluating children's home and school settings. It is always essential to gather information about the child's everyday surroundings and to consider it when interpreting test results and planning intervention programs.

Interpreting Screening Results

The widespread availability of community-based screening programs has contributed significantly to the early identification of children who may have developmental problems. However, the findings are always open to question. In some cases, the screening process itself may have a negative effect on the outcome. Children's attention spans, especially those of young children, are often short and inconsistent from day to day and from task to task. Illness, fatigue, anxiety, hunger, lack of cooperation, irritability, or distractions can also lead to unreliable results. Children may perform poorly if they are unaccustomed to being tested or are unfamiliar with the person who is conducting the test. When children are evaluated in familiar surroundings, such as a classroom or their home setting, they are more likely to cooperate and perform reliably. Consequently, results derived only from screening assessments must be regarded with caution. The following points are intended as reminders for both families and teachers:

- Avoid drawing conclusions based on limited information or a single test score. Such results may not yield an accurate representation of the child's developmental abilities and limitations. A comprehensive and realistic picture of the child's challenges and potentials can only be achieved with data obtained from multiple sources and repeated observations.
- Never underestimate the influence of home and family on a child's performance (Kung et al., 2021; Luo et al., 2021; Oloye & Flouri, 2020). Newer screening procedures are designed to include family participation and to evaluate their concerns, priorities, and resources as well. There is also an increasing emphasis placed on conducting screening procedures in familiar or naturalistic environments where children feel more secure and at ease.
- Recognize the dangers of labeling a child as having a learning disability, intellectual deficiency, speech

▶❚❚ TeachSource Video Connections

Assessing Children's Development

Ongoing and comprehensive evaluation of children's developmental progress is essential. Data gathered in naturalistic environments and from multiple sources yields an objective picture of the child's developmental progress. This information allows teachers and families to tailor interventions that address children's current learning and behavioral needs. Respond to the following questions as you watch the learning video *Observing and Monitoring Perceptual-Cognitive Development in Kindergartners: The Importance of Assessment*:

1. Why is it important to assess children's perceptual-cognitive development?
2. What are the advantages of evaluating children in their natural environments?
3. How did the teacher use her observational data to facilitate children's learning?
4. In what ways does family involvement help children achieve learning goals?

impairment, conduct disorder, or other condition based upon a single test result. Labels can have a negative effect on adult expectations and the way in which they are likely to respond to the child. Labels should be used sparingly and only for professional purposes if they have been validated through appropriate testing channels (Figure 10-5). In any case, **person-first-language**, not labels, should always be used when referring to a child or adult who has a disability or medical condition.

- Question test scores. Test results can be easily misinterpreted. One test might suggest that a child has a developmental delay when nothing may actually be wrong. Such conclusions are called *false positives*. The opposite conclusion can also be reached. A delay that is not evident during the screening process may lead to an incorrect conclusion that a child is developing typically or as expected. This is referred to as a *false negative*. The first situation can lead to unnecessary anxiety and disappointment and may change the way the family and teachers respond to the child. The latter situation can lull a family into not seeking further help and lead to a prolonged worsening of the child's developmental problems. Both situations can be avoided through careful interpretation of test scores and the conduct of multiple observations.

- Understand that the results of screening tests do *not* constitute a diagnosis. Additional information must be collected and in-depth clinical testing completed before a diagnosis is provided or confirmed. Even then, errors can occur. There are many reasons for misdiagnosis, such as inconsistent and rapid changes in a child's growth or changing environmental factors such as divorce, homelessness, the birth of a sibling, trauma, or family relocation.

- Do not use failed items on a screening test as curriculum items or skills to be taught; a test item is simply one isolated example of a broad range of skills to be expected in a specific developmental area at an approximate age. For example, a child who is unable to stand on one foot for five seconds will not overcome a developmental disorder by being taught to stand on one foot for a given amount of time. *Screening test items are not a suitable basis for the construction of curriculum activities.*

- Recognize that test results do not predict the child's developmental future, nor do they necessarily correlate with subsequent testing (Frans et al., 2020; Zysset et al., 2020). The need for *ongoing* observation, assessment, and in-depth clinical diagnosis is always essential when screening tests indicate potential problems or delays.

ECE Library

Figure 10-5 Labels are inappropriate to use unless a child's disability has been documented and confirmed.

IQ Tests: Are They Appropriate for Young Children?

Intelligence tests, such as the Wechsler Intelligence Scale for Children (WISC) and the Stanford Binet Intelligence Scales, were not designed or intended to be used as screening instruments (Mindes & Jung, 2014). Neither are they regarded by most developmental specialists as appropriate to use with young children for any purpose. IQ tests administered during the early years are not valid predictors of future (or even current) intellectual performance (Gygi et al., 2017), nor do they predict subsequent academic performance.

IQ tests do not consider the opportunities that a child has had to learn, the quality of those learning experiences, or what the dominant culture says a child should know at a given age. For example, children raised in poverty or in non-English-speaking homes often do not have the same opportunities to acquire specific information that test items represent (Weis & Saklofske, 2020). Cultural groups may differ in what they believe children need to learn. Researchers have also identified maternal education as an important predictor

person-first-language A respectful way of acknowledging an individual and then referring to their disability or medical condition (e.g., "Alex has autism" versus "Alex is autistic"; "Janay has a hearing impairment" versus "Janay is deaf").

iStock.com/Ridofranz

Figure 10-6 Achievement tests are administered to assess what students have learned.

of children's academic achievement, especially among ethnically diverse and low-income families (Farley & Piasta, 2020; Schochet, Johnson, & Ryan, 2020). Therefore, an IQ test score used as the sole determinant of a child's cognitive or intellectual development certainly must be challenged.

Achievement Tests

The administration of standardized **achievement tests** in elementary and secondary schools has become a widespread practice since the passage of NCLB (Figure 10-6). These tests are designed to measure how much the child has learned in school about specific subject areas. Depending upon the results, each child is assigned a percentile ranking, based on a comparison with other children of the same grade level. For example, a child in the 50th percentile in mathematics is doing as well as 50 percent of the children in the same grade. Test results are increasingly being used to determine children's placement, assess teacher performance, and evaluate a school's overall academic effectiveness (Farley-Ripple, Jennings, & Jennings, 2021; Lockwood et al., 2021). Again, test scores alone do not always provide a reliable representation of a child's abilities. The results should be supported with observational data and samples of children's work (portfolios) before they can have a valid meaning.

Diagnosis and Referral

Information obtained from authentic assessment, including direct observations and samples of children's products combined with screening test results, provides the basis for the next question: Are comprehensive diagnostic procedures required? Not all children will require an in-depth clinical assessment, but many will if they and their family are to receive the best possible referral for intervention services. Families can be directed to early childhood intervention programs (Child Find) in their community for evaluation and services offered under Part B for preschool-age children and Part C for infants and toddlers. Evaluation and assessment services are available to school-age children through their local school system. An interdisciplinary team approach that combines the input of clinicians, child development specialists, and the child's family is always essential for achieving effective and meaningful diagnoses and referrals.

The Developmental Team

Federal law (PL 105-17, IDEA) requires families to be involved in all phases of the assessment and intervention process. They become important members of the child's **developmental team** when they work collaboratively with educators and multidisciplinary professionals. A family-centered approach improves information sharing and enables family members to learn and implement therapy recommendations at home (Kurth, Love, & Pirtle, 2020; Movahedazarhouligh, 2021). Sustained interest and participation in the child's intervention program can be achieved when the developmental team:

- Keeps families informed and encourages their questions
- Explains rationales for treatment procedures
- Uses terms that families can understand and takes the time to explain those that may not be familiar

achievement tests Tests used to measure a child's academic progress (what the child has learned).

developmental team A team of qualified professionals, such as special educators, speech-language pathologists, occupational therapists, social workers, audiologists, nurses, and physical therapists, who evaluate a child's developmental progress and together prepare an intervention plan that addresses the child's special needs.

- Emphasizes the child's progress and helps families to note improvements
- Teaches family members how to work with their child at home
- Provides families with positive feedback and supports their continued efforts and advocacy on the child's behalf

Best practice suggests that the pooling of knowledge and multidisciplinary expertise—in other words, a team approach—is required to manage children's developmental disorders effectively. For example, a team effort provides the most accurate picture of how a delay in one area can affect development in other areas, just as progress in one area supports progress in others. A two-year-old with a hearing loss may experience delays in language as well as in the areas of cognitive and social-emotional development. Thus, appropriate intervention strategies for this child might require the services of an audiologist, speech and language therapist, early childhood teacher, nurse, and, perhaps, social worker. If a team approach is to benefit the child's overall development, effective communication and cooperation among specialists, service providers, and the family is essential. This process is facilitated by the inclusion of an IFSP for infants and toddlers, or an Individualized Educational Plan (IEP) for preschool through school-age children.

Service Coordinator

Many families do not understand the significance of children's developmental problems or find themselves overwhelmed by the process of approaching multiple agencies and dealing with bureaucratic red tape (Rios, Aleman-Tovar, & Burke, 2020; Rossetti et al., 2021). As a result, they often fail or are unable to complete the necessary service arrangements unless assistance is provided. This supportive role was viewed as so crucial to successful intervention that the position of **service coordinator** was written into federal legislation (PL 99-457, Part C) to help families address their infants' and toddlers' developmental problems. A service coordinator or case manager works closely with families, matching their needs and their child's needs with appropriate community services and educational programs. The coordinator also assists the family in establishing initial contacts and provides continued support.

Referral

The referral process involves a multiple-step approach. As described earlier, the child's strengths, weaknesses, and developmental skills are evaluated. The family's needs and resources (e.g., financial, psychological, physical, and transportation) must also be taken into consideration. For example, if a family cannot afford special services, has no knowledge of financial assistance programs, and does not own a car, it is unlikely that they will be able to follow through on professional recommendations. However, such problems are seldom insurmountable. Most communities have individuals and social service agencies available to assist families in meeting these needs and arranging for intervention services.

Placement in an appropriate educational setting frequently is recommended as part of the intervention plan. In these settings, classroom teachers, child development specialists, and other members of the developmental team conduct ongoing assessments of the child's progress (Figure 10-7). In addition, the developmental team continuously reviews the appropriateness of the placements, special services, and progress toward meeting preestablished goals to determine if the child's and family's needs are being met. This step is especially critical with infants and toddlers because their development progresses so quickly. Throughout, there must be effective communication and support among teachers, practitioners, and families to ensure that the child is receiving individually appropriate services and benefiting from the prescribed program.

Did You Know

...that more than 2.5 million students have been diagnosed with a learning disability and account for more than 40 percent of the students who currently receive special education services? A total of 18 percent of these students will drop out of school before they graduate, compared to a national rate of 6 percent.

service coordinator An individual who serves as a family's advocate and assists them with identifying, locating, and making final arrangements with community services.

Figure 10-7 Collaboration among teachers, families, and service providers is essential to an effective intervention plan.

iStock.com/gregory_lee

Summary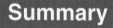

10-1 Legislative acts have established several programs that address prevention, early identification, intervention services, or all three for children who have or are at risk for developmental disorders. Several of the laws discussed in this chapter include:

- PL 88-452; Head Start
- PL 101-239; Early and Periodic Screening, Diagnosis, and Treatment Act (EPSDT)
- PL 94-105; Supplemental Nutrition Program for Women, Infants, and Children (WIC)
- PL 89-10; Elementary and Secondary Education Act (ESEA)
- PL 90-538; Handicapped Children's Early Education and Assistance Act (HCEEAA)
- Section 504 of the Rehabilitation Act
- PL 94-142 (1975); Education for All Handicapped Children Act (EHA)
- PL 99-457; Education of the Handicapped Act Amendments
- PL 101-336; Americans with Disabilities Act (ADA)
- PL 101-476; Individuals with Disabilities Education Act Amendment
- PL 105-17; Individuals with Disabilities Education Act Amendment
- PL 108-446; Individuals with Disabilities Education Improvement Act (IDEA)
- PL 107-110; No Child Left Behind Act (NCLB)
- PL 114-95; The Every Child Succeeds Act (ESSA)

10-2 Several challenges may be encountered when attempting to identify children who have a developmental disability or delay:

- A family may decide to ignore or delay seeking a diagnosis.
- Some developmental irregularities can be subtle in nature and difficult to observe.

continued on following page

Summary

- Maturational and environmental changes may cause temporary fluctuations in a child's development.
- Family values, beliefs, and cultural practices influence what is perceived to be a developmental problem.
- Children may learn to compensate for a developmental irregularity.
- Intermittent health conditions may interfere temporarily with a child's developmental progress.

10-3 The initial step in determining if a child has a developmental problem always involves conducting multiple observations. Data collected from these observations provide a starting point for deciding what additional forms of screening or evaluation are appropriate.

10-4 A multidisciplinary team works cooperatively to obtain a well-rounded, unbiased overview of a child's developmental progress. Individual professionals administer screening tests, interpret and share results with other team members, recommend appropriate services, monitor a child's progress, and inform and support families to assure a successful outcome for the child.

Key Terms

Child Find **p. 261**

otitis media **p. 263**

bilateral **p. 264**

person-first language **p. 267**

achievement tests **p. 268**

developmental team **p. 268**

service coordinator **p. 269**

Apply What You Have Learned

A. Case Study Connections

Reread the developmental sketch about Amita and her family presented at the beginning of this chapter and answer the following questions.

1. Prior to holding a first conference with Amita's mother, what observations and information should her teachers gather and prepare?

2. Why is it imperative that the teachers' initial evaluation of Amita's development include a series of firsthand observations (and recorded notes) conducted in a familiar setting such as the classroom and play yard?

3. Describe three pieces of legislation discussed in this chapter that could be of benefit to a high-risk family such as Amita's.

4. What role might a service coordinator play for Amita's family, and what forms of assistance might this person provide?

B. Review Questions

1. Identify and discuss three concerns that might prevent families from seeking help for their child.

2. What three features must be considered when determining if a screening test is appropriate to use for an individual child?

3. Identify and discuss three reasons why it is important to encourage family involvement in a child's intervention program.

4. Describe three factors that may complicate the early identification of a developmental problem.

5. Describe three reasons why screening test results should be interpreted with caution.

C. Your Turn: Chapter to Practice

1. Observe a child (any age) for approximately 15 minutes with a partner. Focus on a specific behavior and use a frequency count to record your observations. Determine the reliability of your results by comparing them with your partner's.

2. Arrange to sit in on an IEP or IFSP meeting. Briefly describe the purpose of the meeting, the disciplines of team members who were present, how productive you thought the meeting was in terms of achieving the stated objectives, and your reactions to the experience.

3. Write a public service announcement for a local television or radio station informing families of the purpose and importance of early developmental screening and where evaluations can be obtained.

4. Select one of the screening instruments described in Appendix B and administer it to one or two children. Describe your experience. Include any challenges that you encountered and recommendations for others who would use this tool.

Online Resources

Autism Society
The mission of the Autism Society is focused on advocacy, research, and improving the public's awareness and understanding of autism disorders. The site includes extensive resource information in English and Spanish on topics ranging from legal and mental health issues to long-term planning and employment.

Council on Exceptional Children (CEC)
The CEC was established in 1922 and is the largest international professional organization that advocates on behalf of children and youth with disabilities and/or special talents. Chapters are located in every U.S. state and throughout the world. The organization maintains an active role in policy and standard establishment, professional development for special educators, and the provision of extensive information resources for educators and families.

National Center on Secondary Education and Transition (NCSET)
Numerous resources and forms of technical assistance are available to help educators at the secondary and collegiate levels support youth who experience disabilities. Links to national policies, research studies, a special section for youth, and additional resource organizations are provided.

Iris Center
Anyone who works with children who have disabilities or teaches special education courses will find a wealth of resources on this website, including sample syllabi, curriculum modules, videos, case studies, children's books, and evidence-based practices that address important topics ranging from assessment to instructional and intervention strategies.

References

Allen, K. E., & Cowdery, G. (2022). *The exceptional child: Inclusion in early childhood education.* (9th Ed.). Boston, MA: Cengage Learning.

Ballabh, P., & de Vries, L. S. (2021). White matter injury in infants with intraventricular haemorrhage: Mechanisms and therapies. *Nature Reviews Neurology, 17*(4), 199–214. https://doi.org/10.1038/s41582-020-00447-8

Barger, B., Rice, C., Simmons, C. A., & Wolf, R. (2018). A systematic review of Part C early identification studies. *Topics in Early Childhood Special Education, 38*(1), 4–16.

Bevan, S. L., Jianghong, L., Wallis, K., & Pinto-Martin, J. A. (2020). Screening instruments for developmental and behavioral concerns in pediatric Hispanic populations in the United States: A systematic literature review. *Journal of Developmental & Behavioral Pediatrics, 41*(1), 71–80.

Bisiacchi, P., & Cainelli, E. (2021). Structural and functional brain asymmetries in the early phases of life: A scoping review. *Brain Structure and Function.* Advanced online publication. https://doi.org/10.1007/s00429-021-02256-1

Brennan-Jones, C. G., Whitehouse, A. J. O., Calder, S. D., Da Costa, C., Eikelboom, R. H., Swanepoel, D. W., & Jamieson, S. E. (2020). Does otitis media affect later language ability? A prospective birth cohort study. *Journal of Speech, Language, and Hearing Research, 63*(7), 2441–2452.

Broski, J. A., & Dunn, W. (2020). Parent mental models of transition related to their child's developmental diagnosis. *Journal of Child and Family Studies, 29*, 2377–2389.

Cainelli, E., Vedovelli, L., Wigley, I. M., Bisiacchi, P. S., & Suppiej, A. (2021). Neonatal spectral EEG is prognostic of cognitive abilities at school age in premature infants without overt brain damage. *European Journal of Pediatrics, 180*, 909–918.

Camp, B. W., & Bonnell, L. N. (2020). Combining two developmental screening tests to improve predictive accuracy. *Academic Pediatrics, 20*(3), 413–420.

Carome, K., Rahman, A., & Parvez, B. (2021). Exclusive human milk diet reduces incidence of severe intraventricular hemorrhage in extremely low birth weight infants. *Journal of Perinatology, 41*(3), 535–543.

Casagrande, K., & Ingersoll, B. R. (2021). Improving service access in ASD: A systematic review of family empowerment interventions for children with special healthcare needs. *Review Journal of Autism and Developmental Disorders, 8*, 170–185.

Centers for Disease Control and Prevention (CDC). (2020). Preterm birth. Retrieved from https://www.cdc.gov/reproductivehealth/maternalinfanthealth/pretermbirth.htm.

de Almeida, J. S., Meskaldji, D-E., Loukas, S., Lordier, L., Gui, L., Lazeyras, F., & Hüppia, P. S. (2021). Preterm birth leads to impaired rich-club organization and fronto-paralimbic/limbic structural connectivity in newborns. *NeuroImage, 225*, 117440. https://doi.org/10.1016/j.neuroimage.2020.117440

DeCandia, C. J., Volk, K. T., Unick, G. J., & Donegan, L. R. (2020). Developing a screening tool for young children using an ecological framework. *Infants & Young Children, 33*(4), 237–258.

Farley-Ripple, E. N., Jennings, A., & Jennings, A. B. (2021). Tools of the trade: A look at educators' use of assessment systems. *School Effectiveness and School Improvement, 32*(1), 96–117.

Farley, K. S., & Piasta, S. B. (2020). Examining early childhood language and literacy learning opportunities in relation to maternal education and children's initial skills. *Journal of Education for Students Placed at Risk (JESPAR), 25*(3), 183–200.

Fenton, T. R., Nasser, R., Creighton, D., Tang, S., Sauve, R., Bilan, D., Fenton, C. J., & Eliasziw, M. (2021). Weight, length, and head circumference at 36 weeks are not predictive of later cognitive impairment in very preterm infants. *Journal of Perinatology, 41*, 606–614.

Frans, N., Post, W., Oenema-Mostert, I., & Minnaert, A. (2020). Defining and evaluating stability in early years assessment. *International Journal of Research & Method in Education, 44*(2), 151–163.

Gygi, J. T., Hagmann-von Arx, P., Schweizer, F., & Grob, A. (2017). The predictive validity of four intelligence tests for school grades: A small sample longitudinal study. *Frontiers in Psychology, 8*, 375. https://doi.org/10.3389/fpsyg.2017.00375

Kostović, I., Radoš, M., Kostović-Srzentić, M., & Krsnik, Z. (2021). Fundamentals of the development of connectivity in the human fetal brain in late gestation: From 24 weeks gestational age to term. *Journal of Neuropathology & Experimental Neurology, 80*(5), 393–414.

Kung, M., Stolz, K., Lin, J., Foster, M. E., Schmitt, S. A., & Purpura, D. J. (2021). The home numeracy environment and measurement of numeracy in English and Spanish in dual language learners. *Topics in Early Childhood Special Education, 40*(4), 241–252.

Kurth, J. A., Love, H., & Pirtle, J. (2020). Parent perspectives of their involvement in IEP development for children with autism. *Focus on Autism and Other Developmental Disabilities, 35*(1), 36–46.

Lipkin, P. H., & Macias, M. M. (2020). Promoting optimal development: Identifying infants and young children with developmental disorders through developmental surveillance and screening. *Pediatrics, 145*(1), e20193449. https://doi.org/10.1542/peds.2019-3449

Lockwood, A. B., Farmer, R. L., Bohan, K. J., Winans, S., & Sealander, K. (2021). Academic achievement test use and assessment practices: A national survey of special education administrators. *Journal of Psychoeducational Assessment, 39*(4), 436–451.

Luo, R., Pace, A., Levine, D., Igluesias, A., de Villiers, J., Golinkoff, R. M., Wilson, M. S., & Hirsch-Pasek, K. (2021). Home literacy environment and existing knowledge mediate the link between socioeconomic status and language learning skills in dual language learners. *Early Childhood Research Quarterly, 55*(2nd Quarter), 1–14.

Mackie, T. I., Schaefer, A. J., Ramella, L., Carter, A. S., Eisenhower, A., Jimenez, M. E., Fettig, A., & Sheldrick, R. C. (2021). Understanding how parents make meaning of their child's behaviors during screening for autism spectrum disorders: A longitudinal qualitative investigation. *Journal of Autism and Developmental Disorders, 51*, 906–921.

Martínez-Nadal, S., & Bosch, L. (2021). Cognitive and learning outcomes in late preterm infants at school age: A systematic review. *International Journal of Environmental Research and Public Health, 18*(1), 74. https://doi.org/10.3390/ijerph18010074

Mindes, G., & Jung, L. A. (2014). *Assessing young children.* (5th ed.). New York, NY: Pearson.

Movahedazarhouligh, S. (2021). Parent-implemented interventions and family-centered service delivery approaches in early intervention and early childhood special education. *Early Child Development and Care, 191*(1), 1–12.

Nagy, A., Kalmár, M., Beke, A. M., Gráf, R., & Horváth, E. (2021). Intelligence and executive function of school-age preterm children in function of birth weight and perinatal complication. *Applied Neuropsychology: Child.* Advanced online publication. https://doi.org/10.1080/21622965.2020.1866571

National Association for the Education of Young Children (NAEYC). (2021). DAP: Observing, documenting, and assessing children's development and learning. Retrieved from https://www.naeyc.org/resources/position-statements/dap/assessing-development.

Oloye, H. T., & Flouri, E. (2020). The role of the indoor home environment in children's self-regulation. *Children and Youth Services Review, 121*(12), 105761. https://doi.org/10.1016/j.childyouth.2020.105761

Pierce, S. R., Skorup, J., Paremski, A. C., & Prosser, L. A. (2021). The relationship between family empowerment scale and gross motor function measure-66 in young children with cerebral palsy. *Child: Care, Health and Development, 47*(1), 112–118.

Rios, K., Aleman-Tovar, J., & Burke, M. M. (2020). Special education experiences and stress among Latina mothers of children with autism spectrum disorder (ASD). *Research in Autism Spectrum Disorders, 73*, 101534. https://doi.org/10.1016/j.rasd.2020.101534

Rossetti, Z., Burke, M. M., Hughes, O., Schraml-Block, K., Rivera, J. I., Rios, K., Tovar, J. A., & Lee, J. D. (2021). Parent perceptions of the advocacy expectations in special education. *Exceptional Children.* Advanced online publication. https://doi.org/10.1177/0014402921994095

Schochet, O. N., Johnson, A. D., & Ryan, R. M. (2020). The relationship between increases in low-income mothers' education and children's early outcomes: Variation by developmental stage and domain. *Children and Youth Services Review, 109*, 104705. https://doi.org/10.1016/j.childyouth.2019.104705

Trawick-Smith, J. (2018). *Early childhood development: A multicultural perspective.* (7th ed). New York, NY: Pearson.

U.S. Department of Health and Human Services (U.S. HHS). Early Childhood Training and Technical Assistance System. (2021). *Observation, documentation, and reflection.* Retrieved from https://childcareta.acf.hhs.gov/infant-toddler-resource-guide/observation-documentation-and-reflection.

Weiss, L. G., & Saklofske, D. H. (2020). Mediators of IQ test score differences across racial and ethnic groups: The case for environmental and social justice. *Personality and Individual Differences, 161*, 109962. https://doi.org/10.1016/j.paid.2020.109962

Wheelock, M. D., Lean, R. E., Bora, S., Melzer, T. R., Eggebrecht, A. T., Smyser, C. D., & Woodward, L. J. (2021). Functional connectivity network disruption underlies domain-specific impairments in attention for children born very preterm. *Cerebral Cortex, 31*(2), 1383–1394.

Wu, Y., Stoodley, C., Brossard-Racine, M., Kapse, K., Vezina, G., Murnick, J., du Plessis, A. J., & Limperopoulos, C. (2020). Altered local cerebellar and brainstem development in preterm infants. *NeuroImage, 213*, 116702. https://doi.org/10.1016/j.neuroimage.2020

Zuckerman, K. E., Chavez, A. E., Wilson, L., Unger, K., Reuland, C., Ramsey, K., King, M., Scholz, J., & Fombonne, E. (2021). Improving autism and developmental screening and referral in US primary care practices serving Latinos. *Autism 25*(1), 288–299.

Zysset, A. E., Kakebeeke, T. H., Messerli-Bürgy, N., Meyer, A. H., Stülb, K., Leeger-Aschmann, C. S., Schmutz, E. A., Arhab, A., Puder, J. J., Kriemler, S., Munsch, S., & Jenni, O. G. (2020). Stability and prediction of motor performance and cognitive functioning in preschoolers: A latent variable approach. *Infant and Child Development, 29*(5), e2185. https://doi.org/10.1002/icd.2186

Appendix A

Developmental Checklists

A simple checklist, one for each child, can be a useful tool for observing and recording children's developmental progress. Questions on the checklists that follow can be answered during the course of a child's everyday activities and over a period of one week or more. "No" answers signal that further observation and investigation may be in order; several "No" answers indicate that additional investigation is a necessity.

The "Sometimes" category is also important. It suggests what the child can do at least part of the time or under some circumstances. The "Sometimes" category includes space where brief notes and comments about how and when a behavior occurs can be recorded. In many instances, a child may just require more practice, incentive, or adult encouragement. Hunches often provide an effective starting point for working with the child. Again, if "Sometimes" is checked several times, additional observation and evaluation is recommended.

The observation checklists may be duplicated and used as part of the assessment process. They are based on detailed information provided in each of the preceding chapters. The items represent a sampling of developmental milestones associated with each approximate age. When completed, a checklist contains information that members of a developmental team will find useful in evaluating a child's progress and determining appropriate intervention strategies. However, it is important to interpret these findings cautiously and consider cultural, linguistic, and family background variations that may influence children's development.

Child's Name _____   Age _____

Observer _____   Date _____

Developmental Checklist

BY 4 to 6 MONTHS	Yes	No	Sometimes
Does the child . . .			
Show continued gains in height, weight, and head circumference?			
Exhibit a blink reflex?			
Begin to roll from stomach to back?			
Raise up on hands and knees? Begin to crawl?			
Babble, coo, and imitate sounds (*ba, ba; da, da*)?			
Turn to locate the source of a sound?			
Focus on an object and follow its movement vertically and horizontally?			
Rise up on arms, lifting head and chest, when placed on stomach?			
Sit with minimal support?			
Stop crying and relax when held and cuddled?			
Recognize and respond to familiar faces?			
Reach for toys or objects when they are presented?			
Transfer objects from one hand to the other? Put toys in mouth?			
Use a pincer grip to pick up food pieces and small items?			
Smile, babble, and laugh out loud?			
Begin to sleep six to eight hours through the night?			
Suck vigorously when it is time to eat?			
Enjoy (splash, coo) playing in water during bath time?			

Note: Cultural differences may alter the timetable when some developmental skills are acquired and should be taken into consideration.

TeachSource Digital Download

Child's Name _____ Age _____

Observer _____ Date _____

Developmental Checklist

BY 12 MONTHS	Yes	No	Sometimes
Does the child . . .			
Walk with assistance?			
Roll a ball in imitation of an adult?			
Pick objects up with thumb and forefinger?			
Transfer objects from one hand to the other?			
Pick up dropped toys?			
Look directly at an adult's face?			
Imitate gestures: peek-a-boo, bye-bye, pat-a-cake?			
Find an object hidden under a cup?			
Feed self crackers (munching, not sucking on them)?			
Hold a cup with two hands; drink with assistance?			
Smile spontaneously?			
Turn head or come when name is called?			
Respond to "no" and "come"?			
Show hesitation with strangers; want to be picked up only by familiar persons?			
Respond differently to sounds: vacuum, phone, doorbell?			
Look at a person who speaks to them?			
Respond to simple directions accompanied by gestures?			
Make several consonant–vowel combination sounds?			
Vocalize back to a person who is talking?			
Use intonation patterns that sound like scolding, asking, exclaiming?			
Say "da-da" or "ma-ma" or similar terms?			

Note: Cultural differences may alter the timetable when some developmental skills are acquired and should be taken into consideration.

TeachSource Digital Download

Child's Name _____ Age _____

Observer _____ Date _____

Developmental Checklist

BY 2 YEARS	Yes	No	Sometimes
Does the child . . .			
Walk alone?			
Bend over and pick up a toy without falling over?			
Climb up and sit in a child-size chair?			
Walk up and down stairs with assistance?			
Place several rings on a stick?			
Place five pegs in a pegboard?			
Turn pages of a book two or three at a time?			
Hold a marker in a fist and scribble?			
Follow a one-step direction involving something familiar:			
"Give me ___"			
"Show me ___"			
"Get a ___"?			
Match familiar objects?			
Use a spoon with some spilling?			
Drink from a cup unassisted, holding it with one hand?			
Take off coat, shoes, socks?			
Zip and unzip a large zipper?			
Name and point to self in a mirror?			
Refer to self by name?			
Imitate adult behavior in play (e.g., feeds "baby," shaves, cooks)?			
Help to put things away?			
Respond to specific words by showing what was named: toy, pet, family member?			
Ask for desired items by name: ("cookie")?			
Name an object when asked "What is that?"			
Make and maintain eye contact when asking or responding to questions?			
Utter some two-word statements: "Daddy bye-bye"?			

Note: Cultural differences may alter the timetable when some developmental skills are acquired and should be taken into consideration.

TeachSource Digital Download

Child's Name _____ Age _____

Observer _____ Date _____

Developmental Checklist

BY 3 YEARS	Yes	No	Sometimes
Does the child . . .			
Run with coordination in a forward direction; avoid running into objects or people?			
Jump in place, two feet together?			
Walk heel to toe (not on tiptoe)?			
Throw a ball (but without direction or aim)?			
Kick a ball forward?			
String four large beads?			
Turn pages in a book one at a time?			
Hold a crayon: imitate circular, vertical, horizontal strokes?			
Match shapes?			
Demonstrate number concepts of 1 and 2? (Can select 1 or 2; can tell if there are one or two objects.)			
Use a spoon without spilling?			
Drink from a straw?			
Put on and take off coat?			
Wash and dry hands with some assistance?			
Watch other children; play near them; sometimes join in their play?			
Defend own possessions?			
Use symbols in play (basket placed on head becomes a helmet, box turns into a spaceship)?			
Respond to "Put ___ in the box," "Take the ___ out of the box"?			
Select the correct item on request (big versus little; one versus two)?			
Identify objects by their use (show their own shoes when asked "What do you wear on your feet?")?			
Ask questions and make eye contact?			
Tell about something with functional phrases that carry meaning ("Daddy go airplane," "Me hungry now")?			

Note: Cultural differences may alter the timetable when some developmental skills are acquired and should be taken into consideration.

Child's Name _____ Age _____

Observer _____ Date _____

Developmental Checklist

BY 4 YEARS	Yes	No	Sometimes
Does the child . . .			
Walk in a straight line?			
Balance on one foot briefly? Hop on one foot?			
Jump over an object six inches high and land on both feet together?			
Throw a ball with direction?			
Copy circles and Xs?			
Match six colors?			
Count to 5?			
Pour well from a pitcher?			
Spread butter or jam with a knife?			
Button and unbutton large buttons?			
State own gender, age, last name?			
Use the toilet independently and when needed?			
Wash and dry hands unassisted?			
Listen to stories for at least five minutes?			
Draw a person with a head and at least one other body part?			
Play with other children?			
Share and take turns (with some assistance)?			
Engage in dramatic and pretend play?			
Respond appropriately to "Put it next to," "Put it under"?			
Respond to two-step directions: "Give me the sweater and put the shoe on the floor"?			
Respond by selecting the correct object (hard versus soft object)?			
Answer "if," "what," and "when" questions?			
Answer questions about function: "What are cups for?"			
Make and maintain eye contact?			

Note: Cultural differences may alter the timetable when some developmental skills are acquired and should be taken into consideration.

Child's Name _____ Age _____

Observer _____ Date _____

Developmental Checklist

BY 5 YEARS	Yes	No	Sometimes
Does the child . . .			
Walk backward, toe to heel?			
Walk up and down stairs, alternating feet?			
Cut on a designated line?			
Print some letters?			
Point to and name three shapes?			
Group common related objects: shoe, sock, and foot; apple, orange, and plum?			
Demonstrate number concepts to 4 or 5?			
Cut food with a knife: celery, a sandwich?			
Read from a picture storybook (look at the pictures and tell a story)?			
Draw a person with five or six body parts?			
Play and interact with other children; engage in dramatic play that is close to reality?			
Build complex structures with blocks or other building materials?			
Respond to simple three-step directions: "Give me the pencil, put the book on the table, and put your feet on the floor"?			
Respond correctly when asked to show a penny, nickel, and dime?			
Ask "How" questions?			
Respond verbally to "Hi" and "How are you?"			
Describe an event using past and future tenses?			
Use conjunctions to string words and phrases together ("I saw a bear and a zebra and a giraffe at the zoo")?			
Show interest in trying new things?			
Dress self with minimal assistance?			

Note: Cultural differences may alter the timetable when some developmental skills are acquired and should be taken into consideration.

Child's Name _____ Age _____

Observer _____ Date _____

Developmental Checklist

BY 6 YEARS	Yes	No	Sometimes
Does the child . . .			
Walk across a balance beam?			
Skip with alternating feet?			
Hop for several seconds on one foot?			
Cut out simple shapes?			
Copy their own first name?			
Show well-established handedness; demonstrate consistent right- or left-handedness?			
Sort objects on one or more dimensions (color, shape, or function)?			
Name most letters and numerals?			
Count by rote to 10; know what number comes next?			
Dress self completely; button buttons?			
Brush teeth unassisted?			
Have some concept of clock time in relation to daily schedule?			
Cross street safely, holding an adult's hand?			
Draw a person with head, trunk, legs, arms, and features; often add clothing details?			
Play simple board games?			
Engage in cooperative play with other children; participate in group decisions, role assignments, and rule observance?			
Use construction toys such as Legos and blocks to make recognizable structures?			
Do fifteen-piece puzzles?			
Use all grammatical structures: pronouns, plurals, verb tenses, conjunctions?			
Carry on conversations using complex sentences?			

Note: Cultural differences may alter the timetable when some developmental skills are acquired and should be taken into consideration.

Child's Name _____   Age _____

Observer _____   Date _____

Developmental Checklist

BY 7 YEARS	Yes	No	Sometimes
Does the child . . .			
Continue to grow in height and weight?			
Exhibit good balance? Walk across a balance beam?			
Use a pencil and scissors with reasonable skill?			
Catch a tennis ball?			
Hit a ball with a bat?			
Reproduce words and numbers with reasonable skill?			
Concentrate on completing puzzles and board games?			
Ask many questions?			
Use correct verb tenses, word order, and sentence structure in conversation?			
Correctly identify right and left hands? Days of the week?			
Make friends easily?			
Show some anger control, using words instead of physical aggression?			
Participate in play that requires teamwork and rule observance?			
Seek adult approval for efforts?			
Enjoy reading and being read to?			
Sleep undisturbed through the night?			
Plan and carry out simple projects with minimal adult help?			
Show some understanding of cause-and-effect concepts?			
Draw pictures with greater detail and sense of proportion?			
Care for own personal needs with some adult supervision? Wash hands? Brush teeth? Use toilet? Dress self? Tie own shoes?			

Note: Cultural differences may alter the timetable when some developmental skills are acquired and should be taken into consideration.

Child's Name _____   Age _____

Observer _____   Date _____

Developmental Checklist

BY 8 YEARS	Yes	No	Sometimes
Does the child . . .			
Have energy to play?			
Continue to grow and experience few illnesses?			
Have a good appetite? Show interest in trying new foods?			
Use a pencil in a deliberate and controlled manner?			
Use eating utensils with ease?			
Express relatively complex thoughts in a clear and logical fashion?			
Carry out multiple four- or five-step instructions?			
Become less easily frustrated with own performance?			
Seem confident in own ability most of the time?			
Interact and play cooperatively with other children?			
Show interest in creative expression (telling stories, jokes, writing, drawing, singing)?			
Know how to tell time?			
Read and comprehend the story?			
Participate in some group activities (games, sports, choir)?			
Want to go to school? Seem disappointed if they must miss a day?			
Demonstrate beginning skills in reading, writing, and mathematics?			
Accept responsibility and complete work independently?			
Handle stressful situations without becoming overly upset or aggressive?			

Note: Cultural differences may alter the timetable when some developmental skills are acquired and should be taken into consideration.

Child's Name _____ Age _____
Observer _____ Date _____

Developmental Checklist

BY 9 AND 10 YEARS	Yes	No	Sometimes
Does the child . . .			
Continue to gain in height and weight?			
Exhibit improving coordination (running, climbing, riding a bike, writing)?			
Handle stressful situations without losing control or becoming overly upset or aggressive?			
Construct sentences using reasonably correct grammar (nouns, adverbs, verbs, adjectives)?			
Understand concepts of time, distance, space, volume?			
Express thoughts clearly?			
Understand simple abstract concepts?			
Have one or two "best friends"?			
Maintain friendships over time?			
Approach challenges with a reasonable degree of self-confidence?			
Play cooperatively and follow group instructions?			
Begin to show an understanding of moral standards (right from wrong, fairness, honesty, good from bad)?			
Look forward to and enjoy school most days?			
Appear to hear well, listen attentively, and respond appropriately?			
Enjoy reasonably good health with few episodes of illness or health-related complaints?			
Have a good appetite and enjoy mealtimes?			
Take care of own personal hygiene without assistance?			
Sleep through the night, waking up refreshed and energetic?			

Note: Cultural differences may alter the timetable when some developmental skills are acquired and should be taken into consideration.

Child's Name _____ Age _____

Observer _____ Date _____

Developmental Checklist

BY 11 AND 12 YEARS	Yes	No	Sometimes
Does the child . . .			
Continue to grow (gain in height and maintain a healthy weight, not too thin or too heavy)?			
Understand changes associated with puberty or have an opportunity to learn and ask questions?			
Have good vision or wear glasses; not complain of headaches or blurred vision?			
Have straight posture (no curving of the spine or other abnormality)?			
Seem energetic and not chronically fatigued?			
Remain focused on tasks and able to complete assignments?			
Remember and carry out complex instructions?			
Sequence, order, and classify objects?			
Use longer and more complex sentence structure?			
Engage in conversation; tell jokes and riddles?			
Enjoy playing organized games and team sports?			
Respond to anger-invoking situations without resorting to violence or physical aggression?			
Begin to understand and solve complex mathematical problems?			
Accept blame for actions on most occasions?			
Participate in, and enjoy, competitive activities?			
Make and keep friends?			
Accept and carry out responsibility in a dependable manner?			
Go to bed willingly and wake up refreshed?			
Take pride in personal appearance and hygiene?			

Note: Cultural differences may alter the timetable when some developmental skills are acquired and should be taken into consideration.

Child's Name _____ Age _____
Observer _____ Date _____

Developmental Checklist

BY 13 AND 14 YEARS	Yes	No	Sometimes
Does the child . . .			
Continue to experience growth and changes associated with puberty?			
Have sufficient energy to participate in school and extracurricular activities?			
Demonstrate improved hand–eye coordination?			
Think through situations and anticipate the potential outcomes and/or consequences?			
Like school and show interest in learning new material?			
Plan and manage time wisely; complete homework and projects on time?			
Understand right from wrong and accept responsibility for own behavior?			
Begin to develop empathy and consider others' viewpoints and perspectives?			
Read and comprehend material?			
Express thoughts and ideas clearly?			
Work cooperatively with classmates on projects?			
Have friends and do things with them outside of school?			
Understand and engage in humorous antics and interactions?			
Approach daily activities and unfamiliar tasks with reasonable self-confidence?			
Get adequate sleep (8–9 hours) and appear well rested?			
Take pride in personal cleanliness and appearance most of the time?			
Maintain a healthy weight and consume a nutritious diet?			

Note: Cultural differences may alter the timetable when some developmental skills are acquired and should be taken into consideration.

Child's Name _____ Age _____

Observer _____ Date _____

Developmental Checklist

BY 15 AND 16 YEARS	Yes	No	Sometimes
Does the child . . .			
Continue to gain and exhibit self-confidence?			
Make and keep friends who have a positive influence on behavior?			
Set and achieve established goals?			
Understand complex problems and cause–effect relationships?			
Use deductive reasoning to solve abstract problems?			
Communicate and express ideas logically?			
Take pride in personal accomplishments?			
Exhibit good hand-eye coordination?			
Make independent decisions and follow through?			
Express emotions and resolve conflicts in a constructive manner?			
Develop improved emotional control and stability? Limit impulsivity and aggression?			
Show interest in school and extracurricular activities?			
Experience relatively good health (infrequent illness, energetic, maintain an appropriate weight)?			
Respect limits and rules set by adults (on most occasions)?			
Have a trusted and supportive adult with whom to talk?			
Avoid peer pressure to engage in drugs and alcohol? Bullying? Promiscuity?			
Use appropriate protective gear when participating in sports, outdoor activities, or work?			

Note: Cultural differences may alter the timetable when some developmental skills are acquired and should be taken into consideration.

Child's Name _____ Age _____

Observer _____ Date _____

Developmental Checklist

BY 17 AND 18 YEARS	Yes	No	Sometimes
Does the child . . .			
Make independent decisions and assume personal responsibility for outcomes?			
Set realistic goals and take steps to achieve them?			
Have and acknowledge a clear sexual identity?			
Demonstrate effective work and study habits?			
Use analytical thinking to solve complex problems?			
Express ideas with clarity and logical thought? Answer questions appropriately?			
Have a positive outlook on life?			
Exhibit emotional stability and decreased conflict with family?			
Seek advice appropriately?			
Show initiative in achieving independence from family?			
Maintain a healthy lifestyle (diet, physical activity, sleep, safety)?			
Demonstrate moral maturity in social behaviors?			
Possess problem-solving, communication, and intellectual skills and use them when confronted with adversity?			
Demonstrate functional reading and writing skills?			
Attend school consistently?			
Experience good health and relatively few illnesses?			

Note: Cultural differences may alter the timetable when some developmental skills are acquired and should be taken into consideration.

Appendix B

Selected Screening and Assessment Instruments

Examples of Screening Tests

Ages and Stages Questionnaires (ASQ-3) provide a system for monitoring children's developmental progress between the ages of one and sixty-six months. The series of twenty-one questionnaires is used to assess the child's strengths and limitations in five major areas: communication, personal-social, problem-solving skills, fine motor, and gross motor. Families complete the brief questionnaires based on their observations. Forms require two to three minutes to score. Versions of the questionnaires are available in English, Spanish, French, Arabic, Chinese, and Vietnamese.

Battelle® Developmental Inventory (BDI-3)™ is a play-based screening tool that can be used to assess children (from birth to eight years) in five domains: communication, cognitive, personal-social, motor, and adaptive. This instrument is effective for evaluating typical development, school readiness, and children with disabilities.

Beck Depression Inventory-Second Edition (BDI-II) provides a quick (approximately ten minutes) screening test for identifying depression in adolescents and adults and rating its severity (number values are assigned to the individual's responses).

Denver Developmental Screening Test (Denver II) is appropriate for screening children from two weeks to six years of age in four developmental areas: personal-social, language, fine motor, and gross motor. Ratings of the child's behavior during testing can be recorded. Available in English and Spanish.

Developmental Activities Screening Inventory (DASI II) screens children from one month to five years old; a nonverbal test is especially useful for children with hearing or language disorders; adaptations for children with vision problems are also offered.

Developmental Indicators for the Assessment of Learning™, 4th Edition (DIAL™-4) is designed for screening individual children ages three to six years, eleven months, in five developmental domains: motor, concepts, communication, self-help, and social-emotional. The test requires approximately 30 to 45 minutes to administer. A Spanish-language version is available. *Speed DIAL-4* is an abbreviated version of the test that includes items for motor, language, and concept development and can be administered in less than fifteen minutes. The instrument is aligned with the National Education Goals, National Association for the Education of Young Children standards, and Head Start Domains and Standards.

Early Screening Profiles (ESP) can be used to screen children two to seven years of age for cognitive, language, social, self-help, and motor skill development; includes information provided by families, teachers, and child care providers.

First Steps: Screening Test for Evaluating Preschoolers can be used with children from two years, nine months to six years, two months to assess cognitive, communication, and motor skills; an Adaptive Behavior Checklist and a Social-Emotional Scale are included, as well as a Parent–Teacher Scale related to the child's behavior at home and at school. The test takes approximately fifteen minutes to administer.

Examples of Assessment Instruments

APGAR Scoring System is administered at one minute and again at five minutes after birth; the APGAR assesses muscle tone, respiration, color, heartbeat, and reflexes for a maximum score of 10. The information is used to determine which infants may require special care.

Assessment, Evaluation, and Programming Systems (AEPS) for Infants and Children, 2nd Edition (volume 2, birth to three, three to six; volumes 3 and 4, curriculum interventions for birth to three, three to six) is an authentic, family-friendly system for assessing very young children. The activity-based test covers six developmental domains (e.g., fine motor, gross motor, cognitive, social, social-communication, and adaptive) and can be used with children who have disabilities or are at risk for developmental delays. It ties together assessment outcomes and early intervention strategies that are activity-based and family-centered. Test results can be used to determine a child's eligibility for intervention services, establish IEP/IFSP goals, and evaluate intervention effectiveness.

Audiology, that is, hearing assessment of infants and children, requires clinical testing by a trained technician. It is *imperative*, however, in terms of early identification, for teachers and families to record and report their observations whenever they suspect a child is not hearing well. Warning signs include:

- Pulling or banging on an ear
- Drainage from the ear canal
- Failing to respond or looking puzzled when spoken to
- Requesting frequent repetitions—What? Huh?
- Speaking in too loud or too soft of a voice
- Articulating or discriminating sounds poorly

Bayley Scales of Infant and Toddler Development III Assessment® (Bayley-III®) is used to evaluate all developmental areas: cognitive, motor, language, social-emotional, adaptive, and behavior. The age range has been expanded to cover children from one month to three years, six months.

Brigance Inventory of Early Development® III (IED-III®) is a criterion-referenced instrument for assessing children, birth through seven years, in multiple developmental domains: physical development, language development, literacy, mathematics and science, daily living, and social-emotional development. Test results can be used for assessing school readiness, goal setting and curriculum planning, and monitoring a child's progress toward achieving early learning standards, but they are not intended for determining a child's eligibility for special services.

Child Behavior Checklist (CBCL) is a standardized rating scale commonly used to assess children for emotional, social, and behavioral problems (e.g., aggression, defiance, attention deficit, anxious-depressed, or withdrawn). Two versions of the test are available—one for two- to three-year-olds and another for four- to eighteen-year-olds. Parents rate the child on 113 items, which are then scored and used to develop a behavioral profile. A *Teacher's Report Form* and *Youth Self-Report Form* also are available.

Environmental Rating Scales are available in four versions: *Early Childhood Environment Rating Scale®, 3rd ed. (ECERS-3™); Infant-Toddler Environmental Rating Scale®, 3rd ed. (ITERS-3™); Family Child Care Environmental Rating Scale®, 3rd ed. (FCCERS-3™); and School-Age Care Environmental Rating Scale®, Updated (SACERS-U™)*. These well-respected, culturally sensitive assessment tools can be used to evaluate classroom environment quality, including space, materials, learning activities, schedules, health and safety conditions, communication, program structure, and family/staff interaction.

Hawaii Early Learning Profile® (*HELP*®) is a user- and family-friendly curriculum-based assessment instrument designed for evaluating, developing play-based interventions, and monitoring the developmental progress of children (birth through age three). Developmental milestones for each of the six domains are outlined on an easy-to-read chart. Domains are aligned with Head Start, Office of Special Education, and school readiness goals. HELP fosters an interdisciplinary and family-centered approach.

Home Observation for Measurement of the Environment (*HOME*) is a widely used in-home inventory tool to assess the quality and quantity of stimulation and support a child receives at home. Several versions are available: infant/toddler (0–3 years), early childhood (3–6 years), middle childhood (6–10 years), early adolescent (10–15 years), and late adolescent (16–21 years). Each version evaluates the quality of the physical environment, as well as the social, emotional, and cognitive support available to the child. A modified version, *Child Care (CC) Home Inventory*, can be used to assess children in home-based child care settings. The *Disability (DA) Home Inventory* is useful for evaluating the environment of children who have a disability.

Kaufman Assessment Battery for Children, 2nd Edition Normative Update (*KABC*™-*II NU*), is a "culturally fair" test developed to assess the cognitive abilities of children ages three to eighteen years. Test items are designed to minimize the effects of verbal, gender, and ethnic bias.

Kaufman Survey of Early Academic and Language Skills (*K-SEALS*) is used to assess children's (3–7 years) receptive and expressive language skills, as well as concepts related to numbers, counting, letters, and words. In addition, the test can be used to identify children who are gifted, assess children's school readiness, and evaluate program effectiveness.

Learning Accomplishment Profile—Revised (*LAP-3*™) is a criterion-referenced instrument designed to assess children's on-going development across seven domains (e.g., language, gross motor, fine motor, cognitive, prewriting, self-help, and social-emotional). A modified version, the *Early Learning Accomplishment Profile* (*E-LAP*™), is available for use with children whose functional development ranges from birth to three years.

Minnesota Multiphasic Personality Inventory®—*Adolescent* (*MMPI*®-*A*) is a self-reporting questionnaire tool that can be used to evaluate adolescents (14–18 years) for a variety of mental health disorders, including family conflict, substance abuse, defiant behavior, and depression.

Neonatal Behavioral Assessment Scale (*NBAS*), developed by the late Dr. T. Berry Brazelton, is often referred to simply as the *Brazelton*. *The instrument* is used to evaluate neurological and behavioral responses in full-term infants, birth to two months of age.

Peabody Developmental Motor Scales (*PDMS-2*) are used to evaluate children from birth through five years of age in fine motor (e.g., grasping, eye–hand coordination, and manual dexterity) and gross motor development (e.g., reflexes, balance, locomotion, throwing, and catching). Strategies for remediation are also included.

Peabody Picture Vocabulary Test™, *5th Edition* (*PPVT-5*™), is a norm-referenced test that can be administered to individual children in approximately 10–15 minutes. The test is used to assess receptive language (based on standard American English) and verbal ability; appropriate for use with children thirty months and older. A Spanish version is also available.

Preschool Language Scale-5 (*PLS*™-*5*) can be used to assess the language skills (e.g., auditory comprehension, articulation, grammatical forms, and basic concept development) of children from birth to age seven years and eleven months. A Spanish version based on cultural variations is also available.

Temperament and Atypical Behavior Scale (*TABS*) is a screening instrument that can be used to identify children 11–71 months for potential or existing problematic behaviors related to temperament and/or self-regulation. Test results can be used to determine eligibility for special intervention services, for developing remediation programs, and to help families manage children's challenging behavior.

The *Snellen E* or *Illiterate E* eye test is an instrument commonly used for assessing young children's visual acuity (knowing the alphabet is not required). Observation of the following behavioral indicators also plays an important role in identifying children who may have a vision problem:

- Rubbing eyes frequently, or closing or covering one eye
- Stumbling over or running into things often
- Complaining of frequent headaches
- Blinking excessively when looking at books or reading
- Brushing hand over eyes as if trying to get rid of a blur

Healthy eye development has important long-term implications. An on-going nationwide public health program called InfantSEE® was initiated in 2005. Its purpose is to promote the early detection and treatment of vision problems. Infants six to twelve months-of-age can receive free screening and eye care provided by participating doctors of optometry. The following observations are also useful for noting early behavioral signs of potential vision problems:

- Observing the infant's ability to focus on an object
- Watching for uncoordinated eye movements such as crossed or wandering eyes
- Checking for a blink reflex
- Seeing if the infant can visually follow (track) an object, such as a toy, as it is moved in a 180-degree arc

Woodcock-Johnson® IV consists of a battery of individually administered diagnostic tests designed to assess the cognitive abilities, oral language skills, and academic achievements of children and adolescents. The tests are used to identify children's strengths and potential learning disabilities, as well as appropriate interventions.

Work Sampling System®, 5th Edition (WSS), is a unique approach for documenting authentic and ongoing evaluation of children's developmental progress; it uses a combination of portfolio development (with samples of child's work) and checklists for observational data collection. Assessments are conducted three times during a school-year and provide teachers with feedback on effective instructional strategies, as well as how children are responding. The assessment instruments are customized for Pre-K through grade six.

Appendix C

Resources for Families, Educators, and Service Providers

Many resources are available to families, teachers, and service providers who work with children. These resources are provided at the community, state, and national levels and fall into two major categories: direct services and information sources.

Direct Services

Developmental screenings are available through several local agencies and organizations. In addition, most communities offer an array of services and programs designed to help families cope with and meet the special needs and challenges of caring for a child with developmental disabilities. Some agencies also provide technical assistance to educators and other professionals who are working with these children. Often, the agencies themselves serve as a valuable networking resource because they are familiar with other community-based services, assistance programs, and trained specialists.

Examples of Community Services and Resources for Families

- Child Find screening programs
- Interagency Coordinating Councils (ICCs)
- Early childhood centers and therapeutic programs for exceptional children
- Public health departments at the city, county, and state levels
- Local public school districts, especially the special services divisions
- Hospitals, medical centers, and well-child clinics
- University-Affiliated Programs (UAPs)
- Head Start and Even Start programs
- Mental health centers
- State-supported, low-cost health insurance for children
- Parent support groups
- Service groups that provide respite care, transportation, or financial assistance
- Marriage counseling programs
- Philanthropic organizations such as the Lion's Club (glasses), Shriners, and Make a Wish Foundation
- Professional practitioners: pediatricians, nurses, psychologists, audiologists, ophthalmologists, early childhood specialists, educators, social workers, speech-language therapists, and occupational and physical therapists.

Examples of National and Professional Organizations

There are also many national organizations that offer extensive information, as well as direct assistance, to children and families with specific needs. Contact information can usually be found in local telephone directories, the *Encyclopedia of Associations* (which you can find at the library), or on the Internet. For example:

- Allergy and Asthma Foundation of America (AAFA)
- American Council of the Blind (ACB)
- American Diabetes Association (ADA)
- American Foundation for the Blind (AFB)
- American Heart Association (AHA)
- American Society for Deaf Children (ASDC)
- Autism Society of America
- Autism Speaks
- Children's Craniofacial Association (CCA)
- Cleft Palate Foundation (CPF)
- Council for Exceptional Children (CEC)
- Epilepsy Foundation of America (EFA)
- National Down Syndrome Society (NDSS)
- National Center for Learning Disabilities (NCLD)
- National Easter Seals
- National Institute on Deafness and Other Communication Disorders (NIDCD)
- United States Cerebral Palsy Athletic Association (USCPAA)

Examples of Technical Assistance Programs

In addition, there are many organizations whose purpose is to provide direct technical assistance to educational programs and agencies serving children with disabilities. A sample of such organizations includes:

- *American Printing House for the Blind.* This group produces materials and services for children with visual impairments, including talking books, magazines in Braille, large-type books and textbooks, as well as curriculum guides and classroom materials intended for educators of children who are blind or visually impaired.

- *Center on Positive Behavioral Interventions and Supports.* This center, established by the Office of Special Education, assists schools in creating environments that promote positive mental and social-emotional health and equality for all children, especially those who have disabilities. Attention is also focused on cultural sensitivity, the provision of family support, and establishing community advocacy. Extensive resources (e.g., handouts, assessment tools, videos, recorded presentations) can be accessed on their website.

- *Head Start Training and Technical Assistance Centers.* Their purpose is to assist Head Start programs in providing high-quality, comprehensive services to children and their families. At present, four major centers are operational: Early Childhood Development, Teaching, and Learning; Health, Behavioral Health, and Safety; Parent, Family, and Community Engagement; and, Program Management and Fiscal Operations.

- *Early Childhood Technical Assistance Center (ECTA).* This agency provides many forms of assistance to state-funded early childhood programs serving infants and toddlers who are eligible to receive Part C (IDEA) services. The national center works with states to increase public awareness and improve the quality of special education programs and intervention services provided to young children.

- *National Dissemination Center for Children with Disabilities.* This organization serves as a central source for information about specific disabilities, early intervention practices, research, educational law, transition to adulthood, professional organizations, and parent resource materials. Information on expulsion prevention is also available.
- *National Technical Assistance Center for Children's Mental Health.* Information, training, and technical assistance are available to programs serving children and youth. The center's goal is to assist programs in improving mental health outcomes for children and their families.

Information Sources

Extensive information is also published and available online for families, teachers, and professionals who work with children who have developmental disorders. Many professional journals, government publications, and reference books are available in public and university libraries. Special-interest groups and professional organizations also offer printed and online material focused on high-risk children and youth who experience developmental delays.

Selected Examples of Information Resources

- Professional journals and periodicals (in print and online), such as the *Journal of Early Intervention, Topics in Early Childhood Special Education, Young Exceptional Children, Teaching Exceptional Children, Developmental Psychology, Early Childhood Research Quarterly, Early Childhood Education Journal, Child Development, Journal of Adolescent Research, Journal of Learning Disabilities, Journal of Autism and Developmental Disorders, Contemporary Issues in Early Childhood, and Young Children.*
- Trade magazines for families, such as *Young Exceptional Children, Parenting Special Needs,* and *Parenting Children with Special Needs.*
- Government documents, reports, and pamphlets. These materials cover almost any topic related to child development, childcare, early intervention, nutrition, parenting, and specific developmental problems. Most items are accessible from the various agencies' website.
- The Center for Parent Information and Resources website serves as a collection point for publications, webinars, and research. Materials are provided in English and Spanish and available to families of children who have a disability, educators, and other professionals. Regional Parent Centers are located throughout the United States to provide information, support, and training to families of children with disabilities.

Examples of Professional Organizations that Focus on Child and Adolescent Issues

- American Academy of Pediatrics (AAP)
- American Association on Intellectual and Developmental Disabilities (AAIDD)
- American Public Health Association (APHA)
- American Speech, Language, Hearing Association (ASHA)
- Association for Childhood Education International (ACEI)
- The Arc of the United States

- Center for Effective Collaboration and Practice (CECP)
- Center on Technology and Disability (CTD)
- Child Care Aware® of America
- Children's Defense Fund (CDF)
- Council for Exceptional Children (CEC)
- Early Childhood Resource Center (ECRC)
- Early Head Start National Resource Center (ECLKC)
- March of Dimes (MOD)
- Military Child Education Coalition (MCEC)
- National Association for the Education of Young Children (NAEYC)
- National Association for Family Child Care (NAFCC)
- National Center for School Mental Health (NCSMH)
- National Council on Disability (NCD)
- National Head Start Association (NHSA)
- Positive Behavioral Interventions and Supports (PBIS)
- Special Olympics
- Zero to Three

Conclusion

Finding help for children with developmental delays and disorders is not a simple matter. The issues are often complex; some children present tangles of interrelated developmental problems that tend to become more complex when not addressed during the crucial first five years of life. Therefore, effective intervention must begin early and be comprehensive, integrated, ongoing, and family centered. It also must take into account multiple developmental areas at the same time. This effort requires teamwork on the part of specialists from many disciplines, service providers, and agencies working in partnership with the child and family. It also requires an awareness of legislative acts and public policies that affect services for children with developmental challenges and their families, as well as available resources and effective means of collaboration. Only then will children and families fully benefit from a comprehensive early intervention team approach.

Glossary

A

abstract The ability to think and use concepts; an idea or theory. *p. 215*

achievement tests Tests used to measure a child's academic progress (what the child has learned). *p. 268*

amniocentesis Genetic-screening procedure in which a needle is inserted through the mother's abdomen into the sac of fluids surrounding the fetus to detect abnormalities such as Down syndrome or spina bifida; usually performed between the twelfth and sixteenth weeks. *p. 59*

analytical thinking A cognitive process used when attempting to solve problems or make plans; identifying and evaluating the pros and cons of alternative solutions. *p. 245*

anencephaly A birth defect resulting in malformation of the skull and brain; portions of these structures might be missing at birth. *p. 56*

at risk A term describing children who may be more likely to have developmental impairments due to certain predisposing factors such as low birth weight (LBW), neglect, or maternal drug addiction. *p. 11*

attachment A strong emotional connection usually formed between a child and parent(s). *p. 32*

authentic assessment A process of collecting and documenting information about children's developmental progress; data is gathered in children's naturalistic settings and from multiple sources. *p. 13*

autonomy A sense of self as being separate from others. *p. 113*

B

bilateral Affecting both sides, as in loss of hearing in both ears. *p. 264*

binocular vision Both eyes working together to send a single image to the brain. *p. 157*

bonding The establishment of a close, loving relationship between an infant and adults (usually the mother and father); sometimes called attachment. *p. 80*

bullying Verbal and physical behavior that is hurtful, intentional, and repeatedly directed toward a person or child who is viewed as being weaker. *p. 189*

C

cephalocaudal Refers to bone and muscular development that proceeds from head to toe. *p. 40*

cervix The lower portion of the uterus that opens into the vagina. *p. 65*

cesarean section (C-section) The delivery of an infant through an incision in the mother's abdomen and uterus. *p. 66*

Child Find A screening program designed to locate children who have developmental problems through improved public awareness. *p. 261*

chorionic villus sampling (CVS) A genetic screening procedure in which a needle is inserted and cells removed from the outer layer of the placenta; performed between the eighth and twelfth weeks to detect some genetic disorders, such as Down syndrome. *p. 59*

chronological Refers to events or dates occurring in sequence over the passage of time. *p. 27*

cleft lip/cleft palate Incomplete closure of the lip, palate (roof of the mouth), or both, resulting in a disfiguring deformity. *p. 56*

conception The joining of a single egg or ovum from the female and a single sperm from the male. *p. 51*

concrete operational thought Piaget's third stage of cognitive development; the period when the concepts of conservation and classification are understood. *p. 206*

conservation The stage in children's cognitive development in which they understand that an object's physical qualities (e.g., weight and mass) remain the same despite changes in its appearance; for example, flattening a ball of play-dough does not affect its weight or amount. *p. 183*

constructivism A learning approach in which individuals form their own meaning through active participation. *p. 5*

continuity Developmental progress that gradually becomes increasingly refined and complex. *p. 26*

cyberbullying Sending hurtful, threatening, or harassing messages via the Internet or cell phone. *p. 220*

D

deciduous teeth The initial set of teeth that eventually fall out; often referred to as baby teeth. *p. 174*

deductive reasoning A process of considering hypothetical alternatives before reaching a conclusion. *p. 238*

depth perception The ability to determine the relative distance of objects from the observer; recognition of objects as being multi-dimensional. *p. 94*

descriptive praise Words or actions that describe to a child specifically what they are doing correctly or well. *p. 12*

development An increase in complexity, from simple to more complicated and detailed. *p. 25*

developmental sequence A continuum of predictable steps along a developmental pathway of skill achievement. *p. 40*

developmental team A team of qualified professionals, such as special educators, speech-language pathologists, occupational therapists, social workers, audiologists, nurses, and physical therapists, who evaluate a child's developmental progress and together prepare an intervention plan that addresses the child's special needs. *p. 268*

developmentally appropriate A term describing learning experiences that are individualized based on a child's level of skills, abilities, and interests. *p. 11*

discontinuity Development that occurs in irregular periods or stages; not a smooth, continuous process. *p. 26*

discrete behaviors Actions that can be observed and described clearly, such as hitting, pulling hair, laughing, or spitting. *p. 16*

domains Areas of development such as physical, motor, social-emotional, and speech and language. *p. 16*

dysfluency Repetition of whole words or phrases, uttered without frustration and often at the beginning of a statement, such as "Let's go, let's go get cookies." *p. 126*

E

eclampsia A serious pregnancy complication related to preeclampsia. Causes and symptoms are the same as those of preeclampsia with the addition of seizures, agitation, and the potential for stroke. Pregnant teens, older women, and women of color are at highest risk. *p. 58*

ectopic pregnancy Pregnancy that occurs when a fertilized egg attaches itself outside the uterus, most often in one of the fallopian tubes located between the ovaries and uterus. *p. 59*

egocentricity Believing that everything and everyone is there for your personal benefit. *p. 114*

egocentrism Adolescents' belief in their own self-importance. *p. 232*

embryo The cell mass from the time of implantation through the eighth week of pregnancy. *p. 53*

emerging literacy Early experiences, such as being read and talked to, naming objects, and identifying letters, that prepare a child for later reading, writing, and language development. *p. 170*

essential needs Basic physical requirements such as food, shelter, and safety, as well as psychological needs, including love, security, and trust, which are required for survival and healthy development. *p. 11*

executive function The cognitive processes that control working memory (planning, organizing, problem-solving), thinking (ability to focus and shift attention), and behavioral regulation (self-control). *p. 212*

expressive language Words used to verbalize thoughts and feelings. *p. 42, 117*

F

figurative language Words or statements that have meanings other than their literal definitions. *p. 245*

fine motor Refers to small muscle movements; also referred to as *manipulative skills*; includes the ability to stack blocks, button and zip clothing, hold and use a pencil, and brush teeth. *p. 40*

fontanels Small openings (sometimes called "soft spots") in the infant's skull bones; covered with soft tissue; eventually, they close. *p. 76*

food jag A period when only certain foods are preferred or accepted. *p. 26*

formal operational thinking Piaget's fourth stage of cognitive development; the period when children are capable of using abstract thought to predict, test, and reason to arrive at a logical conclusion. *p. 231*

functional language Language that allows children to get what they need or want. *p. 38*

G

gender Reference to being either male or female. *p. 142*

genes Genetic material that carries codes, or information, for all inherited characteristics. *p. 51*

genomics The study of a person's genes, including their structure, function, environmental interactions, and role in health. *p. 148*

gestational diabetes A form of diabetes that occurs only during pregnancy and places the fetus at increased risk; often associated with excess maternal weight gain, a family history of diabetes, and certain ethnicities (e.g., Latina, Native American, African American, Asian, Pacific Islander). *p. 58*

gestational hypertension High blood pressure that develops after the 20th week of pregnancy. Symptoms include headache, swelling, nausea, fluid retention, and vision changes. Pregnant teens, older women, and women of color are at highest risk. *p. 58*

gross motor Refers to large muscle movements such as locomotor skills (walking, skipping, or swimming) and nonlocomotive movements (sitting, pushing and pulling, or squatting). *p. 40*

growth Physical changes leading to an increase in size. *p. 25*

H

hand dominance   Preference for using one hand over the other; most individuals are said to be either right-handed or left-handed. *p. 142*

hands-on learning   A curriculum approach that involves children as active participants, encouraging them to manipulate, investigate, experiment, and solve problems. *p. 171*

head circumference   Measurement of the head taken at its largest point (across the forehead, around the back of the head, and returning to the starting point). *p. 25*

holophrastic speech   Using a single word to express a complete thought. *p. 117*

I

imaginary audience   A component of egocentrism whereby adolescents believe that others care about and notice their behavior and appearance. *p. 232*

implantation   The attachment of the blastocyst to the wall of the mother's uterus; occurs around the twelfth day. *p. 52*

intelligible   Language that can be understood by others. *p. 117*

interdependent   Affecting or influencing development in multiple domains. *p. 38*

intrinsic   A feeling of personal satisfaction, pride, or pleasure. *p. 12*

intuition   A thought or idea based on a feeling or hunch. *p. 206*

in utero   Latin term for "in the mother's uterus." *p. 75*

J

jargon   Unintelligible speech; in young children, it usually includes sounds and inflections of the native language. *p. 26*

jaundice   A yellow discoloration of the infant's skin and eyes caused by excess bilirubin (a yellow pigment that results when red blood cells are broken down in the liver) circulating in the bloodstream. *p. 76*

L

linguistic code   Verbal expression that has meaning to the child. *p. 125*

logic   A process of reasoning based on a series of facts or events. *p. 203*

logical consequence   A planned response that is implemented in response to misbehavior. *p. 221*

low birth weight (LBW)   An infant who weighs less than 5.5 pounds (2,500 grams) at the time of birth. *p. 55*

N

natural consequence   An outcome that occurs as a result of a certain behavior. *p. 221*

naturalistic settings   Environments that are familiar and part of children's everyday experiences, such as classrooms, care arrangements, and the home. *p. 13*

nature vs. nurture   Refers to whether development is primarily due to biological–genetic forces (heredity–nature) or to external forces (environment–nurture). *p. 3*

neophobia   Fearful of, or unwilling to try, something new such as a novel food. *p. 119*

neural connections   Organized linkages formed between brain cells as a result of learning. *p. 30, 229*

neurodevelopmental disorders   Conditions that affect how the brain functions, including autism spectrum disorder, learning and intellectual disabilities, attention deficit hyperactivity disorder (ADHD), and conduct disorders. *p. 213*

neurological   Refers to the brain and nervous system. *p. 28*

norms   Age-level expectancies associated with the achievement of specific developmental skills. *p. 4*

nurturing   Refers to qualities of warmth, loving, caring, and attention to physical and emotional needs. *p. 11*

O

obesity   Although no uniform definition exists, experts usually consider a child whose height-weight ratio (otherwise known as body mass index, or BMI) exceeds the 85th percentile for their age to be overweight, and obese if it is greater than the 95th percentile. *p. 193*

object permanence   Piaget's sensorimotor stage in which infants understand that an object exists even when it is not in sight. *p. 86*

otitis media   An infection of the middle ear. *p. 263*

ova   Female reproductive cells (eggs) that contain reproductive materials. *p. 59*

P

parallel play   Playing alongside or near another person, but not involved in that person's activity. *p. 121*

person-first-language   A respectful way of acknowledging an individual and then referring to their disability or medical condition (e.g., "Alex has autism" versus "Alex is autistic"; "Janay has a hearing impairment" versus "Janay is deaf"). *p. 267*

placenta   A specialized lining that forms inside the uterus during pregnancy to support and nourish the developing fetus. *p. 53*

plasticity   The brain's ability to change and reorganize its structure as a result of learning. *p. 30*

preeclampsia   A serious maternal condition linked to the development of high blood pressure after the 20th week of pregnancy. Symptoms include headache, swelling, nausea, vision changes, and fluid retention; kidney and liver failure and premature birth may occur unless treated. *p. 58*

premature infant   An infant born before thirty-seven weeks following conception. *p. 56*

proximodistal   Refers to bone and muscular development that begins closest to the trunk, gradually moving outward to the extremities. *p. 40*

pruning   The process of eliminating unused neurons and neural connections to strengthen those that the child is actively using. *p. 30*

psychoactive stimulants   This category of drugs includes antidepressants, stimulants, narcotics, hallucinogens, and marijuana (cannabis). *p. 237*

pupil   The small, dark, central portion of the eye. *p. 78*

R

receptive language   Understanding words that are heard. *p. 42*

reciprocal   Refers to exchanges between individuals or groups that are mutually beneficial (or hindering). *p. 11*

refinement   Progressive improvement in the ability to perform fine and gross motor skills. *p. 40*

reflexive   Refers to movements resulting from impulses of the nervous system that cannot be controlled by the individual. *p. 40*

S

scientific reasoning   Critical thinking skills (identify, analyze, and conclude) used to achieve a solution. *p. 239*

self-esteem   Feelings about one's self-worth. *p. 12*

sensory   Refers to the five senses: hearing, seeing, touching, smelling, and tasting. *p. 170*

sensory information   Information received through the five sensory organs: eyes, ears, nose, mouth, and skin. *p. 41*

separation anxiety   Extreme fear or distress that a child experiences when separated from their primary caregiver; occurs most commonly between 9 and 24 months of age. *p. 32*

service coordinator   An individual who serves as a family's advocate and assists them with identifying, locating, and making final arrangements with community services. *p. 269*

sexting   Sending sexually explicit messages or pictures of yourself or friends via a cell phone. *p. 220*

small-for-gestational age infant   An infant whose weight and length are significantly less at birth than an infant of the same gestational age. *p. 58*

social referencing   Observing another person's expressions to determine what they may be thinking or how they are likely to respond. *p. 43*

socio-ecological   Refers to the interactive exchanges that occur between children and their family, other significant adults, and everything in the broader community that affects their lives. *p. 36*

solitary play   Playing alone. *p. 114*

sonogram   A visual image of the developing fetus, created by directing high-frequency sound waves (ultrasound) at the mother's uterus; the procedure is used to determine fetal age and physical abnormalities. *p. 59*

sphincter   The muscles necessary to accomplish bowel and bladder control. *p. 39*

spina bifida   A birth defect caused by a malformation of the baby's spinal column. *p. 56*

stammering   To speak in an interrupted or repetitive pattern; not to be confused with stuttering. *p. 26*

stranger anxiety   A cross-cultural phenomenon in which infants begin to show distress or fear when approached by persons other than their primary caregivers. *p. 95*

T

telegraphic speech   Uttering two-word phrases to convey a complete thought. *p. 117*

temperament   An individual's characteristic manner or style of response to everyday events, including degree of interest, activity level, and regulation of behavior. *p. 51*

teratogens   Harmful agents that can cause fetal damage (e.g., malformations, neurological, and behavioral problems) during the prenatal period. *p. 60*

theory of the mind   The ability to recognize and understand that other people have feelings, beliefs, emotions, and motives that may differ from one's own intentions. *p. 139*

transactional process   The give-and-take relationship between children, their primary caregivers, and daily events that influences each other's behavior and developmental outcomes. *p. 37*

tripod grasp   A hand position whereby an object, such as a pencil, is held between the thumb and first and second fingers. *p. 142*

typical   Refers to the achievement of certain skills according to a fairly predictable sequence, although with many individual variations. *p. 28*

V

voluntary   Refers to movements that can be willed and purposively controlled and initiated by the individual. *p. 40*

Z

Zone of Proximal Development   Vygotsky's term for tasks that initially prove too difficult for children to master by themselves but that they can perform with adult guidance or assistance. *p. 7*

zygote   The cell formed as a result of conception; called a *zygote* for the first fourteen days. *p. 51*

Index